Self Destructive Behavior

A National Crisis

Edited by

Brent Q. Hafen
Department of Health Science
Brigham Young University
Provo, Utah

and comments by

Eugene J. Faux
Director, Youth Center
Utah State Hospital
Provo, Utah

Burgess Publishing Company
426 South Sixth Street · Minneapolis, Minnesota 55415

1   2   3   4   5   6   7   8   9

This book was set in Press Roman by Burgess-Beckwith,
Inc., printed and bound by The Colwell Press, Inc. The
book was designed by Burgess Publishing staff; the cover
was designed by Dennis Tasa. The editors were Robert E.
Lakemacher and Dora Stein. Priscilla Barnes supervised
production.

Self-Destructive Behavior

A National Crisis

Preface

One of the most neglected areas in the education and training of educators and those in the helping and health professions is suicide and self-destructive behavior. Therefore, it seems timely to compile a series of writings representing current thought on self-destructive behavior. The 1960s and early 1970s have been years of social unrest and agonizing political and civil conflicts. Some suggest that we are witnessing a hedonistic generation of young people who seem to have idealized their purposes in a confused combination of pleasure seeking, indignation, and regressed primitive behavior mounted upon prime moralistic concepts, while others suggest that these types of behaviors are a natural outgrowth of the value conflicts being experienced in our society.

Nevertheless, many are saying that cherished value systems have been ridiculed and crushed through a combination of street riots and Supreme Court rulings. In the face of this confusion and agonizing there has been a startling increase in social ills, and one is accustomed to hearing the social ills lumped together—alcoholism, divorce, suicide, crime, juvenile delinquency, venereal disease, and drug abuse. Some like to include mental illness in this category of "evils" and if one uses broad scopes of criteria in defining mental illness this may possibly be appropriate.

Suicide as a phenomenon tends not to get the public attention accorded other social and health problems. There is nearly always the tendency on the part of the press to tone down death details out of respect for the individual and their families. There is also a tendency on the part of institutions to suppress details and statistics in the interest of their own public image. After all, which social arena or institution will launder its dirty linen in public when it is so easy to remain prideful and covert?

Who are the people willing to delve into this topic? What does self-destructive behavior mean? What can and should be done? Just who should be involved in self-destructive behavior prevention, and what can they do? Can we identify suicidal persons, and what are the appropriate preventive and interventive techniques that should be taught? The following papers represent a fair sampling of this fraternity which from the motivational standpoint are self-explanatory. Coming from most of the helping professions these papers represent medical, theological, psychological, sociological, educational, and lay thought. As a compilation, the papers deserve scrutiny by all public minded citizens and the readings should serve as a resource and a supplemental text to teachers in the above disciplines as well as to interested lay persons and students.

The articles have been gathered from numerous sources and represent a broad range of material. The readings have been organized into six parts according to the general content of the articles. The organization of each section is presented in what seemed to the editors to be the most logical sequence.

Part I deals with a description of self-destructive behavior as a health and social problem in the United States. Classification of suicidal phenomena as well as philosophical and ethical considerations are presented. Motivational and suicidal behaviors and the characteristics of self-destructive people are discussed in Part II. Part III takes a close look at self-destructive behavior among youth and adolescents. Particular emphasis is directed towards the reason for youth and adolescent suicidal behavior.

A description of the incidence of student suicides introduces Section IV. This section stresses the role of school personnel as preventive agents to self-destructive behavior as well as the need for education on death and suicide prevention. Part V deals with the critical issue of how you and I as laymen and professionals can help prevent some of the thousands of completed suicides that occur each year. Part VI is an overview of how individuals and institutions, particularly those that deal with the young, may play a significant role during periods of individual stress and crisis.

Appreciation is extended to the authors and publishers for permission to reprint the materials selected for this volume.

Brent Q. Hafen
Eugene J. Faux

January, 1972

Contents

SELF-DESTRUCTION:
A HEALTH AND SOCIAL PROBLEM

The classic writings in suicidology have an established place in the literature and textbooks appropriate to this subject. It now seems timely to document some of the later and possibly more current writings, which should be of interest to the University curricula, Community Mental Health Centers, Suicide Crisis Centers, the various practitioners, and interested laity.

Our particular era seems to bring sociological crises almost faster than they can be appropriately confronted. Self-destructive behavior is a subject with sociological and psychiatric overtones, and many less apparent cross-currents. The editors have attempted to compile a series of papers which represent this complex phenomena, and offer this manual in what should be the first of a series of collected writings where continuity is not intended.

The purpose of this introductory section is to discuss types of self-destructive behavior, self-destruction as a health and social problem, and ideas about death and dying.

The following excerpts from a paper written by a suicidal student point directly or indirectly to some of the sociological and psychiatric overtones that seem to exist in this particular case.

"This paper is nothing of what I had hoped it would be. I wanted, just once, to explain to someone what it was like to live in a world of nothing but fear—to feel different from everyone around—to want desperately to belong—to want to find a peace that would let one's mind stop running. To live just one day and not wonder what everyone around is thinking . . . not to have to weigh carefully each friendship to be sure it is a safe one . . . not to expect the world to fall in at any minute.

While contemplating suicide I have thought of myself:

> I have been running from you all these years. You never run, but when I stop, you are always with me. I hate your gaze. I hate to see myself twisted and broken like that, afraid, and reaching out to grasp my own hand. No, I can never run from you and get anywhere that is away from the me that is you. Am I to fall to the ground, as dirt already stepped on, having never given or received of beauty?

"I have tried in a desperate way to change things and have forced myself to live in a world that has no place for me. I have never been able to rid myself of the feelings I have but have only lost them for a while, having faith that they would not return. Then, when they did return, I was left with a little less faith that my goal was possible.

"The future has never really been on my mind. I have nothing to build on. For a while I found a great deal of new hope. Four years ago I would have spent hours convincing others that they could change. I still feel that others can. Myself, I feel completely broken of any faith, but I still have not been able to rekindle fai within myself. Going to the counseling center has kept me alive—knowing that others have problems. Thoughts of suicide are a constant part of my life. A few years ago I had overcome them; but now they are back, and, as much as I thought they would never return, it is now difficult to remember them ever being gone. I love and enjoy life; I have many friends. Yet I refuse to try again, to hope, to have faith, to become excited and expectant toward the future. It hurts to fail, and fail, and fail. It makes me feel as if it were better to not even try. I am afraid to watch the world around me progress but not me. It hurts to be left standing.

"My mind was completely converted to suicide, and in many ways still is. It seems like such a right thing to do. I had already committed it in my mind and only waited to do it physically in exactly the way I wanted. I see myself as tragic, not in a single sense, as I see other tragedies around and apart from me. Yet I have a great deal to give, and a great deal I want to give; yet it may never happen because of one single aspect of my life. I am afraid of being counterfeit in my feeling. I feel that many people have been counterfeit in their feeling toward me. I was never really fooled, and perhaps for that reason I never wanted to pattern my life after any of them."

"If someone came to me with a similar problem, I would hurt for him. I would cry inwardly, yet he would know my feelings even though they did not come to the surface. He would have to know my feelings and to feel they were sincere or I could do nothing for him other than add myself to the endless chain of 'uninterested' listening ears.

"I wouldn't tell him that everything will be O.K. I wouldn't tell him that God loved him unless I meant it, and not as a way to avoid giving him reasons and answers. I would give him my heart. I would give this person a feeling of self-worth. I would help him not to see himself as different or evil but only as on the wrong behavior pattern to make him happy. I would help him to believe in himself. I would caution him to be patient and not to expect an overnight miracle. I would prepare him to accept slip-backs to previous behavior. I would tell him not to be hurt by the remarks of others made in the ignorance of inexperience. I would tell him that people don't understand or they wouldn't show a counterfeit of love and understanding which hurts more than hate. I would tell him to wisely seek the guidance of someone who he felt could make a sincere effort to help him.

"I would listen, I would love, and I would pray that the efforts of the person would be rewarded. I would love the person no matter what his failures. Hopefully I would love him in such a way that, if all the other reasons to live were gone, he would have so much faith and respect in me that it would make up for the lack of it in himself."

Self-Destruction: A National Problem

Calvin J. Frederick and Harvey L. P. Resnik

In one sense of the phrase, self-destructive behavior is unequivocally suicidal while, in another, the suicidal intent is less clearly defined. Such behavior varies widely from shooting oneself to smoking excessively. Somewhat narrowly viewed, suicide can be seen as a catastrophic illness; more broadly, it constitutes a complex psycho-social problem for virtually every society in the world.

The National Center for Studies of Suicide Preventions, as part of the Division of Special Mental Health Progams in the National Institute of Mental Health, has a mandate to examine the problem of suicidal behaviors. The Center provides research and training funds to qualified investigators throughout the country. In addition, the staff members provide consultation with the assistance of the NIMH Regional Offices and assist local communities in developing crisis intervention programs to deal with suicidal persons. This is often done in collaboration with the emergency services of the local community mental health center.

Most investigators believe overt unequivocal suicides comprise the minority of those which actually exist. Currently some 23,000 deaths from suicides are officially recorded yearly. Experts believe that numerous other deaths are actually self-destructive although they are often recorded under a variety of categories such as accidental deaths, or deaths due to undetermined causes. Apparently, there are a vast number of psychological equivalents of suicide such as the behavior of alcoholics who almost literally drink themselves to death or die in accidents and heavy smokers with known respiratory ailments who markedly hasten the day of their demise.

Suicide ranks as the tenth most common cause of death while accidents rank at least fourth among the nation's killers. Research has begun to indicate that many fatal accidents, especially those by automobile, are really self-destructive. The 53,000 deaths occurring each year from motor vehicle accidents alone are more than twice the recorded suicidal deaths. If these deaths were counted more accurately, then self-destruction would rank much higher among our leading causes of death.

If viewed in a circumscribed fashion, suicide fits the usual criteria employed

Reprinted by permission from *Social Service Outlook,* Vol. 6, No. 17, January 1971.

in describing a catastrophic illness since it is the only mental health problem where immediate life-and-death decisions are a necessity and most suicides are both treatable and preventable. Most suicidologists perceive suicidal behavior as a complex psycho-social public health problem requiring both community and professional attention.

The Center at the NIMH does not limit the programs it supports solely to suicide or even to suicidal behaviors. There is interest in all the parameters of self-destruction, death and dying, mourning and bereavement. There is reason to believe that attitudes toward death differ for various populations and it is important to study them.

RESEARCH UNDER WAY

Among the numerous interesting areas of research supported by the Center are the following examples. One investigator with his colleagues at Harvard and the University of Pennsylvania compared suicide and accidental death in former college students in a 17 to 51-year follow-up after they left college. Antecedent characteristics of suicide included: college education and professional occupation of the father; loss of the father before the son entered college; boarding school during secondary education; heavy cigarette smoking in college; failure to graduate from college; and self-assessed traits of insomnia, worry, and mood swings.

Another researcher in Los Angeles is examining those patients who enter the Los Angeles County General Hospital as a result of near-fatal one-car auto accidents. They are clinically examined and tested psychologically in an effort to ascertain the psycho-dynamics which influence such seemingly self-destructive behavior.

The possible relationship between homicide and suicide is being studied by a research worker in the Northwest who is examining the records of policemen who have been shot during various altercations occurring in their work.

A sociologist who is studying the suicide problems in Cook County, Ill., has challenged one of Emile Durkheim's classic theories—namely, that when external constraints in one's life space are strong, the suicide rate may be low but another form of externally directed aggression, such as homicide, may increase. Stronger constraints from within the person himself and relatively weak ones from without are more likely to lead to suicidal behavior according to this sociological investigator. This is one reason often given for the relatively low rate reported among blacks when compared with whites.

THE BLACK SUICIDE PROBLEM

A psychoanalyst from New York has investigated the black suicide problem in that area and has found that suicide is twice as frequent among New York black males between 20 and 35 as it is among white men from the same area and age group. Thus, some of the older notions that suicide is a white phenomenon occurring among urban middle classes primarily, need revision. This investigator suggests that the problem of being black and the introjected feelings of hostility and resentment contribute to aggressive behavior including suicide. Living itself is seen as a violent act and death is regarded as the only way to control rage.

A pediatrician in Nebraska has been intrigued with repeated self-poisonings occurring in children and has begun to investigate the reasons for that problem. Moreover, a child's concept of death, especially in regard to self-destructive behavior, is being studied in order to shed light on age levels at which children are likely to grasp the concept of death and suicide. The National Center at the NIMH is in the process of investigating a relationship between drug abuse and addiction and suicidal behavior. While this is an obvious area of study, very little has been done on it to date due, in part, to the fact that drug addicts live such short lives and are not available for follow-up study.

The senior author has investigated the handwriting disclosed in suicide notes left by people who had taken their own lives. It was found that expert graphologists in Europe could distinguish genuine suicide notes from controls at a statistically significant level whereas untrained persons such as American detectives and secretaries could not. This result may have predictive value in future studies of behavior.

A different type of NIMH Center support has resulted in the production of a one-act play, *Quiet Cries,* dealing with suicide prevention as a study and training aid for use by a wide range of groups in order to examine suicidal behaviors.

TRAINING PROGRAMS

Two dramatic new training programs are under way which hopefully may set an example and serve as a model for the nation in the field of crisis intervention and suicide prevention. The first consists of week-long Institutes held alternately on the East and West Coasts twice yearly. It brings together experts from all over the country from among the various disciplines of social work, sociology, psychiatry, psychology, medicine, public health, and the law. The area of crisis intervention and suicide prevention is truly one of the most interdisciplinary of all the health professions. An expertise is required in a collaborative approach from all these disciplines in order to research, train, and render service to society effectively. This program covers four broad areas of study, namely (a) a general systematic approach; (b) clinical studies and practice; (c) community organization; and (d) training and education problems. Since research is related to all these areas, it is a common thread which runs through the program and is dealt with according to specific needs. The participants from this program will range all the way from those who are serving as volunteers in clinics to professionals with doctorates in the mental health specialties. There is a great need to supply information appropriately to indigenous gatekeepers and dedicated volunteers as well as established professionals.

Secondly, a highly specialized one-year fellowship program is being carried out in the Washington area, and based at St. Elizabeth's Hospital. This training grant has been awarded to St. Elizabeth's and will receive collaborative support from the Vestermark Training Division of that hospital as well as the staff of the Center for Studies of Suicide Prevention. There is a complement of 12 full-time fellows to be trained in addition to 16 fellowships granted on a part-time basis. This program is a more elaborate and highly specialized version of the summer institute with much more intensive study in the relevant areas of interest. Lacunae in crisis intervention training represent one of the great deficiencies in the problem of suicide prevention. A body of knowledge has been accumulated which can be taught and should be included in the curriculum for trained specialists in social work, psychiatry, psychology, sociology, and allied areas. This will assist the nation in utilizing the mobilizable volunteer force to more optimum efficiency. Prevention through training and research is a time-honored and still valuable approach to public health problems. There is every reason to believe that such procedures used in a creative and innovative manner can lend themselves to an effective effort in the new realms of crisis intervention and suicide prevention.

HIGH RISK GROUPS

One must consider high-risk individuals as those exceeding the national average in both frequency and rate of suicide and those where a marked increase in suicide has occurred recently. In evaluating rate alone, clearly those in the older age groups, namely persons above 65 years of age, have the highest suicide rate of recorded deaths per 100,000 persons yearly. The 40 to 50 age group outranks all others in frequency or the total number of reported deaths from suicide yearly simply because there are almost 11 million white males in that age group. They constitute the largest categorical number of persons who take their lives. Thus, the wage-earning white male who comprises the bulk of the country's work force and contributes most heavily to the gross national product is the greatest risk. It has been estimated that the total economic loss to the nation from wage-earning males who complete suicide is something in excess of $4 billion per year. The loss is in payment of taxes, dollar productivity to his family, and possible welfare to his survivors. This does not take into account human suffering and potentially adverse psychologic effect on survivors.

An alarming rate increase has been noticed among young persons between 15 and 24 years of age and in some minority groups, particularly non-white females. As an illustration, those females in this age group showed an increase of

185 percent over the decade from 1957 to 1967. The incidence among non-white females is increasing at a greater rate than among white females. Traditionally, males in all racial groups have taken their lives two to three times as often as females. Of recent concern is the fact that teenagers and young adults in all sex and color combinations have experienced increases in their suicide rates between 1950 and 1967. Especially dramatic increases to be noted are those among white men of college age from 9.4 per 100,000 in 1950 to 14.9 in 1967 at ages 20 to 24 years; and those for non-white men of the same ages from 8.5 in 1950 to 14.4 in 1967. In fact, nationally there now appears to be virtually no difference between black and white male suicide rates under the age of 35. Only in the later years is there a significant drop in the rate among blacks.

Among other minority groups such as Indians and Mexican-Americans, there appears to be an increase in suicidal behavior, particularly among the underage group. Violent behavior of a self-destructive nature has become increasingly more common among young minority group members placed in restrictive seclusive incarceration. It is not uncommon for one of these youngsters to hang himself in jail. Self-destruction works a different pattern for victim-precipitated homicides who may provoke a fatal fight. If one asks a young black male how he expects to die, there is a good chance that he will say through some sort of violence. This is clearly not the perception held among the white population. Young Indians between 14 and 20 years of age who live on certain reservations are showing a striking increase in suicidal behavior and related maladjustive patterns. As noted earlier, violent deaths from auto accidents are frequent. Other special populations which constitute high risks are the aged, who kill themselves three to four times more often than the general population; almost all professionals, such as dentists, lawyers, and physicians, whose rate is several times the national average; and persons with physical ailments requiring careful personal discipline if life is to be prolonged. Examples are individuals with heart trouble or diabetes who do not adhere to a regimen, and those who habitually take numerous drugs, especially of the "hard" variety. All such behavior can be described psychodynamically as increased risk-taking behavior.

We want to encourage social works and other professionals to become more active in this relatively new field with the suggestion that truly rewarding and monumental strides can be made in an area laden with virgin soil. All of the traditional areas of professional endeavor such as service, training, and research hold much promise, but, in addition, there is a great need for vital, innovative new approaches to the field which require input from social work, as well as the other mental health disciplines.

Classifications of Suicidal Phenomena

Edwin S. Shneidman

With all the current interest in suicide prevention, it remains a fact that *definitions* of suicidal phenomena are ambiguous and that *classifications* of suicidal phenomena remain essentially unsatisfactory. It would seem to be axiomatic that adequate definition and classification are fundamental to good science and praxis, that is, to the kind of understanding that permits effective prevention, intervention, and postvention. In the current scene, it is interesting to reflect on the classification of suicidal behaviors.

In the professional literature the most frequently quoted classification of suicide is that of Durkheim.[1] The durability of this schemata is something which itself deserves special study in the sociology of knowledge. Considering that it was published in 1897 (although it was not generally available in English until 1951); considering further that suicide *per se* was not the primary focus of Durkheim's interest, but rather that the explication of his sociological method, using suicide as the prime example, was Durkehim's main concern; and, considering that Durkheim's classification of types of suicide—anomic, egoistic, altruistic, and fatalistic—has relatively little applicability or power for the clinician on the "firing-line" who is faced by a self-destructive person, its vitality is surprising. It is a classification scheme used and reused in the text books and the technical literature; sometimes there seems to be almost no other.

By *altruistic* suicide, Durkheim meant those self-inflicted deaths which involve a disciplined attachment to the social group of such magnitude that the obligations of the group override the individual's own interests, even his interests in his own life. Durkheim used statistics primarily from various European armies to illustrate this point. By *egoistic* suicide, he meant those deaths in which the individual's relationship to the organized group was such that he was permitted (i.e., forced) to turn against his own conscience and to assume responsibility for his own acts in such a way that he could not rely on canon rule or ritual to bail him out of a personal predicament. To demonstrate this concept, Durkheim contrasted the suicide statistics in religion, especially those between the Catholic

Reprinted from *Bulletin of Suicidology,* July 1968. Published by National Institute of Mental Health.

who is subjected to a group authority and the Protestant who is forced to assume individual responsibility. By *anomic* suicide, Durkheim meant those acts of self-destruction which involve individuals who suddenly have been thrown out of kilter with the important relationships to their group, especially their expectations relative to their moral standards of living. Durkheim used this concept to explain why individuals committed suicide when they lost their income, as well as other individuals (in a seemingly antiutilitarian act) who killed themselves when they became the recipients of large fortunes.

Fatalistic suicide—which Durkheim discussed only in a footnote—is suicide deriving from excessive regulation, as in the suicide of slaves or "very young husbands."

The best exegesis of Durkheim is that of Douglas (1967).[2]

There are a number of other studies generally classified as "sociological" (in the sense that they present statistical or ecological data, but not in the sense that they follow Durkheim's interest in explaining the varieties of man's moral commitments to his society), which are worthy of note—among them Sainsbury[3] (1955) and Stengel[4] (1958) in England, and Dublin[5] (1963) in the United States. Dublin's book, especially, furnishes the student with an encyclopedia of statistical information about suicidal phenomena.

In large part, the currency of the Durkheimian scheme may be due to the absence of any viable competitor. The major alternative conceptualization, that of the Freudian and psychoanalytic theorists, yields not so much a classification as it does a formula—i.e., self-destruction as hostility directed toward the introjected love object (what I have called murder in the 180th degree)—a formulation which sounds globally etiological and universally explanative. As such, this formulation does not help with sorting the multifarious suicidal phenomena which include (in addition to hostility) such psychodynamic constellations as dependency, anguish, hopelessness, helplessness, perturbation, shame, paradoxical striving, etc.

The classic Freudian[6][7][8] approach not only tended rather systematically to ignore social factors, but also tended to focus on a single complex or psychodynamic constellation. But we now know that individuals kill themselves for a number and variety of psychologically-felt motives—not only hate and revenge, but also shame, guilt, fear, hopelessness, loyalty, fealty to self-image, pain, and even ennui. Just as no single pattern is sufficient to encompass all achievements, creativities, or self-actualization, probably no single psychological formula is able to contain all human self-destruction. Many studies of suicide in the psychological genre, more or less following Freud's tradition, have been published. Some of the outstanding ones include those of Hendin[9] (1964), Kubie[10] (1964), Zilboorg[11] (1936), and most especially Karl Menninger[12] (1938).

How do we synthesize these two major theoretical positions—the sociological, with its emphasis on the "social fact" (Durkheim,[13] 1895), and the psychological, with its clinical emphasis on the individual internal drama within the single mind? A recent study bearing on this point (Shneidman and Farberow,[14] 1960) emphasized the interplay between both the social and psychological factors as mutually enhancing roles in each individual's suicide. This finding is consistent with that of Halbwach[15] (1930) whose position—unlike that of his mentor, Durkehim—was that the "social" and "psychopathological" explanations of suicide are complementary rather than antithetical. A synthesis between these two lies in the area of the "self," especially in the ways in which social forces are incorporated within the totality of the individual. In understanding suicide, one needs to know the thoughts and feelings and ego functionings and unconscious conflicts of an individual, as well as how he integrates with his fellow men and participates morally as a member of the groups within which he lives.

Not many classifications of suicidal phenomena *per se* have been proposed. One scheme of note, in addition to Durkheim's classification, is Menninger's[12] classification of the sources of suicidal impulses, namely, the wish to kill, the wish to be killed, and the wish to die. Menninger also classified subsuicidal phenomena into chronic suicide (asceticism, martyrdom, addiction, invalidism, psychosis); focal suicide (self-mutilation, malingering, polysurgery, multiple accidents, impotence, and frigidity); and organic suicide (involving the psychological factors in organic disease). There are other modified-psychoanalytic classifications of types of suicide, especially those by Jackson[16] (1957), Hendin[9] (1964), and Meerloo[17] (1962). A composite listing of their rubrics would include the following: suicide as communication, suicide as revenge, suicide as fantasy crime, suicide as unconscious flight, suicide as magical revival or reunion, suicide as rebirth and restitution.

Another approach to the classification of suicidal types is in terms of cognitive or logical styles, which includes a consideration of the structural and semantic aspects of suicidal communications. Within the framework of this model, a classification scheme, which stemmed from an analysis of the logics contained in suicide notes, has been proposed (Shneidman, 1957,[18] 1961[19]). This approach is based on the Sapir-Whorf hypothesis, which suggests that the ways in which one perceives and thinks are ultimately related to (and inexorably filtered through) the structure of one's language. (Indeed, it might follow that the differences in the per capita suicide rate between, for example, Hopi and Standard-Average-European groups may be attributable to differences in their language structures.) In the Western culture, with its essentially Aristotelian view, three different types of suicidal logic are distinguished: logical, catalogical, and paleological.

Logical (or surcease) suicide tends to occur in individuals who are in physical pain, who show no gross aberrations in their reasoning, and who do not indulge in either deductive or semantic fallacies.

Paleological (or psychotic) suicides are those who use "more primitive" forms of reasoning, are often delusional, and employ deductive gambits of reasoning such as syllogizing in terms of attributes of the predicate (or the use of the "undistributed middle term") as in the following syllogism implied in a suicide note: "Death is suffering; I am suffering; therefore: I must die."

Catalogical suicides are victims of their own semantic errors and especially of their tendency toward dichotomous thinking. Consider the semantic confusion surrounding the word "I" in the following syllogism reconstructed from a suicide note: "If anyone kills himself, he will get attention; I will kill myself; therefore, I will get attention." the "I" that kills and the "I" that is attended to are not only two different "I's"; indeed, the second one is a difficult-to-conceptualize "Non-I." All this is related to the difficulty of conceptualizing death as total cessation.

Oftentimes the semantic confusions ·and dichotomous thinking are related to religious beliefs, especially beliefs about the hereafter, which permit the victims to view suicide not as cessation but rather as transition to another life. Such an individual is haunted by his own polarities; when he cannot tolerate some present *aspects* of his *life,* he dichotomously thinks not of some other ways of living, but of death as the "logical" (and only) alternative to life.

A number of other current investigators have dealt with similar (cognitive) approaches to suicidal phenomena. Osgood[20] (1959) has employed his own Semantic Differential to analyze the communication aspects of suicide notes. His studies indicated that suicide notes contained a usual stereotype, frequent action expressions (nouns and verbs), few discriminating qualifiers (adjectives and adverbs), and tended to use polarized "all-ness" terms. Neuringer[21] (1964) is also interested in the dichotomous and bipolar aspect of suicidal thinking: the polarizations between hope and frustration, fulfillment and renunciation, life and death. In his comparisons among suicidal, psychosomatic, and normal hospitalized subjects, he found that bipolar shifting and dichotomous thinking were higher in both suicidal and psychosomatic subjects, while only excessive rigidity was characteristic of suicidal thinking—the kind of rigidity often related to self-punitive superego functioning and strict conscience control.

A more recent extension of the logical approach to the analysis of suicidal materials is one which details all the *idiosyncrasies of reasoning* in terms of idiosyncrasies of relevance (e.g., irrelevant premise, irrelevant conclusion, argumentum ad hominem, complex question, etc.); idiosyncrasies of meaning (e.g., equivocation, indirect context, mixed modes, etc.); enthymematic idiosyncrasies (e.g., false suppressed premise, suppressed conclusion, etc.); idiosyncrasies of logical structure (e.g., isolated predicate, isolated term); and idiosyncrasies of logical interrelations (e.g., logical type confusions, contradictions, etc.). These idiological patterns are then related to the individual's *contra-logic* (his private epistemology and cosmology which underlie his thinking patterns), to *psycho-*

logic (the "personality" traits related to reasoning which are consistent with his ways of mentating), and his *pedago-logic* (the optimal ways of teaching or dealing with him; i.e., the logical styles in which materials should be presented to him in order for him maximally to resonate or "understand" them (Shneidman,[22] 1966). The hypothesis is that there is a finite number of identifiable logical styles related to a comparable number of specific types of suicidal persons.

Is there any way in which the logical, psychological, sociological, phenomenological, and transactional approaches to suicidal phenomena might be brought together? Perhaps by being cognizant of the relevance of these dimensions and by incorporating elements of each approach into one relatively simple classification, one might prepare a synthesis of the important elements of each, delineating an approach which, in its various parts, would reflect the intra-psychic stress, the inter-personal tensions, the strained ties with groups, idiosyncratic modes of thought, inner pain and hopelessness, and even one's role in the family of man. No current proposal can claim adequately to encompass all of these dimensions or to meet the total criteria for comprehensive classification. But suggestions, prompted by the wish to be heuristic, if not catalytic, should always be welcome, and it is in this spirit that the following tentative classification of suicide behaviors is proposed.

It is suggested that all (committed) suicides be viewed as being of one of three types: (a) egotic; (b) dyadic; or (c) ageneratic.

Egotic suicides are those in which the self-imposed death is the result, primarily, of an *intra-psychic* debate, disputation, struggle-in-the-mind, or dialogue within one's self in the "congress of the mind." The impact of one's immediate environment, the presence of friends or loved ones, the existence, "out there," of group ties or sanctions become secondary, distant perceptual "ground" as compared with the reality and urgency of the internal psychic debate. The dialogue is within the personality; it is a conflict of aspects of the self, within the ego. Such deaths can be seen as egocide or ego destruction; they are annihilations of the "self," of the personality, of the ego. At the time it happens, the individual is primarily "self-contained" and responds to the "voices" (not in the sense of hallucinatory voices) within him. This is what one sees in the extremely narrowed focus of attention, self-denegating depression, and other situations where the suicide occurs without regard for anyone else including especially the loved ones and "significant others."

Such individuals are often seen as delusional, although sometimes the agitated obsessional quality is what is seen most clearly. They are self-contained, in the sense that the person's torment is "within his head," such as the anguish of a Virginia Woolf, the torment of an Ellen West; many of the "crazy" (i.e., "psychotic," gifted, excessively "neurotic," "special," private, inwardly convoluted, highly symbolic) suicides—suicides that can be conceptualized in a number of ways, such as nihilistic, oceanic, reunion, Harlequin, magical, etc.

Egotic suicides are primarily *psychological* in their nature. Suicide notes pertaining to this kind of suicide contain explanations of these special inner states; are filled with symbolism and metaphor (and sometimes poetry); and are special windows not so much into the ideation or affect of the anguished person as they are private views of either pervasive or idiosyncratic existential struggles and *inner* unresolved philosophic disputations. Although they are often meant as diaries to the self, these suicide notes are often addressed to specific persons and as such are meant as didactic "explanations" of the victim's inner world of choice.

Individuals who commit this type of suicide have in common a phenomenon which we shall call "boggling." The person boggles (i.e., stops, hesitates, startles, and refuses to go on because of doubt, fear, scruples, confusion, pain, etc.). It is as though he says to himself, "So far and no further." Colloquially translated, it comes out as, "I've had it," which means that he has "taken" as much of the world's assaults as he can, and that his limits or tolerance for continuing his bargain with life have been reached and that he is now abrogating that relationship.

Here are three examples of *egotic* suicide notes.

(From a 31-year-old single male)

Mr. Brown:
   When you receive this note, call the police.
   Have them break down the door panels of the cabinet nearest the window in room 10. My body will be inside. *Caution—carbon monoxide gas!* I have barricaded the doors shut so that if for any reason the guard becomes suspicious and tries to open the doors, there will be enough delay to place me beyond rescue.
   It seems unnecessary to present a lengthy defense for my suicide, for if I have to be judged, it will not be on this earth. However, in brief, I find myself a misfit. To me, life is too painful for the meager occasional pleasure to compensate. It all seems so pointless, the daily struggle leading *where?* Several times I have done what, in retrospect, is seen to amount to running away from circumstances. I could do so now—travel, find a new job, even change vocation, but why? It is *Myself* that I have been trying to escape, and this I can do only as I am about to!
   Please take care of a few necessary last details for me. My residence is—100 Main Street.
   My rent is paid through the week.
   My only heirs and beneficiaries are my parents. No one else has the least claim to my estate, and I will it to my parents.
   Please break the news to them gently. They are old and not in good health. Whatever the law may say, I feel I have a moral right to end my own life, but not someone else's.
   It is too bad that I had to be born (I have not brought any children into this world to suffer). It is too bad that it took me more than 31 years to realize that I am the cause of whatever troubles I have blamed

on my environment, and that there is no way to escape oneself. But better late than never. Suicide is unpleasant and a bother to others who must clean up and answer questions, but on the whole it is highly probable that, were I to live, it would cause even more unpleasantness and bother to myself and to others.

Goodbye.

Bill Smith

(From a 47-year-old married male)

Mary Darling,

My mind—always.warped and twisted—has reached the point where I can wait no longer—I don't dare wait longer—until there is the final twist and it snaps and I spend the rest of my life in some state run snake pit.

I am going out—and I hope it is out—Nirvanha, I think the Bhudaists (how do you spell Bhudaists?) call it which is the word for "nothing." That's as I have told you for years, is what I want. Imagine God playing a dirty trick on me like another life! ! !

I've lived 47 years—there aren't 47 days I would live over again if I could avoid it.

Let us, for a moment be sensible. I do not remember if the partnership agreement provides for a case like this—but if it doesn't and I think it doesn't, I would much prefer—I haven't time to make this a legal requirement—but, I would much prefer that you, as executrix under my will, *do not* elect to participate in profits for 2 or 3 years or whatever it may be that is specified there. My partners have been generous with me while I worked with them. There is no reason why, under the circumstances of my withdrawal from the firm, they should pay anything more.

I could wish that I had, for my goodby kiss, a .38 police special with which I have made some good scores—not records but at least made my mark. Instead, I have this black bitch—bitch, if the word is not familiar to you—but at least an honest one who will mean what she says.

The neighbors may think its a motor backfire, but to me she will whisper—"Rest—Sleep."

Bill

P.S. I think there is enough insurance to see Betty through school, but if there isn't—I am sure you would out of the insurance payments, at least—

I hope further and I don't insist that you have the ordinary decency—decency that is—to do so—Will you see Betty through college—she is the only one about whom I am concerned as this .38 whispers in my ear.

(From a 21-year-old single female)

12:00 P.M.

I can't begin to explain what goes on in my mind—it's as though there's a tension pulling in all directions. I've gotten so I despise myself for the existence I've made for myself. I've every reason for, but I can't seem to content myself with anything. If I don't do this or some other damned thing, I feel as tho I'm going to have a nervous collapse. May God forgive me, and you too, for what I am doing to you, my parents who have always tried so beautifully to understand me. It was futile, for I never quite understood myself. I love you all very much.

Mary

Dyadic suicides are those in which the death relates primarily to the deep unfulfilled needs and wishes pertaining to the "significant other"—the partner in the important current dyad in the victim's life. These suicides are primarily *social* in their nature. Although suicide is always the act of a person and, in this sense, stems from within his mind, the dyadic suicide is essentially an interpersonal event. The cry to the bootless heavens refers to the frustration, hate, anger, disappointment, shame, guilt, rage, impotence, and rejection, in relation to *him* or to *her*—either the real him or her or a symbolic (or even fantasied or fictional) person in the life. The key lies in the undoing: "If only he (or she) would . . . ." Most suicide notes are dyadic in their nature. Suicide notes, usually prefaced by the word, "Dear," are typically addressed to a specific person, an ambivalently loved love-one. (A prototypical example: "Dear Mary: I hate you. Love, George.") In this country most suicides seem to be dyadic in nature; that is, they are primarily *transactional* in nature. The victim's best eggs are in the other person's flawed basket. He (and his figurative eggs) are crushed. The dyadic suicidal act may reflect the victim's penance, bravado, revenge, plea, histrionics, punishment, gift, withdrawal, identifcation, disaffiliation, or whatever—but its arena is primarily interpersonal and its understanding (and thus its meaning) cannot occur outside the dyadic relationship.

Here are some examples of *dyadic* suicide notes.

(From a 35-year-old single male, who committed suicide after he killed his girl friend)

Mommie My Darling,
   To love you as I do and live without you is more than I can bear. I love you so completely, whole-heartedly without restraint. I worship you, that is my fault. With your indifference to me; is the difference. I've tried so hard to make our lives pleasant and lovable, but you didn't seem to care. You had great plans which didn't include me. You didn't respect me. That was the trouble. You treated me like a child. I couldn't reach you as man and woman or man and wife as we've lived. I let you know my feelings toward you when I shouldn't have. How I loved you, what you meant to me. Without you is unbearable.
   This is the best way. This will solve all our problems. You can't hurt me further and anyone else. I was a "toll" while you needed me or thought you did. But now that I could use some help, you won't supply the need that was prominent when you need it. So, good bye my love. If it is possible to love in the hereafter, I will love you even after death.

May God have mercy on both our souls. He alone knows my heartache and sorrow and love for you.

Daddy

(From a 66-year-old divorced male)

Mary:
We could have been so happy if you had continued to love me. I have your picture in front of me. I will look at it the last thing. I do love you so much. To think you are now in the arms of another man is more than I can stand. Remember the wonderful times we have had—kindly—Good bye Darling. I love you, W. Smith.

Your boy friend Pete Andrews, is the most arrogant, conceited ass I have every known or come in contact with. How a sensible girl like you can even be with him for 10 minutes is unbelievable. Leave him and get a real fellow. He is no good, I am giving my life for your indescressions. Please don't let me pay too high a price for your happiness. All your faults are completely forgotten and your sweetness remembered. You knew I would do this when you left me—so this is no surprise. Good bye darling—I love you with all of my broken heart.

W. Smith

(From a 38-year-old divorced female)

Bill,
You have killed me. I hope you are happy in your heart, "If you have one which I doubt." *Please* leave Rover with Mike. Also leave my baby alone. If you don't I'll haunt you the rest of your life and I mean it and I'll do it.

You have been mean and also cruel. God doesn't forget those things and don't forget that. And please no flowers; it won't but mean anything. *Also keep your money.* I want to be buried in Potters Field in the same casket with Betty. You can do that for me. That's the way we want it.

You know what you have done to me. That's why we did this. It's yours and Ella's fault, *try* and forget that *if* you can. But you can't. Rover belongs to Mike. Now we had the slip and everything made out to Mike, he will be up after Rover in the next day or so.

Your Wife

Ageneratic suicides are those in which the self-inflicted death relates primarily to the individual's "falling out" of the procession of generations; his losing (or abrogating) his sense of membership in the march of generations and, in this sense, in the human race itself. This type of suicide relates to the Shakespearean notion of "ages" or eras within a human life span, and a period within a life in which an individual senses at one level of consciousness or another, his "belonging" to a whole line of generations; fathers and grandfathers and great-grandfathers before him, and children and grandchildren and great-grandchildren after him.

Erikson[23] has used the term "generativity" to represent the concern of one generation for the next—"the interest for establishing and guiding the next generation"—in which the general idea is one of transgenerational relationship. He further points out that where this sense of generativity is absent in the adult individual, there is often "a pervading sense of individual stagnation and interpersonal impoverishment." In most of the important interpersonal exchanges in which an adult engages, he does not ordinarily expect direct or reciprocal reward or repayment, but, rather, as in parenthood, the most that he ordinarily desires is for the next generation to do at least the same for their next generation as he has done for it. The person who falls out of his society or out of his lineage is a person who has lost investment in his own "post-self." This kind of suicide grows out of a sense of alienation, disengagement, familial ennui, aridity, and emptiness of the individual in the "family of man." The sense of belonging to the stream of generations is illustrated in a recently published letter dated October 1967 by Arnold Toynbee in which he said, "I am now an old man and most of my treasure is therefore in future generations. This is why I care so much." The ageneratic suicide has lost this sense of treasure and this is why he cares so little.

This sense of belongingness and place "in the scheme of things," especially in the "march of generations," is not only an aspect of middle and old age, but it is the comfort and characteristic of psychological maturity, at whatever age. To have no sense of serial belongingness or to be an "isolate" is truly a lonely and comfortless position, for then one may, in that perspective, truly have little to live for. This kind of hermit is estranged not only from his contemporaries, but much more importantly, he is alienated from his forebears and his descendants, from his own inheritance and his own bequests. He is without a sense of the majestic flow of the generations—he is ageneratic. Ageneratic suicides are primarily *sociological* in nature, relating as they do to familial, cultural, national, or group ties. Suicide notes of this type are often (although not always) addressed "To whom it may concern," "To the police," or not addressed at all. They are truly voices in a macrotemporal void.

Here are some examples of *ageneratic* suicide notes.

(From a 43-year-old divorced male)

To Whom It May Concern, and the Authorities:
    You will find all needed information in my pocket book. If the government buries suicides please have them take care of my body, Navy Discharge in pocket book. Will you please seal and mail the accompanying letter addressed to my sister whose address is: 100 Main Street.
    My car is now the property of the Jones Auto Finance Co. (You will find their card in my pocket book.) Please notify them of its location. You may dispose of my things as you see fit.

W. Smith

P.S. The car is parked in front of the barbershop. The gear shift handle is broken off, but the motor is in high gear and can be driven that way.

Dear Mary,

The fact of leaving this world by my own action will no doubt be something of a shock, I hope though that it will be tempered with the knowledge that I am just "jumping the gun" on a possible 30 or 40 years of exceedingly distasteful existence, than the inevitable same end.

Life up to now has given me very little pleasure, but was acceptable through a curiosity as to what might happen next. Now I have lost that curiosity and the second half with its accompaniment of the physical disability of old age and an absolute lack of interest in anything the world might have for me is too much to face.

The inclosed clipping seems to tell it much better than I.

My love to both you and mama, for what it's worth.

Sorry,

Bill

"Clipping"

The question, then, as to whether life is valuable, valueless, or any affliction can, with regard to the individual, be answered only after a consideration of the different circumstances attendant on each particular case; but, broadly speaking, and disregarding its necessary exception, life may be said to be always valuable to the obtuse, often valueless to the sensitive: while to him who commiserates with all mankind, and sympathizes with everything that is, life never appears otherwise than as an immense and terrible affliction.

(From a 50-year-old single male)

To the Authorities:

Excuse my inability to express myself in English and the trouble caused. I beg you not to lose time in an inquest upon my body. Just simply record and file it because the name and address given in the register are fictitious and I wanted to disappear anonymously. No one expects me here nor will be looking for me. I have informed my relatives far from America. *Please do not bury me!* I wish to be *cremated* and the ashes tossed to the winds. In that way I shall return to the nothingness from which I have come into this sad world. This is all I ask of the Americans for all that I had intended to give them with my coming into this country.

Many thanks.

Jose Marcia

(From a 58-year-old married female)

I have been alone since my husbands death 14 years ago. No near relatives.

I am faced with another operation similar to one I had ten years ago, after which I had many expensive treatments.

My friends are gone and I cannot afford to go through all this again. I am 58 which is not a good age to find work.

I ask that my body be given to medical students, or some place of use to some one. There will be no inquiries for me.

Thank you.

(From a 61-year-old divorced female)

You cops will want to know why I did it, well just let us say that I lived 61 years too many.

People have always put obstacles in my way. One of the great ones is leaving this world when you want to and have nothing to live for.

I am not insane. My mind was never more clear. It has been a long day. The motor got so hot it would not run so I just had to sit here and wait. The breaks were against me to the very last.

The sun is leaving the hill now so hope nothing else happens.

One last reflection: The general suggestion to eschew the category of "suicide" entirely and to reconceptualize all deaths in terms of their being intentioned, subintentioned, or unintentioned (Shneidman,[24] 1963)— reintroducing the role of the individual in his own demise—would seem to have its own special merits. Indeed, anything said about the classification of suicidal deaths would apply directly to intentioned deaths and, with appropriate modifications, to subintentioned deaths as well.

REFERENCES

1. Durkheim, Emile. *Suicide*. Translated by John A. Spaulding and George Simpson. Glencoe: The Free Press, 1951. (Originally published as *Le Suicide* in 1897.)
2. Douglas, Jack D. *The Social Meanings of Suicide*. Princeton: Princeton University Press, 1967.
3. Sainsbury, Peter. *Suicide in London: An Ecological Study*. London: Chapman and Hall, 1955.
4. Stengel, Erwin, and Cook, Nancy G. *Attempted Suicide*. London: Chapman and Hall, 1958.
5. Dublin. Louis I. *Suicide: A Sociological and Statistical Study*. New York: Ronald Press, 1963.
6. Freud, Sigmund. The psychogenesis of a case of homosexuality in a woman. *Collected Papers*, 1920, 2:202-231. London: Hogarth Press, 1920.
7. Freud, Sigmund. Mourning and melancholia. *Collected Papers*, 1925: 152-170. London: Hogarth Press. (First published in German, 1917).
8. Litman, Robert E. Sigmund Freud on suicide. 1967 In: Shneidman, Edwin S., ed. *Essays in Self-Destruction*. New York: Science House, 1967.
9. Hendin, Herbert. *Suicide and Scandinavia*. New York: Grune and Stratton, 1964.
10. Kubie, Lawrence S. Multiple determinants of suicidal efforts. *The Journal of Nervous and Mental Disease*, 1964, 138:3-8.
11. Zilboorg, Gregory. Differential diagnostic types of suicide. *Archives of Neurology and Psychiatry*, 1936, 35:270-291.

12. Menninger, Karl A. *Man Against Himself.* New York: Harcourt, Brace and Company, 1938.
13. Durkheim, Emile. *The Rules of Sociological Method.* Translated by Sarah Solovay and John H. Mueller, Glencoe: The Free Press, 1938. (Originally published as: *Les Regles de la Methode Sociologique* in 1895.)
14. Shneidman, Edwin S., and Farberow, Norman L. A socio-psychological investigation of suicide. In: David, Henry P., and Brengelmann, J. C., eds. *Perspectives in Personality Research.* New York: Basic Books, 1960.
15. Halbwachs, Maurice. *Les Causes du Suicide.* Paris: Librairie Felix Alcan, 1930.
16. Jackson, Don D. Theories of suicide. In: Shneidman, Edwin S., and Farberow, Norman L., eds. *Clues to Suicide.* New York: McGraw-Hill, 1957.
17. Meerloo, Joost A.M. *Suicide and Mass Suicide.* New York: Grune and Stratton, 1962.
18. Shneidman, Edwin S. The logic of suicide. In: Shneidman, Edwin S. *Clues to Suicide.* New York: McGraw-Hill, 1957.
19. Shneidman, Edwin S. Psycho-logic: A personality approach to patterns of thinking. In: Kagan, Jerome, and Lesser, Gerald S., eds. *Contemporary Issues in Thematic Apperceptive Methods.* Springfield: Charles C. Thomas, 1961.
20. Osgood, Charles E., and Walker, E. G. Motivation and language behavior: A content analysis of suicidal notes. *Journal of Abnormal and Social Psychology,* 1959, 59:58-67.
21. Neuringer, Charles. Rigid thinking in suicidal individuals. *Journal of Consulting Psychology,* 1964, 28:54-58.
22. Shneidman, Edwin S. *The Logics of Communication: A Manual for Analysis.* China Lake, California: U.S. Naval Ordnance Test Station, 1966.
23. Erikson, Erik. *Childhood and Society.* New York: Norton, 1950.
24. Shneidman, Edwin S. Orientations toward death: A vital aspect of the study of lives. In: Robert W. White, ed. *The Study of Lives.* New York: Atherton Press, 1963.

The Enemy

Edwin S. Shneidman

This may be an age of youth but it is also an age of *death*. Death is in the air; none of us is more than minutes away from death by nuclear incineration. Life has become both more dear and more cheap. And if it can be taken by others it can also be thrown away by oneself. Senseless killing and the wanton destruction of one's own mind reflect the same debasement of man's basic coin; life itself. In the Western world we are probably more death-oriented today than we have been since the days of the Black Plague in the 14th Century.

The young reveal an acute sensitivity to life-and-death issues. I believe that they can best be seen as children of The Bomb. At Harvard last year my course on death was scheduled in a room with 20 chairs. Having been for over 20 years one of the few researchers who concentrated on death phenomena—my original focus was on suicide prevention—I had come to assume that only a few would want to deal with the subject. To my surprise more than 200 undergraduates from Radcliffe and Harvard showed up for the first session. Much of my recent work grew out of the introspective reports and papers completed by the participants in that course. The students' painful awareness of death, long before the season regarded as appropriate, has helped me to grasp the difference between individual death as it has long been preceived and the prospect of megadeath in the nuclear age.

At first thought, "death" is one of those patently self-evident terms, the definition of which need not detain a thoughtful mind for even a moment. Every mature person knows instinctively what he means by it. A dictionary defines death as the act or event or occasion of dying; the end of life. As far as the person himself is concerned death is his end—the cessation of his consciousness.

In spite of death's seemingly self-evident character, reflection tells us that it might take a lifetime fully to understand the word "death." As Percy Bridgman pointed out, where either consciousness or loss of consciouness (including death) is involved, we must distinguish between *your* private experiences and *my* private experiences. You (privately) can experience my (public) death; we can

Reprinted from *Psychology Today Magazine,* August, 1970.
Copyright © Communications/Research/Machines, Inc.

both (privately) experience someone else's (public) death; but neither of us can experience his own (inexperienceable) death. You can never see yourself unconscious, hear yourself snore or experience your own being dead, for if you were in a position to have these experiences you would not, in fact, be unconscious, asleep or dead.

If you can never experience your own death, it follows logically that you can never experience your own *dying*. "Now, wait a minute," you might say. "Granted that I cannot experience my being dead but obviously I am still alive while I am dying and, unless I am unconscious, I can experience that." The fact is that you can never be *certain* that you are dying. "Dying" takes its only legitimate meaning from the fact that it immediately precedes death. You may think that you are dying—and survive, in which case you were not dying at that time. You can of course at the present moment keenly experience your *belief* that you are dying, and the experience can be deathly real. You can also in the present anticipate what will happen after you are dead. But these anticipations are at the time they occur always present-moment, live experiences.

All this is not to gainsay the fact that people are often correct in thinking that they are dying because they do then die. During an extended period of dying (or supposed dying), a person, unless he is massively drugged or in a coma, is very much alive. The interval of dying is a psychologically consistent, often exaggerated extension of the individual's personality and life-style. His idiosyncratic ways of coping, defending, adjusting and interacting remain with him, coloring his inner life and characterizing his behavior. A standard textbook on clinical medicine succinctly states: "Each man dies in a notably personal way."

Termination is the universal and obiquitous ending of all living things; but only man, because he can talk about his introspective life, can conceptualize his own cessation. Death is the absence of life—and life, *human* life, is the life of the self, the life of mind. *Your* life is the full accounting of your personal diary, your memory bank, including your experience of the present moment. It is the life of your mind as you look out on the world and reflect upon yourself. Of course by "the life of the mind" I do not mean to limit the notion only to those aspects of mind amenable to immediate or conscious recall.

Death is the stopping of this life. Bridgman said that ". . . my own death is such a different thing that it well might have a different word." I propose that we use the word *cessation*. Cessation ends the potentiality of any (further) conscious experience. It is essentially synonymous with the conclusion of conscious life.

In order to have a full appreciation of the role of cessation, we must understand a few additional terms:

Termination is the stopping of vital physiological functions, including such gross measures as the heartbeat or the exchanges of gases between the person and his environment and such refined measures as what we now call "brain death." Physiological termination is always followed shortly by psychological cessation. The converse however is not always true: it is possible for (private) cessation to occur hours or even days before (public) termination. For example when a person's skull is crushed in an accident, cessation occurs at the instant he loses consciousness for the last time, but he might be kept alive in a hospital as long as he breathes and brainwave patterns are traced on the EEG. But his life ended the instant his mind was destroyed. Loved ones and hospital personnel saw him "alive" in the hospital but that could be an experience only for them. Because the moment of "death" is socially defined by termination, we need that concept even in a psychological approach to death.

Interruption is the stopping of consciousness with the expectation of further conscious experience. It is, to use two contradictory terms, a kind of temporary cessation. Sleep—dreamless sleep—is perhaps the best example of an interruption. Other interruptions include unconsciousness, stupor, coma, fainting, seizures and anesthetic states, and can last from seconds to weeks. By definition the last interruption of a man's life is cessation.

Continuation is the experiencing the stream of temporally contiguous events. Our lives are thus made up of *one* series of alternating states of continuation and interruption.

As one would imagine, *altered continuation* implies the continuation of consciousness in a way that is different from an individual's usual or modal style of functioning. Examples would be intoxication, drugged states, hypnotic states, malingering, role-playing, spying, feigning and even "unplugging." "Unplugging"—a term suggested to me by Professor Erving Goffman—is getting out of one's ordinary track of life by drifting, seceding or uncorking, such as burying yourself in a book, going on a *Wanderjahr,* watching a Western or, more actively, going on an escapade, a binge or an orgy—in short, escaping, as opposed to sweating it out.

A neglected aspect of death is the role of the individual in his own demise. The current traditional (and in my view, erroneous) conceptualization that views death as an experience—noble, religious, frightening, beneficent, malign—makes too much of the individual's role in his own death. We have already decided that for the chief protagonist, death is not an experience at all. But there is still another traditional view of death that, curiously enough, makes too little of man's role in his own demise. That view can be seen in the way we conceptualize death in our official records.

In the Western world "death" is given its operational meaning by the death certificate. The death certificate can be divided into three parts, reflecting the three basic kinds of information that it is intended to convey: a) the top third of the certificate identifies the decedent; b) the second third of the certificate relates the cause or causes of death. The international manual lists around 140 possible causes of death, including pneumonia, meningitis, myocardial infarction; c) the last third of the certificate is perhaps the most important for our interests. It is intended to tell us *how* the person died. It normally indicates one of four conceptual crypts into which each of us is eventually placed. I call this world-wide taxonomic scheme the NASH classification of death, standing for the four *modes* of death: natural, accidental, suicidal and homicidal. The main terms can be combined or modified; e.g., "Accident-Suicide, Undetermined" or "Probable Suicide."

It is evident that the *cause* of death does not automatically tell us the *mode* of death. "Asphyxiation due to drowning" or "barbiturate overdose" does not tell us whether the death was accidental or suicidal or homicidal. The NASH scheme tends to obscure rather than to clarify the nature of human death.

Much of this anachronistic classification can be traced to the 1600s, when the English crown was interested in assigning blame. Natural and accidental deaths were by definition acts of nature or of God. The survivors could only be pitied and the legitimate heirs would come into their rightful inheritances. On the other hand, the culprit must be identified and punished in homicidal and suicidal deaths. Suicide was *felo-de-se,* a felony against the self, and the crown took the dead man's goods. The coroner's judgment thus could affect the fortunes of a family. From the beginning, certification of the mode of death served quasi-legal functions with distinct monetary overtones.

This anachronistic omission of the part that a man plays in his own death ties us to 17th-Century Cartesian thinking and keeps us from enjoying the insights of contemporary psychology and psychiatry. In order to put man back into his own dying—a time of life when he is very much alive—we shall need to call upon social and behavioral science.

It can be argued that most deaths, especially in the younger years, are unnatural. Perhaps the termination of life might properly be called natural only in cases of death in old age. Consider the following confusions: if an individual (who wishes to live) has his chest invaded by a lethal steering wheel, his death is called accidental; if he is invaded by a lethal virus, his death is called natural; if his skull is invaded by a bullet in civilian life, his death is called homicidal. A person who torments an animal into killing him is said to have died by accident, whereas one who torments a drunken companion into killing him is called a victim of homicide. An individual whose artery bursts in his brain is said to have died with a cerebral-vascular accident, whereas it might make more sense to call it a cerebral-vascular natural.

In light of these confusing circumstances, I have proposed that we supplement the NASH classification by focusing on the *intention* of each person *via-a-vis* his own death, that all human deaths be divided among those that are a) intentioned, b) subintentioned or c) unintentioned.

Intentioned. In an intentioned death, the individual plays a direct and conscious role in effecting his own·demise. Persons who die intentioned deaths can be divided into a number of subcategories:

1. *Death-seeker.* He has consciously verbalized to himself his wish for an ending to all conscious experience and he acts to achieve this end. The criterion for a death-seeker does not lie in his method—razor, barbiturate, carbon monoxide. It lies in the fact that *in his mind* the method will bring about cessation, and in the fact that he acts in such a manner that rescue is unlikely or impossible. An individual's orientation toward death shifts and changes. A person who was a death-seeker yesterday might take tender care of his life today. Most of the individuals who are death-seekers ("suicidal") are so for relatively brief periods; given appropriate surcease and sanctuary they will soon wish to live.

2. *Death-initiator.* He believes that he will die in the fairly near future or he believes that he is failing and—not wishing to accommodate himself to a less-effective and less-virile image of himself—does not wish to let death happen to him. Rather *he* wants to play the dominant role; he will do it for himself, at his own time and on his own terms. In investigations among persons in the terminal stages of disease, it has been found that some, with remarkable and totally unexpected energy and strength, take out their tubes and needles, climb over the bedrails, lift heavy windows and jump. When we look at the occupational history of such individuals we see that they have never been fired—they have always quit.

3. *Death-ignorer.* Some people who kill themselves believe that one can effect termination without cessation. But in our contemporary society even those who espouse a religious belief in a hereafter still put the label of "suicide" on a person who has shot himself to death. This is so probably because, whatever *really* happens after termination, the survivors are still left to mourn in the physical absence of the deceased. Thus this subcategory of death-ignorer or, perhaps better, death-transcender, contains those persons who, from their point of view, terminate themselves and continue to exist in some other manner.

   The concept of death-ignoring is necessary; otherwise we put ourselves in the position of making comparable a man who shoots himself in the head in the belief that he will meet his dead wife in heaven and a man who travels to another city with the expectation of being reunited with his spouse. We must consider that cessation is final as far as the human personality that we can know is concerned.

4. *Death-darer.* He bets his continuation (i.e., his life) on a relatively low probability of survival. Regardless of the outcome a person who plays Russian roulette—in which the chances of survival are only five out of six—is a death-darer, as is the uncoordinated man who attempts to walk the ledge

of a tall building. The rule of thumb is, it is not what one does that matters but the background (of skill, prowess and evaluation of his own abilities) against which he does it.

Unintentioned. At the other extreme an unintentioned death is any cessation in which the decedent plays no significant role in effecting his own demise. Here death is due entirely to trauma from without, or to simple biological failure from within. At the time of his cessation the individual is going about his own business (even though he may be hospitalized) with no conscious intention of hastening cessation and with no strong conscious drive to do so. What happens is that something occurs—a cerebral-vascular accident, a myocardial infarction, a neoplastic growth, a malfunction, an invasion—whether by bullet or by virus—that for him has lethal consequences. *It* happens to *him.*

Most traditional natural, accidental and homicidal deaths would be unintentioned, but no presently labeled suicidal deaths would be. Persons who die unintentioned deaths can be subcategorized as follows:

1. *Death-welcomer.* Although he plays no discernible (conscious or unconscious) role in hastening or facilitating his own cessation, he could honestly report an introspective position of welcoming an end to his life. Very old persons, especially after long, painful, debilitating illness, report that they would welcome the end.
2. *Death-accepter.* He has accepted the imminence of his cessation and is resigned to his fate. He may be passive, philosophical, resigned, heroic or realistic, depending on the spirit in which this enormous acceptance is made.
3. *Death postponer.* Most of the time most of us are death-postponers. Death-postponing is the habitual orientation of most human beings toward cessation. The death-postponer wishes that cessation would not occur in the foreseeable future; that it would not occur for as long as possible.
4. *Death-disdainer.* Some individuals, when they consciously contemplate cessation, are disdainful of death and feel that they are above involvement in this implied stopping of the vital processes. They are in a sense supercilious toward death. Most young children in our culture, aside from their fears about death, are probably death-disdainers—as well they might be.
5. *Death-fearer.* He fears death—and even topics *relating* to death—to the point of phobia. He fights the notion of cessation, seeing reified death as something to be feared and hated. His position may relate to his wishes for omnipotence and to his investment in his social and physical potency. Hypochondriacs are perhaps death-fearers. (A physically well death-fearer might, when he is physically ill, become a death-facilitator.)

Image five older men on the same ward of a hospital, all dying of cancer, none playing an active role in his own cessation. Yet it is possible to distinguish different orientations toward death among them: one wishes not to die and is exerting his will to live (death-postponer); another is resigned to his cessation (death-accepter); the third will not believe that death can take him (death-disdainer); still another, although he takes no steps to hasten his end, embraces it (death-welcomer); and the fifth is frightened and forbids anyone to speak of death in his presence (death-fearer).

6. *Death-feigner.* It is of course possible to shout "Fire!" where there is no conflagration. It is also possible to yell or to murmur "Suicide!" when clearly there is no lethal intention. Calls like "Fire!," "Suicide!" or "Stop thief!" mobilize others. They are grab-words; they force society to act in certain ways. An individual who uses the semantic blanket of "Suicide!" in the absence of lethal intent is a death-feigner. A death-feigner simulates a self-directed movement toward cessation. He might ingest water from an iodine bottle or use a razor blade without lethal possibility or intent. He may seek some of the secondary gains that go with cessation-oriented behavior. These gains usually have to do with activating other persons— usually the "significant other" person in the neurotic dyadic relationship with the death-feigner.

Subintentioned. The most important death category—the one that I believe may be characteristic of a majority of deaths—is the *subintentioned* death, in which the decedent plays some covert or unconscious role in hastening his own demise. The evidence lies in a variety of behavior patterns that include poor judgment, imprudence, excessive risk-taking, neglect of self, disregard of medical regimen, abuse of alcohol, misuse of drugs—ways in which an individual can advance the date of his death by fostering the risk of his own dying.

Subintention is a somewhat mysterious concept, resting as it does on the powerful idea of unconscious motivation. It is "the subterranean miner that works in us all." The question is, as Herman Melville asked, ". . . can one tell whither leads his shaft by the every shifting, muffled sound of his pick?"

Many deaths certified as natural have a subintentional quality about them. Many of us know of cases in which persons with diabetes, peptic ulcers, colitis, cirrhosis, Buerger's disease or pneumonia have, through psychologically laden commission, omission, disregard or neglect, hastened their own demise. In addition "voodoo deaths," inexplicable deaths in hospitals (especially in surgery), and some sudden declines in health can be considered subintentioned. There is a notion that the speed at which some malignancies grow may be related to deep inner psychological variables.

And if some natural deaths are subintentioned (and thus not entirely natural), many deaths certified as accident are even more so—and not entirely accidental. A run of inimical events in one person's life can hardly be thought to be purely accidental. Sometimes we see someone drive a car as though he were afraid that he might be late for his own accident; he may be hurling himself toward a subintentioned death. Many automobile fatalities are not quite accidents and may not comfortably be called suicides; they can be more meaningfully understood as subintentioned deaths.

Some suicides show aspects of the subintentioned-death category. (This is especially true for many cases certified as probable suicides.) Indeed the entire concept of subintentioned death—which asserts the role of the unconscious in death—is similar in many ways to Karl Menninger's concepts of chronic suicide, focal suicide and organic suicide, except that Menninger's ideas have to do primarily with self-defeating ways of continuing to live, whereas the notion of subintentioned death is a way to stop the process of living. Cases of subintentioned death may in general be said to have permitted suicide.

Many fatal incidents certified as homicides might be better considered subintentioned deaths. It is obvious that in some close dyadic pairs (married couples, lovers, friends), the victim—like the chief mate of the *Town-Ho* in *Moby Dick*—"sought to run more than halfway to meet his doom." To provoke another person to kill you is an indirect participation, at some level of personality functioning, in the manipulation of one's date of death.

The hypothesis that individuals may play unconscious roles in their own failures and act in ways that are inimical to their own welfare seems to be too well documented from both psychoanalytic and general clinical practice to be safely ignored. Often death is hastened by the individual's seeming carelessness, imprudence, foolhardiness, forgetfulness, amnesia, lack of judgment or another psychological mechanism. Included in the subintention category would be many patterns of mismanagement and brink-of-death living that result in death.

Subintentioned death involves the psychosomatics of death: that is, cases in which essentially psychological processes (fear, anxiety, derring-do, hate, etc.) seem to play some role in exacerbating the catabolic processes that bring on termination (and necessarily cessation). Several types make up the subintentioned death groups:

1. *Death-chancer.* If a death-darer has only five chances out of six of continuing, then a death-chancer's chances are significantly greater but still involve a realistic risk of dying. It should be pointed out that these categories are largely independent of method, in that most methods (like razor blades or barbiturates) can legitimately be thought of as intentioned, subintentioned or unintentioned depending on the circumstances. Individuals who "leave it up to chance," who "gamble with death," who "half-intend to do it," are subintentioned death-chancers.

2. *Death-hastener.* He unconsciously exacerbates a physiological disequilibrium so that his cessation (which would ordinarily be called a natural death) is expedited. This can be done either in terms of his life-style (the abuse of his body, usually through alcohol, drugs, exposure or malnutrition), or through the mismanagement or disregard of prescribed remedial procedures. Consider the diabetic who mismanages his diet or his insulin, the individual with cirrhosis who mismanages his alcoholic intake, the Buerger's-disease

patient who mismanages his nicotine intake. Closely allied to the death-hastener is the death-facilitator who, while he is ill and his psychic energies are low, is somehow more than passively unresisting to cessation, and makes it easy for termination to occur. Some unexpected deaths in hospitals may be of this nature.

3. *Death-capitulator.* By virtue of some strong emotion, usually his great fear of death itself, he plays a psychological role in effecting his termination. In a sense, he scares himself to death. This type of death includes voodoo deaths, the deaths reported among southwestern Indians and Mexicans in railroad-sponsored hospitals who thought that people went to hospitals to die, and other cases reported in psychiatric and medical literature.

4. *Death-experimenter.* A death-experimenter often lives on the brink of death. He consciously wishes neither interruption nor cessation, but—usually by excessive use of alcohol and/or drugs—he pursues a chronically altered, often befogged continuation. Death-experimenters seem to wish for a benumbed or drugged consciousness. They will often experiment with their self-prescribed dosages (always increasing them), taking some chances of extending the benumbed conscious state into interruption (coma) and even (usually in a lackadaisical way) running some minimal but real risk of extending the interruption into cessation. This type of death is traditionally thought of as accidental.

It is important to distinguish between subintention and ambivalence. Ambivalence is perhaps the single most important psychodynamic concept for understanding death—or any of life's major psychological issues. Ambivalence represents at least two simultaneous movements within the mind of one person toward divergent, even opposite, goals. Examples of such contradictory activites would be loving and hating the same person, yearning for both autonomy and dependence, and, at rock bottom, moving toward both life and death. The concomitant movement toward each of these diverse goals is genuine in its own right. One can ingest pills, genuinely wishing to die, and at the same time entertain earnest fantasies of rescue. The paradigm of suicide is one of the deepest ambivalence: to cut one's throat and to cry for help—in the same breath.

On the other hand subintention does not emphasize the dual character of man's behavior so much as, in its own way, it emphasizes the unconscious aspects of man's being. Subintentioned acts, whether toward death or toward the expansion of life, are essentially movements toward outcomes that are not conscious goals. They are life's maneuvers that well up out of unconscious motivations and thus are more subtle in their appearance and more difficult to account. Is smoking suicidal? Drinking? Driving? Skiing? These questions cannot be answered yes or no. The answer is "It depends," and it may depend on a number of factors including the individual's orientations toward death and toward others in his life.

With some passionate emphasis Arnold Toynbee makes the point that death is essentially dyadic—a two-person event—and that as such the survivor's burden is the heavier. When he considers his own situation, he writes:

"I guess that if, one day, I am told by my doctor that I am going to die before my wife, I shall receive the news not only with equanimity but with relief. This relief, if I do feel it, will be involuntary. I shall be ashamed of myself for feeling it, and my relief will, no doubt, be tempered by concern and sorrow for my wife's future after I have been taken from her. All the same, I do guess that, if I am informed that I am going to die before her, a shameful sense of relief will be one element in my reaction . . . .

This is, as I see it, the capital fact about the relation between living and dying. There are two parties to the suffering that death inflicts; and, in the apportionment of this suffering, the survivor takes the brunt."

In focusing on the importance of the dyadic relationship in death, Toynbee renders a great service to all who are concerned with death, particularly with suicide. The typical suicide is an intensely dyadic event. The crucial role of the "significant other" in prevention of suicide is one aspect of the new look in suicidology.

Although it is difficult to take a stance counter to Toynbee, I believe that in emphasizing the dyadic aspect of death he seems to leap from a sentimental attitude of burden-sharing in a love relationship—the noble husband's wish to save his beloved wife from the anguish of bereavement—to an unnecessarily romantic view of death itself. In cases of absolutely sudden and precipitous deaths, the total sum of dyadic pain is borne by the survivor (inasmuch as the victim cannot experience any of it). But in protracted dying the present pain and anguish involved in the frightening anticipation of being dead may very well be sharper for the dying person than the pain suffered then and afterward by the survivor. The algebra of death's suffering is complicated.

For all his wisdom I believe that Toynbee indulges in the romanticization of death. In my view the larger need is to de-romanticize death and suicide.

Certainly one of the most remarkable characteristics of man's psychological life is the undiluted and enduring love affair that each of us has with his own consciousness. Trapped as he is within his own mind, man nurtures his conscious awareness, accepts it as the criterion for mediating reality, and entertains a faithful life-long dialogue with it—even (or especially) when he takes leave of his senses. Often man communicates with his mind as though it were a separate "other," whereas he is really communicating with himself. Indeed, the other to whom he talks is in large part what he defines himself to be. Death preemptorily decrees an abrupt, unwelcome and final adjournment and dissolution of what Henry Murray has aptly called "the Congress of the mind." Death—i.e., being dead—is total cessation, personal nothingness, individual annihilation. Should one traffic with one's greatest mortal enemy, rationalize its supposed noble and saving qualities and then romanticize it as an indispensable part of dyadic life?

One difficulty with death is that within himself each man is noble—indestructible and all-surviving. Being conscious is all one has. That is what one's life is. Consciousness defines the duration and the scope of life, and the scope can be rich or the scope can be arid, a partial death that can come long before one's cessation.

Our current attitudes toward death are unconscionably sentimental. The several notions—of "heroic death," "generativity" and "wise death" in mature old age — are culture-laden rationalizations, as though the cerebrator could ever be truly equanimous about the threat of his own naughtment or his annihilation.

Although there are undoubtedly special circumstances in which some individuals either welcome their own cessation or are essentially indifferent to it, for almost everyone the heightened probability of his own cessation constitutes the most dire threat possible. By and large the most distressing contemplation one can have is of his own cessation. Much of religion is tied to this specter—and perhaps all of man's concern with immortality. We must face the fact that completed dying (i.e., death or cessation) is the one characteristic act in which man is forced to engage.

In this context, the word *forced* has a special meaning. It implies that a characteristic that death shares with torture, rape, capital punishment, kidnapping, lobotomy and degradation ceremonies is the quality of impressment. The threat of being reduced to nothingness can be viewed reasonably only as the strongest and the most perfidious of forced punishments.

In all this I do not believe that I am echoing Dylan Thomas' "Do not go gentle into that good night. Rage, rage against the dying of the light." Rather I am saying that one should know that cessation is the curse to end all curses, and *then* one can, as he chooses, rage, fight, temporize, bargain, compromise, comply, acquiesce, surrender, welcome or even embrace death. But one should be aware of the dictum: Know thine enemy.

Death is not a tender retirement, a bright autumnal end "as a shock of corn to his season" of man's cycle. That notion, it seems to me, is of the same order of rationalization as romanticizing kidnapping, murder, impressment or rape.

Nor does it mollify the terror of death to discuss it in the honorific and beguiling terms of maturity, postnarcissistic love, ego-integrity or generativity, even though one can only be grateful to Erik Erikson for the almost perfectly persuasive way in which he has made a generative death sound ennobling and nearly worthwhile.

I wonder if it would not be better to understand generativity as reflecting pride and gratitude in one's progenitors and perhaps even greater pride and faith in one's progeny, without the necessity of deriving any pleasure from one's own finiteness and the prospect of one's demise. There is (or ought to be) a reasonable difference between experiencing justifiable pride in what one has been and is and has created, on the one hand, and, on the other hand, feeling an unwarranted equanimity when one reflects that he will soon no longer be. Maturity and ego integrity relate to the former; the latter is supported largely by the romantic, sentimental rationalization that one's cessation is a blessing. Such a rationalization is nothing less than psychologically willing what is biologically obligatory. It may be more mature to bemoan this fact and regret it.

All this means that death is a topic for the tough and the bitter—people like Melville, in "The Lightning-Rod Man": "Think of being a heap of charred offal, like a haltered horse burned in his stall; and all in one flash!" Or Camus, especially in Meursault's burst of antitheistic and antideath rage just before the end of *The Stranger*.

A look at another culture might throw some light on this problem. When I was in Japan a few years ago, it seemed to me that one of the most pervasive religio-cultural features of the country was the romantically tinged animism that infused the religious thinking. It was not a more primitive feeling, but rather a more personal and spirited feeling, especially about nature. For example the Japanese feelings about a cherry tree in its ephemerally beautiful bloom seemed totally different from the feelings that an average American would muster on looking at a blossoming apple tree. The Japanese closeness to nature, akin to deification, seems to lead to a special Japanese feeling toward death—which I would have to call romanticization.

When I addressed a group of Japanese university students, one youth asked me if I could give him any reason why he should not kill himself if he sincerely believed that he would then become one with nature. The very quality of this question illustrates this animizing and romanticizing of death. Further I recall a young engineer who sat beside me on the new Tokáidó train and wrote out: "Cherry blossoms is blooming quickly and scattering at once. Better to come to fruition and die like the blossom." He added: "We have had many great men among our forefathers whose deeds remind us of the noble characteristics of cherry blossoms."

In this country, the romanticization of certain types of homicides is an especially troublesome part of our national heritage. The honorifics go to the man with the gun. We have glamorized our rural bandits and our urban gangsters. The romanticized myth of the Western frontier, built around the image of the man with a gun, has set its homicidal stamp on our culture. The problem for television may not be the effects of violence but the effects of the romanticization of violence.

This romanticization of death goes to the beginnings of our national history. We depict our revolutionary heroes as Minutemen with rifles—as though it were primarily guns that had won the war. Perhaps more appropriate monuments at Lexington and Concord—we have even lost the meaning of the word "concord"—might have been statues of Paine and Jefferson seated, with pens. Unquestionably these representations would have implied quite different values and might have shaped our culture in a somewhat different direction. Our recent inability to amend our gun laws in the wake of a series of catastrophic assassinations has been a national disaster and a grisly international joke, highlighting our irrational tie to our own essentially anti-intellectual legends of romanticized homicide.

Romantic notions of death are obviously related to suicide. Individuals who are actively suicidal suffer—among their other burdens—from a temporary loss of the view of death-as-enemy. This is the paradox and the major logical fallacy of self-inflicted death. It capitulates to the decapitator.

Suicidal folk have lost sight of the foe: they sail with full lights in the hostile night. They are unvigilant and forgetful. They behave in strange, almost traitorous ways. They attempt to rationalize death's supposed lofty qualities and—what is most difficult to deal with—to romanticize death as the noblest part of dyadic love. Loyal-to-life people are inured against nefarious propaganda leading to defection. One should not traffic with the enemy. Suicidal individuals have been brainwashed—by their own thoughts.

How could the deromanticization of death help suicidal persons? Would it be salutary or beneficial to embark on programs of deromanticizing death in our schools—with courses in "death education"—or in our public media? In the treatment of the acutely suicidal person what would be the effects of directing his mind to a view of death as an enemy? Would such a psychological regimen hasten the suicide, have no effect at all, or would it make a death-postponer of him? In my own mind, the nagging question persists: would not this type of effort, like practically every other earnest exhortation in this alienated age, itself be doomed to an untimely figurative death?

But perhaps even more important is the question: how would the deromanticization of death reduce the number of those especially *evil* deaths of murder, violence, massacre and genocide? Here, paradoxically, I am a trifle more optimistic. If only we can recognize that our three crushing national problems— the black citizen, the war in Vietnam, and the threat of nuclear death—all contain the common element of dehumanizing others (and, concomitantly, brutalizing and dehumanizing ourselves), then acting out of the urgent need to reverse our present national death-oriented course, we might bring new dimensions to life. But in order to avert the death of our own institutions we shall, in addition to being the home of the brave and the land of the free, have to become the country of the humane.

SECTION **II**

UNDERSTANDING
SELF-DESTRUCTIVE BEHAVIOR

Perusal of this section will convince the reader that etiological factors in suicide are multiplistic. Each death must be understood in terms of the failure of the merging factors which have produced the involved person. Coping mechanisms seem to involve the following areas, and it will usually be found that there has been a trauma in one or more of them: (a) Physical, (b) Psychological, (c) Inter-personal, (d) Social, (e) Religious, and (f) Economic.

Physical

The termination of far advanced physical disease and infirmity by a suicidal act is understandable under certain circumstances. Inviting a premature death is in some instances reasonable and perhaps even deserves different terminology, especially for medico-legal purposes. Sometimes, however, minor physical infirmities are the crucial factor when disaster has occurred in some other area. The aged are particularly vulnerable, and inability to resign oneself to the possession of physical abnormalities may also lead the individual to a self-destructive act.

Psychological

Depression is by all odds the major cause of suicide and can be associated with many of the different types of mental illness. There are three major categories: (1) psychotic depressive reactions; (2) schizophrenia with depressive elements; (3) personality disorders, particularly as they relate to alcohol and drug addiction.

Depressions in childhood and adolescence command special attention because they tend to be camouflaged, thus frequently escaping professional care and sometimes even occurring without the awareness of the involved parents, relatives, and peer group. Grief, as it relates to the loss of a loved one, either through death or some other direct or indirect separation, may also have core significance.

Interpersonal

Family and peer dynamics operate in this area. Families which sustain unresolved grievances or permit the existence of tyranny, sibling rivalries, excessive striving, impossible value systems, etc., can be the source of great damage and occasional suicide in the case of the unsuccessful member.

Peer dynamics have special significance in the adolescent group, where they seem to be magnified more than at any other time in life. It is at this age that peer approval and acceptance become more important than the home and family. This is a time of impulse, rebellion, idealism, and search for identity. Individual demands can be excessive and, in the case of the vulnerable personality, can lead to tragic eipisodes which no other time in life would permit. Those most vulnerable seem to be the highly suggestible, the explosive, and the withdrawn types of personality.

Social

It is well known that certain societies are more vulnerable than others, as may be reflected in a comparison of suicide statistics and attitudes among various cultures and subcultures. Sociological interpretation varies from writer to writer. Reading the selections presented here may lead to reflection in terms of one's own milieu. Examination of social processes is not a simple matter, for the various institutions of society resist our inspection as they try to preserve their usual image. All societies tend to demand maintenance of and loyalty to their established rules from their members. We find it easier to observe the impossibility of certain life styles from our observation of others than to understand our own sociological characteristics. Minority groups have their own grievances in this area since they must reconcile their own philosophies with the different and contrasting ones of other groups which they encounter.

Religious

There are few religions which fail to serve or to make life easier. Unfortunately, religion also makes death attractive to some people. Youngsters who have been tormented by an unhappy family life or a lack of family interaction may feel the impulse to act out the theme, "If no one loves, me, I'll go to my father in heaven." Children, and even some adolescents, sometimes demonstrate a disregard for the finality of death and take the attitude of "Oh, well, if I'm not here then I'll be there" to the suicide act, or adopt the fairy tale mystique of "Now I'll live happily ever after." Mentally ill adults can regress to the same type of childish thinking—"They'll be sorry when I'm gone. I'll show them."

Churches may define taboos which infringe upon the norm, creating impossible conflicts. Unreasonable religious demands are difficult to confront since they are usually associated with piety, tradition, and the survivors or defenders of a particular taboo. The religion we were instructed in as children seems acceptable to us even though it may be found bizarre or ludicrous by others. There is still no force as powerful as religious expectation defined through family processes. The individual who defies these processes is in jeopardy, depending upon his own maturity and personality strengths.

Economic

To some people it would seem impossible that a man would take his life as a result of financial reversals. The rash of suicides which coincided with the "Great Depression" of the early thirties demonstrated the effect that the economy can have on our vital statistics. Apparently there is no grief like the loss felt by a greedy man.

We are in an era characterized by pleasure-seeking and must contemplate Freud's warning "beyond the pleasure principle." Pleasure-seeking seems to invite taking risks. Taking risks is a flirtation with danger, and encountering danger deliberately has suicidal inferences. Psychiatrists have been conscious of certain types of people who live the life of self-indulgence, excitement-seeking, and eventually develop a disrespect of others. Such people have been labeled "antisocial personalities." As increasing numbers of our society demonstrate disregard for their peers in a pleasure-seeking effort we must wonder at the capacity of the social matrix to sustain continued abuse.

The antisocial personality commands our attention because of his disrespect for life and his own reduced life expectancy. Such individuals appear prematurely in the obituaries after assaultive, seductive, drunken, indifferent, or careless behavior. Their disrespect for the rules and the rights of others points toward a disrespect for life itself. Some of these danger seekers find themselves in the headlines after particular acts of "bravery." One wonders how many dead heroes were produced by the pattern of pleasure seeking, the flirtation with excitement-danger and death, with all of its orgastic implications.

Society must learn how to deal with such individuals because their life style tends to confuse and even paralyze people with their reckless behavior.

Witnessing society's concern instructs the antisocial person that to take chances or to threaten one's life has great impact and manipulative potential. When confronted or detained by society these individuals invariably resort to threats. If all else fails the suicide threat becomes a most potent weapon. Usually the narcissistic, egocentric personality will fall short of real self-damage but on occasion as he flirts with these suicidal gestures he surprises himself cutting deeper than he intended or losing his balance with the noose around his neck in what would properly be termed an accidental suicide. It would be interesting to know sometime what the percentage of pleasure seekers is among the clientele of suicide centers.

Epidemiology of Suicide

Karen Westenskow *

INTRODUCTION

As an introduction to this particular area, the use of Dublin's (1967) words seem appropriate:

> We shall make the epidemiological approach. This has been the way of progress during the past 60 and more years in our study of the infections and other health conditions and in bringing about their control. And there is no reason why it should not be as rewarding in the study and ultimate control of suicide. And so I propose that we take note, as far as our knowledge will permit, of the extent of its ravages and the particular groups that are most directly affected. We shall explore the factual differences in regard to sex, age, race or ethnic group, marital condition, geographic location, economic status, religious application or other variables which may, either singly or in their totality, throw light on our particular problem.

Justification for this type of approach would be that suicide is the tenth leading cause of death among adults and the third leading cause of death among youth. "But most importantly, suicide is the first leading cause of unnecessary and stigmatizing death." (Shneidman, 1967)

MARITAL STATUS

Investigator's evidence suggests a pattern of suicide among the married, formerly married and unmarried that is worthy of discussion.

Dublin (1967) found the lowest incidence of suicide among married people with children and the highest incidence among the divorced. Yahraes (1969) found in 62% of his patient study cases that these households did not include children. Dublin (1967) also found the single and widowed fall between the high and low extremes. (See also, Bureau of Vital and Health Statistics, 1950-1964)

Reprinted from *Self-Destructive Behavior* — Workshop Proceedings. Director Brent Q. Hafen, Health Science Department; Brigham Young University, 1971.

*Prepared in association with: John Christiansen, Jeanne Hatch, Suzanne Roberts, and Kathryn Tryon, Karen Westenskow, Chairman.

Relevant here is Stengal's (1969) observation that the incidence of broken homes during childhood is significantly higher among the suicidal group (speaking of patients involved in previous attempts).

Widowers are more prone to suicide than married men (Rachlis, 1970) and Yahraes (1969) found in his study the "typical" Los Angeles suicide had suffered failure in his marital role. This is further supported by Wold (1970) when he found a greater percentage of his suicide-attempt patients living alone. Also, in the case of females, the principal cause of attempt was loss of the mate in some form (separation, divorce or death).

AGE, COLOR AND SEX DIFFERENTIALS

Age: According to the Bureau of Vital and Health Statistics (1950-1964) the rate of suicide increases until the 65-74 age group is reached. Litman (1970) found high suicide lethality rates correlating with increased age and male sex (see also, Farberow, 1968). As Rachlis (1970) says, "despite euphemisms about the 'golden years', life for the typical older person is a struggle for existence." Dublin (1967) found, however, that "attempts" were more common in young than old. Stengel (1969) found from his observations of motives and causes that two of the major precipitating events among the aged are physical illness and bereavement. Among the younger groups, problems in human relations seemed to be a predominant pattern.

Color: Suicide rates among the Negro are markedly lower than among the whites (Bureau of Vital and Health Statistics, 1950-1964; Breed, 1970; Yahraes, 1969). The Bureau (1950-1964) also stated that suicide occurs more frequently in the white population than in the non-white (this includes other ethnic groups besides the Negro).

Sex: It seems men in this respect are truly the weaker sex (or stronger — depending upon how you look at it). Referring again to the Bureau of Vital and Health Statistics (1950-1964) we read "suicide occurs much more frequently among males than among females" (See also, Farberow, 1968). Generally it is about 3 times as high as in females. Litman (1970) found in his study that the males in the suicide prevention center seemed twice as likely to commit suicide as females. Dublin (1967) adds further support to this; he found 3 times the incidence among men as among women. In Lester's (1969) cross cultural study he found that in 24 countries (with the exception of India) men had higher rates than women.

In conjunction with this heading it is found that the reverse of the above is true with reference to "attempts." Women, by far, seem to make more suicide "attempts" than men (Bureau of Vital and Health Statistics, 1950-1964; Dublin, 1967; Lester, 1969).

GEOGRAPHIC VARIATION

According to the Bureau of Vital and Health Statistics (1950-1964), Nevada and the other Western states were much higher (during these years) than the rates in the Southern States (with the exception of Virginia and Florida). For nonmetropolitan counties the rates were slightly higher than the rate for metropolitan counties.

With regard to the Negro, the rates are higher in Northern cities than those in the South (Yahraes, 1969). This opens the way to a discussion not proper in this section of study. Perhaps this is due to increased competition and strain in the Northern cities, or because their mobility has caused a hardship in the establishment of satisfactory social relationships.

Farberow (1968) reports that rates are high in Denmark, Italy, Japan and the Southern United States.

SUICIDE AND AUTHORITY

Using religion and police involvement as authority, the following are findings worthy of mention.

Breed (1970) found in his investigation that 30 out of 42 Negro suicides had the problem of police involvement in one form or another and to various degrees. Yahraes (1969) found similar results in his study with 3 out of 4 cases having had trouble with authority (Negro and White). He felt the Negro bears a double burden of social regulation. He must live within the designated regulation of the whites as well as the blacks. The frequency of suicide was lower among the male whites than among the male blacks when involving this authority stress-factor.

In regard to religion, Dublin (1967) found that where church authority was strong the suicide rate was lower than where church power was tenuous. Yahraes (1969) confirmed this hypothesis when he stated that religion "seemed" to be a protective device.

SOME COMMON CAUSES/ACCOMPANYING CONDITIONS

A predominate pattern among suicide attempts and completions is that of a personal loss of some sort. Among the Indians, the U. S. Department of Health, Education and Welfare (1967) report an external loss, of a loved one (see also, Farberow, 1968), or a fantasied departure of a loved one, loss of a job, good health, etc. Internally the main problem appears to be the loss of hope. A predominant factor in almost every suicidal situation. Farberow (1968) supports the existence of hopelessness and depression in his writings (not in reference to any racial group in particular). Similarly, in the 1969 report by the National Institute of Mental Health, it was reported that there is frequently a real external trauma or loss (threatened, fantasied or actual) and almost invariably an internal loss of hope. Again, with reference to caucasian subjects only, Breed (1967) found that "loss or the absence of something wanted predominate these occurrences." Also brought out in the Institute's report is a high incidence of extreme feelings of self-digust and low self-esteem, and that very often they have had previous records of suicidal behavior. In almost every case an attempt was preceeded by severe depression. Interestingly enough, this depression is quite often not communicated to others and neither is the plan nor intention of a suicide attempt.

Among several African tribes (Litman, 1970) it was found that females committed suicide predominantly in domestic situations. That is, they were unable to play the role of wife and mother adequately (barenness), illness, or the death of some loved person. The male has a similar pattern in addition to other factors. Impotence, or its fear, often leads to suicide. By way of faulty relationships, disease or other misfortune, a threatened domestic situation is a predominant characteristic.

Another predominant pattern is that of exhausted support and/or resources (Farberow, 1968; Litman, 1970).

Most suicide attempts occur in the context of communication. This is because the intention to die is almost always accompanied by an intention to live. It is because the individual wishes to live that the suicide attempt is most often made in such a way that someone else learns about the attempter's activity and the distress which lies behind it (National Institute of Mental Health, 1969).

As Shneidman (1967) says, "the typical suicidal person cuts his throat and cries for help at the same time."

EMPLOYMENT, INCOME AND ECONOMIC CONDITIONS

There is a considerable evidence that unemployment and downward change in economic and/or income status is positively related to suicide. The effects of unemployment and income interact with the effects of one varying depending upon the magnitude of the other. (Rushing, 1968)

Rushing (1968) found in his study that the effects of unemployment are clearly stronger at the lower income levels and tend to increase the tendency to suicide.

Breed (1968) found various correlations between employment and the suicide rate. He found that intergenerational mobility downward was prevalent among the suicide cases in his study. Two-thirds of the younger suicides held a position lower than that of their father. Decreasing incomes characterized more than half the suicides under his investigation. He also found that 48% were unemployed, part time, sick or disabled, retired early, etc. (Yahraes (1969) found the "typical" Los Angeles suicide had suffered failure in his work role. Farberow (1968) writes that work is a principal source of self-significance and self-esteem. He goes on to say that in conjunction with income and employment loss is often a socio-economic change. This socio-economic status shift is a contributing factor worthy of note. However, "job failure is not as frequently a crucial stress factor" for Negroes as for Whites (Breed, 1970).

Dublin (1967) reports a very high incidence among the "unskilled, the unemployed and the unemployables." Contrary to everyone's thought, suicide rates decline markedly during wartime, possibly because everyone is more concerned with larger interests besides those of himself.

Breed (1970) reports that "economic depression is accompanied by higher rates mostly among the higher income groups." Perhaps this is because they have the most to lose both by way of status, personal esteem, and finances. (See also, Farberow, 1968)

SEASONAL VARIATION

According to the Bureau of Vital and Health Statistics (1950-1964), suicide occurs more frequently during the Spring than the other seasons, March, April and May have the highest averages (for the above-mentioned years) with April being the highest in general.

The lowest rates of suicide occur in the winter with November, December, and January ranking the very lowest.

MEANS OF INJURY

Reported by the Bureau of Vital and Health Statistics (1950-1964), firearms and explosives are more frequently used than any other means of injury (48%). Hanging and strangulation follow in frequency and accounted for approximately 15% of the total suicides during the above-mentioned years. Twelve percent expired from poisoning and soporific substances (usually barbiturates), and the last 10% from poisoning by gas fumes (9 out of 10 involving motor vehicle exhaust gas). This methodology is further supported by Dublin (1967) who found that more than one half were the result of firearm use.

A distinction comes within this section as to methods used by males differing from those used by females. The male tends to make use of more violent means as opposed to females who use less violent methods with a larger margin for rescue.

Dublin (1967) found women used poisoning and asphyxiation most often whereas men exercised such means as hanging and firearms. Lester (1969) also found that males seem to succeed more in their attempts than females. He went on to say that attitudes toward death definitely affect the method used. Farberow (1968) supports this view. Women use less disfiguring methods than men, perhaps because of our social emphasis on personal beauty (Farberow, 1968). Differences in strength also affect the method. Women use methods that require less physical exertion and strength (Farberow, 1968).

BIBLIOGRAPHY

Bohaman, Paul. *African Homicide and Suicide,* Princeton University Press, 1960. pp. 262-265.
Breed, Warren. "The Negro and Fatalistic Suicide," *Pacific Sociological Review,* 13 (3): 156-162, Summer 1970.
Breed, Warren. "Occupational Mobility and Suicide Among White Males," *American Sociological Review,* 28:179-188, April 1963.
Breed, Warren. "Suicide and Loss in Social Interaction." In E. S. Shneidman (ed.), *Essays in Self Destruction.* New York: Science House, 1967.
Department of Health, Education and Welfare. *Suicide in the U.S. from 1950-1964,* Bureau of Vital and Health Statistics.
Dublin, Louis I. "An Overview of a Health and Social Problem," *Bulletin of Suicidology,* 11-14, December 1967.
Farberow, N. L. "The Psychology of Suicide," *International Encyclopedia of the Social Sciences.* The Macmillan Company and Free Press, 390-396, 1968.
Hendin, Herbert. *Black Suicide.* Basic Books, Inc., Publishers, pp. 132-147, 1969.
Lester, David. "Suicidal Behavior in Men and Women," *Mental Hygiene,* July 1969.
Litman, Robert E. "Suicide Prevention Center Patients: A Follow-up Study," *Bulletin of Suicidology,* (6) Spring 1970.
National Institute of Mental Health, Indian Health Service. *Suicide Among the American Indians,* U. S. Public Health Service Bulletin #1903, 1969.
National Institute of Mental Health, *Suicide Among the American Indians,* U. S. Department of Health, Education and Welfare, 1967.
Rachlis, David. "Suicide and Loss Adjustment in the Aging," *Bulletin of Suicidology.* Fall, 1970, pp. 23-26.
Rushing, W. A. "Income, Employment and Suicide: An Occupational Study," *Sociological Quarterly,* (9) 493-503, 1968.
Shneidman, Edwin S. "Current Developments in Suicide Prevention," *A Bulletin of Suicidology,* pp. 31-34, December 1967.
Stengal, Erwin. "Motives and Causes," *Suicide and Attempted Suicide.* Penguin Books, 1969.
Wold, Carl I. "Characteristics of 26,000 Suicide Prevention Center Patients," *Bulletin of Suicidology,* (6) Spring, 1970.
Yahraes, Herbert. "Characteristics of People Who Commit Suicide," *Mental Health Program Reports 3.* National Institute of Mental Health, January, 1969.

Deaths in a Youth Program

Eugene J. Faux and Blaine Crawford

The authors discuss eleven deaths that occurred in a series of 595 patients admitted to the Utah State Hospital Youth Program over a six-year period. They consider five of these deaths to have been preventable. Since four of these five took place among patients assigned to the same geographic unit, it seems reasonable to assume that they are related to staff attitudes and hospital living experiences.

It is well known that children who have sufficient problems to enter state hospitals have a higher than average death rate. They tend to be accident prone, abrasive and depressed. Since the beginning of the Utah State Hospital Youth Program six years ago, records have been kept concerning all deaths.

This paper will discuss the reasons for these deaths and the possibility that some of them could have been prevented.

This program is the only residential treatment program for children in the state and as such has admitted 595 patients over the six-year period. These children were grossly decompensated and were usually not admitted unless local community services had been exhausted.

During this time children were required to live on the adult wards, which were divided into the geographic unit system. Each unit had its own professional staff, attendants and two to four wards.

Eleven deaths took place—five during hospitalization and six after hospitalization. The causes ranged from a motorcycle accident to three suicides, one possible suicide and one murder. Unit I had two deaths, Unit II had one, Unit III had seven and Unit IV had one. Unit V, with the largest average daily census of young people and adults, had no deaths.

The youngsters in this sample, who ranged from age 13 to 19, had had their professional treatment and schooling in a day program separate from the rest of the hospital. All the hospitalized young people return at night to their respective wards on the adult units. Utmost cooperation is necessary between the two professional teams involved.

The authors will now take great liberties with this paper and record their

Reprinted by permission from *Mental Hygiene* 54, No. 4 (October 1970).

subjective impressions in a general way as it concerned each adult unit, their attitudes about children and the type of experiences with the youngsters and staff.

Unit I

Interested in children, wanted to help, good staff rapport, permissive attitude, always available for conferences about children, some resistance to acting out patients.

Unit II

Positive attitude about children and a desire to help. Cooperative and available at all times, permissive in their approach. The children liked their dorm and staff. Worked well with acting out as well as withdrawn youngsters.

Unit III

Passive cooperation at first with gradual resistance and antagonism to children as responsibilities were felt. Intolerant of acting out patients and insisted only psychotics should be admitted. Antagonized the children and Youth Center staff. Boycotted staff seminars and when there rebelliously insisted that most mental illness was a myth. Finally refused to allow any children on their wards and the other units had to take care of them.

Unit IV

Cooperative and helpful. Positive most of the time. Had some of our most difficult cases to help with and did so without complaining. Permisssive in approach. Available for conferences. Tends to resist acting out patients.

Unit V

This unit has a tremendous morale and handles the largest case load in the hospital. Responsibilities are taken religiously with children, even volunteering additional help or ideas. The children feel they are on a good unit, but complain that the policies are restrictive. There is a disciplinary attitude and strong therapeutic community type program. Personnel work equally well with psychotic and acting out patients.

DISCUSSION

After analyzing this particular series of deaths the authors have concluded that five of them were preventable. Case 1 was in Unit II. The other four were in Unit III.

Case 1

This was a 15-year-old mentally retarded boy who had been in the hospital several years before the Youth Program began. He was taken for granted as a long-term problem and yearly physical examinations were not done. He never complained and took care of himself without much assistance. One day in the shower room an attendant noticed he had a large testicle which proved to be very malignant and the cause of his death.

Case 2

This 14-year-old girl was in the hospital several months before the Youth Program was initiated. She came from a broken home, having been deserted by her mother in infancy. She failed to prosper after almost a year's hospitalization. The father and stepmother made it plain they did not want her back in their home. At this point her natural mother appeared at the hospital, having lived all these years in another state. She requested the patient's release, saying she was financially successful and capable of assuming responsibility for her daughter. The father at first objected but later joined his ex-wife in requesting the patient's release. Since she was a voluntary admission she was discharged. One and one-half years later we learned she had hanged herself in a girl's reformatory in the mother's home state.

She was a treatment failure in our institution and we hopefully and naively felt she could adjust when reunited with her mother.

Case 3

This boy came from a broken home, and experienced severe rejection by both of his parents. After unsuccessful private care he was admitted to the Utah State Hospital Youth Program but persuaded the judge to release him when he had his hearing. One and a half years later he was admitted as an adult patient making suicidal threats and cutting himself. He could not get along in the hospital and one night hanged himself after making numerous threats to do so. He had been regarded as a poorly motivated antisocial nuisance who made frequent suicide gestures, but, who seemed unlikely to harm himself seriously. Very few precautions were taken and supervision was lax.

Case 4

This girl was admitted at age 10 when Child Welfare workers claimed she had exhausted her foster home and school. She seemed to only be antagonized by hospitalization but failed also to adjust when another foster home was tried.

On her second admission her regular unit would not accept her and she was transferred to another ward. She and another female teenager went AWOL claiming to have had a sexual escapade with boys they picked up. They called the police afterward and asked to be returned to the Hospital. Subsequently the program for her was restrictive. One night after a temper outburst she was found hanged by a sheet in her seclusion cell.

Case 9

This 19-year-old epileptic girl was extremely paranoid and abrasive. She could never prosper in the Hospital and seemed to go from bad to worse. She was found dead while at home on a trial visit and had taken an overdose of barbiturates.

Psychiatric treatment was a complete failure and she expressed hatred for the Hospital.

CONCLUSIONS

Four, and possibly five, of these cases were suicides. Since they were assigned to the same geographic unit and since no other unit in the Hospital had this difficulty it seems appropriate to relate these tragedies to staff attitudes and hospital living experiences.*

The death study has special significance in the suicidology of this particular microsociety. There are epidemiological inferences which demand our respect. Obviously it was staff attitudes which loaned themselves to patient self-destruction; indifference, alienation, antagonism, and finally rejection.

If such anti-therapeutic elements can exist in what was regarded as a treatment institution, imagine the phenomena in the average society which is uncontrolled, lacks professional compartments, and escapes the processes of inspection.

There is a challenge in this study, not only to the institution involved, but also to the reader and his milieu. Are the institutions of which you are a part reporting statistics and studying the suicides close to you? Are we all covert, or do we have our heads in the sand?

---

*The authors are currently working on a study to further identify living problems for our children as they occur in our Hospital. A later publication will define the social static on the respective units in a less subjective fashion.

Two Types of Suicidal Behavior

Norman Tabachnick

INTRODUCTION

This paper attempts to identify and to discuss treatment plans for two types of suicidal patients seen in clinical psychotherapeutic practice—the interpersonal and intrapersonal types. Experience at the Los Angeles Suicide Prevention Center and with other helping institutions and individuals indicates that most suicidal situations will tend to fall into one of these groups. Therefore, an understanding of the clues to their identification and general treatment procedures for them should help significantly in the overall program of suicide evaluation and treatment.

There is little need at this point to go into great detail regarding the enormity of the suicidal problem in the United States. One might briefly point to the great loss of life (suicide is generally considered the number 10 killer in the United States), the depressing and malignant effect on those surrounding the suicide attempter, and the primary fact which is that the suicidal action is an indication of great emotional distress in the individual.

SOME DEFINITIONS AND CLARIFICATIONS

Before delineating the two clinical syndromes referred to above, it may prove valuable to spend some time defining and clarifying certain aspects of suicidal and self-destructive behavior. Suicidal behaviors are found in that relatively limited group of individuals who have conscious intimations of doing away with themselves and proceed to act on these intimations. Self-destructive behavior deals with a much broader range of activity that tends to shorten the physical life of the individual, including such diverse activities as accident, dangerous vocations, dangerous avocations, addiction to drugs, and a number of other categories. Suicidal behavior is included but as only one category among many. Self-destructive activities are often found to coexist with suicidal

Reprinted from *Suicide Among the American Indians,* June 1969. U.S. Public Health Service Publication No. 1903. National Institute of Mental Health; Indian Health Service.

activities, but the relationship is not an inevitable one. Indeed, there are probably a number of different types of relationships.[1]

There are a number of significant differences between suicide attempts and completed suicides. First is the comparative number; there are at least six times as many suicide attempts as completed suicides. It is, of course, difficult to secure an accurate indication of attempted suicides since in most areas there have been no legal or other provisions made for recording all suicide attempts. In addition, even if such provisions are made, it is doubtful that all people making suicide attempts would cooperate in the reporting procedure. Many suicidal attempts (particularly those which do not result in severe incapacity to the individual) can easily be concealed and, for a number of reasons, concealment is exactly what the suicide attempter wishes to accomplish. However, there have been a number of efforts to estimate suicide attempts, and it is from these that the figure listed above is taken.

One's first impression may be that suicidal behavior has but one intention, and that is the cessation of life for the victim. It becomes evident, however, that a number of intentions are possible. Frequently more than one intention can be inferred from a study of the conscious and unconscious thinking of the individual. The intentions include the following: (a) A wish for relief from anxiety; (b) a wish to be reborn; (c) a wish to communicate a need for help; (d) a wish to punish oneself; (e) a wish to punish someone else; and (f) a wish to enjoy approaching death which is eroticized.

Most suicide attempts occur in a context of communication. This is because the intention to die is almost always accompanied by an intention to live. The strength of these intentions varies in different individuals, but both are usually present. It is because the individual wishes to live that the suicide attempt is most often made in such a way that someone else learns about the suicide attempter's activity and the distress which lies behind it.

An important question in suicidal attempts is: How lethal was the attempt? How does one assess this aspect? In general terms, one could and should use the evidence of how close the person actually came to killing himself. Thus, if he was in a state of coma for several days, one can be sure that he was dealing with an extremely lethal attempt, whereas if no physical disability was noted, the attempt can be judged as mild.

Yet it may be possible to make a more accurate assessment of lethality. This might be done by applying two methods of evaluation to the suicidal behavior:

The Point of No Return. This factor refers to the speed of the suicidal mode utilized. Examples of extremes in this situation would be a .38 calibre bullet fired pointblank at one's heart. (This would have a point of no return of less

[1]"Theories of Self-Destruction," by Norman Tabachnick, Karen Kloes, Phillipa Poze, and Elaine Fielder, was presented at the 1968 Annual Meeting of the American Psychiatric Association.

than 1 second.) Contrast this with the ingestion of 15 Seconal capsules (this would have a point of no return of approximately 8-12 hours).

The Possibility of Rescue. This factor refers to the physical and social possibilities for rescue surrounding the suicidal attempt. There are good possibilities for rescue of a housewife who swallows several barbiturate capsules approximately 1 hour before her husband is scheduled to come home from work. On the other hand, there would be poor possibility of rescue for an individual who told his friends that he was going away for the weekend, then, on leaving them Friday evening, went directly to his home, took 40 barbiturate capsules, and locked himself into a closet.

THE TWO GROUPS OF SUICIDE ATTEMPTERS

After this general description of certain aspects of the suicidal situation, let us move to the characterization of the two important clinical groups already referred to. Let us call them the interpersonal and the intrapersonal groups.

The Interpersonal Group

1. This type of suicide attempter tends to be neurotic.
2. The age group is a relatively young one, ranging from 16 to 35 years.
3. The majority of these attempters are women.
4. They are usually quite involved with other people.
5. They are often at odds with other people, and their suicide attempts reflect a difficulty they are having with a significant other.
6. Their attempts tend to have a fairly low lethality.
7. They generally respond well to attempts by others to help them.

The Intrapersonal Group

1. There tend to be many more psychotic or borderline diagnoses in this category.
2. They fall into a much older age group than the interpersonal attempters. They are usually 50 years of age or older.
3. There are many more men than women in this group.
4. These people tend to be isolated. They have typically encountered a progressive loss of significant esteem-sustaining objects such as jobs, significant other people, good health, etc.
5. There are extreme self-punitive and self-depreciating feelings. These include attitudes of depression and disgust about the self. In general, their self-esteem is quite low.
6. This group of individuals tends to have a relatively high lethality rating in their suicide attempts.

7. They respond relatively poorly to helping activities.

The intrapersonal group is obviously the more serious one. Comparison with individuals who have completed suicide indicates that the intrapersonal group of attempters may be a precursor group to those who have successful suicidal activity.

DANGER SIGNS AND CLUES

There are a number of important diagnostic criteria which are noted in these groups.

Manifestations Characteristic of Both Groups

1. Depression (of almost any kind).
2. Drinking and drug-taking.

Drinking and drug-taking are significant in suicidal people from a number of standpoints. First of all, the very fact of the ingestion of alcohol or other drugs is an indication of lowered reserves of self-esteem in the victim. Secondly, having once taken drugs or alcohol, the individual's ability to organize and integrate his behavior according to self-preservative standards is impaired. Thus, whatever his situation before ingestion, the possibilities of self-destructive behavior are increased after ingestion.

Symptomatology Characteristic of the Interpersonal Group

1. There are frequently suicidal threats, suicidal actions, and intimations of suicidal behavior which occur in interpersonal settings.
2. There are often emotional outbursts.
3. A history of previous suicidal behavior is frequently obtained.
4. The suicide plan which members of this group possess is usually not well defined. Often there is no plan apart from an intention that, if things continue to go badly, some kind of suicidal activity will take place.
5. "Interpersonal attempters" often have very clear and definite ideas as to how their crisis may be easily ended. They may sometimes be reticent in terms of quickly entering into discussion with the helper, but once a bond of trust and confidence has been established, the thought as to what might terminate the emotional crisis is easily forthcoming.

Specific Symptomatology Characteristic of the Intrapersonal Group

1. There is noted in the history a progressive isolation from significant others and from valuable outside situations.
2. Opposed to the "interpersonal" group, the suicidal thoughts and activities of this group of individuals are usually concealed.

3. They tend to have well thought out suicidal plans and have made preparations to implement them.
4. They are almost invariably depressed but, interestingly enough (and perhaps related to the lack of "significant others" in their lives), they have not communicated their depression to others.
5. They are relatively hopeless, quick "bouncebacks" are rarely seen, and they generally have few or no ideas of how their situation might be helped.

THE CAUSES OF SUICIDE

The etiology and predisposing causes of suicide have been discussed at great length in many books and articles. Obviously, a short paper such as this cannot hope to do justice to the many worthwhile contributions. However, from the standpoint of the clinic, suicide can be related to an extremely important duality of causes.

The first factor is that there is almost always a real external trauma or loss. This loss can take many forms. It may involve the death of a loved one, the threatened or fantasied departure of a loved one, the loss of a job, the loss of good health, and many other factors. What I emphasize is that some *real* loss may be identified in almost every suicidal situation.

Secondly, there is almost invariably an internal loss (of hope). This loss complements the external loss and is often accompanied by a disorganization of the personality.

These two factors are found to a greater or lesser degree in practically every suicidal situation. An attempt should be made to identify the specific aspects of each of these factors as a first step in the treatment of a suicidal individual.

THE TREATMENT OF SUICIDE

Coinciding with the formulation of the dual causation of suicide, the treatment of suicide is directed to two concurrent aims. These are the reintegration of the personality and the restoration of hope and objects.

The Reintegration of the Personality

As already stated, there is some degree of disorganization of the personality in every suicidal person. This is reflected by a lack of clear judgment. Often there is an aimless skittering about of the mind. It first latches onto one possible direction for action, but before this can be followed through or indeed even clearly delineated, it quickly moves on to another one. There is a difficulty in organizing an appropriate hierarchy of values. The simplest question "Is it more important to go into the hospital following a near-lethal suicide attempt or to be at home because the repairman for the washing machine is coming?" is often difficult to evaluate for a suicidal person. Other indications of poor judgment abound.

To deal with such a situation, the counselor must be encouraging, supportive, and friendly to the victim. However, more than this is required. After establishing himself as a useful, valuable, and authoritative friend, there should be no hesitation in taking over the task of making important judgments when it seems that the suicidal patient cannot accomplish this task himself.

Furthermore, in the course of making these judgments, the counselor must be logical. He should be able to organize a hierarchy of situations to be acted upon. He must be able to say what should be done first and what can wait until a later time because it is not so important. In the course of doing this, he not only helps the suicide attempter make certain decisions which might be quite helpful and indeed life-preserving for him, but equally important, he shows the victim how "appropriate" thinking proceeds. The treatment of the victim in this way acts as a learning experience. Many victims utilize such activity of the therapist as a model upon which to base present and future activities of their own.

The Restoration of Hope and Objects

The basic aim of restoring hope and objects should be implemented in both the interpersonal and intrapersonal groups. However, certain differences in the two groups call for somewhat different techniques of implementation.

The Interpersonal Group. Since the separation from the significant other person or institution is often, in fact, one that can be repaired relatively easily, a first aim of the therapist is to see if this can be done. He must evaluate the seriousness of the rupture with the significant other situation or person by talking to both the suicide attempter and the other person. In addition, the emotional support which is freely given in the situation tends to act as an important nutrient for the depleted suicide attempter. He "swallows this in" and, in the process, becomes stronger.

The Intrapersonal Group. Emotional support is the keystone of the treatment of suicide. This means that it must be given freely and in great quantities to all suicide attempters.

To restore lost objects is not as easy in this group of attempters as it is in the interpersonal group. This is because reality considerations often make the objects impossible to restore. Suicide attempts here often occur in response to recent or past losses of spouse, children, or important friends. These people may be irrevocably lost. When an older person loses a job or his good health, it is often difficult if not impossible to restore them.

However, one can attempt to find new objects which can replace the lost ones. From this standpoint, moving toward new interpersonal relationships, new occupations, new avocations are all an important part of the therapeutic handling of attempters in this group.

It will be sensed by this time that the treatment of the "intrapersonal" group will likely be more prolonged and often need to be more intensive than that of the "interpersonal" group. One must recognize this at the beginning and be prepared for longer, more drawn out therapy. If one is willing and able to provide this therapy, gratifying results will often ensue. Perhaps one important reason for this is that by providing such help to the troubled individuals, the therapist himself becomes a replacement for those lost objects which brought on the difficulty.

In conclusion, it is much easier to write a paper about therapy than to conduct therapy. In order to make certain points in what I hope has been a clear way, I have necessarily had to simplify and codify a complex and difficult situation. It goes almost without saying that there are many suicidal situations which need and deserve a more elaborate evaluation than I was able to indicate in this paper. However, the attempt has been to provide certain guideposts that can act as an initial orientation to the treatment of suicidal patients.

Characteristics of People Who Commit Suicide

Herbert Yahraes

INTRODUCTION AND SUMMARY

The number of reported suicides in this country is running about 22,000 a year, but authorities believe that the actual figure is two or three times as large. Even on the basis of the reported numbers, suicide ranks as the tenth leading cause of death among adults and the third leading cause among persons from 15 to 19. For every suicide there are probably ten attempted suicides.

The costs of suicide are high in terms not only of lives but also of money and of mental health. Typically, a suicide's death deprives his family and the community of years of service and earnings. And each survivor of such a person—spouse, parents, children, brothers and sisters, friends, associates—must handle feelings of extra shame, bewilderment, or guilt. No other kind of death in our society creates such lasting and widespread scars.

The National Institute of Mental Health has long conducted and supported basic research on the causes of suicide—physiological, psychological, sociological—and it has also supported programs established to try to prevent suicides and at the same time to provide opportunities for research and for the training of workers in prevention. To coordinate the attack on the problems of suicide, the Institute in 1966 founded the Center for Studies of Suicide Prevention. And the Center, to coalesce and sharpen the interest of scientists and help-givers in many fields, has worked for the establishment of suicidology as a profession.

In the research reported upon here, Warren Breed, professor of sociology at Newcomb College of Tulane University, New Orleans, has been collecting and analyzing data on 264 persons who committed suicide in New Orleans between 1954 and 1963. He is looking for common denominators: the situations and personality characteristics that typify sizable proportions of those who take their own lives. Such knowledge will increase our ability to identify and help the potential suicide.

Breed reports that the suicide rate in New Orleans is one of the lowest, for large cities, in the Nation: 7.8 per 100,000 people in 1960. For whites, the rate

Reprinted from *Mental Health Program Reports – 3,* National Institute of Mental Health, January 1969. Department of Health, Education and Welfare.

is under 10 per 100,000, as compared to 11 for the country as a whole; for Negroes, it is less than 2 per 100,000. The lower rate among Negroes, Breed thinks, can be attributed at least partly to segregation, which has kept the Negro from competing with the white and therefore has forced him to accept relatively low goals, which can be reached with less strain. The investigator points out that in northern cities the suicide rate among Negroes is considerably higher than in the South. The factors at work probably include (a) the increased competition, with its increased strain; and (b) migration, which often makes it difficult to establish satisfying social relationships. For the country as a whole, the Negro suicide rate is about one-third the white rate. Incidentally, Breed reports that most suicide attempts the country over are made by women—two or three to one; but most of the successful attempts are made by men, again by two or three to one.

For each of the 264 cases in the New Orleans study, at least one person who had known the suicide was interviewed, and for more than 200 of the cases, at least two persons. The informants included relatives, friends, neighbors, employers, fellow workers, and doctors. A few of the interviews are short, but many are long and detailed and contain information about spouses, children, home life, friends, and problems. Breed also has coroner and police reports on each case. For control purposes in the phase of the study dealing with male suicides, Breed collected information, again through interviews, about men who were of the same age as the suicides and lived on the same blocks (which were well scattered through the city).

With the aid of data from the Los Angeles Suicide Prevention Bureau, where he worked and studied one recent year, Breed also has analyzed 50 suicide cases among Los Angeles men and compared the results with those of the New Orleans study.

So far the analysis of the 264 cases has been concerned mainly with what Breed calls "the failure suicide." He had a hunch that many suicides have failed in a major role: many of the men have failed at work or in business; many of the women have failed in the marital-maternal role. "The role of the man in American society is to work," he says. "It is to have some kind of employment and to be at least adequate at it—preferably to be improving and to be going up the ladder of prestige and income. The role of the American female is to get married and have children. So in suicide, I see as a major cause the failure to carry on one's role."

For a test of this hypothesis, Breed studied no suicide more than 60 years of age and none who had not resided in New Orleans more than six months. (He wanted "New Orleans people," not individuals who had gone to the city just to die; he wanted also to make the best use of Census data in comparing suicides and nonsuicides.) In considering failure suicides, he omitted persons who had been seriously ill, physically or mentally.

The principal findings to date are summarized here:

1. A substantial proportion of the white male suicides had indeed experienced failure, or what they perceived to be failure, in their work role. And a substantial proportion of the white female suicides had experienced failure in the wife-mother role. The investigator believes that failure in the work role or the wife-mother role is the major factor in at least half of all suicide cases in the U.S.

2. Among the Negro men who committed suicide in New Orleans, job problems were often important but seemed less critical than "authority" problems. Only 10 percent of the white men but more than half of the Negroes had been involved with the police or the courts at the time of killing themselves; in fact, almost three-fourths of the Negroes had been facing an authority problem of some kind. Also, the Negro suicides were much more likely than the white (40 percent as against 20 percent) to have been concerned about debt.

3. Most of the suicides in the Los Angeles study, too, had suffered loss of status at work or had failed to reach the status desired. But these men, more frequently than those in the New Orleans sample, had also experienced considerable difficulty in other roles, particularly marital. As a possible explanation, Breed notes that almost all the Angelenos but few of the New Orleanians had come from out-of-State and, therefore, presumably had had greater difficulty in establishing and maintaining social ties.

4. Migration seemed to be associated with suicide among New Orleans women, as among Los Angeles men. The female suicides who had lived in New Orleans less than 10 years were younger than the others, less educated, and of a lower social class. Above all, they showed the least satisfactory family situations. About half were not living with a man, legally or extralegally, at the time of death. Only two were considered to have a good marriage. "The single preeminent difficulty experienced by these recently arrived young women," Breed reports, "was in meeting and marrying the kind of man with whom they could establish and maintain a viable home."

5. The analysis of the influence of religion is incomplete, but Breed's impression from the work to date is that active membership in a church, any church, is a protective device against suicide. In this respect, what is important, he thinks, is the commitment to something, and a commitment to atheism might serve just as well as one to religion. Seventy years ago the French sociologist, Emile Durkheim, found that suicides were most frequent among Protestants and least frequent among Jews, with Catholics in between. "But since then," Breed remarks, "religions have become homogenized."

The findings to date have practical value, the investigator believes, because they suggest what the suicide-prevention worker should look for. In the case of a man, the worker should be interested first in his job history, since failure in the work role is a very good indicator of suicide proneness among men. The worker should next be interested in his family life, because family problems often accompanied work-role failure among the New Orleans suicides and ranked of equal importance with it among the Los Angeles suicides. With a woman, in New Orleans at least, the worker should be interested first in the man in her life.

New Orleans will open a suicide prevention center next year, it is hoped, under the sponsorship of Tulane Medical School. Working with the staff, Breed will then be able to apply his findings. Meanwhile, he seeks further information through a more detailed analysis of his cases.

THE FAILURE SUICIDE: MALE

Studying the interviews, Breed found that the commonest factor in the recent lives of the suicides had been a loss. Among the men it had been most often the loss or expected loss of job or status; among the women, loss of a man or failure to get a man. There was also in many cases what Breed calls "loss of mutuality," or a weakening of social relationships. Sometimes this third kind of loss seems to have been triggered by one of the first two; sometimes it had occurred years before.

To study failure in the work role, Breed used a sample of 103 white males between the ages of 20 and 60, for each of whom he got two controls—men of the same age and living on the same block.

Only 50 percent of the suicides, the investigator found, had been working full time just before they killed themselves. Most of the others were unemployed (21 percent), or working only part time (11 percent), or sick or disabled (5 percent), or retired (5 percent). Among the controls, almost all were employed full time.

By and large, the suicides had been "downwardly mobile," meaning that they were in occupations lower than those of their fathers, or lower than the ones they had previously been in themselves, or that their income had been dropping. Downward mobility as indicated by comparing the occupational levels of fathers and sons was especially prevalent among the younger men, between the ages of 20 and 39, two-thirds of whom held a lower position than their fathers. Even between the ages of 50 and 60, though, 44 percent had not reached their fathers' level. For the group as a whole, the proportion was 53 percent; among the controls it was 31 percent.

For one-third of the suicides, the last job they had held had been lower than the one before. This was true for only 5 percent of the controls. More than half of the suicides, but only 11 percent of the controls, had been making less money than they had 2 years earlier. Only 8 percent, but 35 percent of the controls, had been making more.

Three-fourths of the suicides had suffered at least one of these forms of drops in status—they had been skidding. In some of the remaining cases, other disappointments with work status—such as early retirement, or assignment to a smaller office, or failure to receive an expected promotion—were present.

In the great majority of the cases studied, the investigator believes that the men felt acute dissatisfaction with their work performance and guessed that other persons saw them as failures in their main role in life. One man, for example, a devoted Navy officer, had been discharged from the service following an accident to his ship. Another had been a policeman; dropped for accepting a bribe, he had taken a job as a guard with lower pay and prestige. A construction superintendent had been forced into a less prestigious job when orders fell off. An investment counselor had opened his own business but failed to attract enough clients to make it pay.

Says Breed: "I see the person who commits suicide as having felt, "My God! I am a total loss. I am miserable. I feel ashamed in the community. I've felt this way for some time. I've been asking myself what can I do? I felt shame again today; I don't want to feel shame tomorrow. I'm going to kill myself." If that's aggression—and psychiatrists seem to think that in suicide a person takes his aggressive feelings toward others and turns them against himself—well, O.K. I don't see this very often. It is simply feeling that one would be better off dead than alive. I suspect these people are in great pain—the pain of shame."

There were exceptions: a few of the suicides had been performing adequately on the job, and some of the controls had not. Also, work was by no means the only problem. A number of the men had been having marital trouble. (In at least one case, work and marriage difficulties—and aggression—were intertwined: the man had lost two jobs because of a nagging wife. He left his insurance policies where his wife would quickly find them—made out to her but recently allowed to expire.) Some were alcoholics or had other health problems. "I was trying to show the importance of the work role," Breed remarks, "but I do not say that this is the only major factor involved."

As a check on his findings about "work-role failure" among male suicides in New Orleans, the investigator studied 50 suicide cases—48 white men and two Negroes—in Los Angeles. He found that among this group, too, sizable proportions had been going downhill. About two-thirds were either unemployed or working only part time. Income had been dropping in more than half of the cases.

With these men, though, family problems seemed to have been just as important as job problems. Only 18 of the Los Angeles men were married and living with their wives, not all of them happily. Twenty-one were living alone. Ten had never married. The typical Los Angeles suicide had suffered failure in his marital as well as his work role. Why? The investigator thinks it was because most of the men had come from elsewhere (only one had been born in Los Angeles and only three others in California) and therefore had had more difficulty than the

New Orleans men, most of whom had been born in or near the city, in developing satisfying relations with other people.

SUICIDES AMONG NEGRO MALES

Many of the Negro men who took their lives (42 cases have been studied) were, like the whites, having work trouble. The proportion that was going downhill occupationally was only about 30 percent, as compared to about 50 percent for the whites, but a third of the Negroes were already at the bottom and had been there for at least some time. Also, the Negroes were much more likely than the whites to have expressed concern over money matters.

For the Negro suicides, the most characteristic problem seems to have been involvement with authority, particularly the police. It was present in three cases out of four. Breed reports that the interviews abound with comments about the fear of the police the eventual suicides had expressed. Several of them were quoted as having said they would kill themselves before going to jail. Some of the informants charged that the police had beaten and even killed the "suicide." Others voiced their own fear of the police.

The investigator does not know whether or not the fear was justified, but it was there, and he cites one case as perhaps suggesting one of the ways it arose. This young man had never been arrested. When he was much younger, however, his mother told the interviewer, a white detective had "kidded" him a number of times and had told him he would wind up in jail. The officer would say: "Boy, what have you done wrong? Let's see what you've got on you." His mother said: "He was just like his uncle—afraid of policemen." One night he fought with his girl friend, pulled a gun, and wounded her. His mother called the police. When he heard the approaching siren, he turned the gun on himself.

Several kinds of authorities were involved in addition to the police. One man, for example, had remodeled his cafe but could not reopen it because the Negro church next door had obtained an injunction. A retailer who had bought stolen goods—innocently, it was said—was faced with handing out considerable money to hush up the affair. Two men had been served with eviction notices. Tax agents were proceeding against a man who had claimed exemptions for illegitimate children. One man's wages had been garnisheed for payments on his son's car: $57 a month on a weekly wage of $55.

"What strikes me about such cases," says Breed, "is that the Negro typically had little information about community resources and doubtless less confidence that he could gain access to the potential helper. For example, the man with the tax problem could have called upon the Internal Revenue office; others could have sought Legal Aid if not a private lawyer; still others qualified for assistance from social welfare agencies, clinics, credit bureaus, job advisors, and so on. But they tried none of these resources.

"The Negro is subject to the imperatives of two communities, and when his difficulties extend outside the Negro sphere, he is faced with authorities who are white—to him an alien force. He bears a double burden of social regulation. A white man can feel trapped, too, but the data demonstrate a much lower frequency of the 'authority' stress factor in white male suicide."

However, the investigator points out, many other Negroes who were also targets of authority did not commit suicide. From the available information it is not possible to say why.

THE FAILURE SUICIDE: FEMALE

Among the suicides studied were those of 107 white women between the ages of 18 and 60. In only three percent of the cases was the major problem judged to be related to work—either the woman's own work or her husband's. At least among people who commit suicide, Breed comments, the prestige and sense of well-being gained from occupational status is much less important for women than for men.

The principal, and indeed almost the only, problem in 39 percent of the cases, was the loss of the mate. A number of the other women showed this same problem in combination with additional kinds of family difficulties. Only one-fourth of the women were judged to be having a good marital relationship.

Loss of a man can take many forms. In some of the cases there was an actual loss: the husband had died or had left home. In others the loss was threatened or feared: he had been talking about a separation or had been showing interest in another woman. The few women who had neither married nor taken a common-law husband had also suffered a loss, Breed thinks—a loss of something yearned for but not achieved.

As additional evidence of failure in the marital and maternal role, Breed reports that in a surprisingly large proportion of the cases (62 percent) the household contained no children at the time of the woman's death. The proportion was high even in the younger groups. Of the women in their twenties, half had no children in their households; of those in their thirties, 54 percent; of those in their forties, 62 percent. Only 8 percent had never been married or had a common-law husband, yet 39 percent had never had a child. In fact, more than 25 percent had been unable to have children. The investigator is looking for the reasons behind this last finding.

CHARACTERISTICS OF FAILURE SUICIDES

Millions of people fail in various ways during the year but do not commit suicide. So Breed has thought about the failures who do kill themselves and has tried to find characteristics that set them apart. He believes that the failure suicides share the following four:

1. *The acceptance to an extreme degree of the cultural norms of success.* Breed's reading of the interviews convinces him that the suicides were committed to high aspirations—that they had insisted on trying to do what the culture expected them to do.
2. *An extreme sensitivity to failure.* "The suicides had a high capacity to feel shame," the investigator says, "and small capacity to overcome it. They perceived not merely a goof here and a goof there but a generalized sense of worthlessness and hopelessness, permitting no exit with honor in this life."
3. *The inability to change roles and goals: rigidity.* The suicides, having failed along one line, could not try another: in Breed's words, they could not shift gears in the face of difficult road conditions. A failing investment counselor could have had a job in a bank but had not asked for it; a twice-divorced woman could have moved in with a widowed sister but had not given this possibility even a trial. "Bulldoglike," says the investigator, "the failure suicides wanted to succeed in a certain way in a certain role, and nothing else would do."
4. *Worsening of interpersonal relationships.* The failure suicide believes that everyone near to him knows of his failure. (In many of the cases studied, this was true; in many others, however, those near to the suicide did not agree he had failed.) Fearing rejection, he breaks his social ties. This withdrawal leads to further isolation. So he is deprived of the contact with other persons that most of us need to sustain life. "The decrease of social contact leaves a person without support, internal or external," Breed observes. "In a major sense, his humanness has gone. His goals are unreached, his friends are distancing, his self-conception hits bottom, he is in ultimate danger. He asks, 'What else is there for me to do?' But the only person he asks is himself."

Without doubt, the investigator adds, all the characteristics noted above have been influenced by the individual's early experiences at home, in school, and with his fellows. For the cases studied, there is little trustworthy information about the nature of these experiences.

Breed points out that he does not yet have hard evidence confirming every point in his model of a failure suicide. He believes that his data confirm the importance of the work role for men and the marital-maternal role for women. The assumed inability of the failure suicide to change roles and goals and the increasing withdrawal from social relationships seem to be borne out by the case histories, but quantitative information is generally lacking. (There is a little, about social ties. Each person interviewed was asked to rate the suicide as to "friends and visiting" on a "more or less" basis. "The results, while admittedly crude, are quite clear," Breed reports. Among the men, 45 percent were placed in the "more friends and visiting" category; among the women, 44 percent. The proportion among the men in the control group was almost twice as large.

Frequency of church attendance may be another index of mixing with others. Half of the women suicides and three-fifths of the men attended no more than twice a year; only a quarter of the men in the control group attended so seldom.)

Further analysis of the interviews and research by other investigators, Breed hopes, will supply confirmatory data.

How about the very many people who experience failure in work or in marriage and motherhood and who do not commit suicide?

These people do not show the four characteristics of the failure suicide, Breed answers. Experiencing failure, they rationalize it: It didn't really happen to them; or somebody else was to blame; or they never really had their heart set on that goal; anyway, things like this happen to everybody.

Such a person is still valuable to himself. The man says: "I'm doing pretty well now driving a cab." The woman says: "I'm a divorcee but a successful divorcee." Each adds: "I can see some nice things about to happen to me." Also, the "failure" may have changed his associates so that he need not meet people who suspect him of having failed.

Says Breed: "The suicide accepts the failure situation as terminal. The nonsuicide parries and slips the blows so that the self is grazed instead of being stunned into surrender."

Research Grant: MH 15090
Date of Interview: April 1968

BIBLIOGRAPHY

Breed, W. *Occupational mobility and suicide among white males.* American Sociological Review, 28:2, 1963.

Breed, W. On the social psychology of the suicide process. Delivered at Suicide Prevention Center, Los Angeles, May 1966.

Breed, W. Suicide, migration, and race: A study of cases in New Orleans. *The Journal of Social Issues,* 22:1, 1966.

Breed, W. Suicide and loss in social interaction. In: Shneidman, E. S., ed. *Essays in Self-Destruction.* New York: Science House, 1967.

Breed, W. The suicide process. Delivered at Fourth International Congress on Suicide, Los Angeles, October 1967.

Breed, W. Comparing male suicide in Los Angeles and New Orleans. *Bulletin of Suicidology,* December 1967.

Breed W. The Negro and fatalistic suicide. Manuscript.

Loss of Control Over Suicidal Impulses

T. L. Dorpat

In a discussion on the psychodynamics of suicide, Grinker[5] asked, "What differentiates the wish from the act?" We may postulate that suicide stems from two factors: one is the self-destructive wish, and the other is the failure or impairment of the controls which normally inhibit the acting out of such impulses. Previous studies emphasize the conscious and unconscious pychodynamics of suicide motivation. Meerloo[10] has described 52 motivations for suicide. Few have been concerned with the psychological functions that control or fail to control one's acting upon suicidal impulses.

The following case vignette illustrates some mechanisms involved in the loss of control over self-destructive wishes.

> The patient was a 42-year-old woman who, as a result of birth injury, had moderate weakness on the left side of her body. Partially because of her physical handicap, she became closely attached to and dependent on her mother. One evening while stepping off a street corner, she and her mother were suddenly struck by an automobile. Her mother died. The patient's grief was inconsolable and she developed severe depressive and phobic symptoms, including fear of crossing the street alone. Severe insomnia was especially distressing. She made frequent mention of her wish to die and her longing for her mother. Just 1 year after her mother's death she ingested, in a period of one hour, over 20 barbiturate sleeping pills. Her husband, a seaman, returned unexpectedly from overseas, found her comatose, and took her to the hospital. She survived but remained depressed and suicidal. She said she would not move if she found herself on a street with a car bearing down on her. Her fondest wish was for death and reunion with her "mother in heaven." "We were never separated: we were like one person," she said of her symbiotic tie to her mother.
>
> As a member of a fundamentalistic religious sect, she considered "deliberate" suicide sinful and a sure way of going to eternal damnation. Here, then, was her dilemma. Only in death could she rejoin her mother, but to die by a deliberate act of suicide meant going to hell and continued separation from her "mother in heaven."
>
> Immediately after describing her wish to die and how she had

Reprinted from *Bulletin of Suicidology,* December 1968. Published by National Institute of Mental Health.

taken the sleeping pills, she said, "I *can't* think I deliberately did it." [Italics in this paper are the author's.] Her statement of denial reveals how she was able to make the suicide attempt and still avoid feeling guilty. She could do it because she denied doing it "deliberately." The denial of the intentionality of the act, as shown by her use of the word "can't," was done in the service of avoiding the feared punishment for suicide.

The patient was conscious of suicidal wishes before, during, and after her suicide attempt. The act was planned, intentional, and voluntary. Still, she denied that she had tried to kill herself. She was a rigidly truthful person. The denial was not a conscious effort to conceal from others the nature of her act. Rather, it was a denial unconsciously determined by her fear of being punished for attempting suicide.

Defenses of denial and isolation brought about a "split" in her ego, with part of herself consciously and actively seeking to kill herself, while at the same time another part denied that she had intended to take her own life. By means of the defensive split in the ego, she had hoped to die by means of the sleeping pills and, at the same time avoid being eternally punished and separated from her mother. Freud[4] was the first to describe splitting of the ego in the defensive process.

The patient was conscious of her wish to die and of her wish to commit suicide. What was unconscious was her defense against the awareness that she had tried to kill herself. Not every defense acts in such a way as to bar drive derivatives from access to consciousness. When such defenses as denial and projection are used, the wishes that are being defended against can enter into consciousness and be carried out in action.

She had isolated the wish to commit suicide from the execution of the wish in her suicide attempt. These defensive maneuvers allowed her to avoid responsibility for her act and relieved her fear of punishment for carrying out the suicidal wish. Her statement that she would not move if she found herself on a street with a car bearing down on her described her continuing desire to die and her wish to die passively without responsibility for her death.

Her sense of active intention, deliberateness, and planning in all of her behavior was markedly impaired. This mode of experience formed the basis of her defensive operations. These defenses involved an externalization of responsibility for her life. Related to this were her prominent qualities of impulsivity and passive dependence on others.

DISCUSSION

Many people, perhaps most people, at one time or another have self-destructive impulses which are not acted out in suicide. The majority of depressed patients, despite strong self-destructive trends, do not commit suicide. Reviewing the 23 patients I am now treating in psychoanalysis or psycho-therapy, I find that all but one had spontaneously reported suicidal impulses or wishes. Only one of the remaining 22 had lost control of her self-destructive impulses and had made a suicide attempt. Our more comprehensive understanding of suicide should include not only consideration of the dynamics of suicidal impulses, but also knowledge of the factors which lead to the loss of control over self-destructive impulses. My aim is to discuss our very incomplete knowledge about the psychological and physical factors involved in this loss of control.

In the patient described above, extensive employment of denial of suicide intentionality led to the loss of control over suicidal impulses. The split in the ego between the part that wishes and plans suicide and the part that denies the intentional nature of the suicidal act was aptly illustrated in Eugene O'Neill's play, *Long Day's Journey Into Night.*[12] Mary, the depressed and addicted heroine, says, "I hope, sometime, *without meaning it,* I will take an overdose. I never could do it *deliberately.* The Blessed Virgin would never forgive me, then." (p. 121)

In a study of 121 persons who attempted suicide, the author[2] found that approximately one-fourth had denied their intention to kill themselves. This denial was most often observed in those whose suicide attempt involved drug ingestion. A clue to the denial of suicide intention or suicide motivation may be revealed by statements such as these: "I didn't do it deliberately"; "I didn't know what I was doing"; "I felt confused and not sure of what would happen"; or finally, "I took an overdosage."

Physicians often underestimate the suicidal potential in such patients and sometimes unconsciously collaborate with the patient in denying the lethal intention of their suicide attempts. "Drug overdose" or "drug automatism" and similar euphemistic expressions are sometimes used by mental health professionals to deny and dismiss genuine suicide attempts in their patients.

Modell[11] describes a patient who made a serious suicide attempt and who denied, at the time, the motivation for suicide and also the suicide intentionality of the act. The patient ". . . made a serious, but entirely unconscious, suicide attempt. He overingested sleeping medication, conscious only of a powerful desire to sleep; there was no thought of suicide and it was only upon his subsequent recovery that he recognized with horror the danger of self-destruction which had been denied." (p. 539) The stimulus for his massive use of denial was separation anxiety. Denial was related to a profound ego regression in which he denied his separateness from others and sought through the suicide to achieve an abjectless stage and fulfillment of his wish for reunion with his mother.

Denial reactions take different forms in the suicides. Some, like Modell's patient, deny not only the intentionality of their suicidal act but also their suicidal motivation. In my experience, nearly all suicidal persons deny the meaning of death as a final loss and separation. Rather, they conceive death in terms of a continued existence superior to the life they wish to leave. For most people death means the end of life and separation from loved and needed objects. The suicides reverse the usual meanings of life and death. For them continued living in this world means "death," but dying is a gateway to a new life. The denial of death as the end of life is implicit in their frequent suicide fantasies of rebirth or reunion with lost loved objects. Such wishful and pleasant fantasies are used to deny the painful meaning of death and the fear of death. In the patient presented above, the fear of death was denied by the fantasy of reunion with her mother. Hendin[6] warns that the erotization of death in suicide fantasies is an ominous sign presaging suicidal actions. The suicidal person may deny one or more of the following: the meaning of death, the fear of death, the guilt over killing himself, the wish to kill himself, or the intentionality of his suicidal actions.

In the symbols for death there is an ever-present ambivalence. Death can mean loss, separation, and the end of life; or on the other hand, death can have a pleasurable meaning when it is equated with a peaceful sleep, immortality, and union with the "good" mother of one's infancy. The suicides deny the former meaning of death and cling to the latter pleasurable meaning of death.

How do these denials bring about the loss of control over suicidal impulses? Ordinarily a suicidal impulse will elicit some fear of death or guilt over the contemplated destructiveness. The ego normally responds to such danger signals as fear or guilt by initiating defensive and adaptive tactics to control the self-destructive drive and prevent the anticipated danger. The fear of death in one who has a suicidal wish may, for example, mobilize repressive defenses against not only the fear but also against the self-destructive impulse itself. As Jacobson[7] has shown, the more primitive defense of denial functions differently. Denial defenses act against the fear or other danger signals but do not act against the self-destructive impulse itself. When denial defenses are functioning, the suicidal impulses may enter consciousness and be carried out in action unopposed by defenses or other conscious or unconscious ego controls. Here the ego reacts to the danger signal, e.g., the fear of death, by an immediate attempt to ignore the fear. It is this immediate, initial denial of fear or guilt which prevents the ego from instituting controls over the impulse and over the execution of the impulse.

Denial tends to short circuit ego defensive and adaptive functions. Also, it interferes with other ego functions such as cognitive controls, the synthetic function, reality sense, and reality testing. Impairment of these ego functions leads to the loss of conscious controls over self-destructive wishes.

Factors other than the defense of denial may affect the ego functions necessary for the control over self-destruction impulses. Defects in these ego functions may stem from developmental failure or from disease processes as in the psychoses. The developmental failure of these control and synthetic functions is found most typically in impulsive and passive dependent characters similar to the case presented above. Shapiro[16] explains how the attenuation of the feeling of deliberateness forms the nucleus of the impulsive personality and serves as the basis for their characteristic defensive disavowal of responsibility. In the patient described above, the characterological lack of deliberateness and intentionality in conjunction with her denial reactions brought about the failure of her psychic control functions.

Nearly all persons who commit suicide suffer from previous psychiatric illnesses and severe ego defects. It seems reasonable to assume that these ego defects are causally related to their loss of control over wishes for suicide. In both the author's[1] study of 114 cases of suicide, and in the only other psychiatric case study of an unselected and consecutive series of 134 cases done by Robins et al.,[14] it was found that nearly all subjects suffered from a severe psychiatric disorder. A majority of cases in both studies had either some type of psychosis or alcoholism. More research is needed to clarify the relationship of these ego defects to the loss of control over self-destructive impulses.

In a study of 15 men involved in fatal one-car accidents and 15 men who committed suicide, Litman and Tabachnick[9] suggest that the crucial factor which accident-prone and suicide-prone states have in common is a defect in the synthesizing functions of the ego. In suicide-prone states, passive, masochistic, and immobilization defenses predominate. A suicidal action occurs when there is a functional failure of these defenses. In the accident-prone state, denial, counterphobic and action defenses predominate. Accidents occur when these defenses fail and there is a breakthrough of passivity expressed in a withdrawal of attention or loss of control.

"Object loss" has long been considered a precipitating factor in depression and suicide. In another paper the author[3] has described the dynamics in suicide reactions following the loss of a needed symbiotic **partner**. The suicidal subjects had a dependent symbiotic relationship with the lost object which had served as a substitute for their missing or defective ego functions. Previously, they had maintained a precarious psychic equilibrium and control over their impulses through the help of their "auxiliary ego," the symbiotic partner. With the loss of the partner they also lost the means for the control and integration of their behavior.

Sleeplessness and the ingestion of alcohol, narcotics, sedatives, and hallucinogenic drugs (notably LSD) may lead to loss of controls over self-destructive impulses. It is probable that the ingestion of sleeping pills by the patient presented above further impaired her controls over self-destructive impulses. There are many published reports of individuals who have committed suicide while they were under the influence of alcohol, sedatives, narcotics, and LSD.

Prolonged sleeplessness in the patient described above and in other depressed patients probably contributes to their loss of inhibitory controls over suicidal impulses. A number of recent studies show that prolonged sleep loss tends to impair ego defensive and secondary process functioning.

Other studies suggest that alcohol ingestion may lead to loss of control over suicidal impulses. In the study by Litman et al.[9] cited above, nine of the 15 men who had fatal one-car accidents and 12 of the 15 suicide cases had been drinking heavily before their deaths. Palola et al.[13] found that 28 percent of a group of 114 consecutive suicide cases had been drinking at the time of their suicide.

In a study of all suicides occurring in a 5-year period in San Mateo County, Krieger[8] found that 21 percent of the male suicides and 9 percent of the female suicides at postmortem had blood alcohol levels above 0.05 percent. Selzer[15] studied alcoholics involved in auto accidents and provided evidence that excessive drinking just before the accident had led to the loss of their controls over self-destructive impulses.

SUMMARY

Suicide occurs when there is loss of control over self-destructive impulses. This paper uses a case vignette to illustrate and explain some of the mental mechanisms involved in the loss of control. A depressed woman who had made a serious suicide attempt denied that she had performed the act "deliberately." The denial was unconsciously determined by her fear of being punished for killing herself. This fear had previously mobilized controls over her suicidal wishes. The denial of her suicide intentionality led to the loss of these controls.

This loss of control was also facilitated by sleeplessness, barbiturate ingestion, and by the loss of her mother. The death of her mother constituted the loss of an "auxiliary ego," a source of external controls and a substitute for her characterological defective ego controls.

The execution of suicidal impulses occurs when there is an impairment of ego functions required for the control of self-destructive impulses. The ego functions involved include defenses, cognitive controls, and the synthetic function. Sleeplessness and drugs such as alcohol, barbiturates, and LSD impair such ego functions and may lead to the loss of control over suicidal wishes.

REFERENCES

1. Dorpat, T. L., and Ripley, H. S. A study of suicide in the Seattle area. *Comprehensive Psychiatry*, 1:349-359, 1960.
2. Dorpat, T. L., and Boswell, J. W. An evaluation of suicide intent in suicide attempts. *Comprehensive Psychiatry*, 4:117-125, 1963.
3. Dorpat, T. L. The relationship of object loss to ego defects in patients with suicide behavior. (In preparation.)
4. Freud, S. Splitting of the ego in the defensive process (1938). *Standard Edition*, Vol. 23. London: Hogarth Press, 1964. pp. 275-278.
5. Grinker, R. R. The psychodynamics of suicide and attempted suicide. In: L. Yochelson, ed. *Symposium on Suicide*. Washington, D.C.: George Washington University, 1967.

6. Hendin, H. *Suicide and Scandinavia.* New York: Grune & Stratton, Inc., 1964.
7. Jacobson, E. Denial and repression. *Journal of American Psychoanalytic Association,* 5:61-92, 1957.
8. Krieger, G. Suicides in San Mateo County. *California Medicine,* 107:153-155, 1967.
9. Litman, R. E., and Tabachnick, N. Fatal one-car accidents. *Psychoanalytic Quarterly,* 36:248-259, 1967.
10. Meerloo, J. A. M. *Suicide and Mass Suicide.* New York: Grune & Stratton, Inc., 1962.
11. Modell, A. H. Denial and the sense of separateness. *Journal of American Psychoanalytic Association,* 9:533-547, 1961.
12. O'Neill, E. *Long Day's Journey Into Night.* New Haven: Yale University Press, 1956.
13. Palola, E. G.; Dorpat, T. L.; and Larson, W. R. Alcoholism and suicide behavior. In: Pittman, D. J., and Snyder, C. R., eds. *Society, Culture and Drinking Patterns.* New York: John Wiley & Sons, Inc., 1962.
14. Robins, E.; Gassner, J.; Kayes, J.; Wilkenson, R. H.; and Murphy, G. E. The communication of suicidal intent: a study of 134 consecutive cases of successful (completed) suicides. *American Journal of Psychiatry,* 115:724-733, 1959.
15. Selzer, M. L., and Payne, C. E. Automobile accidents, suicide and unconscious motivation. *American Journal of Psychiatry,* 119:237-240, 1962.
16. Shapiro, D. *Neurotic Sytles.* New York: Basic Books, Inc., 1965.

Black Suicide

Lacy Banks

Peter Churney (this name and others of attempted suicides in this story are fictitious) is determined to kill himself. He has thought of doing so for years. At age seven, he saw his father killed in a shootout with policemen who came to stop him from savagely beating Peter's mother. Now He's 20, and he has already attempted suicide twice. In his latest attempt, he swallowed 30 tranquilizer tablets and probably would have died if his mother had not found him in time.

Harrison Eliot is 33 years old, drinks heavily, can't hold a job and has a habit of fighting policemen who try to arrest him when is is rowdy. His father was robbed and beaten to death when Eliot was four years old. When he was 12, his mother died, but he still remembers the severe beatings she used to give him. His brother has a long arrest record and his sister had a nervous breakdown after she was raped by his half-brother and became pregnant. Eliot's behavior is that of flirting with homicide and suicide.

Ina Tracy, a tall black woman, has been thinking of committing suicide ever since her Alabama childhood. She says her mother used to beat her almost every day, and she wished either she or her mother would die. Now she is 31, and she has tried to kill herself twice—both times following fights with friends.

Even though she has been released by a state mental institution, 29-year-old Glenda Williams still hears "voices" telling her to kill herself. Once she tried to answer those "voices" by swallowing half an ounce of rat poison containing 79 percent arsenic. She became violently ill, changed her mind, and called for help, fortunately just in time.

These four young people are among the many thousands who are labeled "suicidal" and try to kill themselves each year. More than 20,000 of them succeed, making suicide the nation's 10th leading cause of death for people of all ages. But for young people, ages 15 through 19, it is, according to the National Center for Health Statistics, the third leading cause of death. For college students, reports the NCHS, it is the second leading cause of death in the United States.

Until recently, suicide had been most popularly considered a problem

Reprinted by permission from *Ebony*, May 1970.

mainly for whites. Reports of random suicides by blacks were so small, they warranted almost no attention at all. But last year, New York psychiatrist Dr. Herbert Hendin beamed the spotlight of suicide research on New York City and found that, for the last 50 years, black men between the ages of 20 and 35 have been killing themselves twice as fast as white men in the same age group. Financed in part by a grant from the National Center of Studies for Suicide Prevention, a division of the National Institute of Mental Health in Chevy Chase, Md., Dr. Hendin's studies presented general psychological analysis and statistics of black suicides in New York and highlighted personal, in-depth interviews with, and psychological diagnosis of, 24 black suicidal patients there. Churney, Eliot, Tracy and Williams were among the patients treated by Dr. Hendin. Their lives all follow a basic pattern: black and poor, forced to deal with the hardships of New York's ghetto streets, all had leapfrogged childhood and entered their growing-up years without the normal love and understanding from family and friends. Instinctive feelings of tenderness and yearnings for parental discipline were crushed early in life, leaving little more than self-hatred and rage.

Dr. Hendin reports that the New York statistics hold true for other cities as well. In Washington, D. C., Chicago, Los Angeles and Atlanta, it is found that suicides by young blacks proportionately outnumber those by whites below the age of 35. Dr. Richard Seiden, associate professor of behavioral sciences at the University of California, says his research of national death records since 1960 show that blacks between the ages of 15 and 24 commit suicide at a rate higher than that of the total black population of all ages. Only after age 45 do white suicides outnumber black suicides overall by a ratio of 11 to 4. The death of blacks at very early ages obviously is the more acute problem, for the black community is robbed of some 30 to 40 years of useful manpower, earned wages and whatever contributions a young black suicider could have made. Hendin's book gives no special explanation for the high rate of suicides among New York's young blacks, but it may be concluded that for any city, the suicide rate mirrors the pressures and hardships of that city.

Few environments offer more pressures on life than that of New York's Harlem. The unemployment, the cramped quarters, the raw filth, the common toilets, the hunger and the cold of its many tenements are among the horrors that detonate black rage. For blacks, the rage peaks early in life. Young blacks become aware of their condition and are faced with the challenge of an adjustment that means either yielding to their rage or scaling down their aspirations. While most endure, Hendin's study reveals that many do not, and he concludes that it is during those 15 rage-filled years—from ages 20 to 35—that the decisions to face life or escape it through suicide eventually are made.

Dr. Hendin explains: "A sense of despair, a feeling that life will never be satisfying, confronts so many blacks at a far younger age than it does most whites. If things start out bad for young whites, they know that the fact they are white is an asset that is bound to reward them within due time. It is mostly when they have seen for themselves, after living 45 or 65 years, that there is no hope that their frequencies of suicide peak. But young blacks have only to look at their parents and the general situation of their elders in the community to realize that the chance of real improvement for them is scant.

An interesting discovery by Dr. Hendin was that among the choices of method, twice as many blacks as whites choose to jump to their death in New York City. He says: "Although a particular method often will be of unique psychological significance for the individual patient, availability and familiarity are major factors. Scandinavian suiciders choose to drown more than any other people in the world. But the sea is their cultural lifeblood. They live and play in it, write, sing and paint about it. Thus it is not surprising that many of them choose to die in it.

"On the other hand." he continued, "life in Harlem centers on its endless number of five-story tenements and it is a wretched environment for most. Jumping from the top floors of such buildings is possibly the closest that many blacks come to feeling of escaping the miserable tenement life."

Paul Curtis, whose office (the National Center for Studies of Suicide Prevention) is responsible for establishing and supporting suicide prevention centers in many areas of the country, labels the rise in young black suicides as the main challenge of his organization. The National Center—a part of the National Institute of Mental Health, which is a subdivision of the U. S. Department of Health, Education and Welfare—provides research grants each year to individuals and programs working in the field of suicide prevention.

"We are willing to provide financial support and consultation to any individual who comes to us with a valid plan either to do research or establish a center in his community for suicide prevention," says Curtis. "All one has to do is contact us." The National Center has direct liaison with about 130 local centers across the country and provides some type of support for all of them.

Since few blacks can afford the expensive (about $35 per 50-minute "hour") services of a private psychiatrist, most can receive assistance—free of charge—by calling a local prevention center. The centers have 24-hour-a-day emergency telephone services manned by staffs of professional and volunteer counselors who are trained to secure aid for potential suiciders.

These centers are located in every major city of the nation and usually list their telephone numbers under the heading of "Emergency Medical Care" or something similar on the inside cover of telephone directories. Because the majority of suicide clients suffer mental illness and have received psychiatric care in the past, much of a center's work involves referring patients to clinical psychiatrists or other sources of help. Sometimes, if the situation isn't serious, the staff counselor may know the client well enough from previous calls that he can handle his case personally.

"Some of our clients have called as many as 300 times within a year or a dozen times within a single day," says Mrs. Phyllis Clemmons, director of the Suicide Prevention Center in Washington, D. C. Mrs. Clemmons is a registered nurse with 21 years of experience, mainly in the various areas of rehabilitation, especially suicide prevention.

"The training we give our counselors who man the phones is nothing elaborate," she says. "We send them through a suicide prevention course and acquaint them with the various institutions available to help our clients. But a counselor's most important tools—humane understanding, compassion and sincere concern—come naturally. Our clients need those desperately. The typical suicider normally has just experienced a great loss—abandoned husband, wife or lover, loss of job, home or prestige. Many call because they have no one else to talk to, and just to have someone else to listen to their problems sometimes makes the difference between life and death."

With the increase of the urban black population and the high rates of suicides among young blacks, the Washington, D. C., center typifies a new standard in the making: that of increased black involvement in suicide prevention, both from the administrative and client standpoints. For example, all but one of the 11-man staff at the D. C. center is black, including Mrs. Clemmons. And unlike most other prevention centers across the country, all the members of the D. C. staff are capable, paid professionals, not volunteers.

Operating as part of the city's Department of Health, the center is vest-pocketed on the fourth floor of the nine-story health department building. Its two rooms, whose walls of pastel green could stand another coat of paint, are the extent of the center's space. Four of its five desks are equipped with telephone, note pad and pencils for the staff counselors who alternate in round-the-clock shifts. The other desk supports a thick journal into which the counselors have logged more than 43,000 calls placed by some 10,000 individuals since the center opened its doors in 1967 (a third of the calls relate to suicides, the others to domestic and personal health problems). But the most important physical object of the office is its four file cabinets into which thousands of folders holding the highly confidential histories of suicidal patients are stored. The folders keep up-to-date tabs on the lives of the patients and whenever one calls, a staff counselor locates his folder, studies his background and makes new entries.

The information already recorded in the folders not only gives clues on how to deal with the potential suicide's problem (often the caller has the same problem many times and the necessary treatment is already known), but how the problems themselves are standardized according to race. According to Mrs. Clemmons, the problem plaguing most white potential suicides who call is the loss of prestige (jobs, grades, reputation, office, social position); whereas, the black suicides mostly suffer the loss of a lover. Yet, despite the difference of their problem and their race, they all call pleading for the same thing—life. And they usually aren't too particular about where the help is coming from.

"Suicidal persons want both to live and to die in the hour of their death scheme," says Curtis. "One part of them is miserable and it wants unconditional death. The other part is innocent and desperately trying to live. It's a natural combination that is part of the human makeup, but in moments of grave crisis, the balance is upset in favor of the death-yearning portion. One of our main objectives when we intervene into those crises is to locate that part of the individual which wants to live and work to strengthen it and swing the balance back over into its favor. In most cases, it's not difficult at all. In fact, when the individual calls a center, that's the part that wants to live right there calling. We alert the counselors at the prevention centers to be ready to take advantage of that opportunity."

Counselors usually begin the life-saving dialogue by examining the condition of the caller, encouraging him to express himself and offering him vocal consolations like: "You're right," "I know how you feel," "I feel the same way myself sometimes," "You're handling things better than most people" and other positive expressions assuring the patient that he's human and that, no matter how great the problem, he still has mastery over it.

In the field of suicide prevention, there is no "cookie cutter" for standardizing the handling of all suicide cases. Each one boils down to the individual in question, and the case may vary from one would-be suicider who was talked out of his attempt by being told, "Hey come on! It's time to eat!" (as one actually was) to the suicider who said nothing to anyone, smiled and carried on as usual until he was found dead one day with a hole in his head and a gun in his hand. The suicider may explain his harbored confusion and frustration in a note such as that written by a New York victim: "Dear Mary, I hate you. Love, John." Or he may leave no note at all.

Mrs. Clemmons and her staff know that not all the alleged suicides who call are serious. Some call just because they're drunk and others sometimes announce themselves as "Mr. Don't Jump" or "Mr. Kill Myself." She knows that many of the clients call merely to play a joke, but she has her staff to log every call and the content of each. "Some people may call to pull cranks on us, but we give them the benefit of the doubt. It may be an unconscious call for help. There was one case where a crank caller was found dead with our telephone number written in a note beside him."

Except for that and about five other cases, Mrs. Clemmons and her staff have received no real clue as to how many people they have actually saved or lost. They can only judge by the letters they get from people thanking them for the help they received. But all are not grateful. Sometimes a despondent whom the center had saved after he had hustled up enough courage to attempt suicide, calls Mrs. Clemmons afterward and curses her or her counselors for saving his life.

As for other examples of increased black involvement, in Sanford, N. C., a black man, Rev. James Hampton, heads a steering committee of black and white ministers and laymen who manage a new million-dollar suicide prevention center for Lee and Harnett Counties. They've been running it for nine years.

Curtis calls the Sanford center a successful model for rural areas, and Rev. Hampton admits, "We've had a few racial problems trying to get started, but we've endured them. Sanford is a Southern town with some typical racial prejudices, but I believe that this integrated staff working together to strengthen people's will to live has helped to do more than prevent suicides. It has made a very healthful contribution to race relations in this small town."

Another group that seems destined to be heard from in this area of work is the rising corps of black psychiatrists. One of them, Dr. Alvin Poussaint, black psychiatrist of Harvard University Medical School, is cautiously optimistic about new funds being made available for black psychiatrists to engage in more research projects. He feels that the proof of the pudding will come when black scientists not only start receiving major grants as readily as white scientists have, but also when the sponsor and society in general pay serious attention to and actively abide by the conclusions of the studies.

Already, in Nashville, Tenn., Dr. Henry Tomes of Meharry Medical School is working on establishing a comprehensive mental health center which would include a program of suicide prevention. He is getting about 90 percent of it financed through a federal grant.

Although the prevention centers may prove some degree of effectiveness in solving the immediate problem of young black suicides, the real basic causes will still remain. Years of American racism did. But the new remedial efforts of the centers are far from expendable, and the increased involvement of black administrators and black psychiatrists should definitely increase their effectiveness not only in preventing suicides among young blacks, but among all people.

Suicide and Self-Destructive Behavior on the Cheyenne River Reservation

Wilson V. Curlee

The Cheyenne River Indian Reservation is located on the plains of northern central South Dakota and is populated by approximately 3,700 Sioux Indians. The reservation, bordered on the east by the Missouri River, measures about 100 miles in length by 70 miles in width. The character of the reservation is predominantly rural, with much of the population living in small (Indian) communities over the reservation, many of which are very isolated by modern standards of travel and communication. The rest of the population lives either in or around the small towns on the reservation or out on the prairie. Those who live around the small towns on the reservation generally are onlookers into the community life, having little voice in the economic and political affairs of the town.

There is virtually no industry on the Cheyenne River Reservation, and most of the jobs either are temporary, being provided by the agencies of the poverty program, or are seasonal, being available only during the warm months, such as ranch work. For this reason, the Indian is forced either to leave the reservation in search of a job or to stay and accept low-paying jobs or relief. If he stays on the reservation, he is likely to be caught in a crippling web of dependency, which may satisfy his physical needs but which denies him the pride and satisfaction of self-sufficiency.

On the other hand, if he does choose to leave the reservation, the Indian gives up the spiritual security of the familiar and ventures forth into an unfamiliar world for which he is usually grossly unprepared. He lacks the skills and the experience needed to exist in a strange job in an unfamiliar place, he feels utterly alone and isolated, and most importantly, he lacks the necessary confidence in himself. He feels unable to compete with the non-Indians on an equal basis, and the sense of inferiority which he has learned saps his courage and determination. As one Indian lady on the Cheyenne River Reservation stated it, "When I was young I was told, 'Listen to him, he's a white man—he's smart,' and although I know I'm as good as a white person, I don't feel that I

Reprinted from *Suicide Among the Indians.* U.S. Public Health Service Publication No. 1903, June 1969.

am." Thus we see that not only the attitudes of whites towards Indians, but also the attitude of Indians toward themselves and their race, fosters and perpetuates this feeling of inferiority.

On the Cheyenne River Reservation the housing and the living conditions are very poor. Alcoholism and violence rates are high. There is not the feeling of closeness and helpfulness among the Indians that one might hope for, and people suffer from the same feeling of isolation in the small Indian communities that is prevalent in the larger cities across the United States. Social disorganization is rampant, and the family is not the source of strength and comfort it might be.

Admittedly this very brief picture of the Cheyenne River Reservation emphasizes the negative aspect of the total environment, but this is the way it looks to the Indian who considers or engages in suicide or other self-destructive behavior. The picture could easily be painted in a positive light if one ignored these negative aspects, but then it would not be seen in the hopeless way that many of those who are caught in self-destructive behavior view it.

Included in forms of self-destructive behavior other than suicide are chronic disregard for proper care of one's health; extreme violence toward others, which places the self in danger; alcoholism; and other dangerous actions such as drunken and reckless driving.

Forms of self-destructive behavior other than suicide are included in this discussion because the dynamics for them seem to be the same; and although we cannot say that all participants in such self-destructive actions are intent on actually killing themselves, neither can we say that all suicide attempts or "gestures" had death as their anticipated end result. Still, however, such behavior is dangerous both to the self and to others and offers a hint of the depression that is behind it.

In the past year on the Cheyenne River Reservation, 15 suicide episodes were reported to the Public Health Service Indian Hospital, none of which resulted in death. Some of these could be called "gestures," in that the person claimed not to have been trying to kill himself but "just did not know what else to do." Although these cannot be discounted as not being suicidal, their act seemed to be more of a spontaneous, impulsive expression of anxiety and desperation than an actual attempt to escape through death.

Of those cases reported, some where admitted to the hospital because of the seriousness of their self-inflicted injury, some were reported by the tribal police and jail personnel, and some were reported by friends or relatives who were anxious for the safety of the person. It is difficult to estimate the number of attempts which were not reported, but due to the personal nature of the causes of the attempts, certainly the number is large. In addition, a number of others have admitted during counseling sessions about other problems that they have considered suicide at one time or another.

Of the 15 who were reported, 13 were between the ages of 15 and 21, and the other two were in their mid-thirties. Of the 13 younger ones, 10 were girls. Thus the emphasis of this group of reported suicides is on the youth of those involved.

What is involved in these suicide attempts? Why these young people, and why the particular time? My impressions will be given here, and while these dynamics do not operate to such a degree in all young people in the Cheyenne River Reservation, they do seem to be present in a significant portion of them.

One difficulty these young people faced was the conflict of cultural transition. There is very definitely a modification, if not a complete change, of the old organization of values held by the Indian people. While many of the older people may be able to retain their identity with the old Indian ways, and to gain stability from this identification, the younger Indian has difficulty adopting these ways because of the great changes in the society over the years, and because he has already adopted some, but not all, of the ways of the white man. These two systems of morals and values do not always fit together, so that gaps and conflicts result, and the younger Indians grow up without being able to identify themselves either with their Indian heritage or as a white person. This lack of identity and stability causes tremendous difficulty to the adolescent who is already caught up in a sea of impulses, needs, wishes, and uncertainty.

The cultural transition causes difficulty not only in identification, but also in knowing how to handle the temptations and stresses of entering adulthood. As the ways of his parents do not always fit the situation in which he finds himself, often the younger Indian is not able to use his parents' behavior as a way of knowing how to handle the situation, and thus the prevalent way of teaching children by example often does not suffice. Several of the 13 young people who attempted suicide complained that they had never been told what to do and not to do by their parents. One girl expressed this thought by saying desperately, "What am I supposed to do? I don't know! My mother never talked to me about what is right and wrong. She left me to find out for myself." Apparently this conflict robbed them of the sense of security that comes from direction by others before the individual feels ready to make his own decisions.

Closely related to this practice of child instruction by example is a profound respect for individual autonomy, even to the point of allowing a child to make his own decisions regarding school attendance and medical care. This dates from an era in which the role expectations were fairly well defined in the tribe, so that by observing the available models of behavior and by imitating them a child was socialized. With patterns of behavior less clear-cut and with the vastly changed situations, such autonomy apparently is often taken advantage of by some children, and in some cases is perverted into giving the child his way all of the time, thus making him into a small tyrant in the family. Several of these who attempted suicide were able to verbalize the complaint of having been given their way too often, having been overindulged in getting whatever they wanted, and stated they felt this had been harmful to them. The fact that it was harmful can be seen by the fact that at least half of the young people, who attempted suicide did so in such a fashion as to manipulate those around them in order to get what they wanted. This spoiling resulted in very self-centered and immature reactions to others, in which other people were objects to be manipulated to get one's own way. As the result, these young people were left with an inability to take no for an answer, and with a lack of any ability to govern their own impulses or to accept any limitation imposed upon them.

Evident in most of these reported cases was an extremely low self-concept. There was no pride in being Indian. Rather there was a feeling that being Indian was of little value. There was a feeling that neither their parents nor anyone else around them cared for them, and part of the low self-image seemed to be due to the fact that since they felt that no one else valued them, they did not adopt any concept of themselves as being valuable. This lack of self-worth or self-respect was most evident in the remark of one girl, "Did you notice that I don't give a damn about myself?" and may be important in the choice of a target for aggression, whether it will be the self or another.

This dynamic of low self-concept is important among the older people on the Cheyenne River Reservation also, although associated more with alcoholism and violence in this group than with suicides. Especially for the man in the older age group—meaning those over 30—there is a crippling lack of lasting satisfaction available in any form. The previously mentioned inability to be the bread winner for the family; the fact that the mother and grandmother are the significant teachers and disciplinarians of the children; in some cases the inability even to father children where the mother elects birth control measures without consulting the father; the dependency on others to provide all services to his family—all of these combine to prevent the man from gaining a feeling of satisfaction or self-importance. He has no role, and often is not important to the family in any concrete way. In addition to increasing his futility, the uselessness and dependency generate more hostility and result in more frequent turning to alcohol as an escape or release. In some cases, alcohol and violence provide a way to gain esteem in the eyes of others by the only means available—through rough or daring behavior. As this reliance on alcohol usually only makes the problems worse, it may then be relied on to an even greater degree, setting up a vicious cycle of drinking and disorganization.

Also important in almost every one of the cases of suicide and violence related to the use of alcohol was the practice of holding in all of the pain, anger, worry—holding in every emotion—until the emotional pressure became so great that some problem triggered a response that was out of all proportion to the incident that caused it. Often these people gave the impression that they were well adjusted, and frequently there was no hint of the inner stress until the pressure became so great that it could not be held back. This dynamic also seems most relevant in drinking and brutality, when a person who is very retiring while sober becomes very abusive and even brutal while drinking.

The Indians on the Cheyenne River Reservation who were reported for being involved in suicide episodes did seem to fit the traditional picture of the Indian as one who endures great pain without crying out, at least until the pain becomes unendurable. This way of handling stress has proved to be used as much for aggression as for anxiety, and often the actual attempt at suicide was an outlet for aggression, much as drinking and fighting provide an outlet for the aggression of other people. The suicidal act might take the aggression out on the self, but often it was directed toward another person, in an attempt to hurt that person by making him feel responsible for the act, thereby producing in him a feeling of guilt.

How can the Indian be assisted to resolve some of the underlying causes of self-destructive behavior described above? There are the long-term goals of better housing, providing jobs through industry on the reservation, and upgrading the environment as much as possible through better sanitation, health care, recreation, and education.

There is also a need for data collection so that approaches toward solutions will be based on accurate knowledge of the problem rather than on descriptive materials alone. Indians must be involved in the solutions to their problems, and solutions must not be imposed upon them in such a way as to cause rejection by those they are designed to help.

ADDITIONAL BIBLIOGRAPHY ON INDIAN SUICIDES

Devereux, George. *Mohave Ethnopsychiatry and Suicide. The Psychiatric Knowledge and The Psychic Disturbances of an Indian Tribe,* Bureau of American Ethnology, Bulletin 175, Washington, D.C., 1961.

Dizmang, Larry H. "Observations on Suicidal Behavior Among the Shoshone-Bannock Indians." Presented at the First Annual National Conference on Suicidology, Chicago, Ill., March 1968.

Fenton, William N. Iroquois suicide: A study in the stability of a culture pattern. *Bureau of American Ethnology Bulletin,* 128, 1941.

Levy, J. E. Navajo suicide. *Human Organization,* 24:308-18, 1967.

A Theoretical Approach to "Accident" Research

Norman D. Tabachnick

For some years, the workers at the Los Angeles Suicide Prevention Center have concentrated their efforts upon the understanding and treatment of suicide. Numerous studies have concerned themselves with the distribution of suicide in various populations, the opportunities which can be offered or created to identify active and potential suicides, and communication and therapeutic efforts with individuals so identified. Although all these efforts deserve and, in fact, are receiving continued attention by the SPC staff, it has not escaped our attention that suicide is only one manifestation of a broader movement toward death which might be called "self-destruction." In some ways, our sphere of interest was forced to spread from a consideration of those who were suicidal (a group that is, at times, difficult to identify and designate) to this larger group of people and this larger group of behaviors. As we attempted to understand suicide and the other self-destructive behaviors, it became necessary for us to develop a general theoretical understanding of the broad area of self-destruction.

The purpose of this paper is twofold. First, we will deal with general issues surrounding the establishment of a classification of self-destructive behaviors; then we will describe some of the past, present and proposed research of our group in the phenomenon called "automobile accident." In the latter part of the article, we will attempt to relate the various researches in accident to the different theoretical approaches to self-destruction.

A DEFINITION FOR "SELF-DESTRUCTION" AND SOME COMMENTS ON THE PLACE OF "VALUES"

First of all, we need to define self-destruction. Immediately we think of a definition which deals with the basic physiological facts—something like this: "Any activity over which man has some (actual or potential) volitional control, which moves him in the direction of an earlier physical death than would otherwise occur, is designated self-destructive."

Let us expand for a moment on the troublesome word, "volitional." What

Reprinted from *Bulletin of Suicidology,* Spring 1970. Published by National Institute of Mental Health.

we wish to imply here is the *actual* or *potential* ability to change the behavior so that it would no longer be self-destructive. As an example, an individual may be involved in a self-destructive activity. He may not realize his activity is self-destructive; furthermore, he may be unaware that a particular force (say, an unconscious need to expiate through being hurt) is pushing him into the activity. If, however, it is judged that he could become aware of the deadly implications of the activity and, moreover, that he has the potentiality (perhaps with the assistance of certain auxiliary measures, such as the support of friends or the services of a psychotherapist) to change the behavior, we would call such behavior *self*-destructive.

Thus, although the definition entails certain problems, it seems fairly straightforward. Our first impression is that it would not be to difficult to use.

However, on further reflection, it becomes apparent that our definition would not include many activities which have been called self-destructive. Let us call to mind self-doubting and self-torturing life styles, turning down opportunities to advance in business, avoiding close personal relationships, and certain occupations such as prostitution or various forms of criminality. (The list could be greatly expanded.) All of these activities have been called self-destructive, yet they are not clearly or inevitably associated with decreased life expectancy. Why then the "self-destructive" appellation? The answer would seem to be that, to the individuals who call these activities "self-destructive," they represent modes of acting, living and feeling which are as self-destructive as the actual loss of life itself.

Thus, we have unintentionally but necessarily entered into the area of "values" (those things which a person considers valuable) and the issue of the hierarchical placement of values. Most people consider life "valuable," but there are other aspects of the human condition which are "valuable" also. Each individual (whether he is intellectually aware of this structuring or not) has placed his values in rank order. Thus, many of us come to realize that there are certain values which are as or more important than life. If someone acts so as not to implement those values, we call him (through identifying him with ourselves) "self-destructive."

There is certainly no quarrel with each person selecting "values" which he deems to be important. Furthermore, we know that there are certain values which large groups of individuals would agree are important. However, at this place in our discussion, we must point out that there is perpetrated an important semantic and practical error if one deems one's personal preferences and values to have some *general* life affirmative meaning. It is just such a decision, of course, which allows one to label all activities which move in a contrary direction (to one's own values) self-destructive.

Having made this detour through the "value" issue, we can return to the comfortable specificity of our first definition—the one which links self-destruction with a movement away from the physical extension of life. Let us therefore adopt that definition as the first "ground rule" of our discussion.

Next, let us turn to the issue of "overdetermination" of actions. Many, if not all, human activities have more than one meaning for the individual. Thus, a particular activity may be self-destructive (in the "physical" sense referred to above). It may well be that the individual does not favor the self-destructive tendencies of his action. However, at the same time as the action is tending to destroy him, it may be advancing certain of his positive values.

Let us illustrate this situation with the example of driving. Newspapers, actuarial tables, and psychoanalytic observations all attest to the significant self-destructive implications of automobile driving. Yet, although many individuals in our country know this, driving is neither exclusively nor generally considered self-destructive. Why not? Because the important practical value of driving, the status value of owning one or more automobiles, and often the unconscious symbolic and erotic gratifications of driving all combine to neutralize and, indeed, to override the self-destructive aspects.

Similarly, in understanding any "self-destructive" act, it is valuable to know something (indeed, a good deal) of the positive and negative values which are associated with it, to the individual, in the culture, and at the time it is taking place.

A CLASSIFICATION FOR SELF-DESTRUCTIVE BEHAVIORS

A recent effort at the SPC was the review of literature and research in the fields of psychiatry, psychology, psychoanalysis and sociology.[3] The effort was to discern in the various descriptions of self-destructive acting and thinking what, if any, general theories of self-destruction might be found. Our efforts indicated that there were three broad theoretical approaches to the understanding of self-destruction. They were: (1) The theory of the death instinct: (2) The theory of mental illness; and (3) The theory of adaptational mishap. There were many instances in which a particular explanation of a self-destructive occurrence overlapped two or three theoretical approaches. Also, in some instances, there might be debate as to which of these three theoretical approaches would most appropriately categorize a particular type of occurrence. Yet, in our review, we did not find theoretical approaches other than these three.

Next, we would like to briefly define each of the categories in our classification.

The Death Instinct. The best-known theory of self-destruction is that of the death instinct. Although alluded to by previous authors, the most explicit statement of the death instinct was made by Sigmund Freud.

In "Beyond the Pleasure Principle,"[1] Freud put forth his last great classification of human instincts. All instincts could be divided into two main categories, those moving toward life and those moving toward death. The death instinct was conceptualized as a primary force in all living matter to return to a state of complete inertia, ultimate rest, and death. This force was combatted from two main sources. First of all, there were opposing life instincts within the organism which attempted to extend life and to bring about higher unities of living matter. An example of these would be procreative sexual activity.

The second interference with the workings of the death instinct came from situations external to the individual, such as his society with its particular forces and values. These forces interfered with the individual's death instinct moving on to its inexorable expression.

Paradoxically, these external forces were often destructive in themselves. For example, enemies might attack an individual and illnesses or nutritional deprivations might afflict him. These external forces would be rigorously combatted by the ego forces of the individual which might, from this standpoint, be seen as manifestations of the life instinct. But Freud felt that, at the deepest level, these ego or life forces worked actually in the service of the death instinct. This paradox was explained by Freud's conception that the death instinct wanted to impose its *own individual pattern* of death upon the person in whom it existed. Therefore, any external or foreign cause of death had to be combatted in order that the individual's death instinct should have its own way and be the victor in the struggle of competing forces to kill the individual.

Mental Illness. Our second category is mental illness. The kernel of this conception is that as an accompaniment of certain mental illnesses, self-destructive actions take place.

Most readers will know that attempts to define mental illness and mental health have undergone numerous vicissitudes. Definitions of these terms are all felt to be less than perfect (often less than adequate) and at best we have a number of definitions, all delineating some aspect or other of mental health or mental illness.

"Mental Illness," as defined by us, means changes in function (in individuals, small groups or larger societies) in which there is less achievement than usual of life-preserving and other "valuable" goals. Such deficits are noted in association with or following the imposition of a foreign and unusual circumstance, virus, culture change, or other motivator of behavior in the person or group in question. The crux of the concept is that as an accompaniment or result of a "new overwhelming responsibility," the organism loses some of its ability to judge and organize.

This theoretical approach does not necessarily exclude death instinct and adaptational concepts. For example, one could say that mental illness which produces self-destructive behavior is but a manifestation of the death instinct.

One might also hold that mental illness produces self-destruction by virtue of interfering with life-preserving adaptational patterns.

Adaptational Mishap. The third category of psychological theories of self-destruction deals with disorders of adaptation. Very briefly, the adaptational theory considers man's behavior from the learning standpoint. Man's important task is seen to be learning to fit his own needs, capabilities, goals and limitations into the various opportunities and limiting aspects of the environment in which he lives. If a particular course of behavior does not prove to result in some successful adaptation for the individual, one of several things may happen.

First, under some conditions he may give up trying to adapt, may enter a period of hopelessness and passivity, and sooner or later be overwhelmed by an environment which refuses or is unable to take care of him in this condition. Secondly, he may try some new pattern of behavior in order to effect a more successful adaptation. This new pattern of behavior may be repetition of something he had done in the past or may represent a creative attempt to synthesize an entirely new solution to his problem.

Under these conditions, there are a number of theoretical possibilities of self-destruction. If the individual gives up all active efforts, the self-destructive implications are quite obvious. Without some effort to actively master them, internal and external forces probably would overwhelm one. Suppose the individual turns to a regressive mode of behavior (i.e., a behavior which was utilized in an earlier time of life). He may perceive his present situation as if it were a repetition of previous events. If he does not suitably take into account the *actual aspects* of his current situation, partial or complete self-destruction may occur. In the creation of a new solution, even though this new solution may successfully or even brilliantly deal with some aspects of the problem, it may fail to take into account certain self-destructive possibilities.

ACCIDENT RESEARCH

Next we would like to discuss automobile accident research at the SPC from the standpoint of these three self-destructive themes.

The Death Instinct. If Freud's theories concerning the death instinct are valid, then we would assume that in a relatively large population, there would be what might be called a constant death rate. The assumptions here are as follows: The death instinct in a large population is one of the important determining factors of the death rate. Assuming that a certain proportion of this rate is due to one factor, for example, suicide, what would happen if the suicide rate were drastically reduced? If the death instinct hypothesis is valid, one would expect that there would have to be a complementary rise in other death rates to counterbalance the declining suicide death rate.[4]

One of the future clinical research plans of the Suicide Prevention Center calls for a saturation suicide prevention program in an area of large population. We intend to center on this area all the preventative measures, communicative measures, and help of interested potential life-savers (medical personnel, ministers, concerned laymen) which can be mobilized. Our hope and anticipation is that these activities would effect a significant reduction in the suicide death rate. At the same time, however, we will be evaluating the changes in the death rate following automobile collision and other kinds of accident. If there are certain numbers of individuals who must die "by their own hand," according to the dictates of the death instinct, and certain efforts are brought to bear to stop their dying by their own hand through suicide, then they may effect their demise by accident. At any rate, should there be an inverse change in the suicide and accident death rates, it would provide interesting support for the death instinct theory.

Mental Illness. Mental illness has been one of the treasured research hypotheses in psychological aspects of automobile accident. (It should be stated at the outset that almost no researchers, including psychological ones, feel that psychological factors are totally responsible for accidents, including automobile accidents. It is generally held that psychological forces are but one in a field that includes many others, such as the condition of mechanical contrivances—automobile, weather and atmospheric conditions, road conditions and a number of other factors.) However, in terms of mental illness, it is one of the few established research findings that many of the drivers responsible for automobile accidents have what is called anti-social, psychopathic or asocial characters.

A second treasured psychological accident hypothesis is that of the accident-prone individual. Although this term has gone through a series of redefinitions, it generally refers to a person who, because of some tension within himself, has developed a pattern of getting himself involved in repeated accidents. These accidents seem temporarily to blind his tension, but it arises again and an additional accident ensues. (For a review of the accident-prone concept, see reference.[5])

A final hypothesis worthy of consideration follows from the possibility that accidents may represent concealed suicides or may be "suicide equivalents." If this is true, one would expect to find a relatively high rate of depressive illness in individuals responsible for the production of accident.

Previous research studies[2,6] by our group investigated, among other things, the comparative incidence of depression and victims of accidental and suicidal death. As expected, a large majority of the suicidal victims were judged as being depressed. Although the percentage of depression in the accident victims was much less than in the suicide group, one-third of them were designated as depressed. This pilot study would then lend support to the concept that a significant number of accident victims suffer from a mental illness—depression.

We are currently involved in an intensive psychoanalytic investigation of attempted accident and suicide victims. One sector of the interview devotes itself to a consideration of the presence, during the entire life history and during the time immediately preceding the accident or suicide attempt, of depression. This study should not only help tell us whether depression is present in accident victims but also give us another estimate of how often it is to be found and, most important, reveal some of its similarities and differences to the depression that is seen in suicide victims.

An additional type of "mental illness" is confusion. Confusion may be defined as an impaired ability to use the judgmental and integrative neuro-muscular apparatuses of the body. Confusion may be linked with either organic or psychogenic illness. The first category would include various kinds of brain disease. In the second, we would have the confusional states sometimes associated with depression or psychosis. In a presently planned research study, we intend to develop indices of safe and unsafe driving as measured on a traffic simulator. Our research plan then calls for the "running" of a number of test subjects in the simulator. During their test runs, they will be subjected to various traffic stresses. (These will be reproduced on the films which are part of the simulator driving experience.) One group of subjects will be selected so as to test the effect of varying degrees of confusion on the simulator driving scores. The results of this study should give valuable information as to the degree to which "confusion" might be responsible for automobile accidents.

Adaptation. We believe that the adaptational approach to the understanding of automobile accident offers much promise. We have described two research studies, the psychoanalytic investigation presently in progress and the contemplated research utilizing a traffic simulator. We would like to point out that these two approaches are, in a sense, complementary. The first attempts to get at matters bearing on accident in a retrospective way, while the second has a prospective approach. Although one could point to general deficiencies and shortcomings in either of these approaches, the establishment of a common research finding in both of them will have increased significance.

Our hypotheses in these two studies are adaptational. In general, we believe that automobile accident, from the psychological standpoint, may be the product of two interlocking sets of variables. On the one hand, we believe that certain aspects of the character or life style may be important. The second set of variables has to do with precipitating life situations. Some of the life characteristics which we feel may be important include impulsiveness, tendency toward action, tendencies to relieve anxiety through action, and absence of introspective judgmental states of being. Some of the life stresses which we feel may be important are recent loss, being slighted or offended by others, and the movement into new areas of responsibility (particularly when the feelings of unsureness associated with these new movements have not been sufficiently mastered).

Some of these hypotheses have been partially supported by previous research; some are new ones which stem from the previous research.

REFERENCES

1. Freud, Sigmund. *Beyond the Pleasure Principle,* Standard Edition of the Complete Psychological Works. London: The Hogarth Press, 1920.
2. Osman, Marvin. Psychoanalytic study of automobile accident victims. *Contemporary Psychoanalysis,* 5:1, 1969.
3. Tabachnick, N.; Kloes, K.; Poze, P.; and Fielder, E. "Theories of Self-Destruction," unpublished.
4. Tabachnick, Norman, and Klugman, David. Suicide research and the death instinct. *Yale Scientific Magazine,* March 1967.
5. Tabachnick, Norman. The psychology of fatal accident. In: Shneidman, E.S. (ed.), *Essays in Self-Destruction.* New York: Science House, Inc., 1967.
6. Tabachnick, Norman. Comparative psychiatric study of accidental and suicidal death. *Archives of General Psychiatry,* 14:60-68, 1966.

Suicide — Evaluation, Assessment and Prediction

Jana Wahlquist and Dorothy Pack

Unfortunately, the areas of evaluation, assessment, and prediction of suicides seem to be new and relatively unexplored and the available data are often inconclusive. It appears that very few suicide experts can provide us with any definite procedure, questionnaire, or test to actually predict or evaluate suicidal behavior in an individual. However, there are some general concepts and methods that can be placed in four categories: 1) General Evaluation; 2) Psychological Tests; 3) Emergency Evaluation; and 4) Evaluation of Specific Groups.

The first area considered in this paper, then, is general evaluation and prediction. A very prominent idea in this area is the verbalization of the desire for suicide. Doctors Richard G. Singer and Irving J. Blumenthal[1] claim that 70% of all people who attempt suicide express ideas of self-destruction. Jan. A. Fawcett[2] provides us with another percentage: 50 − 70% of the individuals who communicate suicidal feelings actually kill themselves. It is true, of course, that many people who kill themselves do not previously threaten verbally to do so, and many who say they will, do not actually follow through. However, it is a significant fact that a great number of persons who attempt and complete suicide do make some kind of verbal indication of this desire. This is one clue to predicting and evaluating suicidal behavior.

The communication of suicide intent occurs in a variety of ways. The most common is by direct and specific statement. Some indirect expressions include: "better off dead;" desire to die; references to methods; dire predictions; putting affairs in order; "can't take it any longer," and references to burial. In a study make by Eli Robbins[3] of 119 cases, 65 per cent used more than one type of expression, and in 67 per cent of the cases communications were repeated. Again, it is important to qualify this information. All of us make statements such as, "Oh, I could have killed myself!" or "I just can't stand it any longer," in reference to school or work. However, any of these statements become significant only when in excess and accompanied by other suicidal symptoms.

Reprinted from *Self-Destructive Behavior* – Workshop Proceedings; Brent Q. Hafen, Director, Health Science Department, Brigham Young University, 1971.

There are some particular personality characteristics which are indicative of suicide patients. One of those most frequently mentioned is depression.[4] This sympton is of major importance to physicians because of its serious disability and danger to life; suicide should be considered as a possibility whenever depressive symptoms are present. The symptoms are physiological, psychological and social.

Physiological symptoms include sleep disorder, especially sleeplessness; appetite disorder, especially loss of appetite; constipation, headaches, other aches and pains; and fatigue.

The psychological symptoms include loss of energy, loss of initiative, and absence of interest in usual pleasures such as sex, sports, books, and television. The patients are sad; they often feel guilty, and have low self-esteem. They tend to feel hopeless and helpless.

Social withdrawal completes the depression. The patient loses interest in social gatherings and other people. Often physicians or families suggest a vacation. The patients realize that they are unable to enjoy a vacation and this may be the precipitator of suicidal crisis.

Even though these evaluative symptoms are proposed for use by doctors specifically, they can also be used by laymen. This brings us to the next characteristic. There is a great emphasis placed on interpersonal communication or lack of it, and dependency in suicidal individuals. There is a general belief that suicide is committed by persons who are unable to express and satisfy needs in an open manner. Also, these people show a great need for dependency. Norman Tabachnick[5] has devised two different outlines; one delineates factors in determining suicide potential, and the other outlines characteristics of suicide attemptors. Both are similar in emphasizing communication and dependency:

A. Factors in determining suicide potential
1. Interpersonal incapacity—inability to maintain warm, inter-dependent relationships
2. Marital isolation—disengagement in spite of appearances; lack of involvement
3. Distorted communication of dependency wishes
4. Help negation—person rejects helpful relationships
5. Psychosis—loss of reality
6. Previous attempts at suicide
B. Characteristics of suicide attemptors
1. Often more than usually dependent—person expects others to make decisions and do things for him
2. Masochism—person becomes angry as a result of frustration, but unable to express anger toward object of frustration because he is afraid of losing dependent support

3. Will tend to seek out others who are
   a. Eager and willing to give and to allow himself to be imposed on
   b. Someone who might punish him
   c. Other person also dependent and masochistic
   d. Both persons in this relationship express anger in some rejecting way—suicide is a result of such rejection
   e. These persons may not display these characteristics except in this particular relationship

Often, it seems that a suicide attempt is a person's effort to make a change in his relationships with persons important to him, or a form of communication to or about these persons.

The necessity of communication and involvement with suicide patients cannot be overstressed. It is a basis for more accurate recognition of suicidal intent. Physicians play the major role of involvement with suicide patients. They can approach the suicidal motivation through a series of questions, working from general to specific. Such a series of questions might be: How is your life going? How are you feeling in general? How are your spirits, your hopes? If answers indicate low spirits, pessimistic attitudes or much confusion, another series of questions would follow: Would you sometimes like to give up? Do you ever wish you were dead? A final set of questions is: Have you ever thought of ending your life? How would you do it? Even though these questions are designed for physicians as tools in determining the mental states of patients, if tactfully and subtly employed, they can be valuable to laymen as well. At this point, the need for communication and involvement acquires its importance. Anyone can and should be alert to the feelings and behaviors of those around him, especially those with whom he is frequently associated.

There are six general items which experts at the Los Angeles Prevention Center have considered important in assessing and predicting suicidal tendencies:[6]

1. *Suicide Plan—proposed method, place and time.* If the person has decided upon a specific, highly lethal method of suicide with an instrument which is readily available to him, there is a serious emergency. It also should be taken seriously when a patient sets a deadline for his action. Vague suicide plans and methods of low lethality are somewhat reassuring. Direct denials, such as, "Yes, I thought of suicide, but I would never do it," are usually truthful and can be relied on.

2. *Severity of Symptoms.* Danger signals are: severe agitation with depression; helplessness; hopelessness which gets worse in response to helping efforts from others; confusion; and paranoid trends.

3. *Basic Personality.* People who have led stable, responsible lives generally

respond well to treatment and return to their previous levels. By contrast, many unstable, immature, addictive, alcoholic and deviant persons are chronically on the edge of self-destruction.

4. *Precipitating Stress.* If the suicidal crisis is a reaction to an overwhelming stress, the patient needs emergency protection and support.

5. *Resources.* These include physical, financial, and interpersonal assets. The willingness and ability of other persons to aid the patient often is the difference between life and death.

6. *Special Indicators.* Family history of suicide. Recent suicide of a close friend or relative. Anniversary of a divorce or death in the family. Complete social isolation. History of psychiatric treatment, especially recent discharge from a mental hospital. Recent suicide attempt, unrecognized or untreated.

Richard G. Singer and Irving J. Blumenthal, in studying psychotic patients particularly, formulated fourteen specific clues for evaluating ideas of self-destruction:[1]

1. Suicidal ideation including dire predictions and morbid dreams—discussion of various methods of suicide, dreams of death or funerals.

2. Verbalization of aggression and revenge—express feelings of revenge toward family, strong anxiety at sight of knife because, "I might kill somebody," suicide and homicide intimately related.

3. Strong tones of recrimination of self-accusation—suicide attempt often represents impulsive acting out in attempt to get rid of unbearable fear.

4. Despair following realization of functional incapacity—the patient feels that he is too dependent, will be unable to care for himself.

5. Loss of elan vitale—profound resignation, indifference to death.

6. Anorexia, insomnia, impotence mask a more serious depressive state—intense preoccupation and tension.

7. Doubts regarding worth of existence—patient decides that life is not worthwhile, indicates that he deserves punishment, yearning for better life.

8. Loss of loved one—may be delusion concerning the loss of love, projected feeling of longing, overwhelming disappointment to which they seem unable to adjust.

9. Loss of emotion in sexual fantasies—losing sexual powers is synonymous with losing power of life.

10. Psychosomatic delusions with morbid content—may feel that his somatic illness is incurable and might as well hasten his departure.

11. Emergence of smiling depression—at the moment a patient decides he will kill himself he may become overtly cheerful; a tremendous relief of tension occurs when a solution is decided upon.

12. Breakthrough of latent homosexual trends—because of this the patient verbalizes desperate need to get out of the hospital without knowing why.

13. Significant statements in correspondence—sometimes implicit in letters that the patient is tidying up affairs, instructing persons to deal with certain details after his death.

14. Changes in attitude toward personal possessions—refuses to spend money on new things because he won't be around to use them.

These fourteen clues can further aid our attempts to evaluate and predict suicidal behavior in individuals.

The past section has dealt with general characteristics of suicidal behavior and some basic danger signals. It is the purpose of the next section to discuss suitability and effectiveness of psychological tests in assessing suicidal tendency. David Lester has evaluated several psychological tests according to their usefulness in predicting suicide. Most of this material will be taken from Lester's article.[7]

The Rorschach Test. Research using the Rorschach to identify and predict suicidal behavior was reviewed by Neuringer (1965). He concluded that the data were equivocal, inconsistent and contradictory. He attributed this state of affairs to the non-comparable nature of the studies, which differed in the conditions under which the test results were obtained and in the different ways in which suicidal behavior was defined by the different authors.

Since Neuringer's review research has been carried out on two Rorschach signs. Applebaum and Colson (1968) have reported a replication of a finding by Applebaum and Holzman (1962) that the use of the shading of color as a determinant of at least one response was more frequent in those who had attempted suicide than in comparison groups.[8] The second sign reported by Sapolsky (1963) is that a response to area D6 on card VII was found more frequently in persons with suicidal ideation than in those without suicide ideation.

The Thematic Apperception Test (TAT). Shneidman and Farberow (1958) collected samples of neurotic and psychotic patients, both male and female, who were tested after an attempt at suicide or before a successful suicidal act and compared them with non-suicidal groups. Of twenty-one possible between group comparisons only four were significant and these four seemed to be caused through differences between the themes of males and females and between the themes of neurotics and psychotics.

Friedman (1958) in commenting on this study, noted the possibility that the basic suicidal impulses may be present in all people and that this may lead to negative results on studies attempting to identify suicidal risk. In any case, the TAT at present is of little value in assessing suicide behavior.

The Rosenzweig Picture-Frustration Test. Comparison of studies of this test shows that only the E score is found by more than one study to differentiate groups of patients. Farberow reported that attempted suicides have lower scores than threatened suicides. However, some studies failed to find that the E score was significant. It appears that this test is of little use in the identification of suicidal risk.

The Minnesota Multiphasic Personality Inventory (MMPI).

a.   Standard Scales. Rosen, et. al. (1954) compared 50 patients who had attempted suicide, 100 patients who had thought about suicide, and a non-suicidal control group. The general trend appears to be that the thought group scored higher on most scales than either the attempted suicides or the control group. However, this is the only significant finding and occurred in only a limited number of the studies.

b.   Profile Analysis. Devries and Farberow tested patients who had threatened suicide, those who had attempted suicide, and a non-suicidal group (1967). They considered only the Pa, Sc, Pt, Ma, Pd and D scales. It was found that the groups differed significantly. The suicidal groups could be distinguished from each other by means of the MMPI than without the test.

   However, a study done by Devries and Shneidman (1967) found that patients respond idiosyncratically and general trends for all suicidal patients are not identifiable.

c.   Item Analysis. Devries has attempted to differentiate those items of the MMPI that are useful in differentiating suicidal from non-suicidal persons. In the first study, groups of psychiatric patients tested before completing suicide, after threatening suicide and after attempting suicide were compared with a control group of non-suicidal patients. The number of items differentiating the completed suicides, the attempted suicides and the non-suicidal group did not exceed chance expectations and so Devries concluded that the MMPI could not be used to predict suicidal attempts.

The Bender-Gestalt Test. Nawas and Worth (1968) compared 17 hospitalized psychiatric patients who had made a suicide attempt within six months prior to hospitalization with a group of non-suicidal patients matched for age, sex, race, marital status, diagnosis, education, and length of hospitalization. Ten signs were hypothesized to differentiate the two groups, and the tests were scored independently by three experienced clinicians for the presence or absence of these ten signs. None of the signs, alone or in combination, differentiated the groups.[9]

The Semantic Differential. Blau, et. al. (1967) compared male psychiatric patients tested after attempting or threatening suicide with a group of non-suicidal patients. Thirteen concepts were rated on 10 scales. Of the 130 possible tests for differences, eight reached significance at the .05 level or better which is no more than would be expected on the basis of chance alone.

Potential Suicide Personality Inventory (PSPI). Devries (1966) studied the suicide literature using the critical incident technique and collected all characteristics of suicidal individuals mentioned in the study. From this collection, 55 items were written and these were administered to a group of non-suicidal psychiatric male patients and to a group of previously suicidal male psychiatric patients. Thirteen of the items were found to differentiate the suicidal patients from the non-suicidal patients at the .05 level of significance or better. This test is one that can be used by professionals or laymen alike. The actual test items and explanations are found below:

POTENTIAL SUICIDE PERSONALITY INVENTORY ITEMS[10]
Answer true or false

   1. I feel worse during the spring or fall than at other times of the year.
   2. There were no heavy drinkers in my family.
   3. I have not yet decided where I will make my home.
   4. Weakness in myself or others makes me uncomfortable.
   5. My nearest relatives understand the troubles that I am going through.
   6. I wish I could be with someone I once loved very much.
   7. I do not have serious financial difficulties.
   8.* I like sunny weather.
   9. I do not become emotionally upset when I am sick in bed.
  10. I cannot foretell changes in the weather.
  11. Some of the people whom I liked and admired have died.
  12. I feel that the people who supervise me tend to be too strict.
  13. I feel much better now than I have felt in some time.
  14. I have the feeling that if someone would pinch me I would not feel it.
  15. I am seldom sick.
  16.* I like watching some television programs.
  17. My sexual frustrations have not worsened lately.
 +18. My future happiness looks promising.
  19. I would rather follow than lead others.
 +20. Recently I have difficulty sleeping.
  21. I have had much pain when I was ill.
  22. I seldom engage in social activities.
  23. My interest in sex has not declined recently.
 +24. My future looks secure.
  25. I think that I am to blame for almost all my troubles.
  26.* I enjoy listening to music.

+27. When I am ill the doctor frequently prescribes sedatives for me.
28. Sometimes I am angry for a whole day.
29. I think that I have had more difficulties throughout life than most people.
+30. Sometimes I am really very much afraid.
31. I often become very impatient.
+32. I sometimes fear that I will lose control over myself.
33. I often feel that I am unwanted.
34. Lately things have happened to me that are enough to discourage anyone.
35.* I like flowers.
+36. Lately I have not felt like participating in my usual activities.
37. I am not actively religious.
+38. I go on occasional drinking sprees.
+39. Within the last two years I changed my jobs at least twice.
40. I have no more family ties.
41. I did not grow up in a broken home.
42. I always feel poorest in early morning than at any other time of the day.
43. There often has been disharmony in our family.
44. Making sexual adjustments is not easy for me.
+45. I have someone whose welfare I very much care for.
46. I never have great fears about the hereafter.
47. Lately I feel quite restless and fidgety.
+48. I never feel that I am completely worthless.
+49. I frequently have a drink in the morning.
50.* I enjoy having a vacation.
51. I feel that I am more tenderhearted than most people.
52. In the last 5 years I have moved at least once every year.
53. I have no habits that are leading me into repeated difficulties.
54. I like to have most things done very precisely.
55. I am not interested any more in the things that I used to enjoy doing.

---

*buffer items
+items which significantly differentiate suicidals from non-suicidals.

An individual who scores more than seven on the items which significantly differentiate should be considered seriously suicidal.

A recent trend in the identification of suicidal risk is the use of personal data about the individual's social history and current psychiatric status. There are many factors that significantly differentiate the suicidal from the non-suicidal patients: age, sex, race, marital status, employment status, physical health, history of disturbed sexual adjustment, recent change in family unity, previous suicide attempt, season of attempt and time of day, presence or absence of suicide note.

A typical schedule has been devised for this type of assessment. It is often used by suicide prevention centers and is valuable in any emergency evaluation situation:

ASSESSMENT OF SUICIDAL POTENTIALITY[11]

This schedule rates suicide potentiality. Listed below are categories with descriptive items which have been found to be useful in evaluating suicidal potentiality. Some items imply high suicidal potentiality, while others imply low suicidal potentiality.

The numbers in parentheses after each item *suggest* the most common range of values or weights to be assigned that item. None is highest, or most seriously suicidal, while one is lowest, or least seriously suicidal. The rater will note that some categories range only from one to seven.

For each category the rater should select the item(s) which apply and place the weight he would assign it in the parentheses at the right of the item. (More than one item may apply.) The rater should then indicate his evaluation of his subject in that *category* by placing a number from one to nine (or one to seven) in the column headed, Rating for Category. In those categories where the descriptive item is not present for the subject being rated, write the item in and assign a weight in the parentheses following.

The overall suicidal potentiality rating may be found by entering the weights assigned for each category in the box, front page, totaling, and dividing by the number of categories rated. This number, rounded to the nearest whole number, should also be circled at the top of the front page.

Name_____Age_____Sex_____Date_____

Rater_____Evaluation _____ 1 2 3 4 5 6 7 8 (9)
                                                      L   M   H

SUICIDE POTENTIAL:

A&S _____	Res _____	TOTAL_____
Sy _____	PSB _____	
St _____	MedSta_____	No. of categories rated_____
AvC _____	Comm _____	
SIP _____	RoSO _____	Average_____

Rating for Category

1. AGE AND SEX (1-9)   (　)
   Male
      50 plus (7-9)   (　)
      35-49 (4-6)   (　)
      15-34 (1-3)   (　)
   Female
      50 plus (5-7)   (　)
      35-49 (3-5)   (　)
      15-34 (1-3)   (　)
2. SYMPTOMS (1-9)   (　)
   Severe depression: sleep disorder, anorexia,
      weight loss, withdrawal, despondent, loss
      of interest, apathy. (7-9)   (　)
   Feelings of hopelessness, helplessness, ex-
   haustion. (7-9)   (　)
   Delusions, hallucination, loss of contact,
      disorientation. (6-8)   (　)
   Compulsive gambler. (6-8)   (　)
   Disorganization, confusion, chaos. (5-7)   (　)
   Alcoholism, drug addiction, homo-
      sexuality. (4-7)   (　)
   Agitation, tension, anxiety. (4-6)   (　)
   Guilt, shame, embarrassment. (4-6)   (　)
   Feelings of rage, anger, hostility, revenge.
      (4-6)   (　)
   Poor impulse control, poor judgment. (4-6)   (　)
   Frustrated dependency. (4-6)   (　)
   Other (describe):   (　)
3. STRESS (1-9)   (　)
   Loss of loved person by death, divorce, or
      separation. (5-9)   (　)
   Loss of job, money, prestige, status. (4-8)   (　)
   Sickness, serious illness, surgery, accident,
      loss of limb. (3-7)   (　)
   Threat of prosecution, criminal involvement,
      exposure. (4-6)   (　)
   Change(s) in life, environment, setting.
      (4-6)   (　)
   Success, promotion, increased respon-

Rating for Category

sibilities. (2-5)   ( )
No significant stress. (1-3)   ( )
Other (describe):   ( )
4. ACUTE VERSUS CHRONIC (1-9)   ( )
   Sharp, noticeable, and sudden onset of spec-
     · ific symptoms. (1-9)   ( )
   Recurrent outbreak of similar symptoms.
   (4-9)   ( )
   Recent increase in long-standing traits.
   (4-7)   ( )
   No specific recent change. (1-4)   ( )
   Other (describe):   ( )
5. SUICIDAL PLAN (1-9)   ( )
   Lethality of proposed method — gun, jump,
     hanging, drowning, knife, poison, pills,
     aspirin. (1-9)   ( )
   Availability of means in proposed method.
   (1-9)   ( )
   Specific detail and clarity in organization of
     plan. (1-9)
   Specificity in time planned. (1-9)   ( )
   Bizarre plans. (4-6)   ( )
   Rating of previous suicide attempt(s). (1-9)   ( )
   No plans. (1-3)   ( )
   Other (describe):   ( )
6. RESOURCES (1-9)   ( )
   No sources of support (family, friends,
     agencies, employment). (7-9)   ( )
   Family and friends available, unwilling to
     help. (4-7)   ( )
   Financial problem. (4-7)   ( )
   Available professional help, agency or thera-
     pist. (2-4)   ( )
   Family and/or friends willing to help. (1-3) ( )
   Stable life history. (1-3)   ( )
   Physician or clergy available. (1-3)   ( )
   Employed. (1-3)   ( )
   Finances no problem. (1-3)   ( )
   Other (describe):   ( )

Rating for Category

7. PRIOR SUICIDAL BEHAVIOR (1-7)   ( )
   One or more prior attempts of high lethality.
      (6-7)   ( )
   One or more prior attempts of low lethality.
      (4-5)   ( )
   History of repeated threats and depression.
      (3-5)   ( )
   No prior suicidal or depressed history. (1-3)   ( )
   Other (describe):   ( )
8. MEDICAL STATUS (1-7)   ( )
   Chronic debilitating illness. (5-7)   ( )
   Pattern of failure in previous therapy. (4-6)   ( )
   Many repeated unsuccessful experiences
      with doctors. (4-6)   ( )
   Psychosomatic illness, e.g., asthma, ulcer,
      etc. (2-4)   ( )
   Chronic minor illness complaints, hypo-
      chondria. (1-3)   ( )
   No medical problems. (1-2)   ( )
   Other (describe):   ( )
9. COMMUNICATION ASPECTS (1-7)   ( )
   Communication broken with rejection of
      efforts to re-establish by both patient
      and others. (5-7)   ( )
   Communications have internalized goal, e.g.,
      declaration of guilt, feelings of worth-
      lessness, blame, shame. (4-7)   ( )
   Communications have interpersonalized
      goal, e.g., to cause guilt in others, to
      force behavior, etc. (2-4)   ( )
   Communications directed toward world and
      people in general. (3-5)   ( )
   Communications directed toward one or
      more specific persons. (1-3)   ( )
   Other (describe):   ( )
10. REACTION OF SIGNIFICANT OTHER
   (1-7)   ( )
   Defensive, paranoid, rejected, punishing
      attitude. (5-7)   ( )

Rating for Category

Denial of own or patient's need for help. (5-7)	( )
No feelings of concern about the patient; does not understand the patient. (4-6)	( )
Indecisiveness, feelings of helplessness. (3-5)	( )
Alternation between feelings of anger and rejection and feelings of responsibility and desire to help. (2-4)	( )
Sympathy and concern plus admission of need for help. (1-3)	( )
Other (describe):	( )

It seems that the personal history method has been most reliable and effective in evaluating and predicting suicidal tendencies. Most of the psychological tests utilized for this purpose have proven of little value or accuracy.

The third category considered in this paper is that of evaluation of suicidal potential in emergency situations. This is most likely to occur as a telephone call to a suicide prevention center. However, anyone might be involved in such a crisis, especially those of the helping professions. Therefore the material in this section will include a "Short Schedule for Assessment of Self-Destructive Potentiality,"[1] and each item will be followed by pertinent comments:

I. Case History: Factual

A. Age and Sex

Older males are more serious about committing suicide than females or younger males. If a male is over fifty years old he is immediately high risk. A young woman, 15-35 is least lethal, and middle age and older women are moderately lethal.

B. Onset of self-destructive behavior: Is there a chronic repetitive pattern of suicide, or recent behavior change? Any prior suicide or recent behavior change? Any prior suicide attempts or threats?

The more acute the onset of suicide behavior, the better the ultimate prognosis, but the greater need for immediate intervention. If a suicide pattern has existed over a long period, it is crucial to determine whether the person has completely exhausted his emotional resources. If he has, there is a high risk situation.

C. Method of possible self-injury: Availability, lethality?

A specific choice of time, place and method is a serious indication, but if the method is aspirin ingestion or cold pills, the emergency is dissipated. The person who owns a gun and proposes to use it should be the object of immediate efforts. Ideas of jumping from a high place should also be taken seriously. One should determine the location of someone who is planning to jump.

D.   Recent loss of a loved person: Death, separation, divorce?

When there has been a definite loss of a loved person (spouse, parent, child, lover, etc.) within the last year, the potentiality for self-destruction is increased. Some widows of ages 40-60 who were extremely dependent on their husbands display exaggerated mourning and grief reactions creating a high suicide risk.

E.   Medical symptoms: History of recent illness or surgery.

History of recent hospitalization or medical consultation, especially in older persons, may indicate increased self-destructiveness. Medical conditions most often associated with suicidal reactions are psychosomatic diseases, polysurgery, malignant tumors, and various symptoms associated with depression. If cancer or other chronic, debilitating diseases actually exist, suicidal reactions tend to be precipitated by incidents that the patient sees as rejection from physician and family.

F.   Resources: Available relatives or friends, financial status.

A recent loss of job or sudden drop in financial status may constitute a traumatic loss to certain persons, especially middle-aged men and career women. Persons who have a lifelong history of direct self-destructiveness (illustrated by unstable interpersonal relationships, alcoholism, impulsivity, hostile dependency) often reach a crisis between the ages of 40-55 when they find they have exhausted themselves financially and interpersonally; they are emotionally bankrupt. This may be a point where such people actually do commit suicide.

II.   Judgmental-Evaluative

A.   Status of communication with patient

When a patient is able to express his troubled feelings and cry for help, the self-destructive danger may be high, but it is never so extreme as when the patient has given up and withdrawn and is no longer communicating.

B.   Kinds of feelings expressed

The most serious suicidal risk is associated with feelings of helplessness and hopelessness, exhaustion and failure, and the feeling, "I just want out." A combination of agitation and confusion, however, particularly in a person who has had a previous psychotic episode, may constitute an emergency. When the predominent feeling is one of frustration, anger, or rage, without overwhelming confusion, the lethal danger is usually somewhat lessened. Suicidal threats designed primarily to taunt or punish the recipient or to gain a distinct goal or objective are usually low in lethality.

C.   Reactions of referring person

A defensive, paranoid, punishing, moralistic attitude on the part of the referring person indicates that little help can be expected from that source. It is generally encouraging when the referring person expresses sympathy and concern.

D.   Personality status and diagnostic impression

It is important to evaluate the possible presence of psychotic thinking and severe depressive affect. If either of these are present and especially if alcoholism is also present, emergency hospitalization should be considered. Also, a previous pattern of failure in therapy is a signal.

This outline, if associated with these preceeding factors and some of the general trends already mentioned, can be useful in a brief, emergency analysis of suicide potential.

The last section deals with the evaluation of suicide in specific groups. We will consider schizophrenics, cardiovascular patients, patients with cancer, patients with anxiety or depressive reactions, and various ages:

Schizophrenics. [13] There are three sub-types of schizophrenic suicidals, the unaccepting suicide patient, the dependent-satisfied suicide patient, and the dependent-dissatisfied suicide patient.

The unaccepting suicide patient rejects or resists hospitalization. He does not believe he is mentally ill and there is a lack of somatic complaints and an absence of feelings of guilt or anxiety. When put under stress this patient reacts with agitated acting out behavior but he still feels that there is nothing wrong with him. Suicide usually occurs on pass or leave from the hospital. The patient is anxious to leave, he feels he is all right, and should be released. He has unrealistically optimistic plans about the future.

The dependent-satisfied suicide patient exhibits a high degree of dependency on the hospital and the patient seems fairly satisfied with hospitalization. He realizes that he is ill. When put under stress there is considerable tension, anxiety and restlessness. The patient is overtly depressed and often expresses feelings of guilt. He also expresses a number of somatic complaints.

The dependent-dissatisfied suicide patient is an individual who begins to feel that the hospital is not giving him the help he needs. He becomes increasingly tense and depressed, and frequent expressions of guilt, anxiety and worthlessness are characteristic. If put under stress this type of an individual experiences restlessness, depression, suicidal ideation, criticism, and hostility. There are increased demands for attention and reassurance and an intense dissatisfaction is felt by the patient. The patient has a number of very ambivalent feelings and suicide is most often committed inside the hospital.

As an over-all concluding comment, it was found that suicide does not occur in the depth of psychosis, but rather, when the patient is improving.

Cardiovascular Patients.[14] Cardiovascular patients who have committed suicide have been more emotionally disturbed and have poorer relationships with hospital staff and family. They were seen as problem patients because of their provoking, complaining, and demanding behavior. In general, a "dependent-dissatisfied" pattern emerged. Compared to patients who did not commit suicide they were emotionally more hostile, anxious, agitated, apprehensive, depressed, and distressed over their illness; they had physical symptoms of insomnia and often obtained relief from placebos. The patients who were suicidal had poorer interpersonal relationships with the hospital staff and more often lacked family support during their illness.

Patients with Cancer.[15] High suicide potential was found among older men with cancer of the throat; younger men with Hodgkin's disease or leukemia; and a person of any age with cancer at the same time as heightened stress, severe anxiety, loss of tolerance for pain. It was found that suicide occurred during all stages of the disease. A general "dependent-dissatisfied" also seemed to emerge.

Patients with Anxiety or Depressive Reactions.[16] When anxiety and/or depression become so marked that they can be characterized as psychoneurotic syndromes suicide can be expected to occur proportionately more often. However, among persons who are depressed it is still possible to make some differentiations between those who are likely to commit suicide and those who are not so likely. Clues that set suicidal depressives apart are:

1. Poor response to therapy.
2. History of suicidal behavior.
3. Discomfort when released from a hospital on leave or pass.
4. Changes in family unity—lack of support or acceptance.
5. Severe psychiatric symptoms.
6. Negative reaction to the hospital.
7. Severe sexual disturbances—this reflects general deterioration in interpersonal relationships.
8. Social isolation.
9. Relative ineffectiveness of somatic complaints—patient feels there is no other way except suicide to express his problems.
10. Ineffectiveness of usual psychological defenses.
11. Negative reactions to hospital staff.
12. Lack of adaptation to illness—suicide is taken as a mode of adjustment.
13. Lack of physical well-being.

14. No plans for the future.
15. Psychological symptoms more marked or prolonged.

Children. The pattern of disturbance in childhood follows two general paths, general feeling of rejection and loss of a loved one. The feeling of rejection is found in relationship to a method or mother surrogate. As a result of depressive reactions following the death of a parent, the child identifies with this lost object; he wishes to be reunited with the parent. Suicide is an attempt to escape from an unbearable loss.

Signs to watch for are dullness and apathy in a normally bright child, inability to study, little response to other children, temper tantrums, agitation, and delinquent behavior.[17] Any profound unhappiness in a child calls for thorough investigation and treatment.

Adolescents. The various deeds of adolescents may be seen to contain not only anger directed against the environment, but punishment for their own acts as well. A few highly intelligent, solitary, and misguided teen-agers who live in a world of false romanticism are likely to have notions about self-destruction. They seem to think that dying will be a great adventure.

Old Age. Suicide in old age is based on feelings of futility, loneliness, mental illness, feelings of being unwanted, social isolation, death of a loved one, and retirement.

In conclusion, four areas of importance in evaluation, assessment and prediction of suicides have been considered in this paper. They are: 1) General Evaluation; 2) Psychological Tests; 3) Emergency Evaluation; and 4) Specific Groups Evaluation. There is no one-two-three rule book for evaluating and predicting suicides. However, there do seem to be some helpful general suggestive trend and characteristics which we have tried to present here.

REFERENCES

1. Singer, Richard G., M.D. and Blumenthal, Irving J., M.D. Suicide clues in psychotic patients. *Mental Hygiene,* 53:346-350, 1969.
2. Fawcett, Jan A. Suicide: clues from interpersonal communication. *Archives of General Psychiatry,* 21:129-137, 1969.
3. Robbins, Eli, et. al. The communication of suicidal intent. *American Journal of Psychiatry,* 115:724-733.
4. Litman, Robert E., M.D. Management of acutely suicidal patients in medical practice. *Los Angeles Suicide Prevention Center.*
5. Tabachnick, Norman. Interpersonal relations in suicidal attempts. *Archives of General Psychiatry,* 4:16-21.
6. Farberow, Norman L., Hirleg, Samuel M., and Litman, Robert E. Evaluation and management of suicidal persons. In: Shneidman, Edwin S., ed. *The Psychology of Suicide.* New York: Science House, 1970.
7. Lester, David. Attempts to predict suicidal risk using psychological tests. Suicide Prevention and Crisis Service, Inc., Buffalo.

8. Applebaum, S. A., and Colson, D. B. A re-examination of the color-shading Rorschach Test Response and suicide attempts. *Journal of Projective Techniques,* 1968, 32, 160-164.
9. Nawas, M. M. and Worth, J. W. Suicidal configuration in the Bender-Gestalt. *Journal of Projective Techniques,* 1968, 32, 160-164.
10. Devries, A. G. A potential suicide personality inventory. *Psychological Reports,* 1966, 18, 731-738.
11. Assessment of Suicidal Potentiality. Available through the Los Angeles Suicide Prevention Center, Los Angeles, California.
12. Litman, Robert E. and Farberow, Norman L. Emergency evaluation of suicidal potential. In: Shneidman, Edwin S., ed. *The Psychology of Suicide.* New York: Science House.
13. Farberow, Norman L., Shneidman, Edwin S. and Leonard, Calista V. Suicidal risk among schizophrenic patients. In: Shneidman, Edwin S., ed. *The Psychology of Suicide.* New York: Science House, 1970.
14. Farberow, Norman L., McKelligott, John W., Cohen, Sidney, and Darbonne, Allen. Suicide among cardiovascular patients. In: Shneidman, Edwin S., *The Psychology of Suicide.* New York: Science House, 1970.
15. Farberow, Norman L., Shneidman, Edwin S., and Leonard, Calista V. Suicide among patients with malignant neoplasms. In: Shneidman, Edwin S., ed. *The Psychology of Suicide.* New York: Science House, 1970.
16. Farberow, Norman L. and Cevoy, Theodore L. Suicide among patients with anxiety or depressive reactions. In: Shneidman, Edwin S., ed. *The Psychology of Suicide.* New York: Science House, 1970.
17. Clark, Marguerite. Suicide in childhood and adolescence. *NEA Journal,* 54:32-33, 1964.

SELF-DESTRUCTIVE BEHAVIOR AMONG YOUTH AND ADOLESCENTS

Throughout this section the reader will observe the drama and dynamics of suicidal behavior enhanced, sometimes incredibly so. Adolescence magnifies many suicidal elements, feelings of inadequacy and worthlessness, impulsivity, guilt, rage, and desire for revenge, loneliness, fear, hypersensitivity and suggestibility. Oddly enough, with adults depression is a common denominator in suicide studies but depression as seen in adults is infrequently found in childhood or adolescence. Object loss or grief is often masked by behavior which has no resemblance to depression on the surface.

The following papers point up the fact that suicide is a very real problem among young people and is tending to increase. Counselors who work with youngsters have particular obligations to remain sympathetic to the acting out impulsive noisy teen-ager whose history suggests he has all of the entitlements to grief. This type of adolescent frequently gets shunted from agency to agency and foster home to foster home without any real opportunity to express the depression which lies beneath his anger or hyperactive, unstable behavior. Juvenile court workers are accustomed to seeing such youngsters in great number, perhaps even to the point that they become calloused to the misfortunes of the youth. The concept of grief entitlements without surface depression in young people is one worth respecting in the suicide prevention field. To detect the depressions of childhood among the so-called "delinquency group" is a diagnostic obligation and if such a child is found early the acting out, cover-up mechanisms can be dealt with before they become an indelible part of the personality.

Self-Destructive Behavior in Adolescents and Adults: Similarities and Differences

James T. Barter

The thesis of this paper is that self-destructive behavior in adolescents and adults differs because of the differences in the psychology of the adolescent and the adult. The similarities in self-destructive acts of adolescents and adults are perhaps more superficial and related to sociocultural roles. One must constantly keep in mind that the adolescent has not had the experience of being an adult and that adults have experienced and passed through adolescence.

The tasks which normal adolescents must successfully master before they attain maturity and adulthood are various. We shall contrast some of these with the adult state and show where they relate to adolescent suicidal behavior.

The problem of control of impulses for the adolescent is different from that of the adult. Adolescents fight for precarious control of unconscious drives which are held in check by relatively weak defenses. This is in contrast to the adult whose unconscious drives are more successfully repressed and controlled by stronger defenses. Impulsivity as a factor in self-destructive behavior in adolescents is fairly common as compared to the adult.

Achieving a sense of autonomy and separation from the family is a major preoccupation of young people. This is difficult because at the point where the adolescent begins to grasp the meaning of the task he is being simultaneously pulled back into the family. He is locked into various complex relationships within the family and is treated at one moment as an immature child and the next reminded to grow up. He must struggle with the problem of gradual separation from the family members, realizing that he is still dependent upon them. Only a slight intensification of this normal struggle for independence and autonomy with attendant feelings of rejection and loss of love are often enough to precipitate self-destructive behavior in the adolescent. By contrast, adults generally have achieved some sort of emancipation and have invested in other relationships such as result from marriage and the beginning of their own families. A mature love relationship for the adult is protective against self-destructive behavior. It is only with the real or threatened breakup of a marriage

Reprinted from *Suicide Among the American Indians,* U.S. Public Health Service Publication No. 1903, June 1969.

or in the older adult who is faced with the dissolution of his family that the risk of self-destructive behavior is increased.

The adolescent has to struggle with the question of who he is, whom he wishes to be like, and what is to be his role in society. This is one aspect of choosing and preparing for a vocation and commitment to life. The adolescent is constantly reminded that he has not yet finished his schooling and is not yet ready to participate in adult society. The adult has a sense of who he is, his vocational choice is usually stabilized, and he is functioning in his job rather satisfactorily. His preoccupations with the future are more apt to deal with raising his family and achieving financial security. The intensity of his concern with the future may be less than that observed in the adolescent. Failure on the part of the adolescent to cope with identity problems increases risk of self-destruction.

Both young boys and young girls have to learn how to identify with members of their own sex while simultaneously being involved in the process of developing affectional bonds with members of the opposite sex as a preliminary procedure in selection of future marriage partners. Adults have presumably worked through these conflicts and have greater sexual freedom and better understanding of the relationship between sexuality and love than have adolescents. Lack of friends of one's own sex and disappointments in adolescent love relationships are well known precipitating causes in suicidal behavior.

CHARACTERISTICS OF THE PRESUICIDAL BIOGRAPHY

Teicher and Jacobs described the biography of the child who eventually arrives at the conclusion that self-destruction is the only solution to his problem. They describe a three-stage progression leading up to a suicide attempt: (1) A longstanding preadolescent history of problems of various kinds, such as broken homes, rejection by parents, and placement in foster homes or juvenile hall, which seem progressively to isolate the adolescent from meaningful social relationships; (2) a period of escalation which is coincident with adolescence, often associated with the appearance of new problems (I see these as essentially involving a series of failures in the solution of the normal tasks of adolescence, such as the struggle for autonomy, failure to achieve an adequate identity, school failure with attendant lack of self-esteem, and inadequate working out of sexual conflicts); (3) the final stage which is described as a chain reaction dissolution of any meaningful social relationships. This final stage is often mistaken as a reason for the suicide but represents only the precipitating cause. Frequently mentioned precipitating causes are a fight with the family, an inadequate romance with its final breakup, school dropout, pregnancy, and perhaps the exodus of older siblings from the household. Teicher and Jacobs further make the point that the suicide attempt, instead of resolving the problem for the adolescent, only adds to his alienation and serves to isolate him further from those sources of support and gratification that he is seeking to attain.

A comparable biography of the adult suicide cannot be as well delineated, although we do feel that there are many clues to self-destructive potential in the adult. Most often, the adult self-destructive behavior takes place in the context of a disrupted marital status brought on by separation, divorce, or death. Frequently the person is living alone and suffers from emotional and/or physical illness for which medical help has been sought in the immediate preself-destructive period. The self-destructive behavior is apt to occur in the setting of waning abilities and/or loss of people close to the individual, resulting in an inability to face the threat of oncoming helplessness or loneliness. Factors which seem to increase the risk of lethal self-destructive behavior include unemployment, alcoholism, and prior attempts at suicide, especially if the suicide attempt was by one of the more lethal methods, and if the prior attempt was associated with psychiatric hospitalization.

SYMPTOMATOLOGY ASSOCIATED WITH SELF-DESTRUCTIVE ACTS

Depression

It is often alleged that depression is covert or absent in the suicidal adolescent. This is not really true. What has been true is that we have largely ignored symptoms. All of the symptomatology of classical adult depression can be seen in the suicidal adolescent—loss of interest in friends and family, lack of initiative and drive, feelings of sadness, emptiness, and loneliness, and eating and sleeping disturbances. But delinquent behavior, sexual promiscuity, and frenetic activity can be as indicative of adolescent depression as the more classical symptoms. In an adult, depression is more often clearly seen and interpreted correctly as such by both the physician and the patient and is useful clinically in judging self-destruction potential. We have learned to recognize that the depressed patient who suddenly loses his depressive symptoms may be at peace with himself because he has determined to die and is no longer in conflict about this decision. But a self-destructive attempt by an adolescent may come as a surprise to the family and physician who did not recognize the depression which the adolescent could not mention.

Impulsivity

Impulsivity is characteristic of the adolescent suicide. Self-destructive acts are usually not well thought out and may represent a whim on the part of the adolescent. As pointed out by Gould (1965) this impulsivity often is the determining factor in the lethality of the suicide attempt of the adolescent; that is, unplanned and poorly executed attempts may result in a high number of "accidental suicides." But on the other hand, an inexpert or imperfect knowledge of lethal methods makes the likelihood of successfully completed suicides less certain. Adult suicide can be an impulsive act as well, but a determination to end life seems more characteristic of adults. In completed adult suicides, methods of high lethality are often chosen with careful planning and much forethought before the attempt. There is apt to be more rumination about suicide over a longer period of time in the adult than in the adolescent. I think, as an illustration of this, one might consider suicide by automobile. Adolescents and adults both attempt suicide by automobile. We can speculate that in the adolescent such suicide may be very impulsive and related to a sudden whim to turn the wheel, whereas an adult suicide by automobile may more frequently represent a deliberate attempt to cover up the suicide for insurance purposes or other personal reasons such as sparing the feelings of the family.

Interpersonal Relationships

Although we have described adolescent suicide attempts as a result of progressive alienation from the family, one has to remember that we are referring to emotional alienation. Suicidal behavior on the part of adolescents may take place in the house with parents and friends in the next room. The attempt may be used to effect changes in the relationships within the family, to get back at the family, or as a reaction to the threat of loss of love. The adolescent attempt often is precipitated by a seemingly trivial event such as an argument over an exam mark or bed time.

Younger adult self-destructive acts may be similar to the adolescents but are most often a reaction to failure in marriage, work, or parenthood. Older adults suicide in the setting of waning abilities, sickness, or loss of a supporting environment. A precipitating cause may be less obvious, and the suicide may appear to be a reaction to a total life situation more than to a single event. Adult suicidal behavior may be a secret affair and rarely occurs in a family setting.

Similarities

There are some aspects of self-destructive behavior which do not seem to be differentiated by age. For example, females attempt suicide three times more often than males, whereas males complete suicide three times more often than females.

Males at all ages who exhibit suicidal behavior seem to be more ill psychologically than are females. Explanations for this seem to be related to sociocultural factors. Our society judges male and female behavior differently in regards to expression of aggression. Because there are adequate approved outlets for aggression by males they are less apt to turn aggression in upon themselves and therefore less apt to make trivial attempts. The expression of aggression in females is frustrated, resulting in a greater number of attempts at suicide. For a male to turn aggression in upon himself represents a more severe state of psychological decompensation.

Males, by and large, favor lethal "masculine" methods such as firearms or hanging.

Method of attempt may well be more related to culturally determined sex roles than to any age factor.

TREATMENT IMPLICATIONS

Adolescent Treatment

The adolescent suicide most frequently takes place in the context of family problems and often is directed at bringing about a resolution of these problems. The attempt often has the opposite effect, however, and further alienates the adolescent from the source of supportive gratification that he is trying to reach. However, it seems extremely important to involve the family in the treatment process from the very beginning. One particularly tries to get the family to help in the process of reversing the alienation of the adolescent. In a followup study of adolescent suicide attempters who had been hospitalized (Barter, 1967), we observed that those adolescents who had sustained a real or threatened parent loss, who lived alone after hospitalization, and who had poor social relationships had a great likelihood of continued suicidal behavior and represented in essence a high-risk population.

Because a suicidal adolescent often does not appear to be terribly ill, his plea for help may be ignored.

The first attempt should be taken seriously and not passed off as a gesture or attention-seeking device, which leads to lowered self-esteem and a higher likelihood of further suicidal behavior, possibly lethal. Do not reassure a suicidal adolescent falsely that everything is going to be all right. Make an honest attempt to understand the agony the patient is going through. It does not pay to be sarcastic or to use techniques which essentially diminish the patient's self-esteem and further increase his suicide-proneness.

It is my feeling that adolescents who make self-destructive attempts should be hospitalized much more frequently than they are. In the study alluded to before, most of these adolescents made more than one attempt prior to the attempt which led to their hospitalization. The hospitalization serves to remove the adolescent from the stressful situation and allows both the patient and the family to reconstitute to an extent. The patient feels supported, protected, and cared for.

Discharging the adolescent from the hospital before he is ready to go or before significant changes have been brought about in the family increases the risk of further suicidal behavior. Antidepressive medications can be used with the suicidal adolescent. However, I feel that such medications have a much more prominent role in the treatment of the depressed suicidal adult. When one is dealing with a suicidal patient, any therapeutic modality which has potential usefulness should not be overlooked, including, of course, drug therapy.

Finally, I would like to say a few words about the problem of suicide prevention in adolescents and in adults. It is important to remember that the suicidal adult is apt to seek professional help, as contrasted with the suicidal adolescent who often feels help is not available and who makes the suicide attempt in an effort to involve his family. The physician is apt to be involved rather late in the game, frequently after the adolescent has made more than one suicide attempt. It seems to me that in many ways we have an understanding of the warning signals and danger signs in the adult suicidal patient. We have been able to identify those factors which seem to increase the risk of lethality, and we can readily set up suicide prevention services on a rather rational basis.

I do not believe that we have a good criteria for assessing suicidal potential in the adolescent nor for picking up the suicide-prone adolescent. Teicher and Jacobs (1966) had stated that they do not believe that the physician can distinguish a potentially suicidal adolescent from other adolescents. First attempts at suicide among adolescents come as a great surprise to parents and friends, as well as physicians involved with adolescents.

I feel we have to be thankful that the great majority of adolescent suicidal attempts are of low lethality. We must recognize that we have a greater responsibility for heeding the cry for help represented by the first suicide attempt of the adolescent and not placing him in a position where he has to make repeated attempts in order to gain the help that he needs. It is particularly important to educate families and family physicians not to ignore self-destructive behavior in the adolescent but to treat self-destructive attempts as a plea for help which, if denied, will lead to further acting-out of suicidal behavior.

BIBLIOGRAPHY

Barter, J. T.; Swabach, D.; and Todd, Dorothy. Adolescent suicide attempts, a followup study of hospitalized patients. Paper presented at Eighth Western Divisional Meeting of American Psychiatric Association, October 1967.

Gould, R. E. Suicide problems in children and adolescents. *American Journal of Psychotherapy*, 19:228-46, April 1965.

Teicher, J. D., and Jacobs, J. Adolescents who attempt suicide: Preliminary findings. *American Journal of Psychiatry*, 122:1248-57, May 1966.

Teicher, J. D., and Jacobs, J. The physician and the adolescent suicide attempter. *Journal of School Health*, 36:406-15, November 1966.

Children and Adolescents Who Attempt Suicide

Joseph D. Teicher

There are no accurate figures on the incidence of attempted suicide in children and adolescents. Families and physicians often conceal such attempts. Suicide is the fourth most frequent cause of death in the 15 to 19 year old age group, and the general impression is that the attempted suicide rate is increasing throughout the western world. Suicide attempts in children are not common if one judges only by hospitalized patients. At the Los Angeles County–University of Southern California Medical Center, increasing numbers of children under 12 are admitted for "accidental overdose." A high rate of accidents in children is common knowledge and it should not be surprising that many are sub-intentioned suicide attempts. One to 5 per cent of all children under 10 years of age admitted to child psychiatric facilities have a history of a threat or attempt to kill themselves. (1)

In general, childhood suicide attempts appear to be impulsive acts mostly motivated by poor treatment and the desire to punish those who would grieve their death. Running in front of cars, jumping from roofs, attempting hanging, placing one's head in a plastic bag, and more recently ingestion of pills are common modes. The relative frequency of suicidal attempts is so much greater in the teen-age period that far more attention is paid to the adolescent era. In general, the child who threatens to kill himself is expressing his rage toward his parents, usually his mother. But death is not permanent to the young child and often means to him a better life or a wish to reunite with the all-giving, good mother, somewhat like the phoenix myth. Those who actually seriously attempt to kill themselves are usually very disturbed, with very disturbed family situations and usually a very disturbed mother.

To indicate the international nature of the problem, one agency reports an international rise in suicide in recent years. (16) "The most striking feature of this world-wide upsurge in suicide is that, with few exceptions, the largest increases were registered among young persons." An 8 per cent increase occurred in the United States (p. 4). "In this country, suicide in recent years has

Reprinted by permission from *Pediatric Clinics of North America* Vol. 17, No. 3, August 1970.

alternated with homicide as the third ranking cause of death at ages 15 to 24, after accidents and cancer" (p. 5). "It is of additional interest that the rates have risen more sharply for females than males and for nonwhites than whites" (p. 6). "Nonwhite teen-agers and young adults showed only slightly lower suicide rates than white ..." (p. 6). There were over 20,000 suicides reported in the United States in 1964, and it is reported that one out of every thousand teen-agers in the United States attempts suicide.

No racial groups are without this problem. In two western American Indian tribes, half the men who take their own lives do so before the age of 20. Indian figures of suicide are near epidemic proportions, with a rate 10 times higher than that for the United States population as a whole. "And in Idaho, the suicide rate among Indian teen-agers is 100 times the national average." (12) Among Chinatown residents in San Francisco, the suicide rate was higher than the San Francisco rate, "itself about three times the national average. The general dissolution of time-honored, traditional values and institutions, the loss of faith in the elders, and the lack of home life because of economic conditions are all factors." (6)

According to Louis Dublin, (2) nonfatal suicide attempts occur seven to eight times more frequently than fatal ones. Data are probably inaccurate, for many cases are concealed by parents and physicians as accidents. In contrast to the higher incidence of suicide among adolescent males, there is apparently a higher incidence of suicidal attempts among adolescent females. Conservatively, Jacobziner (9) estimated that 60,000 suicide attempts are made each year in this country by persons under the age of 20.

VIEWS OF FACTORS IN ATTEMPTED SUICIDE

Some consideration of some of the factors in attempted suicide follows: In general, they substantiate the work done at the Los Angeles County—USC Medical Center to be discussed below.

Anna Freud (4) states that suicidal wishes may occur during adolescence stemming from the reversal of the affect of love to hate toward parents, with displacement to the self. Mason (11) reviewed the cases of four girls between the ages of 18 and 20. He concluded that these girls were reacting to incestuous wishes, but that, unlike children, adolescents have the physical attributes which can make the wishes come true.

Erikson (3) considers adolescent suicide an attempt at an identity based on negative identity choice, i.e., "an identity perversely based on all those identifications and roles which, at critical states of development, had been presented to the individual as most undesirable or dangerous, and yet, also as most real" (p. 87). Schneer and Kay (14) conclude from their series of 84 cases that, "In addition to the anxiety or exaggerated guilt and aggression, the loss of, or separation from, one or both parents, in varying degrees, at crucial periods in development predisposes the adolescent to suicide" (p. 198).

Schrut (15) emphasizes the disturbed relationship between the parents, especially mother and child. He points out that "basic feelings directed toward the child of being a burden were conveyed unconsciously" (p. 1103), and were evidenced from infancy. Moreover, the self-destructive acts are partial fulfillment of the mother's unspoken "demand that he be nonexistent" (p. 1106).

Sabbath (13) basically confirms our work (10) in his article. He too points out the long history of parent-child difficulties and the crisis in adolescence. The parents perceive their child's sexuality and hostility as a threat to "their sanity, marital stability, and even their very existence" (p. 285). They react by wishing him dead "that he could be dispensed with." "He had become expendable" and, feeling abandoned, complies with a suicidal attempt. Marvin Stein, in a communication, reports observations on a group of 330 patients at Kings County Psychiatric Hospital, Brooklyn, New York. Apparently there is a greater frequency of both childhood and antecedent separations in suicide attempters.

Gould, (5) in an excellent review, points out that rejection and deprivation resulting from a loss of love and support is the common theme underlying the variety of precipitating events. Walton's study (21) found consistently as distinguishing characteristics in suicidal, depressive patients loss of a parent before the child was 14, or prolonged estrangement from a parent because of gross conflict. Toolan (20) observed a larger number of suicidal attempts in those from homes where a parent was physically absent.

Universally, there is reported a higher incidence of suicide attempts in girls, which may have to do with the cultural attitudes about aggression in girls which differs from the latitudes afforded boys. As indicated above, no race is free from suicide attempts, but in New York City, Puerto Rican youngsters have a much higher attempt rate than do Negroes or whites. Gould attributes this to the hysterical traits more common in Puerto Rican adolescents. In almost all studies of suicide, Catholics had a lower rate than other religious groups.

The various writers wrestle with the primary factors in attempted suicide. Most modern students agree that separation during critical periods of development is a primary predisposing and unique event which, together with identification with a sado-masochistic, rejecting mother, comprise the major determining factors. Parental loss per se does not predispose to depression and suicide in later life. It is the loss of love, the loss of the reciprocal intimacy, spontaneity, and closeness, that is the key, for separation or absence of the parent or the love object need not be physical. The alienation of an adolescent from his parents is an emotional experience. A comment is in order concerning the state of depression in adolescent suicide attempters. Their depression stems from a series of real life experiences, one full of "downs."

As the reader can see, the relationship of broken homes and loss of a love object to suicide and suicide attempts has been an issue of central concern in the psychiatric literature. The significance of these concepts is better explained as a *continuing process* to which the individual is subject, rather than some unique traumatic event of early childhood which in and of itself predisposes the individual to depression and suicidal tendencies in later life. This perspective helps explain why other adolescents who also experience a parental loss in early childhood were not disposed to suicide in later life and far less disposed to depression.

ATTEMPTED SUICIDE

Our studies at the Los Angeles County–USC Medical Center show that 75 per cent of the adolescent suicide attempters between ages 14 and 17 are girls, whose average age is 16, and the usual mode of attempt is ingestion of pills, which are readily available. Also, that the 5 years previous to the attempt were marked by many personal, medical, social, and family difficulties. In viewing the total biographies of the adolescent suicide attempters studied, we concluded that it is not enough to dismiss a suicide attempt as an "impulsive act"; a crisis situation resulting from a "temporary upset" where each suicidal episode is considered as an independent event; an insincere gesture, i.e., death is not intended; or an action for which the individual is not responsible or he would not have elected to do as he did.

In the great majority of cases, the suicide attempt is considered in advance and is — from the conscious perspective of the suicide attempter — weighed rationally against other alternatives. It is selected, but not before other alternatives for solving a series of long-standing problems have been tried, such as rebelling, withdrawal, running away from home, and lying. These methods have been tried but having failed, suicide (where death is intended in the attempt but does not result) or the suicide attempt (where only an "attention-getting device" is intended) is perceived by the attempter as the only way left. It is not surprising that a high percentage of suicide attempts eventually conclude in successful suicides. More often than not, those who adopt the drastic measure of an attempted suicide as an attention-getting device find that this too fails to gain attention or to open an avenue to a possible solution to their problems. The adolescent is convinced or soon becomes convinced that death is the only solution to what appears to him as the chronic problem of living. Such a view does not necessarily constitute an arbitrary or irrational conclusion on the part of the adolescent. It is based on the adolescent's very real experiences with life and a biography characterized by a progressive social isolation from meaningful social relationships. They would, if they could, choose to live. The potential suicide felt he had no choice.

The biographies of the adolescent suicide attempters are characterized by a three stage progression to the social isolation which results in a suicide attempt: (1) "a long-standing history of problems" from childhood to early adolescence; (2) a "period of escalation" during which many new problems associated with achieving adolescence are introduced; and (3) a final stage, the weeks and days immediately preceding an attempt, characterized by a chain-reaction dissolution of the adolescent's few remaining primary associations. All adolescents are subject, in one sense, to the same processes in the first and second stage. All adolescents have, to one extent or another, a long-standing history of problems, which are normally associated with the exigencies of everyday life; and adolescents gradually experience the onset of a new set of problems associated with becoming an adolescent. The distinguishing factors will, at least in part, be found in the answers to the following questions: How many problems are there? What is their nature? Under what circumstances did they occur? What is their sequential ordering? To what extent did the adolescent feel that there was access to a resolution of these problems as they occurred? It is also necessary to consider how the parents reacted to these problems and how this reaction affected the adolescent-parent interaction. Finally, to what extent are suicidal adolescents as well as others subject to the experiences which characterize the final stage – the unexpected rapid disintegration of meaningful social relationships on all fronts?

Long-Standing History of Problems

A partial list comprising a "long-standing history of problems" which characterize the biographies of the adolescent suicide attempters follows:
1. 20 per cent of all adolescent suicide attempters had a parent who attempted suicide.
2. 40 per cent had a parent, relative, or close friend who attempted suicide.
3. 72 per cent had one or both natural parents absent from the home (divorced, separated, or deceased).
4. 84 per cent of those suicide attempters with step-parents felt that they were contending with an unwanted step-parent.
5. 58 per cent of all cases had a parent who was married more than once.
6. 62 per cent had both parents working (or one parent at work when there was only one parent present).
7. 50 per cent of the suicide attempters' families had a net annual income of $3600 or less, and 52 per cent of those families with annual income of $3600 or less had net annual income of $2700 or less.
8. The average number of serious problem-making environmental changes experienced by the adolescent suicide attempter was 10.42 (e.g., parents remarrying, family members in hospital, death in family, changing schools, siblings leaving home, foster home placement, being in Juvenile Hall, etc.).

9. 74 per cent of the suicide attempters viewed their family conflict as "extreme."
10. 16 per cent had serious problems with a parent due to alcoholism of the parent.
11. Large numbers lived with persons other than parents (foster home placement, left with relatives for prolonged periods).
12. There was marked residential mobility, an abnormal number of school changes, and siblings leaving the home.

Escalation Stage

The problems of the suicide attempters tend to extend into universal proportions in this stage. Most of the problems associated with this stage seem to revolve about the parent trying experimentally to contend with a new and unfamiliar stage of development — adolescence. Often, what are viewed as "behavioral problems" by the parent are regarded as usual adolescent behavior by the teen-ager.

Disciplinary Techniques. The reciprocal effects of the disciplinary process on the adolescent and the parent of our study group are illuminating. On the one hand, the parents' efforts at reforming the adolescent often seem inappropriate to the latter and are considered to be "nagging" — a form of discipline which our study reveals to be used very frequently, especially by the mother. On the other hand, the parents' failure to discourage behaviors that the adolescent feels are bad and which he would gladly forgo with parental aid is taken by him as a sign of rejection. The net result, from the perspective of the suicide attempter, is constant and inappropriate nagging, i.e., unfair discipline and rejection. The net result, from the perspective of the parent, is "getting nowhere in a hurry" and increased frustration, which in turn leads to the vicious cycle of trying to reduce the dilemma by trying harder.

The parents of suicide attempters who begin to exhibit many new behavioral problems, believing that the adolescent would get into less trouble if he is watched more closely, frequently question him about his activities and whereabouts. More often than not, the parents do not accept the adolescent's answers and — in order to reassure themselves — make unannounced "spot checks" on their teen-ager's whereabouts and activities. The adolescent is aware of this procedure, and family quarrels often ensue. This does little to establish respect or basic trust in the adolescent for the parent and goes far toward denying the adolescent an essential and universal criterion for successful social interaction — secrets.

Illness in the Family. A significant situation contributing to the escalation of problems is physical or mental illness in the family. In 48 per cent of all cases, either the adolescent, parent, or sibling was treated for mental illness or serious physical complaints within the last 5 years. Fifty-four per cent of adolescent suicide attempters had been treated for some physical complaint or mental disturbance (including previous suicide attempts) or both within the past 5 years; 32 per cent had some serious physical complaint; 16 per cent had some emotional disturbance; and 6 per cent suffered both physical and mental disturbances. Thirty-six per cent of the parents of adolescent suicide attempters had been treated for either a serious physical complaint or mental disturbance within the last 5 years (including four suicide attempts made by parents). In 14 per cent of all cases, suicide attempters had a sibling or close relative other than parent living with them who had been treated for a serious physical complaint or mental disturbance within the past 5 years.

These illnesses and hospitalizations serve to seriously disrupt the usual composition and interaction of the family and add considerably to the problems faced by the adolescent; e.g., they may result in: (1) his dropping out of school; (2) losing a parent from the household·− often for the first time and for an extended period; (3) possibly losing a parent through death; or (4) assuming a parental role of caring for the sick or for younger siblings and taking care of the household or family business.

The Final Stage

By the end of the escalation period, parents are alienated and the adolescent seeks to re-establish the spontaneity, openness, and intimacy that he feels or fantasies characterized the earlier relationship with the parent. Granted that the above criteria for a meaningful social relationship were only imperfectly realized by the suicide attempter in his childhood, nevertheless, they had now deteriorated to a state of nonexistence.

The Romance. A romance is one of the few possible relationships remaining which provides for re-establishing the above conditions. An adolescent whose biography is characterized by the effects of the first two stages will pursue in earnest what appears to be the last chance to establish a primary relationship. In this pursuit, he (more usually she) spends all his time and energy and has little left for casual friendships or even for a good friend of the same sex. As a result, previous friends − close or casual − are usually alienated during the courtship and with the failure of the romance, the adolescent is left with no one.

The suicide attempters engaged in a serious romance; 36 per cent were all in the terminal stages of the romance. Twenty-two per cent of all suicide attempter girls, as compared with none of the control girls, were either pregnant or believed themselves to be pregnant as a result of the romance. In such cases, pregnancy acts to further alienate the adolescent from society; she is rejected by the boyfriend or his family, abandoned by her parents when help is most needed, and subject to rejection and verbal abuse by her peers. More often than not, her school work suffers as well.

School and Peer Relations. In 36 per cent of all cases, the adolescent suicide attempter was not enrolled in school at the time of the attempt, but in only one case was poor scholarship the reason for dropping out. In 89 per cent of these cases, reasons for nonattendance in school were other than poor scholarship, reasons which, in fact, contributed to the suicide attempt itself. They were illness, pregnancy, prior suicide attempts (44 per cent of all attempters had one or more previous attempts), "behavioral problems," such as acting up in class, "mental instability," or fighting.

Suicide attempters frequently expressed their liking for school for the social life that school provided. It afforded them an opportunity to meet their friends and to discuss school, dates, social activities, today's events, and tomorrow's prospects. To be excluded from school is, for the adolescent, to be excluded from one of his key potential resources for establishing meaningful social relationships. This is even more true for the suicide attempter who has already been excluded from many of the resources still open to the average teen-ager.

The Physician and the Suicide Attempt

In the light of the problems the attempter's biography demonstrates, the importance of the adolescent's contact with his physician in the weeks and months preceding the attempt cannot be overestimated. Forty-six per cent of all suicide attempters had such a contact and, of course, all were seen by physicians immediately following the attempt. Twenty-six per cent were seen previously under similar circumstances on the occasion of a previous suicide attempt. Only 59 per cent of those attempting suicide previously were treated. The remainder were not seen by a physician and kept the event secret. The doctor's interest in and aid to the adolescent and his problems, above and beyond his success in dealing with the specific physical complaint, may, in these cases, mean the difference between life and death.

It is beyond the scope of the physician in a hospital setting or in private practice to undertake to reconstruct the biography of his patient or to get at the attitudes a biography engenders through lengthy interviews or by questionnaire data, etc. However, we believe that short of these procedures and without the insight which one develops by way of constant contact with suicidal persons over a prolonged period, *suicidal persons are not easily distinguished from the "normal" societal member.* Without exception, the suicide attempt where it was a first attempt, came as a great surprise to both the parents and peers of the adolescent. The physicians of these adolescents as well were caught no less off guard. There is no indication in any of the cases that they had given or received any advance warning. This is not surprising since there exists no convenient mechanical means of anticipating a suicide attempt. A good deal must be known in advance about the individual involved; and such information is sorely lacking in the routine contacts of everyday life. One thing mutually agreed upon by both the experimental and control groups was that secrets are an essential part of life, particularly in adolescence. In this respect the adolescent suicide attempter finds himself in a disadvantaged position.

The problems of the adolescent suicide attempters seen by our staff fall broadly into five categories: parents, poverty, peers, broken romances, and pregnancy. All of these are, in fact, problems which one does not readily discuss with others who are in a position to help resolve them. An involvement or failure in these acts or situations brings with it the negative sanctions of society. In addition, by the time the adolescent makes an attempt, he has pretty well convinced himself that "talking about your problems gets you nowhere." It should be added at this point that his past experiences constitute a good reason for him to hold this view. Such an attitude does not represent a spontaneous or arbitrary opinion on his part. In short, *the suicidal youth is not easily distinguished from others because his biography is not common knowledge.* Those events which gave him sufficient good reason to live have, in the course of time, been negated and remain unknown. What is required is that the physician invest the time and effort needed to uncover a minimal amount of information regarding his patient in excess of that necessary for a medical evaluation. Our study reveals that a high percentage of illness for which the suicide attempter sought a doctor's aid fell into the category of "functional physical complaints not given to specific diagnosis."

In many cases the adolescent may seek out the physician, not for his expertise in the healing arts, but because of the high prestige and esteem that the position of doctor occupies in our society and the potential for help implicit in such a position. The analogy of the doctor functioning as "secular priest" in the social order is a common one. Not only is the doctor's position unique in terms of providing the suicide with ready access to what he may feel is a potential source of help when all others have failed, but the doctor is one of the few people in whom one is free to confide and to whom one is free to confess. This is a function of the objectivity, impartiality, confidentiality, and anonymity assured in the doctor-patient relationship. No less important to those seeking help is the presumption that the doctor holds "office" in one of the most powerful existing agencies of help: science. The doctor has a moral obligation to use this privileged position to the best advantage of those seeking his services. Keeping in mind the ready availability of the information which he is in a position to elicit, as well as the experiences and attitudes held by the adolescent suicide attempter as outlined in this paper, the author suggests that it would be helpful for the doctor routinely to compile a thumbnail biographical sketch of his adolescent patients covering the three states already discussed:

1. Is there a long-standing history of problems preceding adolescence?
2. Is there an escalation of problems during adolescence such as described above?
3. Is the stage set for a finale characterized by a chain reaction dissolution of what remains of the adolescent's meaningful social relationships?

One cannot anticipate the potentially suicidal adolescent on the basis of how many problem areas are included in any one stage of the process. It is necessary, rather, to consider how any set of events in time relate to a previous set in the biography of the adolescent and in what manner and to what extent the gestalt has succeeded in isolating the adolescent from meaningful social relationships. An adolescent as a member of a group whose biography is characterized by the above profile and who holds attitudes associated with such a profile has, in our opinion, a high probability of attempting suicide.

Most adults, young or older, do not wish to recapture the emotional turmoil of their adolescent period. This is reflected in the remarkable blindness physicians demonstrate in dealing with troubled adolescents and even those who have attempted suicide. Where the life-line is literally the relationship by which the attempter seeks to escape the dread alienation, doctors all too often "get rid" of the suicide attempter as soon as the medical or surgical problem is eased. The anxiety the disturbed adolescent provokes in the doctor fosters blind spots and a singular unawareness totally uncharacteristic of his other dealings. When one sees how hungry for relationship the attempter is and how, literally, his life is maintained by a firm relationship to an interested human, especially a doctor who holds a special significance, it behooves one to look at how we may remove our blind spots.

The moment the doctor engages with the young person, his effort should be directed at being the "life-line" for the anxious, depressed, insecure, guilty, apprehensive adolescent. There is often active, continued suicidal ideation. The physician must offer himself as an attentive, empathic person who can always be reached and who can begin to develop a beginning trust, an image of a stable, caring significant person in the alienated adolescent's life. The family must be involved to prevent sabotage and to clarify the misperceptions. Psychiatric assistance is usually necessary, but that does not exclude the physician from becoming a dependable, supportive, significant adult in the young person's life.

SUMMARY

Suicidal attempts are far more common in adolescents and three times more frequent in girls than boys. Suicide attempts in children are far less frequent, although many accidents may be suicide attempts. The children's attempts appear to be impulsive and stimulated by poor treatment. Adolescent suicide attempts are viewed as a three stage process: a long-standing history of problems, an escalation of these problems in adolescence, and a final stage characterized by a dissolution of relationships resulting in progressive isolation and alienation. A significant proportion of these young people have a history of physical or mental illness in their family as well as a significant relative having made a suicide attempt. These young people are subjected to a continuing process of deprivation of love and family disruption. Life is a chronic problem; death is the solution. The physician who makes the attempt to help the adolescent must be the dependable, caring adult and thus literally is the "life-line" for the adolescent.

REFERENCES

1. Ackerly, W. C.: Latency age children who threaten or attempt to kill themselves. J. Amer. Acad. Child Psychiat., 6:242-261, 1967.
2. Dublin, L.: Suicide, New York, Ronald Press, 1963.
3. Erikson, E. H.: Identity and the Life Cycle. Psychological Issues Monograph No. 1. New York, International Universities Press, 1967.
4. Freud, A.: Adolescence. The Psychoanalytic Study of the Child, 13:255-278. New York, International Universities Press, 1953.
5. Gould, R. E.: Suicide problems in children and adolescents. Amer. J. Psychother., 19:228-246, 1965.
6. Hospital Tribune, August 25, 1969, p. 22.
7. Jacobs, J., and Teicher, J. D.: Broken homes and social isolation in attempted suicide in adolescents. Int. J. Soc. Psychiat., 13:139-149, 1967.
8. Jacobs, J., and Teicher, J. D.: The role of separation in the adolescent suicide attempt. Presented to the Annual Meeting of the American Psychiatric Association, May 1967.
9. Jacobziner, H.: Attempted suicides in adolescence. J.A.M.A., 191:101-105, 1965.
10. Margolin, N. L., and Teicher, J. D.: Thirteen adolescent male suicide attempts — dynamic considerations. J. Amer. Acad. Child Psychiat., 7:296-315, 1968.
11. Mason, P.: Suicide in adolescents. Psychoanal. Rev., 41:48-54, 1954.
12. Medical World News, April 26, 1968, p. 7.
13. Sabbath, J. D.: The suicidal adolescent — The expendable child, J. Amer. Acad. Child Psychiat., 8:272-285, 1969.
14. Schneer, H., and Kay, P.: The suicidal adolescent. In Lorand, S., and Schneer, H., eds.: Adolescents. New York. Hoeber Medical Division. Harper & Row, 1962, pp. 180-201.
15. Schrut, A.: Suicidal adolescents and children. J.A.M.A., 188:1103-1107, 1964.
16. Statistical Bulletin, Metropolitan Life Insurance Company, New York, March 1967, Vol. 48.
17. Teicher, J. D.: Treatment of the suicidal adolescent — The lifeline approach. Excerpta Medica International Congress Series No. 15, Vol. 1, Proceedings of IV World Congress of Psychiatry. Amsterdam, Excerpta Medica Foundation, 1967.
18. Teicher, J. D., and Jacobs, J.: Adolescents who attempt suicide: Preliminary findings. Amer. J. Psychiat., 122:1248-1257, 1966.
19. Teicher, J. D., and Jacobs, J.: The physician and the adolescent suicide attempter. J. School Health, 36:406-415, 1966.
20. Toolan, J.: Suicide and suicide attempts in children and adolescents. Amer. J. Psychiat., 118:791, 1962.
21. Walton, H.: Suicidal behavior in depressive illness. J. Ment. Sci., 104:884, 1958.

Why Adolescents Kill Themselves

Gay Luce

Using interviews and psychological tests, the grantee and his associates have compared 50 adolescents after an attempted suicide, with unsuicidal peers of the same age, sex, and background. Although economic privation, broken homes, and disciplinary problems were found in the control group—the sequence and timing of events occurred at a different phase in the development of the child. The profile of the suicidal adolescent includes long-standing problems with family, a stage of escalation during adolescence, and a final stage of alienation—a chain reaction that dissolves the adolescent's closest personal bonds. Given detailed biographical knowledge of an adolescent, this study indicates that it should be possible to pick out the youth in danger, for adolescent suicide is not irrational but over-determined by sequences of life events occurring in critical periods.

> " 'Tis because of us children, too, isn't it, that you can't get a good lodging?"
>
> "Well, people do object to children sometimes."
>
> "Then if children make so much trouble, why do people have 'em?"
>
> "Oh, because it is a law of nature."
>
> "But we don't ask to be born?"
>
> * * * "I wish I hadn't been born."
>
> "He got up and went away into the closet adjoining her room in which a bed had been spread on the floor. There she heard him say, 'If we children were gone ther'd be no trouble at all!' " * * *
>
> "At the back of the door were fixed two hooks for hanging garments, and from these the forms of the two youngest children were suspended by a piece of box-cord round each of their necks, while from a nail a few yards off the body of little Jude was hanging in a similar manner."
>
> —Jude the Obscure, *Thomas Hardy.*

Reprinted from: *Mental Health Program Reports — 4.* National Institute of Mental Health, 1970.

BACKGROUND

Adolescent suicide is horrifying, unthinkable, and a little unreal to most adults, for we tend to be complacent about the troubles of the young. To the modern adults, *Romeo and Juliet* may seem only a story. Yet many adolescents cling to one another in similar love, with the desperation of a last hope in a lonely world. A modern Juliet is likely to be a frightened and pregnant little girl: the boy is likely to be rejected, and both may feel totally alone.

Literary descriptions of childhood suicide seem bizarre, yet they resemble modern case histories. In Thomas Hardy's *Jude the Obscure,* the restless wanderings and misery of unmarried parents overcome an unwanted oldest boy. When he hears that yet another unwanted baby is coming, he kills himself and the other children. It is not that such events don't happen, but we are reluctant to believe them.

In 1965, Jacobziner estimated that there were 60,000 attempted suicides among young people under age 20 in the United States each year. Adolescence can be a particularly lonely and difficult period, a time of biological upheaval and social change. A person is expected to emerge from the safety and dependency of childhood into responsible maturity. Even healthy and happy adolescents become moody and oscillate between passions and depressions in a manner that the older people around them rarely understand. Most adolescents have fantasies about killing themselves in moments of rage and frustration or when they feel totally isolated from their families and friends. This is not surprising. Who has not imagined, with some glee, the remorse his parents would feel if he killed himself? Between such imaginings and the act lies the world of pathological events that Doctor Teicher and his associates have begun to define.

Statistics portray great misery among a large population of adolescents. Suicide ranks as the fourth most frequent cause of death for young people 15-19 years old. Fortunately, the vast number of attempted suicides in this age group are thwarted. An estimate of 60,000 suicide attempts a year may seem exaggerated, but hospital admissions offer a convincingly sad picture. In 1960, for instance, at New York's Bellevue Hospital attempted suicide was the reason for admitting 10 percent of the child and adolescent patients. At Kings County Hospital in Brooklyn, 13 out of every 100 children who came to the hospital had attempted or threatened suicide. Each month, the huge Los Angeles County–U.S.C. Medical Center admits about seven patients between 14 and 18 who have attempted to kill themselves, over 80 a year.

THE ATTEMPTED SUICIDES

There has been a general tendency to dismiss a suicide attempt in an adolescent as an impulsive act stemming from a temporary crisis or depression.

Perhaps it is soothing to believe that someone so young with "life ahead of him" could not have intended to kill himself. He could not have considered that he might die. On the contrary, Doctor Teicher and his associates at the Medical Center of the University of Southern California have found many adolescents who attempted to take their lives more than once. At first they may have used the drastic move as a threat to draw attention to their problems. Instead, it generally made matters worse. After an escalation of long standing problems and loss of any meaningful relations, many concluded that death was really the only solution to unsolvable, unbearable, and chronic problems.

Beginning with Freud around 1920, many keen minds in the development of psychiatry have wrestled with the problem of adolescent suicide, but inferences drawn from a few cases or psychological studies did not indicate how to predict a suicide from outside circumstances. In the fall of 1964, the investigator and his associates began to study the life situations of adolescents who attempted suicide, comparing them with control adolescents matched for age, race, sex, and family income—control adolescents who had never attempted suicide. Quite a few interesting patterns have been drawn from this study of 50 young people who attempted suicide. All were between 14 and 18. None of them was mentally retarded or obviously pregnant. All had been brought into the Los Angeles County—U.S.C. Medical Center sometime between September 1964 and May 1965 because of their suicide attempt.

At least one parent, usually the mother, was studied as well. For comparison there was a control group of 32 youngsters and their parents. Three-quarters of the attempted suicides were girls. On the average the suicidal adolescents were around 16 years old. They were white, Mexican, Negro, Protestant, Catholic, and Jewish.

PROCEDURE: CHARTS OF LIFE EVENTS

The procedure called for an interview with the adolescent patient within 24 to 48 hours after the suicide attempt. The parent or parents were also interviewed. Then, the suicidal youngster's therapy sessions in the hospital were taped and transcribed for further analysis.

Two biographies were elicited from structured interviews. There was the parent's version of his child's history, and there was the adolescent's version of his own life. On the basis of the case histories, a life history chart was constructed for each suicide attempter and his matched control. This was done by constructing a chronology (in parallel) on a vertical continuum that depicted all the experiences of the adolescent from birth until the suicide attempt. These graphic charts show residential moves, school changes, the beginnings of various behavioral problems, separation, divorce, or remarriage of the parents, and deaths in the family. The charts were put in a sequence that displayed how the events tended to pile up at a particular point in the adolescent's life. This indicated how the crises had accumulated during the adolescent's life.

What events distinguished those who attempted suicide from those who did not? A simple comparison of events in the lives of the control group and the suicide-attempters might not show that there was a very pronounced difference. The investigators discerned a distinct process leading to progressively deeper unhappiness and pessimism. The suicide-attempters went through a sequence that led to progressive isolation from the important people in his life. The control adolescents did not. The process can be summarized in three stages: The suicide-attempters all had a long-standing history of problems from childhood into adolescence. There was also a period in which problems seemed to escalate, usually at the very beginning of adolescence. Moreover, the problems mounted in a manner that seemed to exceed those of peers and friends. Finally, came a phase characterized by a "chain reaction dissolution of any remaining meaningful social relationships." This isolation occurred in the days and weeks preceding the suicide attempt.

SEQUENTIAL ANALYSIS OF LIFE EVENTS

The advantage of looking at things sequentially can be demonstrated by comparing the two groups. For instance, the life histories of the suicide-attempters showed that 72 percent of them came from broken homes, yet 53 percent of the control group also came from broken homes. Former studies of suicide have emphasized the fact that there were more broken homes among suicide attempters than "control" adolescents. However, none of these studies examined the broken homes of comparison groups. If one looked only at the incidence of broken homes and severed parental relations, there is no great difference between suicidal youths and comparable nonsuicidal youths. However, by looking at the chronological biographies of these two groups, the grantees have seen that the relevance of a broken home depends upon *when* the instability occurred in the child's development.

CRITICAL PHASE

Although 72 percent of the suicide-attempters and 53 percent of the control adolescents came from broken homes, the timing of divorce and remarriage was different. In the suicidal group 58 percent of the parents remarried, but only one-fourth of the control parents remarried. Moreover, these control parents managed to remarry very early in the child's life and remained married. The parents of the suicidal adolescent either remarried quite a bit later in his life, or, if they remarried early, they were subsequently divorced and remarried several times again.

The chronological mapping of biographies shows that the suicidal adolescents had parents who were divorced, separated, or remarried after the onset of adolescence. By contrast, the control families experienced change earlier, if at all. Instability in the home apparently had a differential effect depending upon the age of the child. Both groups experienced the instability of a broken home, but the nonsuicidal adolescents had a stable homelife during their last 5 years, while the suicidal youths had experienced instability then. As the investigators have written,[1]

"This is particularly significant, not only because divorce, separation, or the acquisition of a stepparent is stressful and disruptive event per se, but also because it occurs during a particularly stressful life time in the life cycle, i.e., adolescence."

A great many people who have written about suicide have implied that the loss of a parent in childhood might cause depression and perhaps suicidal feelings later in life. This study would not bear out such a conclusion, since the control group also experienced parental loss in childhood. Perhaps it is not loss of a parent in childhood that predisposes a person to depression and suicide in later life. Loss of a love object, as the grantee has remarked, is an important aspect of the process. But loss must be viewed as a part of the process, and particular attention must be paid to the time when it occurred. Most of the adolescents began their maelstrom descent toward suicide after a long period of alienation from parents. One 14-year-old who had tried to commit suicide twice was asked why. She replied, "It's my mother."[2]

Asked what her mother did, she answered, "We just don't get along. We haven't for 3 years. Before that we were like sisters and then it seems like since she divorced my stepfather it started a lot of trouble."

This girl enjoyed being in the hospital and did not want to return home. It is particularly poignant that she wanted to be committed to a State mental hospital rather than return home. Many of the young suicide attempters described their alienation from parents as a process in which either the mother or father would nag them, would cut them off from their friends, would disapprove of their favorite friends, and thus made it difficult for them to have relationships outside the home, at the same time making life very difficult for them within the home. This was their version.

THE BROKEN ROMANCE

Typically, many of these adolescents had fallen in love and formed very possessive and exclusive romantic relationships. This actually isolated them even more. A girl and boy would concentrate so intensely on one another that they

---

[1] Jacobs, J., and Teicher, J. D. Broken homes and social isolation in attempted suicides of adolescents. *"International Journal of Social Psychiatry,"* 13(2) : 146, 1967.
[2] Unpublished transcript.

tended to cut off all their friends. Then, if the romance failed, they would feel hopeless, lost and despairing.

At the time of the interviews none of the adolescents in the control group was ending a romance, but a number of the "suicidal adolescents" had just broken a romance. Moreover, five of these girls were either pregnant or feared that they were pregnant. As the biographies revealed, pregnancy inevitably led to a great sense of isolation. These girls withdrew and were rejected by their boyfriends. Usually, they were also rejected by their parents at this time when they most needed support. The suicidal adolescents were really in a state of depression compared with their counterparts, and, indeed, as the grantees point out, this seemed to have been prompted by their real experiences in life.

THE WAY THEY SAW IT

Only 38 percent of the suicidal youngsters considered their childhood to have been happy. But about 94 percent of the control group considered childhood to have been a happy time for them. In describing the biographies, the investigators wrote:[3]

"Judging from the verbatim accounts of the suicide-attempters in the interviews as well as the suicide notes left by them, and notes written by other adolescents outside our sample, the decision to suicide was the result of a rational, decision-making process. However, the choice of death is not based on a desire to die. They would, if they could, choose to live. Death, in a sense, is not chosen at all but results from the progressive failure of adaptive techniques to cope with the problems of living, where "the problem" is the maintenance of meaningful social relationships. In short, the potential suicide felt he had no choice, i.e., death is necessary. It is from this recognition of necessity that his sense of freedom stems and immediately preceding the act itself there is often a feeling of well-being, a cessation of all cares. This is evidenced in the matter-of-fact presentation found in suicide notes."

PROFILE OF PROBLEMS: DISRUPTION AT HOME AND DISCIPLINE

Early in childhood or adolescence the suicidal youngsters usually experienced the break-up of their home. In some cases this meant the institutionalization of the child or a family member. Many of them were placed in foster homes or left with relatives. Many of them changed schools and residences frequently. Many of these families were very poor. In some cases, the parents also had been depressed and had attempted suicide. A sizable percent of the suicidal youngsters had either a parent, relative, or close friend who had attempted suicide.

---

[3]Jacobs, J., and Teicher, J. D. Broken homes and social isolation in attempted suicides of adolescents. *"International Journal of Social Psychiatry,"* 13(2) : 148, 1967.

Seventy-two percent had one or both of their natural parents away from home, either because of divorce, separation, or death. Most of those living with stepparents felt they didn't like the stepparent. A great many had a parent who was married several times. In about 62 percent of the cases both parents were working. Half of these families lived on less than $3,600 per year. The background is one of poverty, instability, and unhappiness.

The specific period just preceding a suicide is characterized by a vicious spiral of events. It may begin when a parent feels unable to cope with some behavior in his or her adolescent. The parent begins to nag and use severe disciplinary procedures to prevent the youngster from going out. He may resort to physical punishment. Parents of the suicidal adolescents felt that their children would get into less trouble if they were watched more closely. Therefore, they would question them about their activities and whereabouts. Because the adolescent's trust in his parent somehow depended upon dignity and the maintenance of a certain amount of privacy, questioning set up a vicious circle of mistrust. From the point of view of the adolescents (as revealed on a rating scale), withholding privileges, fussing, nagging, and whipping were considered the worst disciplinary techniques. The suicidal adolescents and their nonsuicidal counterparts agreed on this rating. At the same time, some of the adolescents felt they would gladly forego undesirable behavior, and their parents should have helped them to discourage this behavior. When the parents didn't intervene, the young people took it as a sign of rejection.

As the parent-child situation got worse, the parents grew frustrated, and the adolescent felt that his parents couldn't understand and were punishing him inappropriately. The biographies revealed that this impasse led to the adolescent's rebellion or withdrawal. This stage of deterioration usually led to a breakdown of communication between parent and child, in which the youth's withdrawal was a consequence. Essentially, both parent and adolescent would give up and stop trying to communicate.

Many suicidal adolescents said that they got into the habit of lying and would simply withdraw into their rooms, or withdraw into themselves in order to avoid their parents and conflict.

SCHOOL

A third of the adolescents who had attempted suicide were out of school at the time. Either they were ill because of pregnancy or because of an earlier suicide attempt. An astonishing number had already attempted suicide in the past. A quarter of these suicidal adolescents had been out of school because they were acting up in class, had shown some emotional instability, or had been involved in fights. Half of them had been truant from school during the last 5 years because of lack of interest or active distaste.

TO WHOM DO YOU TURN IN TIME OF TROUBLE?

When asked to whom they turned when they were in trouble, a quarter of the suicidal adolescents said there was no one to turn to. None of the control adolescents felt such isolation. The pathos and the loneliness of the suicidal adolescent is very dramatically shown in some of the figures. Of the 46 percent who reported their suicide attempt to other people, less than half reported it to their parents. Almost two-thirds of them talked to people other than family members. This is particularly significant since 88 percent of the suicide attempts occurred at home, very often with the parents in the next room. In every instance, the lack of communication between family and the child and lack of communication with peers was a very important factor in the period leading to suicide. On interview, these suicidal adolescents conveyed the despairing sense that death was the only solution, there was no other way out. Consider these excerpts from a letter by a 17-year-old Negro boy to his father. This note was written the evening before he made his second suicide attempt:

"Dear Father, I am addressing you these few lines to let you know that I am fine and everybody else is and I hope you are the same. Daddy, I understand that I let you down and I let Mother down in the same way when I did that little old thing [the suicide attempt] that Wednesday night. Daddy, I am sorry if I really upset you, but Daddy after I got back I realized how sad and bad you felt when I came back to California.—I had lost my best girl the week before I did that. I had a fight because some dude tried to take advantage of her when I sped to the store, so I came back and I heard a lot of noise like bumping so I run in and there he is trying to rape my girl, my best one to.—Daddy I tried as hard as I could to make it cheerful, but it does get sad. Daddy I am up by myself. I've been up all night trying to write you something to cheer you up, because I could see your heart breaking when you first asked Sam's wife if they would have room and that Sunday Dad, it was hard but I fought the tears that burned my eyes as we drove off and Daddy part of my sickness when I had taken an overdose I did just want to sleep myself away because I missed you Dad.

"But when I left I felt like I had killed something inside of you and I knew you hated to see me go, and I hated to go, but Daddy, well, I kind· of missed Mother after I had seen her. I miss you and remember what you said, 'settle down,' but Daddy I tried so hard so I went and bought some sleeping pills and took them so both of you could feel the same thing."[4]

When an adolescent has retreated from family problems into a love affair, and then the romance breaks up or culminates in pregnancy, then there is even more isolation than before. A girl is especially alone if her boyfriend disappears and she has already alienated other friends. Parents often become disillusioned

[4]Teicher, J. D., and Jacobs, J. Adolescents who attempt suicide: Preliminary findings. *American Journal of Psychiatry,* 122(11) : 5, May 1966.

and give up at the time their child needs help the most. In a letter to her former boyfriend, a desperate young girl showed the lengths to which she would go for a social relationship and a solution to the problem of pregnancy. She wrote on the night of a suicide attempt. A short excerpt indicates the tragic sense of rejection and isolation.

"Dear Bill, I want you and I to get an understanding about certain things because I think you got the wrong impression of me * * * and believe me it hurt. I knew all the time you were hinting to me I was too young, didn't know nothing about life, but you were wrong. I know a whole lot about life. I'm ashamed of the things I know to be so young. I couldn't tell you this personally, 'cuz I couldn't face what you might have said and I sure it would have hurt my feelings badly. I'm two months pregnant by you. You don't have to admit it, I don't care. You may say anything you like. You don't have to worry about any trouble. It would be a disgrace for me to let people know I threw myself on you knowing you didn't care or feel anyway toward me. Don't worry, no one will ever know my child's father. I will never mention you to him or her whichever it be."[5]

PARENTS AND PHYSICIANS: SURPRISED

Despite the history of increasing problems, the families were inevitably hurt and surprised by the suicide attempt. Parents and physicians who had seen the adolescents would say "it was so unexpected." Actually, some 46 percent of the suicide-attempters had visited their physicians at some time before the attempt. Over half had been treated for some physical or mental disturbance during the prior 5 years. A third had some serious physical complaint, and a third of them had some family member who was sick or had been hospitalized. In screening the adolescents to be included in this study, Doctor Teicher and his associates examined over 100. In the first 30 they found 11 with duodenal ulcers.

In spite of the long history of problems, however, the physician and mothers acted surprised by the suicide attempts. While perhaps expressing some guilt, the mothers would deny that there was anything in the home situation that would cause a suicide. The very people who were closest to the suicide-attempters apparently failed to see the progression of social isolation: the problems with parents, with poverty, broken romances, excommunication from school or peers, especially in the instance of pregnancy. Since these are problems that most people would be reticent to discuss with others, adolescents in such predicaments are especially isolated.

After a period of not communicating, their first suicide attempt came as a surprise to parents, friends, and schoolmates. The physicians who saw them just after the attempt had been taken off guard perhaps because suicidal people are

[5]Teicher, J. D., and Jacobs, J. Adolescents who attempt suicide. *"American Journal of Psychiatry,"* 122(11), 1966.

not easily distinguished from others with severe problems. There seem to be no simple and convenient ways of anticipating a suicidal attempt. No litmus test can determine who is a potential suicide. Clearly a major reason that suicidal attempts are not warded off is lack of communication of the real feelings. The true biography of the unhappy person was not known by anybody around him.

PROFILES FOR PREVENTION

Adolescence is a time of sufficient duress for parents and youngsters as new behavioral problems arise. Moreover, many of the suicidal youngsters in the Los Angeles study also had illness or mental illness in their family during the preceding 5 years. Doctor Teicher and his associates feel that various sets of events must be considered in anticipating suicide. Among them are such factors as economic status, geographic mobility, and the divorce rate in the home. These alone do not predict suicide. However, these events seem to occur at particular times in the adolescent's life and the timing may be critical. Along with an escalation of behavioral problems, a youth who is isolated from family and peers may be in danger of trying suicide.

It should not be surprising to learn that their parents also had unhappy histories. The mothers often got married only because they were pregnant. Some had illegitimate children. Quite a few suffered depression and were depressed after giving birth. This was particularly notable among the mothers of the *boys* who had attempted suicide. Many had illegitimate children or had been forced into marriage because of pregnancy. Seventy percent of them were separated or divorced, a good number of them after short-lived marriages of convenience. Needless to say, a huge percentage had suffered from economic deprivation.

MALE SUICIDE

The number of suicides and suicide attempts among girls far outweighs the number of attempts among boys; and this has been associated with broken romances, rejection, and unwanted pregnancy. In attempting to understand the male suicide attempts, Doctor Teicher and Doctor N. L. Margolin did a special study of 13 of the boys in their group. They were interviewed by one of the authors after their suicide attempt. Identical questionnaires about parent-child relationships and school, about adjustment to peer groups and career aspirations were given to the boys and their parents. Both took a battery of psychological tests in addition.

The boys in the control group also came from broken homes. Many had both parents working and relatives living with the family. However, the vignettes of the suicidal boys differed in that they showed a repeated sequence of events which the authors summarize in this order: They had, first of all, a mother who was angry, depressed, or withdrawn, both before and after pregnancy. Generally it was an unwanted pregnancy. Then, there was the loss of some very significant person or persons in the patient's early life, usually the loss of the father. There was also a reversal of roles with the mother. At the time of the suicide attempt it had seemed to the boy that the mother (or his mother-surrogate) was also going to leave his life forever. During the boy's period of distress his mother was preoccupied with her own depression, up to the time of her son's suicide attempt.

An 18-year-old Mexican-American boy is typical. His mother never wanted him. She became very overprotective until he was about age 12. At age 5 his semi-alcoholic father left the home. At this point he and his mother began to shift around from house to house, mostly living with his grandmother. After the divorce he began to get headaches. His mother thought he missed his father. He always felt rejected, and he made depressed statements such as: "I wish I hand't been born." Then at the age of 15 he was rejected by a girl. This left him emotionally fractured. He would get into romances where he was inevitably hurt and depressed. His mother felt she had never been shown any love or affection by her own family, and she was a chronically depressed person. She explained that, as she was getting older, she had been dating two men. One was a rather selfish man who overlooked her son. She broke up with him. Her boy was than 17 years old.

"I was a very blind and stupid woman. I didn't realize what I was doing to Tom, how sensitive and emotional he was. Well, time went by and Tom started to go to parties and dating, not too often, but he had started to have friendships on the outside. Soon after I met someone at work from the same department and we got along real well. He was divorced also. He has a family of three to support, so we have quite a lot in common. The man moved in. He liked my son and went out of his way to cultivate him, but apparently things went along very well until Tom started to complain that since Sam had moved in with us he was nothing around the house, just in my way, that I didn't love him anymore, but that was not true."[6]

In a pleading letter to the doctor she asked what he could do to undo the damage she had done her son at an early age. Here was the tragic pattern of events—the unhappy circumstances around his birth, the divorce, his father's withdrawal, infantile identification with the mother, frequent moves, repeated loss of peer relationships, the clinging to an angry and depressed mother, and, finally, the threatened loss of his mother to a new man. Case after case revealed this kind of dependency and frustration in the first years of life. In 11 cases the fathers were physically absent from the home. In eight instances the father had left home before the child was 6 years old. Almost all of these boys were prevented from being children. They were thrust into the role of helping their mothers either because they were the oldest or the only child. In each case there

[6]Margolin, N. L., and Teicher, J. D. Thirteen adolescent male suicide attempts. *"Journal of the American Academy of Child Psychiatry,"* 7(2) : 301, 1968.

was also a sense of loss on the part of the child, either because the mother and father had just recently separated, because the mother had a serious illness, or because a stepfather had just recently left home. In one instance, the mother had just recently married, and the boy had been left by his girl friend.

"On the basis of our data we find that the male adolescent suicide attempt seems to have its origins in the mother-child relationships of infancy. Most importantly, these relationships revealed not only early deprivation, but chronic repeated separation threat or object loss. This state of affairs leads to continued, intense, archaic identification with the mother. The lack of a masculine image in the experience of these boys together with the ambivalence of the mothers prevents any working through of the Oedipal phase of development."[7]

A helpless and dependent child needs his mother and cannot "allow" her to be bad. He then blames himself for anything wrong in the environment, which allows him to soak up the badness, as it· were, making things around him all right. The investigators suggest that this situation eventually creates a self-destructive pattern.

"The early and repeated separation trauma resulting in disturbances in early ego and superego development lay the foundation for later pathological identification, and leave their marks on character formation and personality development. As the child enters adolescence, the conflicts over separation intensify due to a number of concurrent reasons, all of which essentially have to do with the biological and psychological need to be autonomous from the mother. The adolescent male tries to defend himself against feelings of helplessness in many ways. He may regress to feelings of omnipotence and pseudoindependence and seek challenging, dangerous situations such as reckless driving, motorcycling, etc. He may act out antisocially as a defense to prevent loss of identity. However, it seems that these defensive attempts cannot be maintained when actual separation from the mother is threatened. This threat can occur in the form of the mother's withdrawing because of her depression, her becoming interested in a new husband, etc. Also significant is the breakup of the adolescent's romance, i.e., experiencing the loss of a mother surrogate. When the mother becomes depressed and suicidal, the adolescent perceives rightly that his very existence is a burden upon her. He acts as if he were saying, 'If I destroy the bad part of myself, then mother will live to care for me.'

"Internally, ego regression with splitting occurs. The split-off part of the ego, representing the bad self, is rejected and persecuted by the parts of the ego and superego identified with the rejecting suicidal mother. *This identification is of great significance in the suicidal adolescents.* Freud (1923) states that the ego, feeling hated and unprotected by the superego, will let itself die, a situation that is similar to the anxiety in infantile separation from the mother."[8]

In these 13 cases, the boys professed to love their nagging and ambivalent

[7]Op. cit. p. 312.
[8]Op. cit. pp. 312-313.

mothers. They did not necessarily feel they were loved, but because of an infantile dependence, the mother's depression, anger, withdrawal, and disapproval had a very devasting effect upon them. In many instances, the mother also had suicidal thoughts, and the boys identified with their mother's depressed and suicidal state. Interestingly enough, the suicidal girls described their mothers in uniformly glowing and idealized terms and denied any flaws, despite the fact that their mothers were often very hostile.

"The suicide attempt is an overdetermined symptom and whether it is an attention-getting or an attempt to die it is always serious. It is an effort to solve a chronic problem, living; a plea for help; an expression of rage and hostility; and at times a symbolic reunion with the pre-Oedipal mother or father."[9]

THERAPY

In many ways the therapist in the hospital has proven to be the lifeline of these youngsters. He maintains his contact with the suicide attempters from the beginning of consultation until final rehabilitation or referral. When they are first brought to the hospital they are shaken, anxious, depressed, insecure, guilty, and apprehensive because of the anger and hurt that they've caused. They feel terribly alone, and this is probably their worst agony. Usually the mother has been angry and sometimes guilty; her next reaction is usually hostile and she will defend herself with great denial. The father, or more usually the stepfather, would consider the suicide attempt a bother and show little concern. Doctor Teicher recommends that suicidal adolescents should be hospitalized, if only briefly, and placed in a ward where there are other adolescent patients to offer warmth, support, and understanding. In many instances the patients of this study didn't want to leave the hospital, and they would cling to the staff and other patients. Adolescents will often talk about the precipitating events, such as their parents' refusal to let them go out, or a broken romance. The rejection by a boyfriend or a girl friend is a most common precipitating factor, but this would be taken in stride as an unhappy experience if there had been some positive experiences earlier in life. The role of the therapist as seen by the investigators is that of a person who provides understanding and love. Slowly the therapist can guide a young person to cope with his conflicts and communicate with his family. Meanwhile he offers support and is always available so that the adolescent doesn't feel so lonely and isolated.

From this study one may clearly see that youth, itself, is no antidote to a hostile environment. The old myth that all suicide attempts are impulsive and irrational is forever banished, and in this study one can see how an accumulation of adverse factors at a critical period shapes the biographical profile of the

[9]Teicher, J. D. The treatment of the suicidal adolescent. *"Proceedings of the IV World Congress of Psychiatry,"* p. 749, Madrid, September 1966. Excerpta Medica International Congress Series No. 150.

potential adolescent suicide. This profile might be used in further studies to predict and prevent suicide attempts.

This brief research has already shown that no simple correlations between life events can predict suicidal despair in a young person. Yet young people—in shockingly vast numbers—are miserable enough and lonely enough that they are brought to hospitals by the tens of thousands each year, after attempting to kill themselves, often in a room right next to their parents.

Further research in this area has implications beyond suicide prevention. The development of biographical profiles may yield techniques whereby informed doctors, social workers, and school personnel might spot the precarious young person in time to obtain therapy for him. However, the import of this research is broader in its implications. It begins to fold back the curtains upon the circumstances and the timing that weaken an individual to the stresses of life and alienate him from all of those who might help him. The chain of misery seems to pass from one generation to the next, and in each case privation plays its part. Moreover, the relations of family members show a psychodynamics that produces instability and separation instead of cohesion and mutual help. Adolescence can be an especially creative and exciting time of life. In this particular era, adolescents are having an ever-increasing impact upon society—they have changed the entire genre of popular music, for example—but exceedingly great numbers of adolescents are having the opposite experience. Suicide prevention studies among the most unhappy of these people may give considerable insight into what it takes to deflect an entire life from misery toward productiveness and participation.

Research Grant: MH 1432
Date of Interview: September 1968

REFERENCES

Jacobs, J., and Teicher, J. D. Broken homes and social isolation in attempted suicides of adolescents. *International Journal of Social Psychiatry*, 13(2):140-149, 1967.

Jacobziner, H. Attempted suicide in adolescence. *Journal of the American Medical Association*, 191(7):11-14, 1965.

Margolin, N. L., and Teicher, J. D. Thirteen adolescent male suicide attempts. *Journal of Child Psychiatry*, 7(2):296-314, April 1968.

Teicher, J. D. The treatment of the suicidal adolescent—the lifeline approach. *Proceedings of the IV World Congress of Psychiatry*, Madrid, September 1966. Excerpta Medica International Congress Series #150.

Teicher, J. D., and Jacobs, J. Adolescents who attempt suicide: preliminary findings. *American Journal of Psychiatry*, 122(11): May 1966.

_____. The physician and the adolescent suicide attempter. *Journal of School Health*, 36(9):406-415, November 1966.

The "Peace Suicides" — Why Did They Do It?

Eliot Asinof

Every small town in America probably has a place like Bees Lane, just outside of Blackwood, New Jersey, a secluded, tree-lined little road where young couples go to park. Howard Anders, a farmer who lived nearby, was accustomed to the sight of an occasional moonlight visitor, even as late in the season as October. On the quiet, misty Thursday morning of October 16, 1969, however, he was surprised to see a pale blue 1962 Falcon sedan, apparently abandoned during the night. So when he ran into Patrolman Joseph Reichert around eight-thirty, he mentioned the car, and Reichert went to investigate.

No, the car had not been abandoned. Two bodies lay crumpled against the door on the driver's side. A boy and a girl. They were teen-agers, clean-cut, neatly and conventionally dressed. The girl wore a dark wool sweater and a plaid skirt. The boy was in a jacket and chino slacks. Beside them lay a pile of envelopes, addressed by name only and unstamped. In the back seat were two guitars.

Reichert immediately called headquarters.

It had been a troubled night for the parents of Joan Fox and Craig Badiali. They had last seen the two seventeen-year-olds around seven in the evening. Craig and Joan had been to the Vietnam Peace Moratorium demonstration at Glassboro State College, the site a few years back of the historic meeting of President Lyndon B. Johnson and Soviet Premier Aleksei Kosygin. Several friends had seen them on their return, late in the afternoon. One classmate, Chris Henderson, a seventeen-year-old girl, had met Joan at school when she had stopped off to pick up a few things from her locker. Joan had told Chris of her disappointment at the ceremonies. Too many kids, Joan said, seemed to be using the day as an excuse to take off from school. "She told me she thought everyone was really more interested in the Mets and the World Series than the forty thousand boys who'd been killed in Vietnam," said Chris.

In the morning the parents made a number of desperate calls, including one to the Blackwood police station where Joan's older brother, Andrew Fox, Jr., was a police officer. But Andrew was on vacation for the day, and others on the small staff had hurried out to Bees Lane. It was close to nine o'clock when the two sets of parents ended up with the State Police at nearby Turnersville and reported that Craig and Joan had not returned home that night.

A few minutes later word came in that Craig and Joan were dead. It was clearly a matter of suicide, premeditated and carefully arranged. Craig had drilled a hole in the rear floor of the family car. Some time around seven-thirty on Wednesday evening, he had driven with Joan to Bees Lane, attached one end of a vacuum cleaner hose to the exhaust pipe, inserted the other through the hole, rolled up the windows and started the engine. According to the coroner, asphyxiation from the carbon monoxide had probably taken less than four minutes.

Since there are many more suicide attempts than completions (experts estimate that the ratio is well over four to one), psychologists theorize that most adolescent suicide attempts—even the successful ones—are designed for failure. They want to try, yes, but they also want to fail, and they manage to omit some necessary ingredient or arrange to be discovered and saved. The deaths of Craig and Joan, however, were swift and sure. There was no leak in the airtight car and no danger of running out of gas before the poison could do its lethal work. At the same time, it was noted that the car doors were not locked. (Did this mean that the two young people really were hoping to be saved?)

Then, too, they had taken the time to prepare twenty-four carefully written and well-thought-out notes to family and friends. (Was their failure to mail those notes an indication of some vague hope of survival?)

One letter, printed neatly by Craig on two thin sheets, four words to a line, had a single word on its envelope: "Why?"

Indeed, why?

Why? Because we see that people just won't do and say what they feel, and you can't just tell someone to. It seems that people are only touched by death and maybe people will be touched enough to look into their lives. And if just one person is touched enough to do something constructive and peaceful with their life, then maybe our death was worth it.

Why—because we love our fellow man enough to sacrifice our lives so that they will try to find the ecstasy in just being alive.

Love and peace,
Craig Badiali
Joan Fox

The parents could not understand. They read the tortured cry for peace and brotherhood, and they couldn't believe that it was their children who had done this incomprehensible thing. Craig's father, Bernard Badiali, is a military man who spent most of his adult life in the United States Air Force, having survived three tours of duty in Vietnam. He loved his son, but this made no sense to him. Andrew Fox, Joan's father, is a truck mechanic, and there is an American flag standing vigil in the front window of his home, a silent tribute to Joan's older brother, Raymond, now serving in Vietnam. Mr. Fox also could not believe what he read. The two mothers were completely shattered, their grief compounded by what they felt to be the senselessness of the tragedy.

Why did they do it? The question ran rampant through the entire community. It was as if the letters explained nothing, for they just did not seem to come from the essence of their young lives. Craig and Joan weren't at all the type to be so "different." They were seniors, better than average students, no more than that. Joan was a sweet-natured, outgoing girl. She was attractive, slender, of medium height. She wore her dark brown hair long, tucked neatly behind her ears. She was a graceful girl who walked tall, her longish neck lending serenity to her style. She had tried for years to become a cheerleader and had finally succeeded. Active in dramatics, she played the clarinet some, participated in tennis and field hockey. Her favorite subjects were history and English, and she was heading for college, presumably at Glassboro a few miles away.

Craig was equally appealing, a big heavy-set boy over six feet tall, with bright brown eyes and straight light brown hair cut short, which he liked to wear slanting down toward his right eye. His round jaw gave his face an oval look, lending a quality of toughness that the gentleness of his eyes betrayed. He was somewhat more complex than Joan and seemed far more serious than she. He was nonathletic, poetically inclined, president of the Dramatic Society; he played the guitar quite well and enjoyed writing songs. He, too, had planned to go to college at Glassboro, hoping to major in dramatics. Both were popular, and everyone thought of them as stable, normal, clean-cut kids. They were not delinquents, drug addicts or peace protesters. They were full of life, enjoyed school and friends and pleasures, just like most other teen-agers. They had no physical maladies or deeply disturbing personal problems that anyone was aware of. Then why?

Psychiatrists specializing in adolescent suicides have found definite patterns. There have been nearly five hundred known suicides annually among American teen-agers in recent years, a conservative estimate since many more are known to be listed as accidents. Most suicides are attributed to quarrels with parents and broken romances. Secondary causes are usually difficulties in school, illegitimate pregnancies, poor health and problems with the law. Though there were no psychiatrists associated with Craig and Joan, there appears to be little doubt that none of these causes were involved here. Dr. Louis I. Dublin, formerly with the Metropolitan Life Insurance Company and a leading contributor to the literature of suicides, has observed: "Some psychiatrists have declared that all suicide victims are psychotic and that no "normal" or [even] neurotic persons actually destroy themselves. This view seems hard to reconcile with such cases in which suicide appears to have been the outcome of considered reasoning." Dr. Klaus Berblinger of the University of California School of Medicine concurs: "Self-destruction is not [always] regarded as the result of a disordered mind."

There is, nevertheless, generally more to explain than meets the eye. Without questioning the sincerity of Craig's and Joan's desire for peace and love, psychiatrists would dig for other forces at work, and it is in the buried tensions of the adolescent struggle for identity that the causes of their suicides are most likely to be found. For example, except in extremely rare cases, adolescent suicides are considered to be acts of hostility against parents. Dr. Robert Porter, associate professor of clinical child psychiatry at the Mount Sinai School of Medicine in New York, comments: "Teen-agers are involved in a normal process of emancipation from parents, striving for emotional independence. They are searching to be the kind of people they want to be, rather than merely the kind of people their parents and the community want them to be. Frequently this creates a conflict that strains their 'frustration tolerance.' "

While Craig's and Joan's "frustration tolerance" appeared to be extremely high (they were not wild or undisciplined; they had not performed rebellious acts of any kind; they did not drink, use drugs, engage in promiscuity or make trouble), at some point approaching October 15 it apparently snapped. Somewhere along the line their struggle for emotional independence failed them. Whatever love they had found was not enough to satisfy them. One can speculate that though they had each other to supply a fundamental need outside their families, they must have sensed some vital personal failure, some disadvantage as a couple that left them feeling less than equal to others.

There were only suggestions of answers to be found at the Highland Regional High School the center of their lives outside their homes. On that tragic Thursday morning their absences had been noted, for they had been a close twosome for a long time (although not without a few separations over the years). Since they were absent together, it followed that some teen-age tongues would waggle and a rumor began to spread that they had eloped. It wasn't until the afternoon that the truth gradually found its way to the school area, for students are not permitted to leave the school building for lunch. One could see the TV trucks, the staff cars of newspapers and radio stations swinging into the huge parking area, only to be firmly directed to drive right on out. There would be no penetrations of the front door by any non-student personnel.

When the news did break out it seemed to simmer like a slow-burning fuse.

"It was crazy," one student said. "Many of us had heard about it. But we went to classes and nobody said much. I guess maybe we were waiting for the teachers to do something, but they didn't. They didn't say a word."

The students finally cut loose at three o'clock, and when it sank in, one could hear them sobbing in the halls, asking the inevitable questions: Why? What for? They stood around in small groups, thinking perhaps that someone would tell them something to help them understand it. But no one did. The principal, Mrs. Virginia Forneron, a youthful-appearing middle-aged woman, assembled the faculty and made the announcement, instructing them all that as little be made of it as possible. School would be held on Friday as usual. There was to be no discussion of the suicides.

The teachers were as bewildered as everyone else. Said Mrs. Ann Walsh, the librarian: "There wasn't a hint of it. I saw them almost every day. Especially Joan. She was a spirited girl. She cared about everything. When she talked about a book, she was so vital you felt the very life of it coming out. The more I think of this, the less sense I can make of it. She was never despondent. Never. In fact, she seemed to infect everyone with her vivaciousness. Even the peace thing confuses me. All these kids were 'realists' about such matters. They weren't demonstrators."

David Towers, in his thirties, was their history teacher. He saw another dimension in them, especially in Craig. "They were both serious kids in class. Without being exceptional students, they were more deeply concerned about the direction society was taking." He noted one instance when the class had been discussing reports of American soldiers in Vietnam having suspended enemy prisoners by their heels from flying helicopters and several boys laughed. "Craig became indignant and said: 'That's the whole problem. Too many laugh about what's happening.' "

Yet they were not radicals. They belonged to no peace organization (indeed, there were no local ones to belong to), though it was noted that Joan had signed the class yearbook in the spring with a peace symbol under her name. In fact, as eighteen-year-old Ed Bonnet pointed out (Ed was the school activist, having organized the LUV—Let Us Vote—campaign for eighteen-year-olds, destined to be defeated in the November New Jersey state elections): "A year ago Craig helped me form what we called Students for America: its purpose was to show support for the men in Vietnam, not to work for withdrawal, and on November 11, 1968 we had a march on Camden. It was in all the papers. Joan was in the group too. But about six months ago they both dropped out. They just stopped coming . . . . I don't know if I can understand this thing."

Chris Henderson added to the mystery: "Craig used to question those protest suicides we'd read about, like the monks in Vietnam and that Czech student. He said he didn't know what they were trying to prove; it was just one more dead person."

There are some who were aware of deeper qualities in each of the two. Chris, for example, had special words for Joan: "She was really a very sincere girl. She wanted to be different, yes, but she had to be real about it. She didn't think it was so important to dress like a mod or a hippie or anything like that. She felt a person could be different by what she felt in her heart." Then there was one of the twenty-four notes that somehow found its way to its addressee, eighteen-year-old Frank DeGenova, a freshman at Rensselaer Polytechnic Institute at Troy, New York. It exposed a raw, troubled spirit:

I waited until last to write you. It's 6:30 now and I'm going to pick·
up Joan . . . . I have found love in Joan. My life is complete except all

my brothers are in trouble—war, poverty, hunger, hostility. My purpose is to make them understand all this trouble. Maybe they will start a chain reaction of awakening, love, communication. I've been so down, so goddam down, I can't get up . . . . Read my poetry and make people understand how I feel. Make them wake up and tell each other how beautiful they are. Take my life into yours. If I sound strange, it's because I am insane with sorrow and distress. Please, make them see!

Frank DeGenova was deeply moved. "I guess I just didn't realize it meant that much to him. After reading this, I'm sure it did. I remember when I went away to school, he gave me a peace medal. He said I was supposed to wear it and think about it—and then pass it on so somebody else could think about it. He said that people are the most important thing of all. He always had a lot of people who would take their problems to him. He tried so hard to understand. He was always so happy himself. He wrote out everything that bugged him. He just spent his time with people trying to make everybody see how wonderful it is to be alive. He saw a lot of beauty that he wanted everybody else to see."

Confusion remained as to the meaning of it. Autopsies revealed no pregnancy or sexual cohabitation, no drug use, no sickness. The coroner's office found nothing, which openly surprised some and secretly disappointed many.

The majority of the notes remained with the police and would not be released to the friends for whom they had been written. It was said that there was a danger of more such suicides, and their distribution would serve no purpose. Two psychiatrists from the National Institute of Mental Health at Bethesda, Maryland, attached to the Suicide Prevention Unit, met with parents, police, ministers, allegedly concurred in this decision, then left quietly.

Suicides, apparently, have a special way of being infectious, tipping the delicate balance of dormant impulses in others and leading them to try for a similar fate. Sometimes it becomes a small but threatening epidemic. When Marilyn Monroe took her tragic overdose of barbiturates in the summer of 1962, there was a wave of similar cases in the weeks that followed. In Blackwood, the initial reaction was to bury the double-suicide story in all its details as quickly and as thoroughly as possible. It was said that the parents wanted it this way, and all such decisions sprang from them. (It is noteworthy, however, that the coroner, Thomas Daley, who had announced the impounding of the suicide notes, received many letters from all over the country, mostly from young people, protesting this suppression.) When a television crew from NBC in New York City tried to film a documentary of the tragedy, the community succeeded in shutting the network out, ostensibly because it was invading privacy.

The mood of Blackwood is, in essence, all of a piece. Part of a conglomerate of small communities spilling over into each other. Blackwood is barely twelve miles southeast of Camden—just across the Delaware River from Philadelphia—but its style suggests a sleepy village far distant from any metropolis, barely contending with the rapidly changing American scene. It is a quiet town of hardworking people who have lived there for generations, none rich and very few poor, a town of small, well-kept frame houses on peaceful streets, of one-car garages and postage-stamp lawns. If there is truly such an entity as the Great Silent Majority, the people of Blackwood would be proud to be part of it.

Highland Regional High School is a spanking new two-story complex of buildings and playing fields on what was once farmland. It is run like a tight ship. Controls on the students are quite rigid. On the day before the Vietnam Moratorium, for example, the students were openly discouraged from participation in it, and the school had the lowest October 15 absentee rate in all of South Jersey. On the day after, there was no discussion of it. In general, the school boasts of the top wrestling teams in the area, the finest band, the best chess team. Its students are said to have contributed the largest sum of money to the United States Olympic fund of any high school in America. There has been no SDS (Students for a Democratic Society) activity, nor is there likelihood of any. The students, part vocationally oriented, part academic, are more neatly dressed than most, their hair shorter, their styles less flamboyant. There are no foreign cars in the parking lot.

When school convened on the Friday following the suicides, students went to their classes as usual. If there was an overhanging somberness in the atmosphere, there was no discussion of the deaths or even an earnest quest for their significance. Some teachers prepared tests to divert attention. Others chose to attack their respective subject head-on. Said one student: "It was ghoulish. It was like it never happened!"

To an educator like Dr. Robert Havighurst of Fordham University, conscious of the idealistic adolescent suicides, this kind of ostrich-like evasiveness is destructive to the young people it seeks to protect. "The sensitive, intelligent adolescent who is declining to settle for a simple, positive identity has a valuable faculty for criticism and nonconformity that is very much needed in our society. Perhaps this kind of person needs these years to grow in his powers of analysis and social criticism, even though he may be somewhat unhappy and may make his family uncomfortable."

Among some students there was resentment at the lack of public concern. A number of them, feeling the need to do something that would be a meaningful tribute to the dead couple, planned a candlelight memorial parade on Wednesday evening, exactly one week after their deaths. Everyone would meet at the high school and march to a field on Black Horse Pike. Classmates would read some of Craig's poetry and sing songs he had written. "We knew it was right that we should do this," one boy said. "Craig and Joan believed in what they did very strongly. They wanted their deaths to mean something. They wanted to make an impact. Well, we were going to try to do what they wanted."

The response was spirited among the students. However, among the adults it was wary and noncommittal. When a report of the memorial parade plan appeared in the Camden *Courier-Post*, the parents of the couple interceded and let it be known that they did not endorse the march. Would it not attract a horde of out-of-towners, long-haired hippies, peaceniks and radicals hungering for a chance to demonstrate? Would that not turn such a march into an insult to the memory of the two? Other adults chimed in. The minister of St. John's Episcopal Church, where Craig's funeral service was held, agreed. In time, the students decided to cancel the event.

So there was no ceremony, no memorial in Blackwood. Several towns, including the city of Camden, conducted their own ceremonies, attended by scores who did not even know the couple—quiet, simple, dignified meetings wherein young people lit candles and sang. "All we want is to give peace a chance." But Blackwood remained silent.

"The people in town," said a friend of Joan's, "Shook their heads and kept asking why, why, why? But what they refused to do was look into their own lives."

So it was that the week went by. The couple was buried according to their last requests, side by side. There would be no official or family statements. When a minister from nearby Collingswood called the suicides an "evil deed" and likened their plea for peace to those who would surrender this country to the Communists, even that evoked no comments. The local weekly newspaper, the *Observer,* had what was called "After Thoughts" on its editorial page: "Although average intellectually, they must have realized that their deaths would accomplish nothing. . . . Whom do we blame? We don't know. We can only question why."

In time, no one seemed to care. The town would be rid of it, once and for all. Columnist Stephen Allen of the Camden *Courier-Post* made this poignant observation: "If a policeman had been killed enforcing the law, there would be black bunting everywhere, and the flags would be at half-staff. But there was not an inch of black anywhere. There was no indication in any of the store windows that they mourned the passing of two of their young who died in the name of peace. Even in front of the Highland Regional High School, the flag fluttered at the top of the staff."

(Maybe this will start a chain reaction of peace," the couple had written.)

It started nothing and ended nothing but their own lives. It would seem that the very forces of inhumanity, fear and repression that possibly drove Craig and Joan to their suicides now conspired to rob them of their purpose. Months would go by and nothing would be said. The parents of the two would maintain a rigid isolation, their silence protected by sympathetic friends. Other parents would concur, frightened that their own children might be spurred to some comparable act of self-sacrifice. It was all too much for them, as they had been all too much for Craig and Joan.

To at least one teacher, this was totally dismaying. "I really believe they were terribly ashamed of those kids," said one lady who wished to remain anonymous. "They wanted to hide the tragedy in a closet and forget about it. To them, Joan and Craig had done a foul and debasing thing in protesting the war, especially since Joan's own brother was in the fighting in Vietnam. The people in this town simply could not face the fact that otherwise normal kids would choose to die for such things as peace and brotherhood. When they couldn't come up with an explanation that the kids were sick or crazy or aberrant, they just went and shut themselves off from it."

As the psychiatrist Dr. Robert Porter commented: "At seventeen an adolescent struggling for his identity also wants to find a common ground with his family and community wherein he can get satisfactions from his activities. If he doesn't, he will inevitably seek alternative ways." It was ultimately clear that Craig and Joan did not find those satisfactions. They responded to their frustration with such despair they could not see their way out of it. It was apparent from their notes that the whole sense of the community overwhelmed them. It was in writing those notes, pleading for a better level of human understanding, that they thought they could find an alternative way.

Craig had written one note to their senior English class: "You are off to see life for us. Try making peace, love and communication part of your life. Don't let us down."

Even among their friends there are some who say it was all in vain. Maybe so. But others, both young people and adults, may have been touched by the tragedy.

As with a pebble dropped in a quiet pool, ripples fan out and stir up the waters.

Studies of Adolescent Suicidal Behavior

Richard H. Seiden

This section is based upon studies which have dealt directly with suicidal adolescents. The format of this section is to cover, in turn, the three major areas of etiology, treatment, and prevention. Within each of these major headings, the material is divided into more specific categories. For example, the etiological factors are categorized according to individual, social, and cultural determinants. The treatment material not only covers the areas of formal psychotherapy and hospitalization but chemotherapy and non-traditional methods as well. The topic of prevention is separated into three levels of preventive approach. Primary prevention, which deals with the prodromata or "warning signs"; secondary prevention which covers crisis intervention and basically concerns the material reviewed in the treatment section; and tertiary prevention which treats the important subject of how the survivors are affected by suicide. Such complicated material presented numerous problems in the arrangement and ordering of the data. These problems were exacerbated by two major considerations: first, the methodological defects and non-comparability of many of the studies, and secondly, the sheer weight of the literature written upon this subject. The etiological section, in particular, includes large numbers of studies, which are very uneven in their quality. Many studies contained imprecise definitions or conclusions that frequently went far beyond their data. Particularly common was the failure to distinguish between attempted, committed, threatened, "partial" and "probable" suicides. Various kinds of self-destructive behaviors were frequently combined without due respect for the important differences which exist between them. In some cases the results from a study based upon one group, such as attempted suicides, were over-generalized to other categories of suicidal behavior as well. In other cases the authors drew conclusions which were not evident from their data but which seemed to have been applied "wholesale" from previous studies. Yet another obstacle to neat, synoptic organization was introduced by the great numbers of factors which had been elicited in the various studies. For example, a prodigious number of psycho-

Reprinted from Suicide Among Youth, A Supplement to the *Bulletin of Suicidology*, published by National Institute of Mental Health, National Clearing House for Mental Health Information, December 1969.

dynamic characteristics have been causally linked to adolescent suicide, including, among others:

Chronic depression (Lawler, Nakielny & Wright, 1963: Cerny & Cerna, 1962),

Hallucinations, delusions, schizophrenic reactions (Lawler, et al., 1963; Toolan, 1962),

Feelings of rage and desire for revenge (Bender & Schilder, 1937; Moss & Hamilton, 1956),

Guilt—self-blame for parent's suicide (Cain & Fast, 1966); over sexual freedom (Jensen, 1955); anxiety and guilt over sexual impulses (Mohr & Despres, 1958); arousing guilt as a means of hurting others (Block & Christiansen, 1966); remorse (Bakwin, 1964); shame about failure and reactions of others (Iga, 1961),

Fear—of punishment (Bakwin, 1964; MacDonald, 1906—7; Zumpe, 1959); failure in school, especially college (Jensen, 1955; Rook, 1959),

Feelings of powerlessness (Porot, Collet, Girard, Jean & Coudert, 1965),

Desire to control environment (Mohr & Despres, 1958); need to force attention and love from others (Bender & Schilder, 1937; Bergstrand & Otto, 1962; Faigel, 1966; Gould, 1965); manipulativeness (Toolan, 1962); blackmail (Launay, 1964; Ringel, Spiel & Stepan, 1955),

Feeling of worthlessness (Hendin, 1964); of inadequacy (Iga, 1961; Lyman, 1961); severely reduced self-esteem (Munter, 1966); sense of failure (Gunther, 1967),

Loneliness and creation of unreal world (Bergsma, 1966; Maycock, 1966); withdrawal (Morrison & Smith, 1967); isolation (Jacobs & Teicher, 1967; Jan-Tausch, n.d.); fantasy life (Lawler, et al., 1963)

Feelings of helplessness—dependency needs, insecurity (Iga, 1966); when dependency removed (Lourie, 1966); lack of love and protection (Zumpe, 1959),

Impulsivity (Geisler, 1953; Gould, 1965); ineffective self-control (Iga, 1966); crisis in control of aggressive urges; hypersensitivity, suggestibility, magical thinking (Schneer, Kay & Brozovsky, 1961),

Identification—wish for reunion with dead parent (Keeler, 1954; Launay, 1964; Mohr & Despres, 1958; Moss & Hamilton, 1956); follow example of parent's suicidal behavior (Lourie, 1966),

Feelings of hopelessness—futility; last resort (Jacobs & Teicher, 1967; Tuckman, Youngman & Leifer, 1966),

Desire for escape from unbearable situation (Bender, 1953); tired of poor treatment (Faigel, 1966); feels unloved (Mohr & Despres, 1958; Peck, 1967a),

Loss of love object, concept of death, puberty (Alexander & Alderstein, 1958; Nagy, 1959).

Our major task was to bring some order into the literature on this subject. We have attempted to evaluate the key studies, and from the numerous papers to select those whose findings had sufficient correspondence to warrant their presentation as a body of consensual knowledge. That is, our criterion was to select the research that was substantially relevant and could be generalized to the study of adolescent suicide.

ATTEMPTED VS. COMMITTED SUICIDE

The most striking defect in many of the studies of adolescent suicides was their frequent failure to distinguish between various self-destructive behaviors, particularly between the general categories of attempted and committed suicides. The only logical way to combine these categories is to assume that cases of attempted and committed suicide come from the same population or are characteristic of the same kinds of persons. This assumption infers that all degrees of self-destructive behavior are essentially attempts at suicide which differ only with respect to how "successful" they are. In other words, the suicidal behavior is regarded as continuous, and fatal attempts simply mark its terminal phase. The unsoundness of this assumption is indicated by a wide body of evidence that persons who attempt suicide do not come from the same population as those who commit suicide. Mintz (1964) conducted the only prevalence study of suicide attempts to be found in the literature. His results indicated that suicide attempters were younger (model age range 14-24) than completed suicides and that the sex ratio for attempts was the reverse (females 3:1 over males) of the sex ratio associated with completed suicides. Shneidman & Farberow (1961) summarized the demographic distinctions between attempters and committers in the following table:

Table 14. Characteristics of Attempted and Committed Suicides.

Variables	Modal Attempter	Modal Committer
Sex	F	M
Age	20-30	40 plus
Method	barbiturates	gunshot
Reasons	marital or depression	ill health, marital or depression

Source: Adapted from Shneidman & Farberow, 1961, p. 44.

On the basis of their investigation they concluded that attempted and committed suicides cannot be combined without masking some extremely important differences. Stengel (1964) also insists that data on attempters and committers should be clearly separated. He points out that less than 10 percent of persons who attempt suicide later kill themselves and that many of the people who commit suicide do so on their first attempt. An important reason for distinguishing attempters from committers is that the problems of persons who survive attempted suicide offer the greatest challenge and hope for remedial action: First, for the obvious reason that these people have survived despite their suicidal behavior, but also because they outnumber committed suicides, especially in adolescence, by a ratio which has been estimated from 7:1 (Dublin, 1963) to as high as 50:1 (Jacobziner, 1960). The problem of suicide attempts is particularly significant in adolescence since it is reported that 12 percent of all the suicide attempts in this nation were made by adolescents, and that 90 percent of these attempts were made by adolescent girls (Balser & Masterson, 1959).

Some of the recent studies in progress (e.g., Peck & Schrut, 1967) demonstrate an increased awareness of the important differences manifested among varieties of self-destructive behavior and, in fact, are utilizing these distinctions for comparative study. In their current research on college-student suicide Peck & Schrut have divided their subjects into four groups: attempted, threatened, and committed suicides and a control group of non-suicidal individuals. Their design calls for comparisons among these four groups to determine differences in demographic factors, factual items, and life style.

Unfortunately, many of the studies encompassed in this review did not make such necessary distinctions. Most of the published studies were based upon suicide attempters (about one-fourth of them were based upon cases of committed suicide, a handful on threatened suicide and other forms of suicidal behavior). Nonetheless, of all the etiological factors presented in the following section, there was only one characteristic which was differentially assigned to one type of suicidal activity. That single characteristic was "social isolation." This determinant was generally attributed to cases of completed suicides but apparently was not seen to be as characteristic of suicide attempters or threateners. Except for this single instance, the causative, dynamic factors were applied to the entire range of suicidal behaviors. More often than not widely different suicidal behavior, ranging from the "partial" suicide of a diabetic who disregarded medical dietary advice (Mason, 1954) to the suicide of an adolescent who killed himself by highly lethal means on his first attempt, was attributed to similar if not identical dynamics.

THEORIES OF SUICIDE

Another deficiency of most of the studies of adolescent suicide is the absence of a theoretical orientation from which testable hypotheses can be derived and verified. This absence is not surprising because no theories of suicide are directly based upon adolescent cases. With the possible exception of psychoanalytic theory, which does emphasize the importance of renewed libidinal impulses at puberty, the theories of suicide were derived from the study of adult cases. Little attention has been paid to the specific dynamics leading to youthful self-destruction.

In general, the various theoretical writings on suicide can be divided into two major categories: (1) those formulations where individual, psychodynamic determinants are emphasized and, (2) those in which socio-cultural factors are accorded a dominant role.

The psychodynamic formulations fall into two main classifications: non-psychoanalytic and psychoanalytic. The nonpsychoanalytic theories are widely diversified, ranging from the view that suicide is caused by a failure in adaptation (Crichton-Miller, 1931) to the idea that suicide is affected by climate (Mills, 1934). The psychoanalytic theories stress the importance of libidinal impulses, particularly dynamic, strongly aggressive impulses directed against an introjected object. Schneer and Kay (1962) specifically apply psychoanalytic formulations to describe the particular dynamics of adolescent suicide. They conceive of adolescent suicide as an immature means of coping with extensive Oepidal conflicts through renewal of infantile primary process thought and action.

Sociocultural theories of suicide place greatest emphasis upon dynamic interrelated social forces influencing the suicide rate. The most important of these formulations was developed by (Durkheim 1899) who stated as a general rule that the suicide potential of a given society varied inversely to the degree of cohesion existing within the society. According to Durkheim, suicides could be classified into three types reflecting an individual's relationships and attachments within his social context. Three types of suicide he described were: (1) Anomic, where a poorly structured, normless society provided few ties for an individual; (2) Egoistic, wherein an individual was unwilling to accept the doctrine of his society and; (3) Altruistic, where an individual was too strongly identified with the traditions and mores of his social group. Gibbs and Martin (1964) likewise propose a theory based upon the durability and stability of social relationships and the degree to which different social statuses are successfully integrated by an individual. Paralleling Durkheim, they state as their major premise that the suicide rate of any population will vary inversely with the degree of such status integration. Henry and Short (1954) also employ a sociocultural frame of reference in relating suicide and homicide rates to shifts and trends in the economic business cycle.

These examples afford a brief description of the major theoretical orientations. The reader who wishes a discussion and review of the various theories of suicide is referred to the informative articles written by Jackson (1957) and Farberow (Farberow & Shneidman, 1961) on psychodynamic theories; Broom and Selznick (1958) and Sorokin (1947) for the sociocultural viewpoint on suicide.

ETIOLOGY – INDIVIDUAL DETERMINANTS

Genetic and Familial Tendencies

The literature records several references to families with a history of self-destruction (A family of suicides, 1901; Manganaro, 1957; Shapiro, 1935; Swanson, 1960). Since, in these cases, suicide seemed to "run in the family," it was speculated that a tendency to suicide may be inherited. However, this speculation has never been proven and there is no evidence that self-destructive tendencies can be transmitted genetically. The only studies specifically designed to examine the possibility of genetic influence were done by Kallman (Kallman & Anastasio, 1946; Kallman, De Porte, De Porte & Feingold, 1949). In these investigations, the case-histories of suicides occurring in sets of identical and fraternal twins (11 sets in the first study, 27 in the second) were compared. Kallman found that suicidal behavior was not consistent among sets of twins even though they might be similar in personality or even when they were handicapped by comparable mental disorders. He concluded that there were no special hereditary traits predisposing a person to suicide. Instead, he reasoned that suicide was "the result of such a complex combination of motivational factors as to render a duplication of this unusual constellation very unlikely even in identical twin partners."

Puberty

There are indications that, at puberty, a sudden significant increase takes place in the number of suicide attempts. Puberty is also the stage of development where characteristic sex-specific differences in suicidal behavior become apparent (a male preponderance for completed suicide, a female preponderance for suicide attempts). This pubertal increase in suicidal activity has generally been linked to the "stress and strain" of adolescence, especially to conflicts over sexuality and dependency. As Gorceix (1963) points out, the adolescent is sexually mature but his environment does not accept this maturity. According to Schneer, et al. (1961), suicidal behavior in adolescence (either attempts or threats) may represent a cry for help in dealing with the problems of sexual identification and with associated libidinal and hostile impulses. A crisis in sexual identity is cited by several authors (Bigras, Gauthier, Bouchard & Tassé, 1966; Schneer & Kay, 1962; Zilboorg, 1937) who propose that a failure in masculine or feminine identity, or concern about possible homosexual tendencies, may lead to serious suicide attempts. In a recent study, Peck (1967b) pointed out that many boys use their fathers' guns (symbolizing masculinity) to commit suicide. He found that if a boy has a father who places a premium on masculinity, commanding his son to "be a man," this directive may frequently have the opposite effect and lead to a weakening of his sense of masculine identity.

Even when sexual identification is adequate, the increased sexual impulses of adolescence, *per se,* may lead to anxiety, guilt, and frustration. Schrut (1967) as well as Winn & Halla (1966), concluded from their studies of adolescent girls that "guilt over sexual acting out" was a major factor precipitating their suicide attempts. Another example of the eroticization of suicide has been described by McClelland (1963) who proposed that there were persons (mostly women) who fantasied death as a lover—"a mysterious, dark figure who seduces and takes them away . . ." McClelland calls this feeling of excitement and anticipation, of "flirting with death," the "Harlequin complex." As such his findings would help to explain the greater preponderance of female suicide attempts, particularly among adolescent girls dealing with the renaissance of their sexual impulses. Increased sexual impulsivity may also be responsible for one very unusual and highly sexualized type of self-destruction. That is, the death by hanging of adolescent males acting out erotic fantasies. One of the earliest studies which mention this peculiar kind of death was published by Stearns (1953) who reported several cases of early-adolescent males who had hanged themselves while dressed in female clothing, in some cases with their feet and hands bound up as well. He made no attempt to explain this phenomenon but regarded it as a case of "probable" suicide. Similar cases where young men hanged themselves while engaging in transvestite activity were also mentioned by Ford (1957); Litman, Curphey, Shneidman, Farberow & Tabachnik (1963); Mulcock (1955); Shankel and Carr (1956). All these instances involved young males who died during autoerotic or transvestite activity. Precautions were frequently taken to avoid disfigurement (e.g., a towel placed around the neck to prevent rope burns). The repetitive history of this unusual activity led these investigators to regard such deaths as accidents caused by excessive eroticized "risk-taking" rather than as clear-cut cases of suicide.

Mental Disorder

The two mental disorders most frequently linked to suicide are depressive states and schizophrenic reactions. However, there are no modern writers who contend that mental disorder is either a necessary or sufficient cause of suicide.

Depression: In the clinical evaluation of suicide potential, the role of depression has always been considered important. But, recent studies indicate that depression defined by internalized aggression and self-hatred may not be as important a factor in younger age groups as it is in cases of adult suicide.

If a pathological state of depression occurs in a young person it is usually associated with the loss of a love-object either through death or separation. For example, after the death of a parent, impairment of ego-functioning coupled with a feeling of helplessness, has been observed. This combination of symptoms may lead to a serious suicide attempt as a means of regaining contact with the lost love-object (Faigel, 1966; Schechter, 1957; Toolan, 1962.) Paradoxically, the critical period for suicidal behavior does not seem to be during the depressive reaction but shortly after the depression lifts. Apparently a patient's mood may improve chiefly because he has resolved his conflict by making definite plans for his own destruction. Some recent studies (Cerny & Cerna, 1962; Lawler, et al., 1963) found depression to be characteristic of half the young people who attempted suicide. Contrary results were reported by Lourie (1966) who stated that younger children making suicide attempts revealed no depression in the usual adult sense. He suggested that it was not until late adolescence that the clinical picture of depression appears as a prime factor. Likewise, Balser and Masterson (1959) concluded that depression was not important among adolescent suicide attempters. They were joined in their dissent by Winn & Halla (1966) who were similarly skeptical as to the importance of depression in children who threatened suicide.

In brief, if depression is simply and circularly defined as normal grief over the loss of significant relationships, then children and adolescents can be considered depressed. On the other hand, if depression is defined as a syndrome characterized by feelings of guilt, worthlessness and pessimism, then such symptoms would not appear to be as characteristic of youthful suicides as they are of adults.

Schizophrenic Reactions: Response to auditory hallucinations or commands may sometimes be the cause of serious suicide attempts among young people (Lawler, et al., 1963; Toolan, 1962). The combination of a rich fantasy life coupled with limited environmental interaction has been proposed as the factor which produces these suicidal hallucinations (Lawler, et al., 1963).

Winn and Halla (1966) diagnosed childhood schizophrenia in 70 percent of the threatened or attempted suicides in their study. Fifty percent of the attempters experienced hallucinations telling them to kill themselves; all of the adolescent boys in their study described "command" hallucinations. Balser & Masterson (1959) found that 23 of 37 adolescent suicide attempters had been diagnosed as schizophrenic, with specific pathology which included dissociation, hallucinations, delusional ideas, withdrawal, suspiciousness, and lack of communicability. These investigators concluded that schizophrenic reactions bear a closer relationship to suicidal tendencies in adolescents than does depression. Maria (1962) supports this hypothesis with his observation that in cases of completed suicides, schizophrenia is diagnosed more frequently in childhood and adolescent cases than it is in adult cases.

Identification, Imitation, Suggestion

Studies of suicide and suicidal behavior have found that children may imitate the actions or follow the suggestions of people close to them who have died, attempted suicide, are preoccupied by suicidal thoughts, or who openly reveal death wishes toward them.

Death may mean to the child a chance for reunion with a loved one, and there are instances where a child has attempted, through suicide, to join a beloved brother, sister, or parent—or even a favorite pet. In his study of children's reaction to the death of a parent, Keeler (1954) reported fantasies of reunion with the dead parent were present in eight of 11 children, and that suicidal preoccupations and attempts in six of these children seem to represent an identification with the dead parent and a wish to be reunited.

Lourie (1966) cited identification (or imitation) as an important dynamic factor for the younger children in his study. A suicide or suicide attempt by a family member may lead the young child to copy his example, even insofar as making the same choice of weapon. Bender & Schilder (1937) suggested that a deep attachment to a mother or father with suicidal preoccupations may spur suicidal preoccupations in a child. Schrut (1964) stated that a young child does not clearly differentiate his identity from that of his mother. If the mother harbors feelings of self-hatred and helplessness, the child may also harbor these same feelings. The opposite case, where lack of identification plays a part in suicidal behavior, was reported by Fowler (1949) on the basis of her work with suicidal children. She cited problems in primary family relationships where the parents provided poor models for the child to identify with as important determinants of suicidal activity.

A child's capacity for responding to suggestion may contribute to suicidal tendencies. Children who are openly rejected by a parent, or whose parents are frequently hostile toward them may respond to these "death wishes" with a suicide attempt. In their study of children who had threatened or attempted suicide, Winn and Halla (1966) found that over 50 percent of the children had experienced hallucinations directing them to kill themselves. Lawler, et al. (1963) described these auditory hallucinations as "hearing a voice, speaking in a critical manner, telling [the child] to kill himself." Occasionally, epidemics of suicides among school children have been recorded. These, too, seem to be at least partly motivated by suggestion and imitation.

It is doubtful whether any very young (under age 9) children actually intend to die. Because of their incompletely developed concept of death, any type of threat or attempt by children is particularly dangerous. If a child does not fully anticipate that he may indeed kill himself, his choice of method (jumping from a window, leaping into a river, or running in front of a car or train) may not leave him any of the chances for rescue which characterize the suicide attempt made in later adolescence.

Death Concept

Integrally connected to suicide is an individual's conception of death. To understand why a person takes his own life, we must also understand what death means to that person. Suicide in the young is particularly tragic since they frequently do not seem realistically aware of their own mortality. Winn and Halla (1966) found that young children often attach as much significance to stealing from their mother's purse as they do to a threat to kill themselves. Paradoxically, a child may wish to kill himself but not to die. That is, death is simply and tragically equated to running away or escaping from an unbearable situation. Without the realization that death is final, a child measures his own life's value with a defective yardstick. While young children do not lack a conception of death, their death concept is qualitatively different and frequently distorted when compared to that of a mature adult. A more realistic concept of death seems to emerge in a predictable, developmental sequence which corresponds to chronological age.

The earliest empirical investigation of this topic was conducted by Schilder and Wechsler (1934). Their findings indicated that even a child who was preoccupied with fantasies of death and violence did not really believe in the possibility of his own destruction. Similarly, Bender & Schilder (1937) believed that a child conceived of death as reversible and temporary. Supposedly, a child has this concept because of his difficulty in distinguishing between reality and unreality. Geisler (1953) emphasized the ambivalence of childhood fantasies of suicide which might be violent and motivated by aggressive-sadistic impulses, but also by a desire not to cease existing but to return to a more peaceful existence.

Nagy (1959) published a definitive study of the developmental sequence of children's death concepts. On the basis of compositions, drawings, and discussions collected from children (ages 3-10), she was able to formulate three major developmental stages: Stage 1 (under 5 years) is characterized by a denial of death. Death is seen as separation or similar to sleep and as gradual or temporary. Stage 2 (ages 5-9 years) is where the child reifies and personifies death. Death is imagined as a separate person or is identified with those already deceased. The existence of death at this stage is accepted but averted. At Stage 3 (age 9 years and older) a child begins to realize that death means a final cessation of bodily activities. This general developmental sequence was confirmed by Lourie (1966). Moreover, he pointed out that among the school age children he studied a frequent awareness of death was expressed in their thoughts and even in wishes for their own death. This awareness was evident not only among 70 percent of the children with emotional problems but among 54 percent of the normal school-age population. Rochlin (1965) also indicated that children are quite concerned with death. He disagrees with other writers in maintaining that by as early as age 3 or 4 a child is aware of his own mortality. It is for this reason, says Rochlin, that a child sees death as temporary or reversible—to defend himself against an overwhelming fear of his own demise. In this regard he agrees with Ackerly (1967) who also sees the childhood belief in the reversibility of death as a defensive maneuver. In a study comparing different age groups, Alexander and Alderstein (1958) measured emotional responses to the idea of death using word-association tasks. They concluded that the concept of death had greatest emotional significance in young children (5 to 8 years) and adolescents (13 to 16 years) as compared to the latency age (9 to 12 years) child. This discrepancy was attributed to the observation that social roles and self-concepts in the latency age child were more well defined than they were in the other two groups. Death attitudes among adolescents were specifically studied by Kastenbaum (1959). He concluded that the adolescent lived in an intense "present" and paid little attention to such distant future concepts as death. When adolescents did regard the remote future they saw it as risky, unpleasant and devoid of significant value. The findings of Alexander and Alderstein and of Kastenbaum seem to indicate that the concept of death achieves a renewed emotional significance in adolescence but that it is handled by displacement or denial in a manner characteristic of much younger children. Denial of death fears by suicidal adolescents has also been cited by Lester (1967) who developed a scale to measure the fear of death. He concluded that suicidal adolescents feared death less than did their non-suicidal adolescent counterparts. These observations are additionally confirmed by the work of Speigel and Neuringer (1963). Through a detailed study of suicide notes they concluded that normal feelings of dreading death were inhibited as a necessary precondition for suicidal activity.

Aggression

All types of suicidal behavior in young children—whether threats, attempts, or completed suicide—have been customarily explained as displacement of frustrated aggression which becomes self-directed (Bender & Schilder, 1937). However, Stengel (1964) argues that aggression directed toward others, not oneself, is more typical of the suicide attempter. He believes that this means of directing aggression is an important difference which distinguishes suicide attempts from cases of completed suicide.

The particular dynamic relationship between aggression and suicide stems from the belief that direct expressions of hostility or rage—usually provoked by disappointments or deprivation of love—are thwarted (Moss & Hamilton, 1956) and are turned inward for several reasons: 1) The motive of spite or revenge is predominant. Faigel (1966) stated that the desire to punish others who will grieve at their death was one of the most frequent motives to suicide in young children. An angry child, powerless to punish or manipulate his parents directly, may take his revenge through an attempt at self-destruction. Zilboorg (1937) found that spite was a frequent motivation to suicide among primitive people.

He suggested that it was a typical and universal reaction. 2) A child may become overwhelmed with guilt, fear, or anxiety about his feelings of hostility, and then direct his aggression against himself (Moss & Hamilton, 1956).

Spite, Revenge, or Manipulation

An almost universal fantasy among children is "If I die, then my parents will feel sorry." Hall (1904) suggested that such desires to punish others were a frequent motive to suicide in young children. Research by Lourie (1966), Bender and Schilder (1937) and Faigel (1966) supported this conclusion. They found that revenge or spite toward a parent was one of the most frequent reasons given by young children for their suicidal behavior. In particular, Lourie maintained that the ultimate goal a child hoped to achieve was the love and attention of the parents while Bender and Schilder declared that suicide threats were frequently used by a youngster to assert his independence.

According to Lawler, et al. (1963), these manipulative attempts were not likely to result in death except through miscalculation.

Impulsivity

Suicide threats and attempts are often attributed to the greater impulsiveness of youth. As such, this impulsivity is considered to be the necessary component which translates youthful suicidal thoughts into actions.

Winn and Halla (1966) designated impulsivity as a prominent feature in the personality of a child and noted its existence in two-thirds of their cases of children who threatened suicide. Lawler, et al. (1963) described the children in their study of attempts as possessing a rich fantasy life leading to little environmental interaction. This combination, they stated, leads to a control by inner impulses sometimes resulting in self-destructive action.

Lourie (1966) concluded from his study of childhood attempters that the vast majority of these children had impulse control problems. Although most of the children had no particular preoccupation with self-destruction, they came from a cultural setting which encouraged or even stimulated general impulsivity. He suggested that the attempts were "mostly based on the pressure of the moment in an individual with relatively poor impulse control." But he also noted that despite their immediate problems of impulsivity, these children had a chronic history of long-standing problems.

Jacobziner (1960) reported that the high incidence of attempts among adolescent girls is "probably due to the greater impulsivity of the young female, who does not premeditate the act . . . it is, in the main, a precipitous impulsive act, a sudden reaction to a stressful situation." In their study of suicide attempts in Sweden, Bergstrand and Otto (1962) likewise concluded that for most adolescent girls, suicidal attempts seem to be impulsive acts connected with small problems.

A strong note of disagreement with these conclusions was reached by Teicher and Jacobs (1966a). They argue with the idea that suicide attempts are impulsive and precipitated by some trivial, isolated problem. Rather, they suggest that a longitudinal view of a person's total life history demonstrates that "the suicide attempt is considered in advance and is ... from the conscious perspective of the suicide attempter ... weighed rationally against other alternatives." In other words, the suicide attempt is not really an impulsive, spur-of-the moment decision but an end-phase to a long history of problems in adjustment.

Drugs

Of all the "psychedelic" drugs currently popular among the youthful generation, LSD has been most frequently linked with suicide. There has been a great deal of heat, particularly by the mass media, but relatively little light, beamed on this subject. According to Cohen (1967), LSD can be related to suicide in the following ways:

Accidental: Where, under the influence of hallucination or delusion, a subject embarks upon an act which leads to his destruction. Examples: the delusion that one has the ability to fly, hallucinations that cars on highways are toys which can be picked up in motion. In this category, there is no true suicidal intent as such.

Exacerbation of suicide proneness: Cases where suicidal thought has taken place before ingestion and the LSD experience intensified such wishes. This condition can lead to:

1. suicide attempts under LDS or;
2. suicide attempts after the "trip."

Intrusion of suicidal ideas in "normal" individuals, usually as a result of a panic state in an individual who has not previously thought of suicide. Under LSD, dissociation of body or thoughts that a "bad trip" will never end can take place. These ideas might result in suicidal attempts made during a drug-induced state of agitated depression.

Suicide as a result of LSD-induced fantasy: These are miscellaneous cases where a subject may sense his death is necessary for altruistic reasons. This type of suicide is sometimes associated with a person's feelings of guilt and his conviction that he "must die to save the world."

Flashback suicide: These are cases where LSD effects recur without the drug-magnifying or distorting psychopathology or depression. Panic is intensified by a confusion over what brought the episode on and whether or not it can be ended. Attempts at suicide in this state may be marked by the same motivation to escape psychic pain that occurs in the drugged state.

In these LSD-related suicides there does not seem to be any underlying depression; rather, the main precipitant is an overwhelming emotional experience beyond an individual's control; an experience which can be exacerbated by suggestibility factors when the drug is taken in social groupings. At this stage the psychopharmacology is still not clear, but it seems reasonable to conclude that LSD may act to catalyze underlying conflicts and emotions including suicidal predispositions and to disorient a person to such a degree that his self-destructive potential (lethality) is increased.

It is unclear whether these LSD suicides are really intentional. Shneidman (1963) considers such individuals to be what he calls "psyde-experimenters." Their motivation is not to die but to be in a perceptually altered and befogged state. They wish to remain conscious and alive but benumbed and drugged. Accordingly they may experiment with dosages, sometimes with fatal consequences but this type of death is traditionally considered to be accidental.

While there is scanty evidence of a direct causal connection between adolescent drug usage and suicide, there have been some anecdotal speculations concerning the observed association. Trautman (1966) reports a case study in which drug abuse and an attempt at suicide were viewed as complementary means of escaping an "unbearable family situation." Schonfeld (1967) blames our affluent society which emphasizes immediate rewards, not allowing adolescents to become tolerant of frustration. Subsequently, he writes, when faced with difficulties, they become overwhelmed and turn to escapist measures such as drugs, withdrawal and suicide.

ETIOLOGY – SOCIAL DETERMINANTS

Family Relationships

Family relationships are particularly important in the etiology of adolescent suicide. Not only because the family represents the most viable social unit in our society, but because of the significance of family relationships in the life of the young. Hardly any studies have investigated the protective values of a favorable family environment; instead, most studies have emphasized sibling position, family disorganization, loss, and types of destructive parent-child relationshps which lead to suicidal behavior.

Sibling Order: Kallmann, ét al. (1949) observed in their studies that the suicide rate of only children did not differ significantly from that of the general population. Several recent investigators, however, have suggested that a child's sibling position may be related to his suicidal behavior. Toolan (1962) found that 49 of 102 adolescent suicide attempters were first-born children. Lester (1966) compared Toolan's statistics on sibling positions with data from the New York City population. He confirmed that the distribution of sibling positions in Toolan's samples—especially the high number of first-borns—differed significantly from the expected distribution.

Another group of investigators (Lawler, et al., 1963) concluded from their study of suicide attempts that a disproportionate number of suicidal children occupy special sibling positions. Fourteen of the 22 children in their study occupied special positions (three only children, seven first-born, four youngest), but the sample was too small for adequately reliable conclusions. Lester recently (1966) re-examined the relationship between sibling position and suicidal behavior. He reasoned that suicide attempts might express an affiliative tendency to communicate with significant others. Noting that such affiliative tendencies are strongest in first-born and only children, Lester predicted an overrepresentation of first-born and only children attempting suicide. His data did not bear out the hypothesized relationship.

Family disorganization: A significant number of young people who commit or attempt to commit suicide have a history of broken or disorganized homes. A correlation between broken homes and suicide has been noted not only in the United States but has been observed throughout the world by investigators in such countries as Canada (Bigras, et al., 1966); Japan (Iga, 1966); Germany (Zumpe, 1959); France (Porot, et al., 1965, Zimbacca, 1965); England (Mulcock, 1955); and Sweden (Bergstrand & Otto, 1962).

But Stengel (1964) injects a note of controversy by pointing out that the definition of "broken home" varies greatly in the discussions of different authors. To some it means lack of at least one parent. Others seem to include all forms of family disorganization, including severe parental discord or extreme family conflict.

However it is generally agreed that the motives for suicide in children cannot be fully understood without carefully considering their family situations. Most young people who exhibit suicidal behavior seem to come from homes with grossly disturbed family relationships. Frequently these family problems constitute the dominant motivations provoking the suicidal behavior.

In study after study, the home lives of suicidal children have been characterized as disruptive or chaotic. Their histories generally include several of the following indices of family disruption: 1) Frequent moving from one neighborhood or city to another, with many changes of school; 2) family estrangement because of quarreling between parents or between parent(s) and child; 3) great financial difficulties and impoverishment; 4) sibling conflict; 5) illegitimate children; 6) paternal or maternal absence; 7) conflict with step-parent(s); 8) cruelty, rejection, or abandonment by parent(s); 9) institutionalization of adolescent or family member (hospital, jail, reformatory, etc.); 10) suicide attempts by parents; and 11) alcoholic parents.

Such poor family life has been hypothesized to lead to the following conflicts: A fear or knowledge of being unloved; fear of harsh punishment; desire to escape from intolerable conditions; lack of meaningful relationships, creation of guilt; spite; depression; loneliness; hostility; conflict; anxiety; and other affective states, any of which can predispose a child to many forms of anti-social behavior. This consequent anti-social behavior may range from stealing, fire-setting, running away, sexual promiscuity, to other forms of juvenile delinquency or, in some youngsters, to suicide.

Despite the general agreement that broken homes are causally related to youthful suicide, a critical view is taken by Jacobs & Teicher (1967) who contend that any valid analysis must place "broken homes" into the context of an adolescent's total life history. In their study of adolescent suicide attempts, they found that broken homes *per se,* were not distinctively precursive of suicidal behavior. Both their suicidal and non-suicidal control groups demonstrated similarly high percentages of broken homes. The real distinction was that the control group had experienced a stable home life *during the preceding five years* while the suicide attempter group had not.

Loss: The loss of a parent or other loved one (through death, divorce, or prolonged separation) seems to have several significant influences affecting suicidal behavior in children. First, a loss through death may lead to a desire for reunion with the lost loved one. A young child may therefore attempt suicide in order to rejoin his dead parent, sibling (or even favorite cat), yet not intend to die permanently. An older child or adolescent who believes in the existence of an afterlife, may make a serious attempt at suicide in order to rejoin a parent, sibling, or friend.

The death of significant persons in the child's life can also stimulate suicidal activity in other ways: 1) Parental suicide may lead a young child to copy his parent's example. 2) A child may blame himself for the death of his parent and be driven by this guilt to make a serious suicide attempt. 3) A child may be predisposed to suicide in later life through parental loss in childhood.

Zilboorg (1937) suggested that "when a boy or girl loses a father, brother, or sister at a time when he or she is at the height of their Oedipus complex, or transition to puberty, there is . . . a true danger to suicide." Several studies support the conclusion that the death of a parent early in a child's life may contribute to his later suicide-susceptibility. Dorpat, Jackson and Ripley (1965) studied 114 completed suicides and 121 attempted suicides. They found that the death of a parent was highest for completed suicides, and concluded from this that unresolved object-loss in childhood leads to an inability to sustain object-loss in later life. Bruhn (1962) compared a group of attempted suicides against a control group without suicidal tendencies. The group of suicide attempters was distinguished by the lack of both parental figures or had experienced the absence or death of a family member. Similar results were reported by Greer (1964) who found that the incidence of parental loss was higher in suicidal than nonsuicidal persons. Paffenbarger and Asnes (1966) discovered that death or absence of the father was the major precursor of suicide among college males. Another consequence of paternal loss or absence is that the mother may be cast in the role of chief disciplinarian. According to Henry (1960), this type of family role structure is associated with children's tendencies toward self-blame. And since the turning of blame inwards has been related to suicide, this type of family structure may predispose children toward suicide.

Again an iconoclastic note is sounded by Jacobs and Teicher (1967), who argue against a simple unitary relationship between loss and suicide. Their research compared the life histories of 50 adolescent suicide attempters with those of 32 control adolescents. Both the suicide attempters and control adolescents had high rates of parental loss in childhood. One group attempted suicide; the other did not. Obviously it was not simply parental loss in childhood which predisposed some subjects to depression and suicides in later life. They concluded that:

> loss of love-object is an important aspect of the process, but it must be viewed as part of a process where particular attention is paid to when it occurred and/or recurred, and not merely to its presence or absence. Furthermore, it seems that it is not the loss of a love object per se that is so distressing but the loss of love.

4) A child who suffers the loss of a love object may be predisposed to states of depression linked with suicidal tendencies (Lawler, et al., 1963). The common denominator in all youthful depression is considered to be the loss of the love-object. When this loss occurs to young children it can lead to difficulty in forming the object-relationships required for healthy emotional development. When the loss occurs during adolescence it does not block the development of object-relationships since the critical years for this development are passed. On the other hand, it can cause an adolescent to hate the love-object, who he feels has betrayed and deserted him (Toolan, 1962).

5) Adolescent girls, who make approximately three-fourths or more of all adolescent suicide attempts, may be especially vulnerable to loss of a father. Lack of a father is frequently noted in their histories and some writers hypothesize that paternal deprivation plays a significant part in the suicidal attempt of young girls (Bigras et al., 1966, Gorceix, 1963; Toolan, 1962; Zimbacca, 1965).

6) Other forms of love-object losses have also appeared to be significant influences leading to youthful suicide. They include:

   a. Loss of close friends through repeated school transfers (Lawler, et al., 1963).
   b. Loss of older siblings through marriage, college, army, or moving (Teicher & Jacobs, 1966a).
   c. Loss of boy-friend or girl-friend, where this love-object has become a substitute for a dependency upon the parent (Peck, 1967a).

d. Loss felt by freshmen at college—a kind of homesickness which overcomes the youngster when he finds himself alone and his dependency needs acutely unsatisfied (Peck, 1967a).

Social Isolation

Of all the psychodynamic attributes associated with suicidal behavior, the factor of human isolation and withdrawal appears to be the most effective in distinguishing those who will kill themselves from those who will not. While withdrawal and alienation can be important determinants of many types of suicidal behavior, they seem to characterize cases of completed suicides rather than suicide attempts or threats.

Jan-Tausch (n.d.) studied New Jersey school children and reported that "in every case of suicide, . . . the child [had] no close friends with whom he might share confidences or from whom he received psychological support." The critical difference between attempters who "failed" and those who "succeeded" was that those who failed had a relationship with "someone to whom they felt close." Jan-Tausch goes on to suggest:

the individual has either withdrawn to the point where he can no longer identify with any person or idea, or (he) sees himself as rejected by all about him and is unable to establish a close supportive relationship with any other individual.

Reese (1966) also investigated school-age suicides and found chronic social isolation to be the single most striking feature of this group. He reported that these youngsters had such a marked lack of involvement with other students or teachers that they were literally "unknown" in their own classrooms. Social isolation was also regarded as a major prodromal sign for college suicides many of whom were described as "terribly shy, virtually friendless individuals, alienated from all but the most minimal interactions" (Seiden, 1966).

Various reasons have been assigned to explain this state of isolation. Stengel (1964) maintains that "lack of secure relationship to a parent figure in childhood may have lasting consequences for a person's ability to establish relationships with other people. Such individuals are likely to find themselves socially isolated in adult life, and social isolation is one of the most important causal factors in the causation of suicidal acts." Schrut (1967) states that, for adolescent females, isolation is a gradual process which takes place over a long period. This process of isolation has also been associated with progressive family conflict which becomes increasingly more severe. He reported that the adolescent female suicide attempter in his studies "characteristically saw herself as being subjected to an unjust, demanding, and often irreconcilable isolation with a typical, chronically progressive, diminution of receptive inter-familial communication." After an adolescent becomes estranged from her parents, she relies upon a boyfriend to become the substitute parental image. A fight with the boyfriend is frequently the final blow and becomes the precipitating factor in her suicide attempt. Jacobs & Teicher (1967) concur with this analysis, adding that suicidal adolescents usually have numerous and serious problems which progressively isolate them. These authors describe a similar chain-reaction of conflicts isolating an adolescent from meaningful social relationships and frequently leading to a suicide attempt: A long period of extreme conflict between an adolescent girl and her parent(s) eventually leads to parent-child alienation; the adolescent girl frequently seeks to re-establish a meaningful relationship through a romance with a boyfriend. During this time she alienates all other friends by concentrating all her time and energy on her boyfriend. When the romance fails, she finds herself isolated from all "significant others," and the possibility of a suicide attempt is likely. The importance of an active social life is emphasized in the research of Barter, et al. (1968) where peer group relations were considered an important barrier to suicide attempts. They note that even though the nuclear family life might remain quite disorganized, when the adolescent has an active social life the prognosis is favorable. Additional support for the significance of good peer-group relations can be found in the research of Harlow and Harlow (1966) in their continuing studies of affective relationships among lower [primate] animals.

Communication

Closely related to feelings of social isolation are problems in communicating with others—difficulties which are characteristic of many suicidal individuals. In some cases the suicidal act itself is a form of communication, a desperate "cry for help." In other cases, an individual may attempt suicide because of the loneliness and despair growing out of his failure to communicate.

In many cases of attempted or threatened suicide, self-destruction may not be the dominant purpose. That is, some suicidal activites are distinguished by features which are not entirely compatible with the purpose of self-destruction: Some suicide attempters give warning of their intention (allowing for preventive action) or the attempts are carried out in a setting which makes intervention by others possible or probable (allowing for rescue). Stengel (1964) calls these attempts "Janus-faced," because they are directed towards destruction, but at the same time towards human contact and life. He believes they are really alarm signals which should be regarded as appeals for help. They should be treated as highly emotional types of communication which are different in style and content from the usual kinds of communication. A recent study by Darbonne (1967) investigating this point, indicated that the communication style of suicidal individual was distinctively different from the non-suicidal individuals.

A large portion of the suicidal behavior of adolescent girls seems to fall into the category of communication attempts. Stengel (1964) thinks these young girls use suicidal threats and acts as appeals to the environment more frequently than males, and that females seem inclined to use the suicidal act as an aggressive manipulative device more often than males.

Why do adolescents resort to this dangerous method of gaining attention and response? Lourie (1966) indicates that they drag with them, into adolescence, poor, distorted answers to the problems of earlier development (i.e., what to do with aggression, how to get attention, etc.) Peck (1967b) commented:

> We must . . . wonder at the condition of poverty of one's inner resources, when suicidal behavior becomes one's sole means of obtaining that attention.

But he goes on to state that these young people are not to be shrugged off merely as attention-seeking, manipulating youngsters, but should be regarded as unhappy, helpless, hopeless young people who are apparently unable to change things in more constructive ways.

These attempts to communicate through suicidal behavior may have two outcomes: change or further impasse. On a hopeful note Peck reports:

> . . . when the kinds of problems that underlie a suicidal behavior are appropriately confronted . . . suicidal behavior often disappears as a coping mechanism.

Yet a high percentage of these attempts do not result in improved conditions and when they do not they sometimes end in suicide. Peck (1967a) states that if the communications go unheeded, they become louder and more lethal, and the consequences, regardless of how nonlethally intended, may be disastrous. The possibility of tragic consequences is also confirmed by Teicher and Jacobs (1966a) who similarly observed:

> More often than not adolescents who adopt the drastic measure of an attempt as an attention-getting device find that this too fails . . . (and) the adolescent is then convinced . . . that death is the only solution to what appears to him as the chronic problem of living.

Socio-economic Status

The relationship between socio-economic factors and youthful suicide is, in general, similar to that of adult suicides. That is, suicides are highest in times of economic depression and lowest during periods of war. However, social upheavals do not seem to affect the suicide rate of the young as much as the rate of adults. The factors predisposing to youthful suicide appear to be much more related to home, family, and school life. Poverty has been associated with suicide and so has wealth but on balance there is no real evidence to suggest that suicide is more frequent among the rich or the poor. As Shneidman and Farberow (1961) pointed out, the distribution is very "democratic" and represented proportionately among all levels of society. Nevertheless, suicide is most prevalent in the transitional sections of a community, which are usually impoverished and run-down areas. Sainsbury (1955) has reported that low income by itself does not lead to high suicide rates. In his ecological studies, he discovered that it was the poor stability of a neighborhood not its poverty which accounted for the high rate of suicide.

Religion

There is little reliable evidence to relate religion specifically to suicide. Among the three major religions in this country, the suicide rate is highest among Protestants, lowest among Catholics. Durkheim (1897) proposed that the higher rate among Protestants was because Protestantism had less social integration and consistency than did Catholicism and therefore the Protestant church had a less moderating effect upon suicides of its members. On the other side of the coin, it is possible that Catholic suicides may frequently be concealed because of religious and social pressures. History indicates that religion has both moderated and facilitated suicidal activity. For example, the history of the Jews is replete with instances of mass suicides which occurred as a consequence of persecution and discrimination. There are also cases of individuals caught up in a religious frenzy or motivated to achieve religious martyrdom through self-immolation.

Simplistic attempts to relate suicide to unitary religious dimensions, e.g., Catholic, Protestant and Jewish, are merely exercises in futility. Questions of religious affiliation do not get at the critical variables influencing suicide. The important unanswered questions concerning religion and suicide were delineated by Shneidman (1964):

> What would seem to be needed would be studies relating self-destructive behaviors to the operational features of religious beliefs; including a detailed explication of the subject's present belief system in relation to an omnipotent God, the efficacy of prayer, the existence of an hereafter, the possibility of reunion with departed loved ones, etc.

Education – the Special Case òf Student Suicide

The subject of student suicide appears throughout the 20th century literature; however, the first thorough study of suicide on United States campuses dates back only 30 years (Raphael, Power & Berridge, 1937). Stimulated by the fact that suicides accounted for over half the deaths at the University of Michigan, Raphael and his colleagues investigated the role and function of the university mental hygiene unit in dealing with this problem. Later research on college suicide described the suicide problem at Yale. (Parrish, 1957), Cornell (Braaten & Darling, 1962), and Harvard (Temby, 1961). The results of these studies indicated that the suicide problem was substantial and implied that the risk of suicide was greater for students than for their nonacademic peers. In addition, these autnors attempted to identify the factors which predisposed students to suicide and to offer suggestions for its prevention. These earlier studies were almost entirely descriptive, and while they did provide informative insights they failed to provide control groups for a baseline against which the validity of their findings could be assessed. This situation was remedied by later studies (Bruyn & Seiden, 1965; Seiden, 1966) which applied the necessary principle of adequate control or comparison groups to answer two basic questions: (1) Are students at greater risk of suicide than non-students? (2) How do suicidal students differ from their non-suicidal classmates?

Students vs. Non-students: Studies by Temby (1961) and Parrish (1957) indicated that students were more suicidal than non-students. Temby reported a suicide rate of 15 per 100,000 at Harvard, and Parrish's work indicated a suicide rate of 14 per 100,000 at Yale. Both of these rates are well in excess of the expected suicide rate for this population (7 to 10 per 100,000). A series of studies in English universities also led to the conclusion that students were more suicidal than their nonacademic age peers. Parnell (1951) published a detailed analysis of suicides at Oxford University comparing deaths due to suicide among Oxford students to those in the population at large. He found that the suicide rate was approximately 12 times as great for Oxford students (59.4:5.0). Carpenter (1959), after reviewing cases of suicide among Cambridge undergraduates, also concluded that the rate of [male] students was higher than for comparable groups. Two years later Lyman (1961) investigated suicides at Oxford University comparing the incidence at various British schools. Her data is summarized as follows:

Table 15. Suicide Rates of British Universities

Populations	Annual suicide rate per 100,000 population ages 20 to 24
England and Wales	4.1
Oxford University	26.4
Cambridge University	21.3
University of London	16.3
Seven unnamed British universities	5.9

Source: Lyman, 1961, p. 219.

To test whether the same relationship held in American universities, Bruyn and Seiden (1965) investigated the incidence of suicide among college students at the University of California, Berkeley campus (UCB) and contrasted this incidence with the figures for comparable age groups in the California population. During the 10-year period they studied (1952-1961) there were 23 student suicides whereas only 13 suicides would be expected if the general population rates held. They concluded that the suicide rate among students was significantly greater than for a comparable group of age cohorts. In addition, they found that the general mortality experience [deaths due to all causes] was significantly lower for students when contrasted to a comparable group of age peers.

There is one study which indicates lower suicide incidence among [male Finnish University] students, when compared to the general population (Idanpann-Hekkila, *et al.,* 1967). Barring this exception, the general rule obtains that students are at greater risk of suicide than their non-student peers.

Suicidal Students vs. Non-suicidal Classmates: This question was investigated by Seiden (1966) who compared students at the University of California, Berkeley (UCB) who committed suicide during the 10 year period, 1952 through 1961, with the entire UCB student body population during this same decade. The main findings of this research were:

> Suicidal students could be significantly differentiated from their classmates on the variables of age, class standing, major subject, nationality, emotional condition, and academic achievement. Compared to the student population at large, the suicidal group was older, contained greater proportions of graduates, language majors, and foreign students, and gave more indications of emotional disturbance. In addition, the undergraduate suicides fared much better than their fellow students in matters of academic achievement.

Another study which distinguished between suicidal and non-suicidal students was published by Paffenbarger and Asnes (1966). Using the college records of 40,000 former students at the Universities of Pennsylvania and Harvard, they examined the records for characteristics precursive of eventual suicide. Early loss of or absence of the father was found to be the dominant distinguishing characteristic in cases of male suicide.

The Effects of School Success or Failure: There is some disagreement about the importance of school success in relation to suicide. This has been a recurrent question over many years. One of the most famous discussions of the Vienna Psychoanalytical Society was held in 1910 to deal with the specific problem of suicide among students. The Teutonic school system was the target of much public criticism and members of the Viennese psychoanalytic group, including Freud, Adler, Stekel, *et al.* applied the newly developed insights of dynamic psychology and psychoanalysis to this controversy. A recent translation (Friedman, 1967) of this classic symposium provides an extremely interesting historical and theoretical contribution to the literature.

In more recent times Otto (1965) examined 62 cases where public school problems were indicated as a provoking cause of suicidal attempts. He found that the school problems, when compared to other difficulties, were factors of relatively slight importance. However, Reese (1966), studying public-school-age suicides to assess the effects of the school environment found that half of the subjects were doing failing work at the time of their suicide.

Reese's study was the only research which showed a relationship between low I.Q. and suicide. He found that in 25 percent of those cases where the I.Q. was available, the scores were borderline or below. In contrast, other studies by various authors have indicated that suicidal adolescents have invariably been of average or better than average intelligence. With college students, the factor of intellectual competence has been characteristically greater in the suicidal students than in their nonsuicidal classmates (Seidan, 1966). Students who committed suicide had higher gradepoint averages (3.18 opposed to 2.50) and a greater proportion of them had won scholastic awards (58 percent as opposed to 5 percent). The transcripts of these students would indicate that they had done splendidly in their academic pursuits. However, reports from family and friends revealed that these students were never secure despite their high grades. Characteristically, they were filled with doubts of their adequacy, dissatisfied with their grades, and despondent over their general academic aptitude. This propensity for some brilliant academic students to feel that they achieved their eminence by specious means was also reported by Munter (1966) who called this syndrome the "Fraud Complex" and indicated that it was a frequent cause of depression among students.

Suicidal Students or Academic Stress? A pivotal question is whether students are at greater risk of suicide because they are initially more suicidal than non-students or because the school environment makes them more susceptible. Is the higher student rate due to selection procedures? Rook (1959) maintained that it was when he wrote that "higher standards of entry are more likely to lead to selection of the mentally unstable." Or is the elevated rate due to the institutional inflexibility and the stresses of academe? The Conference on Student Stress implied this viewpoint when they met to deal with the question: "How do stresses of students affect their emotional growth and academic performance?" (Shoben, 1966). The answer to this question needs further research to follow up college students and record their later mortality experience. Unfortunately, the standard death certificate does not supply information regarding education of the decedent. Such data would be helpful for a definitive answer to the controversial question of which is more significant, the suceptible student or the academic stress?

Variation by College: There is no evidence directly bearing upon this question. A definitive answer would require standardized reporting procedures probably involving a national clearinghouse for information on student suicide. Nonetheless, the data from Lyman's study of English universities (1961) clearly indicated that the Oxbridge schools had a remarkably high rate of suicide compared to the nation in general and to the unnamed "red-brick" British universities in particular. Accordingly, it may be reasonable to hypothesize that the suicide rates at top-ranked American universities, e.g., Harvard, Yale, Cornell, Berkeley, are higher than the suicide rates at schools of lesser academic reputation. The test of this hypothesis is an interesting subject for future research. Other provocative questions which must await future research are the comparison of suicide rates for: Large vs. small schools; public vs. private schools; and co-ed vs. sexually segregated schools.

Mass Media

Youthful suicide has been a subject for novelists and poets throughout the years. Literature is filled with humorous, insightful and sensitive treatments of the conflicts and despair of adolescents (Beerbohm, 1911; Gide, 1926; Goethe, 1774; Hardy, 1923; Ibsen, 1961; Kleinschmidt, 1956; Reid, 1939; Roth, 1963; Shakespeare, 1936; Stevenson, n.d.). Some people believe that the functional, romanticized treatment of suicide and adolescence acts as a stimulant to self-destruction. Perhaps the most vigorous advocacy of this position came from Mapes (1903) who wrote that:

Trashy novels and all kinds of unwholesomely sentimental literature are a very important predisposing cause to suicide in this country. They produce a morbid condition of mind which unfits people for realities.

Mapes' outrage was primarily aroused by one of the most celebrated examples of stormy adolescent love—Goethe's novel, *The Sorrows of Young Werther* (1774). This slim volume became a symbol of 18th century *Weltschmerz* and was vastly popular throughout the world. Soon afterwards Goethe and his book were accused of initiating a wave of schoolboy suicides which followed its publication. Goethe himself came in for various denunciations; his book was lampooned (Thackeray, 1903) and banned from public sale in some cities. Even to the present day, one finds castigating references blaming "Wertherism" for adolescent suicides (Becker, 1965).

Despite the condemnation of "trashy" novels and romantic sentimentality there is no evidence that the treatment of suicide by mass media influences the suicide rate. The only study to directly attack this question was done recently by Motto (1967). To determine whether newspaper publicity about suicides influenced the suicide rate he studied the incidence of self-destruction in cities which had experienced newspaper blackouts due to strikes. No significant changes were noted when the newspaper coverage was suspended. Motto concluded that newspaper publicity was not an instrumental precipitating factor for suicide. The blame for youthful suicide is no longer placed upon literary influences but on the deeper underlying motives which lead children to suicide. Nonetheless, it is of some passing interest and a reflection of the *Zeitgeist* that *The Ode to Billy Joe* (Gentry, 1967) which tells the story of a teenage suicide was, for many weeks, the number one best-selling phonograph record throughout this country.

Despite the inflammatory accusations leveled against the mass media, the educational aspects of a mass media approach have not been overlooked. There have been numerous films, plays and stories designed to educate the public about the general problem of self-destruction. In the specific area of youthful suicide, such a training film has been produced with the cooperation of the Los Angeles Suicide Prevention Center (Peck, 1969). This film is especially geared to help teachers, counselors, parents and others who have frequent contact with adolescents, to recognize and deal with the clues prodromal to adolescent suicide.

ETIOLOGY – CULTURAL DETERMINANTS

Cultural factors may influence the suicide rate in three basic ways: (1) By the acute psychological stresses and tensions produced in its members; (2) by the degree of acceptability accorded to suicidal behavior; and (3) by the opportunity for alternative behaviors provided by the culture.

Stresses: Instances of the first type, where the built-in stresses of a culture may catalyze and aggravate the suicide potentiality of its members, were discussed by Bakwin (1957). Writing on the "Prussian" attitude toward children, Bakwin related the high suicide rate among Prussian children to their fear of punishment and to their strong guilt feelings about failure. Prussian children were reared in an atmosphere which demanded a rigid conformity; punishment was frequent and severe. Overly-strict attitudes with few excuses accepted for "misbehavior" were the dominant codes at home and in the classroom. A comprehensive study of cultural factors influencing suicide was published by Hendin (1964) who used a psychoanalytic frame of reference to study individuals and their culture. Hendin investigated the reasons for the consistent differences in suicide incidence among the Scandinavian countries of Denmark, Sweden and Norway. From his observations of parent-child relationships, Hendin formulated modal "psycho-social character" structures which typified each of the three Scandinavian nations and which he related to national differences in child-rearing orientations. Sweden, where the suicide rate is relatively high, was characterized by "performance" types of suicide due to high achievement expectations, self-hatred for failure, and problems with affectivity resulting from early maternal separation. Denmark, where the suicide rate is also high, was characterized by "dependency" suicides revolving around such conflicts as anxiety about losing dependency relationships, over-sensitivity to abandonment, and difficulty in expressing overt aggression. In contrast, the suicide rate in Norway is quite low. Hendin proposed that this lower rate occurred because Norwegian mothers were more accepting, less concerned with their children's performance, more tolerant of aggression and strivings for independence, then were Swedish or Danish mothers. He believed that those suicides which occurred in Norway were mainly of a "moralistic" type, stemming from guilt feelings precipitated by puritanical aspects of Norwegian culture. Hendin's hypotheses were later tested by Block and Christiansen (1966) who investigated the reported child-rearing practices of Scandinavian mothers. They found general, but somewhat equivocal, support for Hendin's conclusions. In particular, their results were fairly consistent with Hendin's regarding Denmark and Norway; less so with respect to Sweden.

Acceptability: Examples of the second type, where culturally favorable attitudes may affect the suicide rate were presented by Bakwin (1957) who pointed out that countries such as Austria and Germany, where suicide is regarded as an honorable way to die, produce a higher incidence of self-destruction than countries like England or the United States where suicide is looked upon as cowardly or as a sign of mental aberration. The effect of culturally favorable attitudes toward suicide are probably best exemplified by the extreme case of Japan. In past years children of the nobility and military classes were indoctrinated at an early age with the belief that suicide was an acceptable, often highly valued, means for resolving demands of honor or duty, e.g., *kamikaze, seppuku.* Although traditional suicides are no longer as prevalent in Japan, the general attitude toward suicide is still much more tolerant than it is in many other parts of the world. At present, in Japan, suicide incidence has reached the point where it is the number one cause of death below the age of 30. Contrary to the United States pattern where the frequency of suicide increases with advancing age. Japanese suicides reach a peak at the youthful ages of 20-25. During the age range of 15-24, the suicide rates for Japanese youth are 10-20 times the corresponding United States rates (Iga, 1961). Despite the fact that academic competition (Examination Hell, 1962); exaggerated dependency and shame or failure (Iga, 1961); poor family relationships (Iga, 1966); and attempts at symbolic communication (Hayakawa, 1957), have all been cited as significant influences, the singularly distinctive characteristic cited in studies of Japanese suicide is the culturally favorable attitude toward self-destruction.

Alternatives: Conversely, where the cultural attitudes are condemnatory or repressive, one finds examples of the third type where the culture provides for alternative behaviors that indirectly satisfy the same end of self-destruction. Wolfgang's research (1959) supported the belief that the relatively high homicide and low suicide rates among young American Negro males were influenced by common values shared by members of this sub-cultural group. That is, suicide was perceived as cowardly and effeminate whereas death by homicide was considered to be masculine and courageous. Lowie (1935) recorded a somewhat parallel phenomenon among the Crow Indians. He observed a cultural pattern which was geared towards those men who were no longer interested in living. They were allowed to become a "Crazy-Dog-Wishing-to-Die."

> Above all, these warriors were pledged to foolhardiness and they deliberately courted death, recklessley dashing up to the enemy so as to die within one season.

A similar cultural pattern had also been observed in past years among the Northern Cheyenne Indians. Formerly, when a Cheyenne warrior became depressed or lost face, he could deal with the situation by organizing a small war party. During the ensuing battle, he could resolve his conflict through a feat of bravery which would renew his self-esteem or by engaging in an extremely dangerous and courageous act during which he was killed (Dizmang, 1967). As such, these cultural alternatives bear some similarity to the fictitious Suicide Club described by Robert Louis Stevenson (n.d.). Members of this club could manage to die without actually doing the killing themselves. As one of the characters remarked, "the trouble with suicide is removed in that way . . .".

But what happens when a culture comes to a deadend and no longer offers these alternative outlets for its members? Dizmang (1967), writing on the Northern Cheyenne Indians, observed that their traditional ways of acquiring self-esteem were gone, the culturally approved means of expressing aggression (e.g., Sun Dance, buffalo hunt, inter-tribal warfare) had been denied to them and he reasoned that it was these sorts of deprivation which were responsible for a mass epidemic of adolescent suicide attempts. In this case, Dizmang concluded, a whole culture had been "denied means for dealing with instinctual feelings . . . and the result was a feeling of hopelessness and helplessness," stemming from this cultural deadend.

TREATMENT

The methods indicated for treatment of suicidal adolescents are generally different from those most useful for adults. Despite these differences, the subject of specific treatment for youthful suicidal behavior has received singularly little attention in the literature. Surely this is a subject which warrants serious investigation.

Treatment of any kind of suicidal behavior must begin with an evaluation of the seriousness of a child's suicidal desires. Observing the child, interviewing his parents, and examining the child's history and home environment should enable an investigator to determine whether a child presents a significantly dangerous risk. Glaser (1965) offers some criteria to be appraised: depth of the conflict, inner resources for coping with the situation, outer sources available, and severity of the stressful situation.

Hospitalization

For those children who are identified as "high risk," immediate precautions must be taken. Hospitalization is the most effective precautionary measure. Shaw and Schelkun (1965) set forth some of the advantages of temporarily hospitalizing the child: 1) It provides a breathing spell for both child and family; 2) it removes the child from all stressful or anxiety-producing situations; 3) it allows the child to be observed and evaluated; 4) it indicates to the child that he is being helped, and that his problems are being taken seriously; and 5) it enables the child to accept a therapeutic relationship more easily.

The child who is mentally ill or extremely suicidal will require a long period of hospitalization. Moss and Hamilton (1965) present the factors in successful therapy of the seriously suicidal patient. (N.B. although the article by Moss and Hamilton does not refer to adolescents, it is the only extensive discussion available on treatment for seriously suicidal patients). The first phase is directed mainly toward adequate protection, relief of anxiety and hopelessness, and restoration of satisfying relationships with others. A deep, probing approach is postponed. During the next phase—the convalescent stage—the patient remains in hospital. He receives active psychotherapy, with the therapist approaching the problem directly and discussing new solutions. Only during the final phase is the patient allowed to renew contact with his original environment. Moss and Hamilton emphasize that since this is a crucial period for the patient, he should remain in hospital during this time. Although the patient usually considers himself greatly improved, there will be, upon contact with his previous environment, reactivation of the suicidal drive 90 percent of the time. This reactivation must be anticipated, and the patient and his family warned of this probability.

For the less seriously suicidal patient, hospitalization need not be for a prolonged period. Even a week can be beneficial in reducing the despair of a child, and in providing time to formulate a plan of treatment (Shaw and Schelkun, 1965).

Psychotherapy

Psychotherapy can be useful for seriously disturbed youngsters. Schechter (1957) believes that depression is the basis of much childhood suicidal behavior. Accordingly, he sees the treatment of suicide in children as based entirely on the concept of actual or threatened loss of love-object. The suicide attempt is considered to be both an attack on this object and an attempt to regain it. Therefore, he would treat all children by helping them to re-establish adequate object-relationships.

Shaw and Schelkun (1965), on the other hand, feel that the specific direction of the therapy should be highly individualized and dependent upon the predominant conflict: Inward aggression may be rechanneled; grief may be sublimated; fear of abandonment can be relieved. The therapist should work to relieve conflict and stress, to control destructive impulses, and to stimulate the child toward constructive action, but any deep, uncovering therapy should usually be avoided.

Richman (1968) sees the therapy of attempted suicide in a somewhat different perspective. On the basis of his work with adolescent suicide attempters and their families, he sees the suicide attempt as a symptom of disturbed family dynamics. In particular, these crises appear to revolve around handling of aggressive feelings within the family and with disturbed family role-relationships. He concludes that the therapy must involve the entire family as the patient, not simply the adolescent who manifested the suicide attempt.

Electro-convulsive Therapy

The use of electro-convulsive therapy (ECT) is a highly controversial matter. Fawcett (1966) maintains that ECT is probably the most effective treatment there is for severe depressions. Furthermore, Moss and Hamilton (1956) reported that with the advent of ECT, suicidal attempts by disturbed hospital patients are one-tenth as frequent, that the use of ECT significantly shortens the acute phase, and that productive psychotherapy can thus begin at an earlier stage. Toolan (1966), however, states that depressed children and adolescents, in contrast to adults, usually do not benefit from ECT therapy. Schechter (1957) objects to the use of ECT in treating children. He believes that it destroys the chances of the therapist to form an adequate relationship with the child. Even its advocates agree that electro-convulsive therapy does not have long-term effectiveness, and is highly objectionable to many groups (Fawcett, 1966). For these reasons, the anti-depressive drugs are now much more heavily relied upon than ECT.

Chemotherapy

Several authors report on the successful use of anti-depressive drugs in treating young people. Faigel (1966) mentions the iminodibenzyl group, and Lawler, et al. (1963) suggest imipramine for the treatment of depression in children. Phenothiazine drugs have been cited as useful for relieving the anxiety associated with suicidal activity (Shaw & Schelkun, 1965) and for the treatment of suicidal behavior associated with schizophrenia (Lawler, et al., 1963). Lawler also suggests chlorpromazine and trifluoperazine as antipsychotic drugs (the former to control agitation and the latter for suppression of frightening hallucinations).

Shaw and Schelkun (1965) state that mood-elevating drugs seem to be ineffective in children, but may prove helpful in older adolescents. They also declare that authorities "are unanimous in condemning the use of barbiturates for the potentially suicidal patient." Even the best of the psychopharmacological agents are not considered to be the final answer since the general belief is that medication is not as effective in children as in adults (Toolan, 1966), and that medication alone is not effective treatment—only psychotherapy for both the child and his family can lead to a permanent cure (Faigel, 1966).

Nonpsychiatric Approaches

In less dangerous cases, where neither hospitalization, chemotherapy, nor extensive psychotherapy is indicated, family physicans and public health nurses can be valuable sources of treatment.

Many young people can be treated adequately by an alert and interested family physician or pediatrician. Discussions should be held not only with a youngster but also with the parents. These discussions should be directed towards the patient's conflicts, his emotional and social problems, his preoccupations with school, peers and sex, and any other difficulties which may become apparent. If the physician then finds a deep-seated emotional disturbance, psychiatric care can be recommended (Jacobziner, 1960, 1965a).

Powers (1954, 1956), also, comments on the role of the physician in treating young people for suicidal behavior. He contends that any doctor who is willing to listen to a child, accept him, and try to understand him, can provide the proper supportive setting. Powers suggests that it helps the physician to create this supportive setting if he starts with a thorough physical examination. He believes this examination reassures the patient, reduces his tension, and is conducive to an atmosphere of hope and understanding. Once a positive relationship is established, the factors contributing to the child's suicidal activity can be discussed and their relative importance assessed. The physician should point out positive values and points of strength to the patient, thereby assisting the child in mobilizing and integrating his strength so that he can better meet his stresses.

Teicher and Jacobs (1966b) call attention to the unique position of the physician to recognize early symptoms of potential suicidal behavior and to provide a source of help for young people before this behavior becomes serious. An adolescent views a doctor as someone who is readily accessible, and as one of the few people in whom he can confide freely. He may seek out a doctor as the last possible resource for help in resolving his problems. It is emphasized, therefore, that a physician should listen to the complaints of adolescents sympathetically, and be ready to respond to warning signs of suicidal thoughts.

Jacobziner (1960) discusses the contribution of public health nurses in the treatment of suicidal behavior. He has found that in New York City the public health nurse was the logical person to make home visits. She had an intimate knowledge of the existing community resources, of the cultural and social characteristics, and diverse customs and traditions of the residents of the city. Public health nurses are also capable of establishing rapport with families easily. In fact, Jacobziner notes, families tend to accept visits from public health nurses more readily than from any other member of the health professions. The nurse can explain the emotional and social development of adolescents to their families, and can make follow-up visits to provide further guidance. Furthermore, she can help the families with health problems and, if necessary, she is in a position to recommend and make referrals for psychiatric treatment.

Finally, the most succinct and probably the most difficult prescription for treatment of the self-destructive adolescent was advanced by Shneidman. Departing from traditional methods, he proposed that the best therapy was to indulge the adolescent, to "cater to his wants and to help him fulfill his emotional life" (Shneidman, 1966a). Moreover, he states, the problem should not be seen as an individual conflict, but as the expression of a family disturbance, since

> one does not encounter a disturbed, suicidal adolescent without also finding a disturbed, destructive family. Parents as well as child, need a great deal of help. (Shneidman, 1966b).

In this connection, various suggestions relating to the patient's home environment have been made:

1. Before the patient leaves the hospital, his family and community must be prepared for his return home, and acceptance into his family must be assured (Jacobziner, 1960).
2. Destructive environmental factors should be corrected. Family conflicts must be resolved, school-load reduced, and all other serious stresses removed, if possible. If the patient is seriously suicidal, a major change in his environment is usually required (Moss & Hamilton, 1956).
3. If a child's home-life cannot be changed, it may be necessary to remove him from the damaging environment. This can be done by placing him with relatives, in a boarding school or foster home, or returning him to the hospital (Schechter, 1957; Lawler, et al., 1963; Shaw & Schelkun, 1965).

PREVENTION

The primary aim of suicide prevention is the identification and treatment of the presuicidal individual which leads to the ultimate goal, the saving of lives. Unfortunately, it is not always possible to prevent suicide at this primary level. However, preventive efforts can be directed at different levels with different objectives.

At the secondary level, during the acute period of suicidal crisis, the aim is to help the individual deal with his conflicts by providing adequate treatment and crisis-intervention services and to prevent further suicidal behavior.

At the tertiary level, after a suicidal crisis has occurred, the program shifts to the survivors who must cope with the stigma and shame that accrues to the family and even to friends and acquaintances of the suicidal individual. The aim at this level is to help the survivors to live with the condemnatory attitudes of the community as well as to work through the personal feelings of grief and guilt which invariably accompany suicide.

Primary Level

It is now well established that the suicidal person gives many clues regarding his suicidal intentions. Most people who kill themselves give definite warnings of their plans. The first step in preventing suicide is the recognition of these warning signs.

Otto (1964), in an effort to identify a specific presuicidal syndrome, first searched the literature for recorded opinions on the subject. He found that most investigations of this problem only concerned adults, and they they were not able to define a specific presuicidal syndrome. Otto then reviewed psychiatric material on 581 cases of children and adolescents in Sweden who attempted suicide in order to detect changes in behavior during a 3 month period preceding the attempt. He concluded from his study that a specific presuicidal syndrome does not exist in children and adolescents. The most common changes consisted of depressive and neurotic symptoms, such as anxiety, insomnia, anorexia, and psychosomatic symptoms. These presuicidal depressive and neurotic symptoms correspond to the findings of other recent studies of suicidal youth (Bakwin, 1957; Faigel, 1966; Jacobziner, 1960, 1965a; Swiden, 1966; Toolan, 1962).

Balser and Masterson (1959), however, describe reactions which contrast markedly to those described above. They assert that schizophrenic symptoms are much more common in adolescents than depressive symptoms. They describe a presuicidal adolescent as one who is delusional in varying degrees and spends much time in fantasy activity. These adolescents may not show anxiety, sleeping and eating disturbances, nor any of the typical symptoms of depressive reactions.

Literature review indicates that rather than just one particular type of presuicidal syndrome, all kinds of prodromal signs have been reported. As an example, the following prodromal signs have been compiled from the studies of Faigel (1966); Teicher and Jacobs (1966a); Perlstein (1966); Jacobziner (1965a) and Toolan (1962):

Changes in behavior preceding an attempt:
Eating disturbances or loss of appetite (anorexia), psychosomatic complaints, insomnia, withdrawn or rebellious behavior, neglect of school work, inability or unwillingness to communicate, promiscuity, use of alcohol or drugs, truancy or running away, neglect of personal appearance, loss of weight, sudden changes in personality, difficulty in concentration.

Related psychodynamic factors:
Repressed anger, sex anxieties, deflated self-image or self-depreciation, irritability, outbursts of temper, hostility, hallucinations, hyper-sensitivity, hypersuggestibility, low frustration tolerance, despondency.

Other related characteristics:
Broken home or disorganized family life, lack of friends, extreme parent-child conflict, long history of problems and a period of escalation of problems, death or loss of parent or other important person, accident-proneness, chronic disease or deformity, a clinical evaluation of depression or schizophrenia.

Despite the multiplicity of prodromal factors there is widespread agreement with one explicit point made by Jacobziner (1965b) and by Shneidman (1966a), among others. That is, that all suicidal behavior must be taken seriously. Even mere threats or seeming gestures should not be ignored.

Parents have the main responsibility for raising children in such a way that they will not resort to suicidal behavior as a "solution" for problems. Beeley (1929) considered suicide as a form of evasion or escape from crises. His answer to the problem was not to avoid conflict but to teach children early in life how to meet inevitable crises intelligently. Recently, Shaw and Schelkun (1965) have returned to this same theme: A child must learn to live with his conflicts.

Jacobziner (1965a) suggested that parents be better educated to understand the needs of adolescents and the psychodynamics of adolescence if they were to prevent suicidal behavior in their children.

A simpler and more direct way to reduce the number of suicide attempts would be to persuade parents to make guns and poisons inaccessible to their children. Since some authors believe that suicide attempts in adolescents tend to be spontaneous, impulsive actions, they suggest (Roche, et al., 1965; Peck, 1967b; Shaw & Schelkun, 1965) that the lack of immediate access to these two methods would be enough to prevent many of these supposedly impulsive actions.

Expanding preventive efforts into the school setting, Jan-Tausch (n.d.) recommends ways that public schools could help to prevent suicide:

1. Remedial reading courses should be made available, because there seems to be a correlation between poor reading and emotional distress.
2. Children should be encouraged to participate in extra-curricular activities, as a deterrent to withdrawal and isolation.
3. Schools should encourage more personalized teacher-pupil relationships.
4. Counselors should try to see that all pupils have at least one friend or confidant.
5. Guidance counselors should begin counseling children instead of performing administrative duties as a "way up the ladder."

Munter (1966) makes the following recommendations for colleges:

1. Close personal contact between students, faculty, and administrators.
2. Provision of counseling and treatment facilities.
3. Training of faculty and physicians in student health services to recognize prodromal signs, particularly of depression.
4. Encouraging an atmosphere in which emotional difficulties are accepted and support is provided to students.

Shoben (1966) in a report of the U. S. National Student Association Conference on Student Stress (Nov. 11-14, 1965) summarizes the conference's recommendations to minimize academic stress as follows:

1. Increase the relevance of education to the modern world.
2. Encourage more authentic and personalized student-faculty relationships.
3. Revise the campus community from an adversary atmosphere to a coopera-

tive one by allowing greater student participation within decision-making bodies.

Farnsworth (1966) states that the prognosis of students contemplating suicide is good if treatment is obtained. He provides the following suggestions for college psychiatrists:

1. Suspect suicidal preoccupations or actions in anyone who is depressed and anxious.
2. Make it clear to a student that he is free to talk about his feelings without any action being taken against him.
3. Develop a warm and accepting relationship with students suspected of suicidal thoughts.
4. Keep lines of communication open at all times from him to a source of help.
5. Notify parent or next of kin if suicidal signs become ominous.

Finally, Paffenbarger and Asnes (1966), on the basis of their research, proposed that the appropriate guidance by college agencies might provide a substitute for the paternal deprivation which influenced male college suicides.

In connection with student populations, Cohen (1967) has a few suggestions for proper education about drug use: Make accurate information available; make sure the sources are credible; and provide information about alternatives. Only in this way, he concludes, can attitudes toward drugs be changed.

On a community level, Jacobziner (1965a) advocates providing a greater concentration of health services in deprived areas where many of the potential suicides live.

Efforts could be made by communities to disseminate information about how to recognize warning signs and where to go for help. Shneidman (1966b) proposes using all the media—TV, newspapers, billboards, and even signs in public toilets—for providing this information. Concise and inexpensive pamphlets are also useful as a guide for parents, teachers, family doctors, ministers, youth leaders, and others who come into contact with adolescents. Such pamphlets, which discuss the problem of suicide, prodromal clues, and the nature of community suicide prevention services, are *How to Prevent Suicide* by Shneidman and Mandelkorn (1967) and the U. S. Public Health Service pamphlet entitled *Some Facts about Suicide* (Shneidman, Farberow & Leonard, 1961).

Suicide prevention in an unusual setting is described by Dizmang (1967) in his study of young people on the Cheyenne reservation. At present, the VISTA workers, the clergy, the Community Health Workers (Cheyenne who have received special training in public health practices and practical nursing) are the major sources of help used by the Cheyenne youngsters. These three groups have been alerted to watch for cries for help, so that referrals can be made to the Public Health Service. An effort is now being made to help young Cheyenne function in the "white man's world." Through the Neighborhood Youth Corps, the adolescents learn regular work habits and gain approval of the tribe by learning how to improve the reservation. Dizmang comments that response to this program has been "overwhelmingly positive." But the larger problem, he says, will be one of "community organization, through which the latent internal resources of these young people could be tapped and a cultural process of self-renewal rather than self-destruction begun."

Secondary Level

The measures useful at the level of secondary prevention have been discussed previously in the section on treatment. These methods are used during the period when the suicidal tendencies have become apparent, but the person has not yet become a suicide. They include hospitalization, medication, psychotherapy, and environmental intervention.

One topic not yet covered is that of crisis-intervention. That is, methods which deal with the crisis while it is in progress. This is one of the main purposes of a suicide prevention center. Operating around the clock, the center is always available to desperate people. The center attempts to find out what is bothering the person, provides reassurance that solutions can be found, and makes referrals to appropriate community agencies. The goal during this acute phase is not solution of the person's problems, but rather to provide immediate relief and hope since the suicidal mood is usually a temporary state. Thus, the suicide prevention center is primarily directed toward averting the immediate crisis, which then allows time for providing long-term solutions to the person's problems.

Suicide prevention centers in this country are developing rapidly. There are, in 1969, over 100 such centers throughout the nation and the number is increasing annually. As part of this movement, the federal government in 1966 established as part of the National Institute of Mental Health, a Center for Studies of Suicide Prevention. The Center acts as a catalyst for research, training, and community services, and as a guiding force for the development of the newly created, interdisciplinary, field of "suicidology."

Tertiary Level

Tertiary prevention refers to efforts made after a suicide has occurred. It involves working with the survivors of the person who committed suicide—especially those survivors who are children or adolescents.

Appropriate to the idea of tertiary prevention are several articles dealing with children's reactions to the death of a parent.

Keeler (1954) examined eleven children (ages 6-14) who were admitted to hospital after the death of a parent. He found depression in all eleven cases, along with such serious symptoms as fantasies of reunion with the dead parent, visual and auditory hallucinations, and development of conversion hysterias. Of particular significance was the report of suicidal attempts and preoccupations in six of the 11 children. Cain and Fast (1966) studied 45 "disturbed" children (ages 4-14) whose reactions had been caused by the suicide of a parent. Their disturbances were attributed to guilt derived from 1) pre-existing hostile fantasies toward the suiciding parent; 2) feelings of blame for the parent's despair; 3) their inability to prevent the suicide. Cain and Fast found that there had been no opportunity for the children to get relief from these feelings of guilt because of distorted communications regarding the parental suicide. The stigma surrounding suicide had led the surviving parent to do such things as completely deny the fact of the suicide, or to give differing accounts of the death at different times. Lastly, Sugaya (1965) reports the case history of a child whose father hanged himself. She was placed in a foster family, where she later became emotionally autistic and behaved bizarrely.

One of the few published studies in the area of postvention or tertiary prevention consisted of interviews with the parents of adolescents who had committed suicide (Herzog & Resnik, 1968). These interviews occurred from 2 months to 2 years after the suicide deaths. The experiences and recommendations of the investigators may be summarized as follows:

Parental Response

1. Overwhelming hostility directed towards essentially neutral parties such as medical examiners, physicians, hospital attendants, etc. and denial of suicide claiming that it was an accidental death or other non-suicidal death. It was felt that these unresolved emotions led to later feelings of guilt, depression, and failure as parents.
2. Due to the stigma parents were unable to derive the usual social benefits of working through their grief by talking to others about their children's death. In fact, it was felt that the parents rarely were able to talk even with one another about this event.
3. Parents would have appreciated professional help at the time of the suicide in order to deal with their feelings of grief, mourning and bewilderment.

Recommendations

1. Followup interviews in *all* families where a suicide occurs.
2. This function to be performed by mental health personnel operating on an official basis, e.g., through the coroner's office.
3. Early contact in the first few hours after a death occurs.
4. It was concluded that the interviews had therapeutic and cathartic value for the parents and serve as a first step toward an eventual psychological resynthesis and the prevention of subsequent suicides and related mental disorders among the survivors.

Though little work has been published on the subject of tertiary prevention, the lack of studies is by no means commensurate with the importance of the subject. The problem is one of extreme significance for it is quite likely that as Shneidman (1966b) has indicated, positive preventive efforts in the area will "head off the schizophrenias of the next generation."

REFERENCES

A family of suicides. *Medical Record, New York,* 60(17):660-661, 1901.
A student suicide. *Boston Medical Surgical Journal,* 196(2):491, 1927.
Ackerly, W. C. Latency age children who threaten or attempt to kill themselves. *Journal of the American Academy of Child Psychiatry,* 6:242-261, 1967.
Alexander, I. E. and Alderstein, A. M. Affective responses to the concept of death in a population of children and early adolescents. *Journal of Genetic Psychology,* 93:167-177, 1958.
Bakwin, H. Suicide in children and adolescents. *Journal of Pediatrics,* 50(6):749-769, 1957.
Bakwin, H. Suicide in children and adolescents. *Journal of the American Medical Women's Association,* 19(6):489-491, 1964.
Balser, B. H. and Masterson, J. F. Suicide in adolescents. *American Journal of Psychiatry,* 116(5):400-404, 1959.
Barter, J. T., Swaback, D. O. and Todd, Dorothy. Adolescent suicide attempts. *Archives of General Psychiatry (Chicago),* 19:523-527, 1968.
Becker, W. Suicide in youth. *Medizinische Klinik (Munchen),* 60(6):226-231, 1965.
Beeley, A. L. Juvenile suicide. *Social Service Review* 3(1):35-49, 1929.
Beerbohm, M. *Zuleika Dobson.* New York: Dodd, Mead & Co., 1911.
Bender, Lauretta. Children preoccupied with suicide. In Lauretta Bender, *Aggression, Hostility, and Anxiety in Children.* Springfield, Ill.: Charles C Thomas, 1953. pp. 66-90.
Bender, Lauretta L. and Schilder, P. Suicidal preoccupations and attempts in children. *American Journal of Orthopsychiatry,* 7:225-243, 1937.
Bergsma, J. Suicide and suicide attempts, especially in young people. *Nederlands Tijdschrift voor de Psychologie en Haar Grensgebieden,* 21(4):245-273, 1963.
Bergstrand, C. G. and Otto, U. Suicidal attempts in adolescence and childhood. *Acta Paediatrica,* 51(1):17-26, 1962.
Bigras, J., Gauthier, Y., Bouchard, Colette and Tasse, Yolande. Suicidal attempts in adolescent girls: A preliminary study. *Canadian Psychiatric Association Journal,* (Suppl.):275-282, 1966.
Block, Jeanne and Christiansen, B. A test of Hendin's hypotheses relating suicide in Scandinavia to child-rearing orientations. *Scandianavian Journal of Psychology,* 7(4):267-286, 1966.
Braaten, L. J. and Darling, C. D. Suicidal tendencies among college students. *Psychiatric Quarterly* 36(4):665-692, 1962.
Broom, L. and Selznick, P. *Sociology* 2nd Ed. Evanston, Ill.: Row, Peterson, 1958. pp. 20-24.
Bruhn, J. G. Broken homes among attempted suicides and psychiatric out-

patients: A comparative study. *Journal of Mental Science,* 108 (whole No. 457):772-779, 1962.

Bruyn, H. and Seiden, R. H. Student suicide: Fact or fancy? *Journal of the American College Health Association,* 14(2):69-77, 1965.

Cain, A. C. and Fast, Irene. Children's disturbed reactions to parent suicide. *American Journal of Orthopsychiatry,* 36(5):873-880, 1966.

Camus, A. *The Myth of Sisyphus and Other Essays.* New York: Vintage, 1955. (Originally published in 1942.)

Carpenter, R. G. Statistical analysis of suicide and other mortality rates of students. *British Journal of Preventive and Social Medicine,* 13(4):163-174, 1959.

Cerny, L. and Cerna, Marie. Depressive syndrome in children and adolescents with regard to suicidal tendencies. *Ceskoslovenska Psychiatrie,* 58(3):162-169, 1962.

Cohen, A. Y. *LSD and the Student: Approaches to Educational Strategies.* Unpubl. ms., Univ. of Calif. Counseling Center. Berkeley, 1967.

Crichton-Miller, H. The psychology of suicide. *British Medical Journal* 2:239-241, 1931.

Darbonne, A. R. *Dissertation Abstracts,* 27(7-B):2504-2505 [abstract], 1967.

Dizmang, L. H. Suicide among the Cheyenne Indians. *Bulletin of Suicidology,* July 1967:8-11.

Dorpat, T. L., Jackson, J. K. and Ripley, H. S. Broken homes and attempted and committed suicide. *Archives of General Psychiatry,* 12(2):213-216, 1965.

Dublin, L. I. *Suicide: A Sociological and Statistical Study.* New York: Ronald Press, 1963.

Durkheim, E. *Suicide.* Glencoe, Ill.: Free Press, 1951. (Originally published in 1897.)

Examination hell: Japan's student suicides. *[London] Times Educ. Suppl.,* Oct. 26, 1962:2475-2533.

Faigel, H. C. Suicide among young persons. A review for its incidence and causes, and methods of its prevention. *Clinical Pediatrics,* 5:187-190, 1966.

Detecting Depressions in Childhood

Eugene J. Faux and Carl M. Rowley

Depressions are easily diagnosed in adult patients and represent a sizable number of admissions to psychiatric hospitals. The American Psychiatric Association's *Diagnostic and Statistical Manual* classified depressions essentially under psychotic and psychoneurotic disorders. Under psychotic disorders are listed involutional psychotic reaction; manic depressive reaction, depressive type; and psychotic depressive reaction. Under psychoneurotic disorders is listed depressive reaction.[1] These terms are understood and accepted by most practitioners, and adult patients usually fall into one of these categories. We believe, however, that depressive reactions in children, when associated with object loss or rejection, need to be better defined.

Children do not always manifest depression by dejection, lassitude, or unhappiness, but often by other affective and behavioral states. Perhaps "grief reaction" would be a better term than "depressive reaction" to describe the neurotic conditions we have observed.

In our youth center, we are swamped with the most unloved, rejected, miserable children in Utah communities. Most of these children are referred because they have been acting out in a number of ways. As Alt and his associates note, "It is difficult to distinguish between the delinquents and most of the nondelinquents. Defiance and aggression characterize the behavior of both."[2]

The most common diagnoses offered by the referring agencies are "adjustment reaction of adolescence" and "adjustment reaction of childhood." Those terms do not satisfy us, and we feel sure they displease many others in the helping professions. We think that grief reactions are much more common than the literature implies, and although we cannot substantiate our conclusion, we feel that the children we are about to describe might well show the classical symptoms of a depressive reaction when they are confronted by crises during their adult lives.

Reprinted by permission from *Hospital & Community Psychiatry*, February, 1967.

[1] *Diagnostic and Statistical Manual: Mental Disorders,* American Psychiatric Association, Washington, D.C., 1952.

[2] Herschel Alt, *Residential Treatment for the Disturbed Child: Basic Principles and Design of Programs and Facilities,* International Universities Press, New York City, 1960, pp. 30-31.

Oddly, as we investigate the standard works on child psychiatry, we see little reference to childhood depression or grief. The psychoanalytic literature, however, includes a number of papers on maternal deprivation[3] and on grief and depression in very young children and infants.[4] Rene Spitz noted that 19 foundling-home infants developed symptoms of weeping, withdrawal, and a "sad or depressed expression . . . which often impels [the observer] to ask whether the child is sick."[5] Bettelheim describes two children who he thought had clear symptoms of depression.[6] Some of the most significant work on depression in children is contained in some of the literature on school phobia. In fact Campbell says, "Seventy-five per cent if not more of otherwise well-adjusted children who develop school phobia are really suffering from an endogenous depression."[7]

Agras, in his report of seven cases of school phobia at Montreal Children's Hospital, says, "Depressive symptoms were shown by six of the seven children. The most common, which occurred in six cases, was frequent outbursts of weeping coming on for no apparent reason in a previously happy child, together with a great deal of unhappy, miserable, whining behavior. Three manifested both fear of dying and a wish to die, and one made several suicidal gestures. It is suggested that these children show a syndrome comprising depressive anxiety, mania, somatic complaints, phobia, and paranoid ideation."[8]

In reviewing the bulk of psychiatric literature or visiting institutions for disturbed children, however, one gets the impression that childhood depressions do not occur, or, if they do, are of little consequence. Many times visitors to our youth center comment, "This looks like any other school—these children don't seem to be sick. They run and play, laugh and shout, and it's difficult to see anything wrong with most of them." About the surface impression, one must agree, but the insider who is familiar with the plaintive backgrounds, the evidences of indifference and rejection by parents, and the tragedies of divorce and death realizes only too well that a child's veneer of indifference or buoyancy and optimism may hide considerable grief and lonely dejection.

We think workers in child psychiatry have a responsibility to make every

[3]A. M. Earle and B. V. Earle, "Early Maternal Deprivation and Later Psychiatric Illness," *American Journal of Orthopsychiatry*, Vol. 31, January 1961, pp. 181-186.

[4]John Bowlby, "Grief and Mourning in Infancy and Early Childhood," *The Psychoanalytic Study of the Child*, Vol. 15, 1960, pp. 9-52.

[5]Rene A. Spitz, "Anaclitic Depression: An Inquiry Into the Genesis of Psychiatric Conditions in Early Childhood," *The Psychoanalytic Study of the Child*, Vol. 2, 1946, pp. 313-342.

[6]Bruno Bettelheim, *Truants From Life: The Rehabilitation of Emotionally Disturbed Children*, Free Press, Glencoe, Illinois, 1955, pp. 76-77, 136-137, 188-189.

[7]John D. Campbell, "Manic-Depressive Disease in Children," *Journal of the American Medical Association*, Vol. 158, May 21, 1955, pp. 154-157.

[8]Stewart Agras, "The Relationship of School Phobia to Childhood Depression," *American Journal of Psychiatry*, Vol. 116, December 1959, pp. 533-536.

effort to acquire techniques for discovering children in the earlier phases of emotional upset. Which child will become depressed? Which one paranoid, phobic, hysterical, obsessive-compulsive, cyclothymic, sociopathic, sexually deviant? Our belief that early indications of disturbance are discernible is based on our empirical observations of children who, in our opinion, show colorings of depressive reaction that could intensify in adult life.

We believe that the label "adjustment reaction" of childhood or adolescence is a vague diagnostic catchall that fails to communicate enough information. We suggest that when revisions are made in the classifications of childhood disorders, developmental factors should be heavily weighed and childhood depressions be carefully delineated. Categories of depressions of childhood might be:

Grief Response (Functional Depression)
> Overt depression manifested by feelings of futility, guilt, unworthiness, or self-destruction
> Depression masked by manipulative expression
> Depression masked by denial
> Depression masked by hostility
> Depression associated with withdrawal and fantasy

Endogenous Depressive Diathesis (A term that implies an idiopathic constitutional tendency; possibly the early manic depressive should be so categorized.)

Depression Associated with Cultural Deprivation (A circumstance in which there is insufficient stimulation, which results in listlessness and apathy)

Depression Associated With Physical Incapacity
> Medical disorders (diabetes, polio, muscular dystrophy, etc.)
> Mutilation (amputation, burns, etc.)

Drug-Induced Pseudo-Depression (A type of reaction that occasionally occurs when hypnotics, anticonvulsants, or sedatives are used in the treatment of emotional or physical disorders)

Examples of these depressions can be seen in several case vignettes of children admitted to our hospital. Although we realize that children rarely present clear-cut illnesses or syndromes and that no child fits neatly into any one category, the attempt at categorization aids comparison, assessment of treatment methods, and statistical reporting of diagnoses.

Grief Response (Functional Depression). We believe that functional depressions in childhood are not easily engendered. Children seem to tolerate a wide range of family upsets without losing faith or becoming disordered. Their natural resiliency and their magical belief in inevitable happiness permit them to ride out many of life's storms with little feeling of threat or anxiety. The initiation of depressive feelings seems to require tragedy or stark rejection; some youngsters can handle these amazingly well if they find their way to some loving, supportive, predictable environment, where wisdom is provided to absorb expressions of grief or fear without retaliation. But if the child's adult world fails to help him compensate for grief or rejection, his ego development is undoubtedly impaired, although the damage is not always obvious at once.

Instead of expressing feelings or yielding to futility or hopelessness, children seem to act out their inner lives in a variety of ways. Gyomroi, in her account of the analysis of a young girl who had been in a concentration camp, noted how "exaggeratedly cheerful" the girl and her sister were, in spite of their deprivation and trauma.[9]

Under the threat of rejection or grief, children with certain ego defects may act out in various ways that actually mask depression. That is the way in which they deal with a conscious or at least a preconscious death wish.

Overt depression. Occasionally, we see a child, usually an older one, whose response resembles that seen in adults, except that the onset of the depression is usually abrupt and its duration brief. Such children manifest feelings of futility, worthlessness, guilt, and even self-destruction, and they give in to inertia, disinterest, and dejection. Although it is not common, children do commit suicide. In the youth program at Utah State Hospital, a large number of youngsters have made suicidal gestures, usually symptomatic of a depressive reaction. As Karl Menninger has said about suicide, "It does hurt the 'other fellow,' the relatives . . . . The revenge is a childishly dramatic but a fearful and effective one."[10]

Until children are in the prepubescent or adolescent years, their grief rarely leads them to consciously entertain a death wish. We think that certain youngsters experience depression when their egos are too weak to master the anxieties associated with increased sexual drives. We have seen serious suicidal gestures made by youngsters with homosexual orientation and by guilt-ridden perfectionists who cannot accept their budding sexual inclinations.

Roger was an example of the latter. He was 17 when he was admitted and six weeks before had attempted suicide by shooting himself under the chin with a .22 rifle. He did not lose consciousness, and when his parents found him, he said that he wanted to die. After he had spent 35 days in a private hospital, his psychiatrist referred him to us.

Roger's attempted suicide was a surprise to everyone. His parents recalled that he had seemed somewhat discouraged and preoccupied in recent weeks, but they had always regarded him as a predictable, fairly well-adjusted boy, although shy and self-conscious about his acne.

Roger's family lived by the high standards of their church and the

[9]Edith Ludowyk Gyomroi, "The Analysis of a Young Concentration Camp Victim," *The Psychoanalytic Study of the Child,* Vol. 18, 1963, pp. 484-510.
[10]Karl A. Menninger, *The Human Mind,* third edition, Knopf, New York City, 1947, p. 125.

community. Two older brothers had completed missions for the Mormon Church, and other siblings were described as good students or "accomplished." Roger had always been regarded as an optimist; he constantly tried to "build himself up" physically and mentally. He achieved the rank of Eagle Scout and had perfect attendance at church meetings. This struggle for perfection, however, was in contrast to prolonged incestuous feelings for one of his sisters; his parents had also been surprised, on one occasion, to find him looking at photographs of nude women. The day after Roger's last school report arrived, showing one B, two Cs, one D, and one E, he made the suicide attempt. His parents were surprised that the sister was not upset after the incident; on the contrary, she seemed calm and unconcerned, as though it was to be expected.

On admission to our youth center, Roger showed no sign of depression, and his psychiatrist made a diagnosis of "situational adjustment of adolescence." He remained in the hospital for eight months and was a model patient—cooperative, friendly, and eager to do well in school. He was active in the center's program and in group therapy, but denied that he had any problem. It is unlikely that he profited greatly by his experience with us, although undoubtedly he must have learned that perfection is not the only approach to life. When he was discharged, the psychiatrist wrote, "Basically, he continues to be a rather compulsive perfectionist who has little flexibility. This may cause him trouble in the future." Since we last saw him, he has successfully completed one year of college without any problems.

Certain accident-prone children seem to be overtly depressed. We have a group of patients who constantly suffer physical injuries and who sometimes seem to invite the injury. We are not talking about hyperactive youngsters, who are sometimes accident-prone, but not deliberately. We are speaking here of children who invite serious injuries in a way that implies total disregard for life.

Doris, a tall, angular 12-year-old, fits into this category. She had the reputation of being rebellious, defiant, and hedonistic. During her hospitalization she often had to be treated for somatic complaints and minor injuries. Throughout her hospital stay she was hyperactive and accident-prone, and we believe these reactions were basically defense mechanisms against underlying intense depression. When she cut her legs or arms or jumped from stairs or ramps, her basic depression would sometimes be revealed. She seemed to incite other children into similar self-destructive behavior, and for several months we had an epidemic of cut wrists and other injuries.

When Doris was three, her mother had deserted her weak, unaffectionate father, who then placed the child with relatives or a baby sitter while he worked. When she was five, he married a divorcee, who brought with her three daughters, all under eight. She was opinionated and aggressive, and she and Doris constantly clashed. Doris complained bitterly about her stepmother's alleged cruelty, saying she beat her, but at other times she staunchly defended her, saying how much she loved her stepmother and her father.

We made several attempts to involve the family in Doris's treatment and tried to arrange more frequent visits home. The family always had an excuse, which masked basic rejection and an obvious reluctance to take the child back into the home. Doris was aware of this rejection much earlier than we were and used bubbling, effervescent behavior as a defense against her depressive feelings.

In time she improved and developed meaningful relationships with hospital staff. Through these she became able to deal more realistically with her feelings. Her pathological tendency to self-destruction waned. At this time her natural mother became interested in her and came to the hospital, accompanied by Doris's father, to request us to release Doris to her. The father reversed his previous attitude and vouched for the mother's integrity and stability. We crossed our fingers and released the child to her care. Unfortunately things did not go well for Doris. She ran away from home, was placed in a hospital out of state, and finally was referred to a disciplinary school for girls. Recently we received word from that state that she committed suicide while in an institution there.

Depression masked by manipulative expression. After experiencing a depressive insult and perhaps demonstrating a wish to die, hurt children learn that pushing the panic button results in attention and certain gratifications they might not otherwise experience. They learn that by making suicidal threats and gestures, they can achieve secondary gains. A child who acquires that pattern of behavior is most distressing and difficult to deal with. He often has the adults in his life practically standing on their heads to please him. By the time such children reach clinical help, they have learned other manipulative techniques, and some are well on their way toward sociopathic behavior. Those are the most difficult children to diagnose and to treat, because it seems ridiculous that a child who has become callous and indifferent in his relations with others has a depressive core.

Sixteen-year-old Julia was such a child. She came into the hospital under considerable pressure from the juvenile court. She was defiant, uncooperative, sullen, and pseudosophisticated. Many staff members could not believe that this worldly young woman was really an adolescent.

Julia's initial behavior in the hospital was uncooperative. She threatened to go AWOL, sign out, or commit suicide. Previous suicide gestures and severe conflicts with her mother had led to her becoming involved with school social workers and various agencies while she was only in the sixth grade. She had above-average intelligence, and it, plus her deceptiveness, made her an expert in manipulating others and irritating her mother. She was placed in a foster home, from which she and a girl-friend ran away. Their spree culminated in an automobile accident in which a male companion was killed and Julia badly injured. After recovery she was sent back to Utah, and she was threatened with placement in the state industrial school unless she would "voluntarily" come to our hospital.

We tried to maintain a consistent, structured, and yet understanding environment for her. We insisted that she attend school regularly and that her behavior become predictable and responsible before we granted any privileges. Although she tested the limits constantly, she learned that we meant what we said. Her defiance, sociopathic behavior, sophistication, and manipulations gave way to self-examination, and at one point she showed profound depressive feelings that led us to believe that she did indeed have suicidal tendencies. We continued family therapy with Julia, her mother, and her third stepfather. Although the treatment was punctuated by frequent explosions and upsets, it did help effect a more stable family adjustment. Julia was released to return to her family, and she completed the school year at her local high school. During the summer she married a young man and at the time of our last contact was making a good individual as well as marital adjustment.

Depression masked by denial. A number of children seem to require almost constant euphoria to tolerate daily routine. Many of them come from deprived homes where rejection or tragedy has been violent. In the face of an impossible environment, the youngster has resorted to vigorous denial. Such children are lively, effervescent, and restless and in no way express conscious depression. Their friends describe them as lovely, happy children; everyone is incredulous when such a child becomes overtly psychotic or makes a suicidal gesture.

Susan, a 14-year-old, was admitted to our hospital in January 1966. Up to the previous October, she was apparently well adjusted and was described as being an attractive, animated, coquettish young lady with above-average talents. She was popular with her peers and a favorite of teachers and other significant adults. She attended church regularly and received many awards and honors. It was a shock to friends and family when she broke down and showed the depression and disturbance that led to her admission.

The symptoms of this disturbance had become apparent in October 1965 when she experienced uncontrollable shaking spells that lasted three to four minutes. The family doctor diagnosed hypoglycemia, but this diagnosis was not verified by other doctors. However, she was treated for hypoglycemia, without response, and in fact the spells became more severe. In December she was referred to a psychiatrist for evaluation and treatment; he placed her on medication and saw her once a week. She suddenly became depressed; she cried out frequently and spoke of the futility of living. She openly criticized her parents and told school counselors and teachers that she was unhappy at home. She asked several adults at school and at church to take her home with them and not make her return to her parents.

Susan is the oldest of the four girls of her mother's second marriage. All her life she had lived with her natural parents. Two older half brothers, now living away from home, have been in trouble most of their lives. Two of her full sisters are demonstrating some problems. Her parents have had marital problems; the father is a borderline alcoholic. He is unreasonable, demanding, and rejecting. The mother tries to mediate between husband and children but usually gets caught in the middle. She feels guilty about the plight of her daughters, but is helpless to remedy the situation. After a trial separation of six months, the parents worked out some compromises and came back together "for the sake of the children."

By January 1966 Susan's symptoms became more acute, and she made several attempts at suicide. It was at this point that her psychiatrist referred her to us for residential treatment. She adjusted well to our program, made friends on the ward, and was highly regarded by peers and staff. She was cooperative, friendly, and eager to please. She did well in school and was a student government leader. At times, however, signs of depression broke through her friendly veneer. She would cry and utter recriminations against herself and her family.

One of us met with Susan and her family several times. Outwardly the family was gay, friendly, jocular, and cooperative. However, it soon become evident that they were all resisting treatment by refusing to discuss their feelings or the family problems. When the father was not present, the mother and children criticized him; the mother wanted help, but had trouble moving against her husband. The father denied that the family had significant problems, and he attended the sessions only as a way to get Susan out of the hospital.

We finally confronted the family and the father in particular with the many problems in the home, and we frankly discussed his resistance to treatment and his family's fear of him. As a result he signed Susan out of the hospital against medical advice and refused any further treatment effort. He had taken similar action with other agencies that had become involved with the family because of the problems his daughters were having.

Depression masked by hostility. In the face of continued rejection, an unloved, rejected child may be unable to neutralize his depression and may resort to expressing hostility. His behavior is often overactive, which further impairs his relationships with significant adults and results in their rejecting him even more. To all outward appearances, such a child is aggressive, yet the initial insult of being unloved and rejected would foster depression. Depressive feelings can come to the surface when hostilities are adequately dealt with. Once the depression is acknowledged, expressed, and compensated for, ego development can continue.

When Helen was admitted in April 1964, she was 15. Her history reeked of hyperactivity, hostility, and assaultive behavior. "I ran away from home 35 times in the last three years, and I've been in one detention home or another ten different times," she said almost proudly. She had made every effort to be a problem child since her parents' divorce ten years earlier. She was the child of her father's second marriage, and when he married a third time, his wife would not take her to live with them. Helen's natural mother had also remarried, and

Helen had lived with her grandmother, who on occasion told others that Helen was her least-favored grandchild. The parents later moved out of state and surrendered the child to the welfare department.

On many occasions Helen tried to run away from her grandmother's home and even made her way out of the state to contact her father. Each time she was returned to her grandmother. Her disruptive behavior resulted in two hospitalizations before she came to us, and we were told that on each admission she had been delusional and was hallucinating. Just before she was admitted to our hospital, she had been living in a girls' group home, where she was described as being destructive, assaultive, hyperactive, and impossible to control.

Personnel at Utah State Hospital will long remember this child. She proved to be the most rebellious, disruptive, assaultive hospital patient we had had in many years. She struck or bit the attendants, inflicted lacerations on helpless patients, and constantly attempted to elope. She made multiple suicide gestures, usually in the form of superficial wrist lacerations, but on occasion would impulsively thrust her fist through a window or leap from the top of a stairway to a concrete floor below. In spite of her reckless behavior, she sustained no serious injury. She constantly mobilized hostility in other children. Our limits and our patience were severely tested.

Month after month Helen crashed in and out of our program, leaving disarray and confusion behind her. Gradually her hostilities lessened, and she began to take an interest in certain staff members. As her destructive behavior abated, she began to mobilize and express her assets, and she revealed herself as an intelligent, creative youngster, hungry for acceptance and involvement. As she improved, she became more obviously depressed and gave way to quiet, petulant periods during which she spoke of her discouragement and sense of futility. Staff members reached out to her, and the attendants who related best to her helped influence her toward more acceptable goals.

Meanwhile she began to show an interest in some of our younger children and demonstrated a tenderness and empathy for them that prompted us to discontinue her own group therapy and include her as a "subtherapist" with our younger children. Helen was placed in a girls' group home several months ago and began her senior year in high school. Despite several problems she has made a rather amazing adjustment, and we are very encouraged about her prospects.

Depression associated with withdrawal and fantasy. Some children, when rejected or traumatized by tragedy, give way to preoccupation, withdrawal, and fantasy. There may be all degrees of compensation expressed in this fashion, and undoubtedly we are calling some of the severe manifestations schizophrenia. Jerry, 17, originally received a diagnosis of "schizophrenic reaction, schizo-affective type," but we came to regard him as a depressed individual who sometimes made frantic efforts to escape from his unhappiness into a world of unreality.

When he entered our program, his behavior was bizarre. He was hallucinating actively and had a variety of delusions. He thought he could cause
earthquakes, could save or destroy the world, had the cure for cancer, and could
understand all the problems of the universe. He was extremely overactive and
would assume bizarre postures and leap into the air. His affect was inappropriate, and he would glower fiercely or preach to those about him. His stream of
thought was characterized by clanging rhyme, punning, and push of speech that
approached flight of ideas. After he had been in the hospital a few days, he
startled the patients and staff by going quite seriously on a dinosaur-egg hunt.

Family members later confessed that Jerry had been in a similar mental
condition for several years. They had taken him to the county mental health
clinic, but the waiting list prevented his receiving immediate help. By the time
we saw Jerry, he had been out of school for two years, although he had attended
a technical trade school for several months.

Jerry and one sibling had been conceived out of wedlock, and although the
parents married later, their relationship was a stormy one, marked by several
separations. Ultimately they were divorced when Jerry was ten. The father
remarried promptly and lives in an adjacent town. After 18 months the mother
was remarried, to a man who was later sent to prison for writing fraudulent
checks. Jerry's mother has long been a welfare recipient. During these years
Jerry was regarded as a "likeable kid." He became interested in church activities
and a different value system than prevailed in his home.

During his hospitalization the boy recovered from his hypermanic behavior,
but revealed a depressive ego structure with little flexibility. His self-image did
not permit him to think he could make a satisfactory social adjustment. In spite
of that he continued to improve and did well in school. He was well liked by the
staff and patients and also by community acquaintances, notably the mayor and
the police chief, who, much to his surprise, took an interest in him. After a year
in our program, he became an outpatient. He became discouraged, however, and
impulsively enlisted in the army. He stayed in only a few months, and we do not
know the details of the difficulties he had in the service.

During his best periods of adjustment, Jerry's thought processes were
orderly and his affect appropriate. Unfortunately, the last time he paid us a
social call, we noted evidence of impending decompensation. Because he was a
voluntary patient, the responsibility for seeing that he gets further care if he
needs it rests with the community.

Endogenous Depressive Diathesis. Certain youngsters seem to have depressive predispositions with a lifelong proclivity for episodic relapse with no
apparent cause. Such children usually maintain a listless adjustment, but others
demonstrate violent mood swings that might appropriately be labeled manic-
depressive psychosis. Kraines says:

"Manic-depressive attacks may occur at any age. They are found in childhood and in advanced age. Statistically, fewer than 0.1 per cent under the age of 14 are in institutions for this disease. This incidence is probably too low, since many children have manic-depressive attacks which are variously misdiagnosed as 'phases,' 'anemia,' or 'reaction to stress.' Many misdiagnoses, no doubt, occur because children cannot adequately verbalize what they feel."[11]

In spite of treatment by some of the best-trained people in mental health, 15-year-old Dale continued to be victimized by cyclic, recurrent episodes, except within the sheltered environment of a hospital. Obviously environmental factors were important, but his depressive diathesis led to psychosis under the least pressure. He was admitted to our hospital early in 1964 and remained with us for more than two years, except for an experimental period of seven months, when he returned home and went to his regular high school.

Dale is the middle child in a family of five boys. His parents are professional people, talented, intelligent, and sincere. However, there is tremendous striving and competition among the children to achieve intellectually, academically, and athletically. The "family volume" seems to be turned up to a high, nerve-wracking pitch. Dale was never quite able to match the achievements of his brothers, and when under pressure, seemed to resort to fantasy and depression. We made efforts during family therapy to reduce the competitiveness that seemed to trigger his wide mood swings.

The onset of his illness occurred about three years before his admission here. He had an acute psychotic break with reality and expressed grandiose, expansive ideas. He had been hospitalized several times and had been treated individually by a private psychiatrist. He had also been in a private residential treatment center in California, but was so manic and destructive that the staff could not keep him in the program. In desperation his family brought him to us when our program started in March 1964. His early stay was characterized by cyclothymic states of "high" manic grandiose behavior followed by shorter periods of apathy and veiled depression.

Gradually Dale's moods stabilized, and he became one of the most responsible youngsters in our program. It was then that we put him on trial visit to attend his local high school. He got along well for several months, but relapsed, was rehospitalized, and, particularly during the summer, showed depressive features.

Six months ago he developed rheumatic fever and was placed on complete bed-rest. This proved to be a blessing in disguise. He of necessity learned to pace himself better and not to allow himself the luxury of excessive mood swings or unrealistic plans. Dale was released in June 1966 and has re-entered his local high school. Working with the school, we have tried to arrange an academic program with a minimum of competition and pressure. Dale seems to be prospering.

[11]Samuel Henry Kraines, *Mental Depressions and Their Treatment,* Macmillan Company, New York City, 1957, pp. 67-68.

Depression Associated With Cultural Deprivation. We have seen several children, and the literature reports others, who have been diagnosed as mentally retarded, whereas they are suffering from the results of an inadequate environment. Ego development can be strikingly impaired if significant adults fail to meet their responsibilities. The result may be a disinterested, inert, rejected child, whose depression is associated with the retardation of many mental functions. Such children develop almost vegetative self-images. They know they have been rejected, and they have no motivation to learn. Writing of this phenomenon, Publicover states:

"Children begin to learn almost immediately after birth. The basis for their learning is their relationship with the person who takes care of them, usually their mother. If the relationship is warm and nurturant, the child learns to look upon his mother as the purveyor of all good things. When the child is hungry, he cries. His mother comes to him and feeds him, cuddling him and talking sweet talk. The child has the basic need of hunger satisfied, and associates this closely with his mother. He learns to trust his mother. He wants to satisfy her so that she will not deprive him of food and affection. This is the basis of the desire to learn. If the parent thenceforth lets the child know that intellectual tasks, such as speaking and reading, are important, the child will do it. He is rewarded by his mother's affection, concern, and continued support.

"Look at the child who does not have this history. He is hungry and cries, and his mother, if she pays any attention at all, shoves a bottle in his mouth and leaves him. This child does not associate his mother with the feeding. He sees no particular reason to placate his mother or be nice to her. He does learn to be aggressive and active, for aggression and activity pay off. He learns a fatalistic attitude which generalizes to other aspects of life. We say he is emotionally disadvantaged . . . .

"The hypothesis is that these children do not do well because they have been brought up under circumstances in which they had little or no chance to learn the knowledge and attitudes and motivations that are necessary for success in our schools and in our society. For various reasons, they weren't ready for school when they came to school, and they have not been able to catch up, but, instead, get further and further behind."[12]

When nine-year-old Harry was admitted to the youth center, he appeared retarded and showed surface depression and rejection. He had been unable to complete the first grade because of learning difficulties and hyperactivity. He was brought to us dramatically by two police officers who were acting on a court order initiated by Harry's mother. He brought with him a life-sized, fully clothed dummy, which he said he had made so that he could have a friend.

Harry was the youngest of nine children; he had not been planned for and

[12]Robert G. Publicover, "The School and the Culturally Disadvantaged," *Utah State University Special Educator,* Vol. 1, Fall 1965, pp. 14-19.

was not wanted. His mother was an apathetic, uninterested, and inadequate woman. During Harry's first year she took to her bed with "sleeping sickness" and spent most of her time there. The father, a known alcoholic, was untalkative and seclusive unless he had been drinking, when he became garrulous and abusive.

Harry became increasingly active as he grew older, and soon the neighbors were complaining about his neglected state. He would wander around the neighborhood in various stages of undress. He did not get along well in public school, so he was sent to a school for retarded children. He was dismissed from there because his influence was disruptive and he did not seem to be profiting.

When he was admitted to the hospital, we quickly learned of his hat fetish. Perhaps it was symptomatic of his feeling that he was unwanted and was always about to be "sent someplace." At any rate we never saw him without a hat, indoors or out, and his collection seemed inexhaustible. After a few days he gave up his dummy, but never would yield his hats. We observed the hyperactivity that had been described, but when his needs were met, he favored a quiet role, and during thoughtful moments he would be wistfully tearful. He complained of missing his mother, but seemed to know he could not go home.

With time, Harry gave up his depressive tendency and became enthusiastic about the prospect of being in a foster home and going to public school. Nine months after discharge, his adjustment at the foster home has exceeded all expectations, and he is doing admirably in a special education class. The agency that referred Harry to us felt his prognosis was poor. It seems, however, that his ego elements were soon mobilized, and his future is quite hopeful.

Depression Associated With Physical Incapacity (medical disorders such as diabetes, polio, or muscular dystrophy; or mutilation, such as amputation, trauma, or burns). Children can be seriously disfigured or incapacitated and still not become depressed if their significant adults are supportive, interested, loving, and wise enough to help them express their interests and satisfactions in the ways open to them. Unfortunately many children with serious medical problems are managed by parents who are guilty, repelled, or overindulgent. Overt depression is frequently seen in these circumstances.

Drug-Induced Pseudo-Depression. This category must be included in any classification of depressions because many physicians prescribe various "tranquilizers" for emotionally upset children. Youngsters do not respond to medication as adults do; they are unpredictable and atypical and frequently demonstrate the opposite effect to that expected. We have occasionally seen older children who became quite depressed on phenothiazines, and we have seen several epileptic youngsters who were overmedicated and unresponsive.

Some brief comments about the youth center's approach to treatment may be appropriate. The over-all program of Utah State Hospital emphasizes social psychiatry rather than traditional psychotherapy. The therapeutic community model serves as the basic frame of reference from which we approach children. The milieu is well structured, predictable, and accepting. It maintains security of discipline, appropriate permissiveness, and support from warm, interested adults. Our program allows for ego growth, self-reliance, and creativity. It is designed to keep each child involved, to assiduously avoid the neglect that depressive patients seem to invite.

Each child must have tempered opportunities to ventilate and express the ego-alien ideas and feelings that accompany and usually cover his feelings of worthlessness, rejection, or grief. If he acts out, the program provides opportunities for immediate confrontation and support. We feel it is essential to keep pace with peer exchanges and to be aware of the peer dynamics among our patients. This is especially important with the depressed youngster who frequently expects support from his peers, but fails to get it. His needs make it impossible for other children to relate to him, and his failure alienates him even further from the group. His social exchanges are paced according to his capacity to handle them. Group therapy is an excellent pacing device and at the same time meets some of the child's needs for acceptance, belonging, and warmth.

All children require limits and schedules that are totally predictable. Because his acting-out tendencies thrive with idleness, the depressed child must never experience a time lag in his activities. We can reduce our expectations during the early management of these children, but must increase them as ego development occurs. We believe that intellectual tasks are part of the therapeutic process, and that teachers are key members of the treatment team.

We have little respect for drugs in managing depression in children. We have never given a child electroconvulsive therapy, and it has been over six years since an adult received this treatment in our hospital. We have not missed the procedure.

Family repair, through family therapy, has provided startling benefits in many cases, and we intend to expand and refine that program.

STUDENT SUICIDES
AND THE SCHOOL

Public schools and universities have unique responsibilities in the mental health sphere. School officials and teachers must be aware of the particular cultural physical, cultural, emotional, social, and spiritual factors which might make it very difficult for young people and especially adolescents to successfully adjust in various settings. These factors may range from a callous indifference to life to obsessive regard for life and the many responsibilities which might be attendant to attitudes about "sin," superstitions, or myths which impose complications on the developing personality. School officials frequently must deal with many age groups, many cultural representatives, many different religions, and many different value systems. Somehow, common denominators must be found and everyone must be brought to a better appreciation of each other's value system. In many regions of the country this seems like an almost impossible task, but certainly it must be appreciated and efforts made toward resolving the intense conflicts which might come into play as value systems clash or loyalties are stirred. Generations ago the melting pot phenomenon did not exist as dramatically as we see it today. Traveling experiences were limited, and we did not have the type of mass communications media of the modern age. Now it is virtually impossible to bury one's head in the sand, and for this reason a great movement has occurred among the youth who are demanding common sense morality, a common sense value system, defiance of hypocritical superstitutions, less civil contradictions, and insistence upon the worth of each individual. If the schools can sponsor such phenomena in a supervised thoughtful and constructive way future generations stand to benefit from the so-called "youth movement." The mature, well-informed teacher who can stand in the middle of the chaos and come to symbolize understanding, order, justice and discipline is in a position to do a great deal of preventive work in the mental health sphere. Unfortunately many teachers are finding campus life to be noisy, disruptive, disrespectful, and even dangerous. We are asking a lot of school officials when we ask them to cope with the multiple problems and processes at hand. Those who do so with a respectful or even reverent regard for youth will be the first contacts or sources of counsel during times of crisis with their students.

We must keep in mind that the school as an institution offers one of our greatest preventive potentials. The schools should serve as one of the front line defenses against self-destructive behavior. Prevention has to do with building a greater degree of immunity-producing experiences in our schools. This can be done through specific interventions at points where psychological discomfort of an individual can be predicted and where a little help can go a long way. Since school personnel often have close and extended exposure to young people, they are in a position to identify the early stages of crisis and can often intervene by offering adult support and guidance at the most strategic time. Many teachers do this every day, without any special realization of the mental health implications of their help. The teaching profession has never been confronted by a more challenging time and has never had such dramatic opportunities to dignify their profession.

The articles in this chapter deal with the incidence of student suicide, a description of how some schools may be unknowingly contributing to the problem, some plans for preventing student suicides, and suggestions for curricular experiences on death and self-destructive behavior prevention.

Student Suicide

Susan A. Winickoff and H. L. P. Resnik

At 11 P.M., one cold February night, an 18-year-old high school senior said good night to his girl friend, drove to a deserted road, and shot himself. Several hours later, the policeman who found him slumped over the steering wheel took him to a local hospital, where he was pronounced dead.

The whole community was shocked and startled by the news of this suicide, and yet, suicide among adolescents is not uncommon. Their suicide rate has been increasing slowly over the past 25 years until it is now the fourth leading cause of death among young people, exceeded only by accidents, malignancy, and homicide.

Statistically speaking, suicide is a significant problem for 15 to 19 year olds, among whom the rate is 4.0 per 100,000 population. It assumes even larger proportions in the 20 to 24 age group, where the rate is 8.4 per 100,000. Up to 10 years of age, it is virtually unknown; from 10 to 14 years, its rate is 0.5 per 100,000, which makes it a rate occurrence (2). Rare or not, however, suicide ought to be a significant concern in every age group because it is a preventable cause of death.

These figures almost certainly do not indicate the extent of suicide among youth, because suicidal deaths are often not reported. This is probably even more true in the case of youthful suicide than with adult suicide. In an attempt to spare the survivors the stigma of having a suicide in the family, many such deaths are falsely reported as accidental. To have a child suicide seems even more shameful for a family, and attempted concealment is probably more widespread. Nevertheless, available statistics reveal some interesting patterns.

In addition to the age breakdowns mentioned earlier, striking sex differences can be noted. About three times as many boys kill themselves as girls. No satisfactory explanation of this phenomenon has been offered, but it has been suggested that society's less tolerant attitude toward open emotional expression in males—coupled with greater availability of, and familiarity with, guns—may be important contributing factors.

Reprinted by permission from *Today's Education. NEA Journal,* April 1971.

The authors wish to acknowledge the assistance of Carol J. Hartz, fellow in suicidology, Saint Elizabeth's Hospital, Washington, D.C.

Recent findings show that the suicide rate among nonwhite males between the ages of 15 and 24 has increased markedly during the past decade. In fact, the rate is increasing faster than that of any other age group in the population. This very high rate for nonwhite males is accounted for largely by suicide among black adolescents in the cities and American Indian adolescents on reservations. The suicide problem for these groups may be a reflection of the significant degree of hopelessness and helplessness which they feel.

About 90 percent of suicides by young people between the ages of 10 and 14 are committed by means of firearms or hanging, with no appreciable differences between the sexes. In the 15 to 24 age group, males tend to use more violent means, such as firearms and hanging.

Females, on the other hand, use poisoning first, then firearms, then a variety of other means. This tendency of males to use firearms and females to use drugs holds true for all older age groups as well.

The discussion so far deals with completed suicides. The subject of suicide *attempts* cannot be discussed simultaneously, for in a large proportion of cases those who attempt suicide are not those who commit suicide. Fewer than 10 percent of those who attempt suicide later kill themselves; conversely, many people kill themselves without having made a previous attempt. No one knows how many attempts are made, for there is no uniform legal requirement that they be reported. In many cases, suicide attempts are not even recognized as such.

The ratio of attempts to completed suicides has been variously estimated; many people say there are 10 attempts for every completed suicide, but this figure is merely a guesstimate, not one based on hard data. In any case, it is known that adolescents, particularly adolescent girls, make a significant number of suicide attempts. Very few adolescent boys who commit suicide have made a prior attempt. Therefore, the following signals become most significant.

Several studies have been made of adolescent suicide attempts (note references 1, 4, 5, in bibliography). These attempts seem to fall into the following major categories:

A distress signal. The youth is saying, in effect, "Notice me. I need help badly."

An attempt to manipulate another. A teen-age girl may take an overdose of pills to persuade her boyfriend to come back to her.

An attempt to punish another. The youth is saying, usually to his parents, "You'll be sorry when I'm dead."

A manifestation of a mental disorder. In a severely disturbed, mentally ill condition, the child or adolescent may hear inner voices commanding him to kill himself.

An attempt to regain contact with a loved one who has died. A child may attempt suicide in order to join a deceased parent or sibling. This possibility may be stronger on the anniversary of the death of the person who meant a lot to the child.

A reaction to rejection. Children whose parents reject them may act out the wishes of their parents and attempt to kill themselves.

A result of overwhelming shame or guilt. To avoid facing an extremely painful situation, a young person may make a suicide attempt. Any situation could be seen as too painful by the involved student, although it might seem unimportant to the student's teacher or other adults. Such incidents may be as "minor" as the inability to get an A on a test, to turn in a paper on time, or to deal with a particular teacher or peer relationship.

LSD and other drugs may produce hallucinations and delusions which lead to suicide attempts. A youth may feel himself invulnerable to traffic or a bullet, or think he has the capacity to fly. Furthermore, the aftereffect of a nightmarish bad trip may so haunt an adolescent that he may kill himself in complete hopelessness.

Some adolescents with little prior difficulty uncover hitherto unconscious emotional conflicts under drug influence—conflicts that do not resolve themselves after the drug incident is over. Such continuing emotional conflict may precipitate a quick escape through death. There are also increasing reports of young people who are unable to kick the habit and who kill themselves in despair.

Even when the use of hard drugs does not result in attempted suicide, drug abuse should be recognized as grossly self-destructive behavior. When youngsters mix unknown drug combinations and use them indiscriminately, their behavior is as potentially lethal as playing Russian roulette.

Many of the reasons for attempted suicide also appear to have motivated completed suicides. However, the additional factors of social isolation, withdrawal, and inability to communicate are generally present in those who actually commit suicide as opposed to those who only make attempts. Investigations of school-age suicides indicate that chronic social isolation and a striking lack of involvement with either peers or teachers were prominent features (1, 3). Overwhelming loneliness is an intolerable state in which to live.

A suicide rarely occurs without warning. The warning may be in the form of verbal clues or it may be in the form of behavioral changes. Examples of verbal indications are either direct statements, such as "I'm going to kill myself" and "Life just isn't worth living," or indirect statements, such as "You won't be seeing me any more" or "That won't matter where I'm going" or "I'm no good." In any case, remarks like these should not be allowed to pass without some checking.

Bringing up the question of suicide will *not* put the idea into a youngster's head. As a matter of fact, a direct inquiry about suicide ideas, once you have determined something is wrong, can be most helpful. If one has already been thinking about it, it will be a relief to have the subject out in the open.

Behavioral changes which school personnel might notice include the following:

- A dramatic shift in quality of schoolwork;
- Changes in social behavior, including excessive use of drugs or alcohol;
- Changes in daily behavior and living patterns, such as extreme fatigue, boredom, decreased appetite, preoccupation, inability to concentrate;
- Overt signs of mental illness, such as delusions and hallucinations;
- Giving away prized possessions;
- Truancy.

Obviously, most of these warning signals are not specific to a suicidal crisis, but they should alert the sensitive teacher to consider depression and the possibility of suicide. They are signals that something potentially serious is wrong.

In the case of a socially isolated youngster who has no friends or close relationships with others, the presence of one or more of these clues bespeaks a serious situation. The teacher who notices these signals should follow up by finding out more about what is going on ("I've noticed that you can't seem to concentrate. Is something bothering you?") He should also refer the youngster to the school nurse, psychologist, or counselor.

Any action taken by one of these specialists should, of course, involve the child's parents, especially with the younger, school-age child. The teacher ought not to add the role of therapist to his already overburdened repertoire, but he should be able to recognize a child or adolescent who is having emotional difficulty and to take some responsibility for seeing that the youngster is put in touch with an appropriate resource person. In consultation with such an expert, the teacher can provide an ongoing source of emotional support.

Because young people rarely contact established suicide prevention centers or emergency mental health services, teen-agers in many parts of the country have set up their own hot lines, supported by flexible school administrators and teachers. Training and professional consultation provide ongoing support for this youth-oriented and youth-run type of service.

The Center for Studies of Suicide Prevention of the National Institute of Mental Health is sponsoring a National Hot Line Conference in June 1971, where teen-agers and college students will meet to discuss hot lines and their approaches to the crises faced by themselves and their peers. Inquiries should be directed to the CSSP Community Services Section, Room 12A-01, 5454 Wisconsin Avenue, Chevy Chase, Maryland 20015. Copies of a play called "Quiet Cries," which tells the story of an adolescent in a suicidal crisis, may be obtained from "Quiet Cries," CSSP Information Services, at the above address.

A final word is necessary about an often neglected area of mental health intervention. Called "postvention," it deals with the effects of a suicide upon the survivors—family, friends, and classmates.

If the suicide is a parent, counseling of the children is important, for all too often unexpressed guilt, depression, and subsequent suicidal behavior (as an identification) can follow. If a sibling has killed himself, the same intensive help should follow immediately. If a suicide occurs among a school population, it is important that the event be handled in some constructive way, not ignored.

Perhaps the school psychologist or someone from the community can hold an open meeting of the friends or classmates of the student where they can share their sense of loss, guilt, or bewilderment and discuss what action they would substitute for suicide if they felt overwhelmed.

The school psychologist or other school-oriented mental health specialist should be consulted about what kind of school activity, if any, should be planned after one of the students has committed suicide. Any activity must be appropriate to the age group involved and might well demand the consent of the parents of the pupils who are to be exposed. It would seem advisable that a schoolwide policy be established to serve as a guideline in the event of a student suicide.

The family in which a member has committed suicide frequently feels guilty and does not receive the support usually received when a death occurs. The teacher should be aware of this in dealing with siblings who may be in school and in any further dealings which he might have with the deceased child's parents. A notation about any suicidal event within a child's family might become part of that child's cumulative record. Of course, the issue of invasion of privacy would also have to be considered.

Teachers continuously hear the comment, "The whole child goes to school." We will not belabor the point here. However, the reader is reminded that it is the child with whom educators are to be concerned—the typical child and the atypical child, either or both of whom may be suicidal.

Suicide is not responsible for most adolescent deaths now, but the number of suicides is increasing among young people. A youngster in your own town, your own school, perhaps even in your own classroom, may be considering suicide at this very moment. The teacher who is alert to suggestions in this article and who acts accordingly may help prevent an unnecessary death.

REFERENCES

1. *Suicide Among Youth,* a supplement to the *Bulletin of Suicidology.* U. S. Government Printing Office, 1969.
2. *Vital Statistics of the United States—1967.* U. S. Department of Health, Education, and Welfare.

3. Reese, F. D. "School-Age Suicide: The Educational Parameters." *Dissertation Abstracts,* 27(9-A):2895-2896, 1967.
4. Toolan, J. "Suicide in Childhood and Adolescence." In Resnik, H. (Ed.) *Suicidal Behaviors: Diagnosis and Management.* Boston: Little, Brown and Co., 1968.
5. Teicher, J. "Why Adolescents Kill Themselves." *Mental Health Program Reports–4.* U. S. Department of Health, Education, and Welfare, 1970.

Meeting of the Minds

G. Murlin Welch

Why would a young man in the top five per cent of his high school class, who was a school leader respected by everyone, commit suicide? This was the question Shawnee Mission North High School was forced to face about two years ago when a student killed himself for no apparent reason.

Shawnee Mission, Kansas, is a suburb of Kansas City. The 2,300 students who attend North High School come from the upper-middle class. With some 75 per cent of the graduating class enrolling in colleges and universities, curriculum emphasis is on college preparation. Competition for grades is keen.

Besides pressures for grades, there is competition for school leadership and "making the team." All of the activities in the usual large high school are to be found at North High School, which has a proud tradition of scholastic, athletic, and forensic achievements.

This was the situation and the background as shocked teachers questioned why this tragic death occurred. They asked, "What did we do to contribute to this young man's problems?" "What could we have done to reduce the pressures he must have felt?" And, "Are there more students in our school who are potential suicides that we might have the opportunity to help?"

Out of the ensuing concern, a committee of faculty members representing all areas of study volunteered to work with the principal in examining school practices that might create tension in students. Within a short time, they recommended several immediate measures which were adopted for the 1966-67 school term.and are still being used.

A "PRESSURES PROGRAM"

The recommendations by the study committee were to: (1) establish a committee for the English department to provide a statement of acceptable work for all departments to follow; (2) designate a specific day of the week for different departments to give one-hour tests; (3) eliminate overlapping of outside reading among departments; (4) prepare a calendar to stagger deadlines for written reports; (5) regulate outside activities to some degree; (6) reevaluate

Reprinted by permission from *Theory into Practice,* Vol. VII, No. 1, February 1968.

honors classes by more careful screening of students and reduction of class size; (7) devise a procedure to advise teachers (in confidence) of unusual behavior problems; and (8) inform parents of pressures they unwittingly create.

However, the most crucial committee recommendation developed from a teacher's remark that it was "too bad" that the school did not have some way to reach all of the students to help them understand the pressures under which they work. As a result, one entire day was set aside and a "pressures program" was planned in which the student body had the opportunity both to listen to and discuss the complexities of modern life with each other, their parents, their teachers, and mental health experts—the program was called, "Meeting of the Minds."

The program included major addresses by Dr. Karl Menninger, of the Menninger Institute and Clinic in Topeka, and Dr. Frederick Hacker, of the Hacker Clinic, Hollywood, California. In addition, Dr. Donald C. Greaves, Professor and Chairman of the Department of Psychiatry, Kansas University Medical School arranged for ten local psychiatrists and psychologists to help explain the pressures under which teenagers live and work.

Following the talks by Dr. Menninger and Dr. Hacker, the student body, parents, and teachers were separated into ten groups for discussion sessions. For each group, this included a discussion by a psychiatrist or psychologist, a discussion by a parent-teacher panel, and a discussion by a student panel. For the final session of the day, students and parents returned to homerooms for additional informal discussions and evaluation—many remained for further talk even after the bell rang to dismiss school for the day.

Students responded enthusiastically to the idea of the program, and, although it was possible to use only forty students on the panels, over four hundred volunteered to participate. A faculty and student committee screened volunteers so that panels would include problem students, ordinary students, and school leaders. All of the English classes assigned students to write themes on pressures they felt and to express their concerns and submit questions they would like to have answered.

To preserve the contributions of the various persons on the program, every session and each panel discussion was taped. They were placed in the library and are used extensively by college research students, an evaluation team from the Menninger Clinic, students, teachers, and parents.

Although it is difficult and probably impossible to evaluate success in achieving all of the goals the program was designed to accomplish, some things were apparent to everyone—students became aware of their problems and openly discussed them. A comment they often made was, "We didn't know anyone cared." In many instances, students approached teachers, counselors, and administrators with problems that no one had ever suspected. Teachers became more aware of the student as a person, not merely as the recipient of subject matter.

FOUR AREAS OF PRESSURES

From their themes, questions, and comments for the pressures program,[1] it was possible to pinpoint four areas which seemed to produce the greatest pressures on students. These pressures are bound up in the parent's responses to his child, the teacher's responses to him as a student, the student's response to himself and his peers, and the area of psychological response which interacts on all three other areas simultaneously.

From Parents. The students' responses indicated that parents exert pressures which, although based upon a desire to help the child, sometimes bring impossible emotional burdens to bear. Many of these pressures are related to the grade a pupil receives in his classes. Too many parents apparently use their child's grades, if they are high, to feed their own egos—lowering of the child's grade results in a proportionate lowering of parental ego. Parents' response to failure is generally emotional—"O.K., no car this six weeks." The idea of being grounded for something that really cannot be helped results in no benefit either to child or parent.

Parents who expect their child to perform beyond his abilities create an impossible pressure situation for the pupil—this is especially true for the child who desperately wishes to please his parents but only seems doomed to displease them. Insistence upon a course of study which lies completely outside the pupil's interest or ability can have disastrous results.

Although unhappy home situations are often based upon circumstances beyond the school's control, certain efforts could be made to help relieve pressures which are carried into the school surroundings. For example, parents might be invited to a well-planned panel of teachers, counselors, students, and doctors, who could present some basic facts about the pressures young people face. This panel could include not only an outline of the "pressure points," but also an appeal to use wisdom in such things as "groundings," especially when the student is working to capacity. In addition, a closer, continuing parent-teacher relationship should be attempted. Conferences with parents of pupils who have received failing grades or those which have shown a serious and unexplained drop should be a requirement. Parents who are obviously applying pressures the pupil cannot cope with should be made aware of certain facts about the child's ability—painful as the experience might be.

From Teachers. Like parents, teachers, too, try to plan their students' lives—"If you make an A in chemistry, you're a chemist." However, as they were discussed by the students, most pressures from teachers basically resolve themselves into some relationship with grades. Teachers may consider their own assignments as having precedence over other school activities. As a result, they

---

[1]The discussion in the paragraphs which follow is based upon a report by Bob Wootton, English teacher at Shawnee Mission North High School, which summarized and evaluated the pressures students in the school identified.

sometimes create situations which make it nearly impossible for students to complete all of the assignments for a given day or week, if three or four other teachers are also making the same demands.

Students say that some teachers are apathetic or cold. They maintain a "sink or swim" attitude toward students, ignoring that the students may be incapable of doing anything except "sinking." Teachers give the impression that not education, but the "score" is the prime consideration; not learning but testing is the purpose of school. Cheating is a direct outgrowth of this. Emphasis upon grades alone should be relaxed. When "score" rather than the fuller educational potential of a class is primary, unwholesome pressures may result.

The solution to these problems belongs almost entirely with the teacher himself. A deemphasis of the grade as the best and final reward should be attempted. Testing devices and techniques should be subjected to harsh examination. A universally applied grading ideal, if not scale or schedule, should be applied. Ample time should be allowed for major projects. Departmental schedules of major test days should be worked out. Term papers, major themes, or lengthy reading assignments should not fall due in the same grading period.

Teachers should give special concern to the student who has disabilities that have already been identified by parents or psychiatrists. Although difficult, a relaxation of the secrecy between doctor and patient would unquestionably result in a better understanding by teachers of pupils' abilities to withstand the normal and healthy pressures which competition presents. If it were directed through rigidly controlled channels, information about psychiatric patients would be of great benefit to teachers; and, unless this information is available to the teacher, damage may result before the teacher is aware of the student's troubles.

From Students Themselves. Although parents and teachers exert heavy pressures, students also exert pressures both upon themselves and others. Such motivations as clothing, cars, as well as the unnatural pressures surrounding sex and drinking, may lie only vaguely within the province of school. Academic competition is one area over which some control may be exerted, however.

Many students take on unbearable work loads without realizing it. Their attempt to be "in" takes the form of multi-participation, forcing them to realign schedules so that there is little time left for enjoyment, reading for pleasure, listening to music, or just plain loafing. "Overload" may be the fault of parents, teachers, or students themselves—whatever the source, the school can help. In particular, strict examination should be given the practices which result in selection of students for accelerated classes. Standards should be established and maintained which would exclude those not really qualified or capable of competing in the honors program. Students should have the opportunity to indicate an interest in accelerated classes before they are accepted, and a strict limit should be imposed on the number of accelerated classes a student might carry.

Psychological Pressures. Although less apparent than the pressures involving parents, teachers, and students, psychological pressures will yield to intelligent attempts to reduce the number of situations which create such pressure. One student mentioned the "Unsuccess Syndrome." By his definition, this is the result of repeated and unrelieved failure in anything the child attempts. Efforts to create success-producing experiences should be made. Wider course offerings might help—in addition to college preparation, the curriculum could include vocational and industrial arts programs. Unneccessary scheduling pressures should be eliminated. Students should be allowed as much choice as possible in selection of teachers. A certain mobility should be permitted in the movement from one class to another. The "free period" should be freer; lunch periods more relaxed.

Although many problems may seem to resist solution, whatever time and effort is required should be willingly expended. The frank and open discussions which existed within the context of a pressures program at Shawnee Mission North High made it obvious that teachers and persons who work with children and adolescents can no longer dismiss the behavioral patterns they see daily as manifestations of the "spoiled child" or "toad." Schools should be involved in definitive efforts to aid children toward good adjustment, success, and happiness. The task is to shape and mold the child, not to break him.

School Age Suicide and the Educational Environment

Frederick D. Reese

"My report card is in my arithmetic book."

This was a note written shortly before an 11-year-old, Ohio sixth-grader put a .45 caliber automatic to his head, pulled the trigger, and killed himself.

What factors have brought such stress to bear on the life of a young person that he or she has seen no alternative but self-destruction? The fact that youth do kill themselves is in itself a sizeable social and personal tragedy. Suicide is the fourth leading cause of death in the 14 to 19 year age group, surpassed only by the accidents, malignant neoplasms, and homocides. The U.S. Bureau of Vital Statistics indicates that the numerical incidence of suicide in the United States exceeds 600 individuals per year in the age group 10 through 19.[1]

Added to the known suicides must be that unknown but considerable number of youths whose deaths go unreported as self-inflicted. According to Jacobziner and Bakwin, such youthful suicides are not so designated because of family pressure and lack of specific circumstantial evidence to support a coroner's verdict of suicide.[2,3] In addition to the known and suspected suicides, a far larger group of young people make an unsuccessful attempt to kill themselves. Faigel estimates that, for every successful suicide in adolescence, there are between 50 and 100 unsuccessful attempts.[4]

Psychologically, suicide can be viewed as escape behavior resulting from the interaction of the individual's inner emotional makeup with external stress or extreme social pressure.[5] From a behavioristic standpoint, suicide can also be seen as problem-solving behavior based on erroneous assumptions and conclu-

Reprinted by permission from *Theory into Practice,* Vol. VII, No. 1, February 1968.

[1]Vital Statistics of the United States, 1963, Volume II, Mortality, Part A, *U.S.H.E.W.,* Public Health Services, p. 246.

[2]Jacobziner, Harold. "Attempted Suicide in Adolescence," *Journal of American Medical Association,* Jan. 4, 1965, 191, 101-104.

[3]Bakwin, Harry. "Suicides and Children in School," *Journal of Pediatrics,* 1957, 50, 749-750.

[4]Faigel, Harris C. "Suicide Among Young Persons," *Clinical Pediatrics,* March 1966, 5, 187-190.

[5]Jackson, Don D. "Theories of Suicide," in *Clues to Suicide,* E. S. Schneidman and N. L. Farberow, editors. New York: McGraw-Hill Book Co., 1957, p. 16.

sions. Contrary to adult suicide, the young person often acts on impulse in the heat of anger or to some sudden environmental stress. Limited experience prevents him from seeking alternative solutions to problems which might seem of transitory importance to adults. A youth, in his inexperience, tends to view death as either reversible or a magical opportunity for rebirth and restitution for wrongs committed or suffered.[6]

SUICIDE AND SOCIAL ISOLATION

While the reasons for suicide vary from individual to individual, there is evidence that facets of the educational environment are associated with the act of suicide. From January 1960 through June 20, 1965, 164 Ohio youth (between the ages of 10 and 19) committed suicide. Investigation[7] of the educational environments and the circumstances surrounding the deaths of students who committed suicide during the academic years 1963-1964 and 1964-1965 revealed two findings related to the educational setting. The most striking of these was inadequate social identification within the school environment. Case after case revealed students who were, in a literal sense, almost unknown as individual personalities by both faculty and peers. Minimum social identification was particularly pronounced in larger schools where students were seemingly swallowed up in the press of a thousand or more classmates. Students in the large schools were remembered only as persons occupying certain seats and achieving particular academic levels over a given period of time. In not one case was there any significant personal interaction between the teachers and the student—there was a singular absence of knowledge of personal likes, ambitions, habits, and problems. Though less pronounced, in the smaller schools this phenomenon of social isolation was still in evidence. These students were known by the faculty, but in the majority of cases only superficially.

One example of such social isolation was a 16-year-old Caucasian boy, in the eleventh grade of a middle-class high school of 600, who wrapped himself in a plastic shower curtain and hung himself from a coat bar. A moody, withdrawn boy, he rarely participated in class unless called upon. The only exception was in the creative arts where he did outstanding work. He was vaguely seen by his peers as being "different," and, as far as could be determined, he had no close friends and participated in no sports or school activities. Analysis of the art and written work he did prior to his suicide revealed an increasing sense of isolation and despondency, and it is of clinical interest to note that shortly before his death he painted a picture of a shrouded figure hanging from a giblet. The general impression regarding this suicide was of a school and community culture

[6]*Ibid.*
[7]Reese, Frederick D. "School-Age Suicide: The Educational Parameters," doctoral dissertation, The Ohio State University, 1966.

foreign to the boy's personal needs, which resulted in social isolation, rejection, and a preoccupation with death as the means of escape.

One of the psychological characteristics of the adolescent is his involvement in close peer relationships and in conforming to group behavior. The suicides in the study were atypical. It was not that the desire to conform and interact was not present, but, rather, that these students, for the most part, did not function in this manner. As far as could be determined, the majority played no sports, joined no clubs, and had no hobbies. It should be mentioned that these were long-standing patterns of interaction and not of a transitory nature.

One of the primary goals of education is to develop social competency in students and, in these cases, the schools abdicated their responsibility. Meaningful relationships with other individuals are fundamental to the mental health of all persons—this is essential to emotional well-being. In school or after school, no realistic provisions were made to provide opportunities for students to relate with peers and faculty. The students most needing these relationships were the very ones who were least able to find an avenue of approach. In one instance, in a large metropolitan system, much of the student social life centered about a rigid fraternity-sorority organization established on the basis of social class standing. Moreover, these sororities and fraternities tended to be controlled by parents, not the school authorities. The result was that school-centered activities withered, and numerous students were excluded from meaningful social pursuits. Emerging from this study is a picture of students being left to their own devices in establishing relationships and participating in activities. Concentration in most of the schools centered on the academic aspects of education rather than the social-emotional needs of the student.

SUICIDE AND ACADEMIC FAILURE

Another pattern which emerged concerned the academic performance of the students who committed suicide. Half were doing failing or near failing work at the time of death. Intelligence tests indicated that one-quarter of these students scored below the fifteenth percentile, but no particular provisions were made for these students. Here were students who had been exposed to years of academic failure. In this area of academic failure, the educational involvement relating to suicide was indirect and inferential. In terms of the stated purpose of education as a growth-producing emotional and academic experience, it would be difficult to conceive how the educational experiences of these students could be so designated. In half the cases, the scholastic records were an unbroken series of poor and failing letter grades interspersed with notations of grade repetition. Several students were forced to compete in systems in which they could not possibly achieve academic success because they were being compared with more intellectually talented peers.

One case in point was a 17-year-old Caucasian farm boy who lived in a foster home and was in the ninth grade in a small rural school. His school history was one of extended failure dating back to the first grade. He had been held back three times and was doing "F" work at the time of his death. He was not a behavior problem and was seen as a pleasant, if retarded youngster, by the staff. He ranked at the seventh percentile of the Ohio Eighth Grade Achievement Test and was regarded as the poorest student in the school. Socially, he was rejected by his classmates, played no sports, and was in no activities. This boy became involved in an argument with his foster parents and was to be removed from the home—it was Christmas Eve. The prospect of being removed was simply too much. He hung himself from a rafter in a shed. The tragedy is that he was reported to be a likeable child, but in all his seventeen years he had been unable to find one single human being with whom he could form a meaningful relationship. The boy's educational experience, while not directly involved, was not supportive, and this boy desperately needed support.

Extended periods of failure and frustration lower the individual's self-concept to a point where there is little sense of self-worth. These students' educational experiences were nonsupportive and laden with frustration. Thus, this important segment of these individuals' life space was not conducive to personal growth. Since suicide represents a confirmation of negative inner emotional tensions coupled with stressful external factors, education for these children was one stressful external factor.

HELP WITH ADJUSTMENT PROBLEMS

Personal and social adjustment in youth can be looked on as a continuum. On one end of the scale is the young person who is achieving adequately, has meaningful social contacts, has a sense of self-worth, and is successfully able to face the problems inherent in living. On the other end of the scale is the youth who does not achieve and fails to develop growth-producing personal relationships. Such students drop out, some fight back and become delinquents, some withdraw into themselves, and some commit suicide, a tragic manifestation of maladaptive social behavior.

What can be done to alleviate this and concomitant problems of adjustment?

First, school must be recognized as a way of life and not merely an institution. This way of life demands that every student participate meaningfully in some social phase of this environment. In a psychological sense, this aspect overshadows the academic, but apparently little heed is given to it. Athletics, clubs, faculty-student relationships, and other activities should be so organized that no student is left in a social limbo year after year. This would, of course, involve deliberate programing, tact, and careful supervision. It does not mean individual coercion, but helping lonely students to achieve awareness of their worth through participation in school activities. This involvement is extremely necessary in metropolitan schools whose very size is inherently conducive to social isolation.

Second, the academic aspect of school life, traditionally uppermost in educator's minds, should be evaluated in a more realistic manner. Of what use are standards which all cannot possibly meet? This results in built-in academic failure which produces frustration, anger, and resentment. The sacrosanct use of letter grades has an extremely detrimental effect on students who are being compared to their more intellectually gifted peers. There are many alternatives which are more educationally and psychologically defensible and which have as their foundation the concept that learning takes place when students are rewarded for realistic achievement and not punished for unrealistic nonachievement.

Suicide in school-age students is a dramatic and tragic phenomenon which, in part, underscores some of the stressful forces prevailing in the educational environment. Research clearly indicates that social isolation is associated with the act of self-destruction. Educators must direct more effort toward creating the opportunity for all students to achieve meaningful social relationships. Such involvement must not be left to chance, but must be structured if it is to help rectify maladaptive social behavior. It is suspected that the benefits of a structured social program would also carry over into the academic realm. The student who has a satisfying social life is better able to employ his energies in a productive manner in the classroom. Suicide has also, through inference, indited the cumulative effects of academic failure on the student's personality. Many educators have suggested alternatives to the prevailing practice of using failing or near-failing grades to positively motivate behavior. Suicide, tragic as it is, may dramatically serve to highlight the need to nullify destructive stresses in schools and supplant them with systems which enhance social and intellectual growth.

A Plan for Preventing Student Suicide

Donald E. Berg

Any suicide prevention plan rests upon the tripod of knowledge regarding the dimensions of the problem, the superstitions and myths about suicide, and clues to suicide.

The first leg of the tripod is knowledge regarding the dimensions of the problem.

Suicide statistics must be called into question primarily because suicide, generally, is under-reported. Social, financial, religious, and cultural factors often force families to disguise the student suicide, for example, which is more often certified as accidental. Furthermore, certification by the coroner's office or medical examiner is sometimes difficult because of the unclear circumstances of the death and the stigma attached to suicide. An estimate of the under-reporting of suicide statistics runs as high as 200%. Let's look more closely at what the figures reveal.

Suicidal deaths do not occur before age 5 and are almost nonexistent prior to age 9. Between ages 10 and 14, suicide is so rare that the rate is less than one death per 200,000 children. However, in the age group 15 to 19 years old, death by suicide rises to four per 100,000. In the age range 20 to 24, the rate doubles again to more than 8 per 100,000. The national suicide rate for all ages is 11 per 100,000.

Two questions present themselves from this material. First, is the youthful suicide rate rising in the United States? The rate itself is not rising. In comparison with the rate over the past century, the current rate of youthful suicide has actually decreased. The major exception to this is the rate of nonwhite male suicides, which not only is increasing but is increasing faster than the population increase rate. Although the overall youthful suicide rate is not increasing, today there are more deaths by suicide among youth under 24 because this age group constitutes a larger portion of our population.

Second, how does suicide rank as a cause of youthful death? Suicide has increased its prominence not because the rate has increased but because youth die less from other causes. Improvements in sanitation, medical care, and

Reprinted by permission from *School Health Review*, September 1970.

pharmacology have all but eliminated many infectious diseases as major health problems. With this decline in mortality from infectious diseases, the relative importance of chronic diseases and violent deaths, such as suicide, has increased. In the age range 15 to 24, suicide is the fifth leading cause of death.

Furthermore, suicide still remains a special kind of guilt provoking tragedy. While it may rank only fifth overall as a cause of death, suicide is the number one cause of unnecessary, stigmatizing, and preventable death.

The second leg of the tripod consists of myths regarding suicide.

There are many myths of suicide, but I shall discuss nine of the most prevalent myths. The material is based upon an article by Alex D. Pokorny, (1) which I have adapted specifically to the problem of student suicide.

1. The student who talks about suicide won't commit suicide. While not all persons who talk about suicide go on to attempt or commit suicide, as many as 80% of all persons who have committed suicide have communicated their intent. This communication can range in complexity from a simple, straightforward sentence such as "Life isn't worth living anymore" to a much more subtle comment which contains within it the seeds of intent: "How about one last ride?" It is a myth that a person who talks about suicide will not attempt or commit suicide. However, communication of suicidal intent is complex and serves many purposes. Talking about it may be for the purpose of trying out the idea on friends, or appear to threaten or manipulate others. Kobler and Stotland have suggested that talking about suicide represents a plea by a hopeless person to other persons to restore lost hope.(2)

   The student who talks about suicide should be taken seriously. It is a disguised cry for help. It should not be treated lightly or be dismissed. It demands the same response you would give to a student who says clearly, "I need your help. I feel hopeless."

2. A second myth is that suicide happens without warning. Youthful suicides most often happen with advance warning. The warning may be forthright or so indirect as to be indiscernible. I will develop later a list of clues against which to measure the lethality of the suicide-prone student, but for now, any major changes in the behavior of a student accompanied by depression, isolation, and/or signs of mental illness constitute warnings.

3. If you are concerned that a student is considering suicide and ask about it, you may be planting the idea in his mind. This is a myth. If you suspect something is awry, it is because the clues have been clear enough so that you have become alarmed. If you broach the subject you will not be planting the seeds in the student's mind. Chances are great that the response may be positive, and the admission of suicidal thoughts often lessens their impact and opens the door for further discussion. If the student denies having such thoughts, nothing has been lost.

4. Suicide and attempted suicide are the same class of behavior. This appears

to be untrue. One person in 10 who attempts suicide will later go on to complete suicide. This means that nine of the 10 will attempt but will not go on to complete suicide. Also, adolescent girls attempt suicide eight times as often as their male peers, while the adolescent male suicide rate is double that of females. Female attempts are sometimes lightly dismissed as "just trying to get attention." Is there something wrong with needing and wanting attention? The point is that the youth who attempts suicide is shouting silently that all other methods have failed.

5. Another myth is that "good circumstances" will prevent suicide. This myth is the obverse of another: that suicide occurs more among the poor. Neither is true. Economic levels and suicide rates are not directly related. What is true is that suicidal youth are from families which are constantly moving under stress, causing social isolation. Social isolation cuts across all demographic, ethnic, economic, and social lines.

6. Suicide is a crazy or insane act performed only by the mentally ill. The evidence here is as yet unclear. The mentally ill child is a higher suicide risk than his "normal" colleague, but other factors must be present within his life space to predispose him to suicide. These factors include isolation, delusions (particularly "command" delusions in which someone is telling him to die), and the lack of any meaningful relationship. However, many students commit suicide who are not mentally ill.

7. Suicide is inherited. Here the evidence is overwhelming and unequivocal. Suicide is not a biological trait which is inherited. While suicide may occur in successive generations of families, the transmission of suicidality is a social and psychological phenomenon. It is not biologically transmitted. This is an especially insidious misperception. Many persons today live with the fear that, because a relative committed suicide, at some point in their lives they will become susceptible. The knowledge that suicide proneness is not biologically inherited in itself is a relief.

However, the young person who has suffered the loss of a parent early in life by whatever means of death may, because of the nurture which was also lost, find it difficult to develop satisfying emotional relationships later in life. Not the loss of the loved parent, but the loss of that parent's love is what is crucial. If, because of this loss, the young person cannot develop gratifying relationships, the subsequent isolation can lead to thoughts of suicide.

8. The student who attempts suicide is fully intent on dying. Persons who attempt suicide are not fully intent on dying. They are intent on changing something, to restore a lost relationship, to recover self-esteem, to escape from an intolerable situation, or to activate support and a response by significant others. Even at the moment of decision, there is a wish to be rescued, a hope for another way, a counterforce for life.

9. Once a person is suicidal he is suicidal forever. Edwin Shneidman has

described the debate of life versus death that rages within the person who feels hopeless and helpless as "the congress of the mind." (3) At the point of taking one's own life, the debate has temporarily, and I stress temporarily, diminished the voices of hope. The debate has raged long, and this momentary victory may lead to suicidal action.

Who among us has not, however lightly or seriously, considered suicide as an alternative? But it would be grossly unfair to say that all of us are therefore suicidal. Thoughts about and actions leading to suicide come and go depending upon a tapestry of forces, and for most who are suicidal they are so for only a limited period of time. And if, in fact, the forces within their life space change for the better, they may never be suicidal again.

The third leg of the tripod is: What are the clues to suicide?

It is possible to identify the suicide susceptible student? The following clues to suicide (4) must be viewed through a prism on which is printed, in bold type, isolation. None of the following clues to suicide exists separately from isolation. Even combinations of them, apart from the concept of isolation, are not indicative of high lethality.

I shall approach the complex area of clues to suicide from three vantage points: observable changes in behavior, observable changes in emotional factors, and other characteristics within the student's life space.

Observable changes in behavior include the following.

1. Sudden and unexplainable neglect of school work.
   When a good or outstanding student suddenly begins to perform poorly it is a danger sign and requires exploration.
2. Decrease in the ability to communicate.
   When the student dramatically shifts his communication patterns, particularly among peers, the noncommunication is a communication of need.
3. Changes in daily living patterns.
   Decreased appetite, psychosomatic complaints, sudden loss of weight, and insomnia all point clearly to a need for help.
4. Changes in social behavior.
   Sudden, serious use of alcohol or drugs, promiscuity, and violent outbursts complete the picture of behavioral clues to suicide.
   Observable changes in the student's emotional life may involve the following.
1. Low self-esteem or self-deprecation.
   The adolescent, of course, is characterized by mood swings. It is a time of life to be up and to be down as the adolescent gropes for a consistent identity. For the troubled adolescent there are few ups.
2. Depression.
   This depression as a clue is not, again, the prolonged down period of the adolescent mood swing. It is more pervasive, characterized by aloofness and

withdrawal, and the tragedy is that the depression itself further increases isolation.

3. Hallucinations and delusions.

While it is not true that all mentally ill students attempt suicide, it is true that a considerable number of students who commit suicide have suffered from hallucinations and delusions. Fortunately, when these occur within the context of a school setting the evidence is so clear-cut, and the impact on the setting so great, that counseling or psychiatric help is sought immediately. Other characteristics of a student's life space also form clues to suicide.

1. A family life marked by long-standing conflict, accompanied by rootlessness or transience.

Obviously, not all children who come from broken or conflict-ridden homes choose suicide as the only escape. This clue to suicide must always be placed in the context of relationships with other relationships. What is important about conflict and the transience is not that it occurs, but rather how well the student can make new friends, relate significantly to elders and peers, and so seek, in his larger society, that which he is denied within the confines of his family.

2. The death or loss of a parent or significant other.

This is more crucial the younger the child is. Again, the loss needs to be considered within a matrix of other relationships. Unfortunately, many family units move from a community following a loss of one of the parents, particularly by suicide, thus throwing an added weight onto the burden of the loss. Clearly, if a student enters a class at the beginning of the year or in the middle of a year and moving to the community was occasioned by the death of one of the parents or a sibling, the student deserves special attention in terms of concentrated efforts to help him become involved and to develop new relationships.

3. A history of long-standing problems with recent escalation of certain of the problems.

Students presenting the school system with problems over a long period of time suffer the fate of the shepherd who cried wolf once too often. Emotionally draining, constantly requiring some remedial action, the problems of the student come to be seen as a life style. Problems in students, however, may be cumulative unless some intervention is provided. When a student of this kind escalates the level of his dysfunctioning, someone needs to try to find out why.

Perhaps I have approached these clues like one of the blind men trying to describe an elephant. You may have been thinking that any of these clues are characteristic of any problem child in any class. I could not agree with you more. They are. It becomes a question, first of all, of severity, but secondly, and more importantly, of the overall concept of isolation.

It is through isolation that we must view any one or combination of these clues. The student who is peripheral, outside of normal activities; the loner, who may be doing extremely well in school precisely because the classroom work gives him momentary self-esteem; the student seen as odd and different—this is the student most suicide-prone. The teacher does not have to have a sixth sense or specialized training to observe these clues. Clues to suicide are very often clear if we are aware of how they fit together in a student who is isolated from significant emotional involvement with peers, parents, and educators.

We have discussed the extent of the problem of student suicide, we have discussed the myths and realities of suicide, and we have talked about observable clues to suicide. These are the three legs of the tripod upon which we can rest firmly a plan for the prevention of student suicide.

I shall not make the mistake of holding the educational system solely responsible for suicide prevention, as it has been held responsible for maintaining the morals of our society and the mental health of youth. I shall, however, urge a partnership and speak of the teacher's role in the whole cloth, which is student, teacher, administration, family, and community working together.

In discussing a plan for "suicide prevention," it is necessary to think about it in three complementary phases: prevention, intervention, and postvention. (5) Prevention is simply a plan for education: providing knowledge, demolishing myths, and sensitizing individuals to the existence of the problem. Intervention is simply the courses of action open to anyone faced with the problem of a student suicide. Postvention completes the cycle. It is a plan for reintegrating the student who attempts suicide and working with families in which there has been a completed suicide. Postvention is for the purpose of preventing destructive aftereffects.

A PLAN FOR PREVENTION

To begin with the teacher, a first concrete step would be to build into the junior high curriculum of social problems or health classes discussion about suicide. This would reduce the stigma attached to even talking about it. More importantly, it would encourage among students a discussion of two very important areas.

The first is that of the relationship between events and emotions. For all our so-called psychological sophistication, the vast majority of adolescents remain in the dark as to the forces behind their volatile and ricocheting feelings. This is no different than it has always been. Adolescence is such a private turmoil that the young student, beset by powerful feelings, assumes not only that he or she is undergoing those in isolation but that the feelings are without understandable cause. A frank discussion of the roots and causes of suicide leads to emotional self-knowledge.

Second, the sharing by students of similar feelings reduces dramatically the sense of isolation. So while the curriculum topic may be student suicide, the content will focus upon the importance of understanding emotions and how they influence behavior. Picture if you will for a moment an isolated student saddled with guilt, low self-esteem, or serious depression who hears, in a classroom, perhaps for the first time, that his classmates, whom he has viewed as different, luckier, or better off than himself, are beset by some of the same feelings. Picture if you will this same student beginning to understand that his feelings have causes, that he is not strange and that, while his feelings may run deeper, they are nevertheless the same feelings of his classmates. Can you imagine the impact this would have on the isolated student?

It appears there is some fear of introducing the topic of suicide into a curriculum. Actually, adults are more fearful and frightened of this than are students. The experience of the staff at the Crisis Clinic is that when we speak at assemblies or classes, it is difficult to end the discussion when time is up.

If there is difficulty in gathering together information for classwork, try these approaches: consult mental health professionals in the community; call on one of the more than 130 suicide prevention centers throughout the United States; seek out a competent therapist and request help; request back issues of The Bulletin of Suicidology or other information from the Center for Studies of Suicide Prevention, National Clearinghouse for Mental Health, National Institute of Mental Health, Chevy Chase, Maryland 20015.

There is a second role that the teacher can play in prevention. A school is a small society, regardless of how large it may be. The normal tendency is for a community to cover up a suicide attempt, to pretend that it didn't happen, to offer excuses for its happening, or to view the family in which it happened as strange and unapproachable. There is no better time to discuss suicide in a classroom than after a suicide attempt has taken place. It will certainly be talked about among the students—but otherwise in ignorance and fear.

There may be siblings of the deceased student in the same school. Give them the choice to participate or not and to decide upon the level of their involvement. Encourage discussion of the feelings and the ideas of the class. When these feelings and ideas have been expressed, the effective teacher can then present, in a thoughtful and sensitive manner, some of the things covered here.

In a community where student suicide is a continuing tragedy, act as a citizen to obtain information about what can be done. Some communities respond through the creation of emergency telephone services serving and staffed by students. Others have requested consultation and education from community mental health centers. It may be possible to initiate a community-wide suicide educational program.

Teachers are often the first to detect the clues to suicide. Long before the family physician, the clergyman, or even the parents become aware, the teacher may clearly see drastic changes in the life style of a student. A final point to remember is that honest, open, and kind confrontation of a student by a teacher who cares can literally save a life.

What is the role of administrators in suicide prevention? When teachers return from a conference and wish to include in the curriculum a discussion of suicide, the administrator should encourage it. If a student suicide has occurred in the school, seize the opportunity to encourage the staff to discuss it. Listen carefully to the emotional waves the suicide has created among the staff and be sensitive to the fact that those waves affect the student body as well.

Take another look at what the counseling staff is doing. Are they counseling—that is, are they sensitive to the emotional needs of students? Are they obtaining the kind of consultation that will make them better counselors? Are they given the educational opportunities that will enrich their role? Do they have basic knowledge of clues to suicide and steps for prevention? Or are they disciplinarians, only vocational counselors, or points of referral?

A PLAN FOR INTERVENTION

Beginning with the teacher, there are three possible points of intervention. The first is with the student directly. We hesitate to intervene, even though we may see serious clues to suicide, for fear that in some way we will have to assume the responsibility for then doing something about it. Intervention by teachers need not be for the purpose of solving the problem. That's not their role; they don't have time, and it may be impossible. Intervention by a teacher directly with the student is for the purpose of letting that student know that at least one person is aware that there is a problem. To considerately and openly point out that a change has been noticed is the first step toward a solution.

The second line of intervention is with the family, which requires tact. Don't confront a family with a suspicion that a child may be suicidal. It is enough to point out that a significant change in the student has occurred within the school setting. If the family is unaware of this, channels of communication between the teacher and the family need to be kept open to pave the way for the family to accept the need for the student to obtain outside help.

Realistically, since many of these students come from families already beset with many problems, talking to the family may not succeed. I would strongly suggest that the teacher then communicate his concern to someone else. If this means going to the administration of the school or directly into the community to family physician or clergyman, so be it.

The essential task of suicide intervention is to put the student in a relationship with someone with whom he can talk openly and honestly about his feelings. The goal is to find somebody who can serve this purpose, and the task is not to stop until that person is found.

There are several concrete things that can be done by the administrator to achieve the goal of intervention. This may be so basic that it needs no more than passing reference, but it is important that all staff and faculty clearly understand how far a teacher or counselor should go in order to achieve the goal of help for a disturbed student. In short, the system must not prevent the concerned educator from securing help for the suicidal student.

Establish close relationships with those resources in the community from which help can be obtained. The sources of help must extend beyond the boundaries of the school itself and into the community: to the hospitals, the police, clinics, physicians, and others. The liaison between the school and the helping community needs to be a two-way street.

The administrator is still a person of authority who can be called into action to assist in securing help for a child even though the family may be reluctant. The administration of a school sets its tone. The administrator is in a key position to influence the attitude toward emotional problems. It can be repressive, creating a closed system, or enlightened, fostering maturity. The school has a task to educate, and the student has a task to learn. No one succeeds when one or both parties in this partnership is isolated. It takes courage and patience to come to grips effectively with the suicidal student, but the alternatives are frightening.

A PLAN FOR POSTVENTION

For the student who has attempted suicide and returns to school, the teacher can reduce the isolation by reestablishing lines of communication. Perhaps because everyone who has come into contact with a student who has attempted suicide feels in some way responsible and, perhaps, feels somewhat guilty, or for whatever reason, the student who has chosen this type of cry for help often is left more isolated. This student needs to be integrated into the classroom, not in an excessive manner, but with some thought given to the circumstances of his isolation. Some teachers have used group assignments and projects, others have created manageable tasks that require the student to interact more with his peers. Whatever the plan, reduce the isolation.

Although rare, the phenomenon of a suicide epidemic does occur. The chances of this happening can be reduced if, following a student suicide, discussion can be created within the classroom as to the impact this has had on other students. Reach into the community for help with this. The point is that covering up or ignoring what everyone knows has happened is not helpful. Use the event wisely and creatively to tap the repercussions within the student body.

If, even in some small way, the stigma and shame surrounding a student suicide can be reduced, the beneficial repercussions will be great. If there are siblings, they too at this point need the involvement of their peers. This can only happen if the event itself has been openly discussed and rendered less mysterious and frightening.

The administrator's role in suicide postvention follows along the same lines described. The administrator is in a key position to do for the staff and faculty what the teacher can do for the class. By example, he can encourage staff and faculty discussion and develop a well thought out plan for reducing the isolation of the student who has attempted suicide or the family survivors of the student who has committed suicide. His stance will support and encourage or inhibit and discourage postventive attempts by his staff and faculty.

School personnel are in key positions to do something about the tragic problem of suicide among students. Health educators are in the unique position of having the opportunity to develop specialized relationships which cannot be accomplished very often in the more highly structured classes within the educational system. Use these specialized relationships, for after all, isn't that your calling? Doesn't educate mean to lead out? Leading a student out of the labyrinth of isolation with the power of a caring relationship is quite literally the essence of suicide prevention.

REFERENCES

1. Alex D. Pokorny, "Myths about Suicide," in *Suicidal Behaviors,* edited by H. L. P. Resnik (Boston: Little, Brown and Company, 1968).
2. A. L. Kobler and E. Stotland, *The End of Hope* (London: Glencoe Free Press, 1964).
3. Edwin S. Shneidman and Philip Mandelkorn, *How To Prevent Suicide,* Public Affairs Pamphlet No. 406 (New York: Public Affairs Committee, 1967).
4. Richard H. Seiden, "Suicide Among Youth," prepared for the Joint Commission on Mental Health of Children, Task Force III, published as a supplement to *The Bulletin of Suicidology,* National Clearinghouse for Mental Health Information, NIMH, Chevy Chase, Maryland 20015.
5. Edwin S. Shneidman, from a speech delivered to the International Association of Suicide Prevention, Los Angeles, in the fall of 1967.

The School Guidance Counselor as a Preventive Agent to Self-Destructive Behavior

Calvin J. Frederick

The problem of self-destructive behavior among younger age groups is becoming a matter of major concern and is receiving renewed attention from the Center for Studies of Suicide Prevention at the National Institute of Mental Health. Such disturbances create ever-increasing problems for school and college personnel as well. Until quite recently it was generally thought, even by many professionals, that youngsters below the age of 15 years rarely engaged in serious self-destructive behavior to the point of taking their own lives. As more and more evidence comes to the fore, it is clear that youngsters act out their frustrations in a multitude of ways, some of which are self-destructive.

Three terms are often used to describe behavior of this type. One is *self-assaultive behavior* which connotes an attack or an assault upon one's self that may or may not be suicidal. It is actually not uncommon for children to threaten injury to themselves as well as to others and, in some instances, carry it out. They may actually verbalize the fact by warning the parent or some parental surrogate that they are going to hurt themselves. It is *frequently* done by saying, in effect, "I'll punish myself before you can punish me." thus disarming the parent or the authority figure by conveying the message that "You can't do any more to me than I have already done to myself; hence, your punishment is a waste of time." In other instances, the youngsters will injure themselves and become "accident-prone" in order to gain sympathy and love which they feel is not forthcoming in other ways. *Usually* this stems either from sibling rivalry in an effort to draw attention away from the rival at any cost or from past situations which have led the youngster to believe that it is the most effective way of getting real love and affection from the parent.

The term *self-destructive behavior* applies to more serious cases than most behavior labeled *self-assaultive.* Although here too there are varying degrees of intensity, self-destructive, by definition, *ultimately* becomes synonymous with *suicidal behavior.* However, there are "psychological equivalents" of self-destruction which need to be recognized since they are often unconscious on the part of the individual committing such acts. An example of this kind of behavior

Reprinted by permission from *New York State Personnel Guidance Journal,* Vol. 5, No. 1, 1970.

can be found in the youngster who has some physical infirmity such as diabetes and fails to take insulin properly. There are varying degrees of understanding by the youngster regarding ideas of death, even among teenagers. It is not unusual for an obese girl who is diabetic to fail to take her insulin and go into a serious state of shock approaching fatality and in some instances eventuating in her demise. Despite an intellectualized understanding beforehand that she will go into shock and seriously endanger her life, some of these girls have immature and romanticized notions of death. They believe that they will somehow be saved at the last moment even though they have acted upon the situation in such a manner that this is not likely. In other cases, they believe they will live in another after-world in some manner. This belief therefore precludes the behavior from being really suicidal in their own minds.

There is very real doubt about the age at which youngsters really understand the concept of death, particularly suicidal death. The youngest instance in the author's experience is that of a five-year old who was extremely bright and after thorough examination of the youngster himself as well as his parents, it was apparent that he did understand the notion of self-destruction and was engaging in genuine suicidal attempts. Ordinarily, youngsters of that age are not thought to have a grasp of such concepts but it is possible that a small percentage do. The age at which youngsters seem to understand the nature of their actions in self-destructive behavior will vary with their cultural background, relationship to their parents, presence of older siblings who engage in self-destructive behavior, intelligence, and exposure to violence in and outside of the home.

There has been a sharp increase in committed suicides in the age group of 15-24 years over approximately the last decade. Although the suicide rate for males is 2 or 3 times that of females, the rate among non-white females has risen 183 per cent during that time. Among all the younger age groups, the rise has been greater among females than males and greater for non-whites than whites.

Suicidal behavior can be regarded as more unequivocal than the other two types. It is the intentioned cessation of human life. Some authors like Shneidman (Shneidman, 1968) included subintentioned groups as well. Being self-assaultive or self-destructive is not as far out on the continuum towards death as *suicidal behavior*. One can injure or destroy a part of oneself without actually taking one's life, of course. There is a finality to suicidal behavior which sets it apart from the others, even though the difference is only a matter of degree.

THE "GATE-KEEPER" OR PREVENTIVE
ROLE FOR THE GUIDANCE COUNSELOR

Youngsters who are genuinely suicidal usually do not consult directly with a family physician or a clinical psychologist. In the instance of youngsters, they are not likely to consult with parents, clergymen or anyone else *whom they do not trust.* They are more likely to consult with a peer and, thus, may obtain the necessary support and guidance they need. *If the school guidance counselor can establish the image of a stable and trustworthy friend,* then he or she can easily become one to whom a troubled youngster can turn in time of serious need. It is in this role of true friend and counselor, that the school professional in this field can render a unique, unmistakably gratifying and life-saving service to young people today. In order to help promote this role, the various signs of serious mental disorder and psychological first-aid principles will be outlined here.

SIGNS OF MENTAL DISORDER

Traditionally, there are two mental disorders which are often associated with suicidal acts. These are *depressive states* and *schizophrenic reactions.* In the context of self-destructive actions, some descriptive mention of each is worthwhile.

With adults particularly, there are various kinds of *depressive states* which can result in irrational behavior and serious consequences even though the depressive period may be temporary. There is a good deal of question in the thinking of most experts as to whether or not childhood disorders such as schizophrenic reactions and various depressive states constitute the same entity for both youngsters and adults. It is generally believed today that there is a negative correlation in causality with respect to these mental conditions and self-destructive behavior when comparing young persons and adults. While most youngsters appear to be depressed in the sense that they are down-cast and low in mood, one would hesitate to put them into one of the classical depressive states nosologically. Seiden (Seiden, 1969) points out that if depression is defined as a syndrome where there are feelings of pessimism, worthlessness and guilt, then these symptoms would be more likely to characterize adult suicides than those of youngsters. It is also of interest that many adult suicides are missed even by physicians, most of whom are not alert to the symptoms, since this body of knowledge has not been taught in medical schools because of the relatively recent appearance of the entire crisis-intervention field.

Only about one-third of the individuals who have committed suicide were diagnosed as falling into one of the traditional depressive states. These states for adults are: *manic-depressive psychoses,* which are marked by severe mood swings and the tendency to remission and recurrence frequently without any precipitating event; *involutional melancholia* where worry, anxiety and severe insomnia often accompany changes in middle life; *paranoid states* where mood and thought disorders are the central abnormalities without the presence of schizophrenia; *psychotic depressive reactions* where no history of mood swings is present but a severely debilitating depressive mood is attributable to some stressful experience; and *depressive neurosis* which is manifested by an excessive reaction of depression because of internal conflict or because of some identifiable event such as the loss of a loved object or cherished possession. It is difficult to place youngsters into these usual adult categories, simply because their personalities have not formed completely into a cardinal type.

When schizophrenia is operating, the depressive behavior and lowered mood is also accompanied by disorders of thinking which are rather bizarre. In addition, the behavior is likely to show regressive symptoms to a more childlike form along with some withdrawal and isolation. *Schizophrenic reactions* which are most likely to result in self-destructive behavior are: *schizophrenia, paranoid type,* where the individual tends to blame other people and shows a good deal of hostility and hallucinatory behavior which may be turned upon himself; *schizophrenia, schizoaffective type,* where there are symptoms with marked elation or depression accompanied by disordered and bizarre thinking; and *schizophrenia, catatonic type,* which is characterized by excessive and occasionally violent motor activity and excitement and/or by inhibition shown in stuporous behavior, mutism, negativism, and deterioration into a more childlike vegetative state *(Diagnostic and Statistical Manual of Mental Disorders,* 1968).

In schizophrenia as with depressive states, there is *a marked difference between youngsters and adults.* Very few adults who take their lives are diagnosed as schizophrenic, whereas *a sizeable number* of youngsters who have taken their lives have apparently experienced some kind of schizophrenic reaction including hallucinatory behavior.

Because of their lack of maturity, suicidal behavior among children *frequently* reveals that they tend to imitate the behavior of loved ones who have died. This is especially true if the family member himself has committed suicide, such as a parent, older sibling or a favorite uncle or aunt. Death seems to represent the chance for reunion with the lost one. Parents who reject children and in effect wish them dead or out of the way can precipitate self-destructive behavior in these children. This writer is convinced that severe punishment and child-abuse is *likely* to evoke violent behavior on the part of the recipient later, including suicidal behavior.

SYMPTOMS TO LOOK FOR IN POTENTIALLY SELF-DESTRUCTIVE YOUTH

The following list of behavioral clues should prove helpful to guidance counselors in their work with youngsters.

1. Adolescents contemplating suicide are not apt to communicate verbally with their parents at all. This, in fact, is part of the problem. They would be more likely to communicate with a peer or another interested individual in

whom they have some faith and trust. Thus, if the youngster says he cannot talk to his parents, the listener should be alert to the nuances of serious problems.

2. Behaviorally, they are more likely to give signs which are a cause for concern. They may give away a prized possession with the comment that he or she will not be needing it any longer.
3. The individual is apt to be more morose and isolated than usual.
4. While insomnia, worry and anorexia often appear, the youngster may not have all the classical signs of a depression. It is a mistake to feel that an individual will not take his life unless he is clinically depressed.
5. Young males are likely to have experienced the loss of a father either through death or divorce prior to entering college, usually before the age of 16 years.
6. The father of young males is likely to be very successful and heavily involved in his profession or business without having had sufficient time to develop a father-son relationship which is solid.
7. Young males coming from a higher socio-economic class are likely to have spent some time during the period of secondary education at a private boarding school.
8. Girls who attempt suicide are likely to have had much difficulty with their mothers especially when there is a weak and ineffectual father in the home. The girl often turns to a boy friend for support and he in turn lets her down because he is not capable of satisfying her psychological demands. Frequently, the girl may believe she is pregnant.
9. Adolescents are apt to smoke heavily, suggesting the severe tension they are experiencing.
10. General efficiency and school work usually drops off.
11. Recently involvement with various kinds of drugs has constituted an accompanying problem to anxiety, depression and self-destruction. Drinking is likely to be less serious, although it should not be overlooked.
12. Even though apparently "accidental" one should be alert to instances of self-poisoning behavior. Frequently, the same child will continue to poison himself repeatedly and have to be salvaged. Ultimately, this behavior will result in self-destruction.
13. Homes in which the professional suspects child-abuse or the so-called "battered child" syndrome are serious cause for concern since there is a mounting body of clinical evidence which indicates that future violence can evolve including suicide as a result of these early experiences. If the child feels openly rejected by his parents, it should be noted, even if severe physical punishment is absent.
14. Look for something in the youngster's behavior or talk suggesting that he wants to get even with his parents. A prominent component in suicidal

behavior is the wish to take one's own life in order to make those left behind sorry that they did not treat the victim better when he was alive.

WHAT TO DO OR
"PSYCHOLOGICAL FIRST-AID"

1. *Listen.*
   The first thing a youngster in the throes of a mental crisis needs is someone who will listen and really hear what he is saying. An effort should be made to really understand the feelings being expressed behind the words.
2. *Evaluate the lethality or seriousness of feelings of the youngster.*
3. *Evaluate the intensity or severity of the emotional disturbance.*
   It is possible that the youngster may be extremely upset but not suicidal.
4. *Evaluate the resources available.*
   The individual will have both inner psychological resources such as various mechanisms for rationalization and intellectualization which can be strengthened and supported, and the individual can have outer resources, that is, the resources in his environment such as ministers, relatives and other people whom one can call in.
5. *Take every complaint and feeling the youngster expresses seriously.*
   Do not dismiss or undervalue what he is saying. In some instances the difficulty will be presented in a low key, so to speak, but behind it will be very profound and serious distressed feelings.
6. *Act definitively.*
   Do something tangible; that is, give the youngster something concrete to hang onto, such as arranging for him to see someone else or whatever seems appropriate. Nothing is more frustrating than for the youngster to leave the office and feel as though he has received nothing from the interview.
7. *Be affirmative, perhaps even authoritarian, yet supportive.*
   Strong stable guideposts are extremely necessary in the life of a distressed individual. In other words, provide him with some strength by giving him the impression that you know what you are doing and that you intend to do everything you can to prevent him from taking his life.
8. *Do not be afraid to ask directly if the individual has entertained thoughts of suicide.*
   Experience shows that harm is rarely done by inquiring directly into such thoughts. As a matter of fact, the individual frequently welcomes it and is glad the therapist or counselor enabled him to open up and bring it out.
9. *If the individual does admit seriously entertaining such thoughts and then intends to be euphemistic about it and says he is all right, do not be misled by this.*

Frequently on second thought, the individual attempts to cover it up, but the thinking will come back later.

10. *Do not be afraid to ask for assistance and consultation.*

Call in whoever is necessary, depending upon the severity of the case, e.g., the school psychologist or whoever may be in a position to render assistance immediately. Do not try to handle everything yourself, but convey an attitude of firmness and composure to the youngster so that he will feel something realistic and appropriate is being done to help him.

Since a youngster spends the major portion of his day-time, waking hours in school settings, the school counselor is in a good position to be on the front lines of much of his behavior and stressful activities. The school counselor can be of inestimable value in meeting the crisis needs of youngsters on the spot.

REFERENCES

Diagnostic and Statistical Manual of Mental Disorders, (Second Edition). Washington, D.C.: American Psychiatric Association, 1968.

Seiden, Richard H., Ph.D., M.P.H. *Suicide Among Youth: A Review of the Literature, 1900-1967* (Supplement to the *Bulletin of Suicidology*). Washington, D.C.: National Clearinghouse for Mental Health Information, December, 1969.

Shneidman, Edwin S., Ph.D. Orientation Toward Cessation: A Reexamination of Current Modes of Death, *Journal of Forensic Sciences,* January, 1968, 13:1, 33-45.

The Need for Education on Death and Suicide

Dan Leviton

The need for formal and informal education enabling people of all ages to cope with death and suicide is becoming increasingly evident. Still a taboo topic, nonetheless, in recent years there has been a significant increase in both the popular, clinical, and experimental literature. Several books are available which examine the meaning of death to man from a bio-psycho-social (4, 7, 8) and philosophical (3) point of view. Shneidman (19), Shneidman and Farberow (18), and Menninger (16) have made significant contributions to the growing problem of suicide. Besides those studies published in scientific journals, there now exist two sources devoted entirely to the study of death (11) and suicide (20).

Aware of the need to stimulate concern and action preventing suicide has stimulated the National Institute of Mental Health to create the Center for Studies of Suicide Prevention under the direction of Dr. Edwin Shneidman. Some cities, notably Los Angeles and San Francisco have successfully developed Suicide Prevention Centers and Save-a-Life Leagues as a means of helping people, around the clock, who cry for help . . . who contemplate suicide.

Apparently, an understanding of death and suicide, like sexuality is being recognized as an area intimately related to man's ability to live a worthwhile and happy life. To paraphrase Choron, we need to be concerned with the issue of what death means and "does" to the individual (4, vii). Weisman and Hackett (22) have written that how one has lived can determine how he will die; conversely, how one views his imminent death can affect his style of living. A careful study of the literature coupled with my own teaching experience with college-age students leads me to suggest that the study of man's ability to cope with his own imminent death and the death of others is a valid area of concern for health educators.

Death thoughts are frequently found in children's fantasies. Anthony tested children between the ages of 3 and 13 years of age with a variety of techniques including parents' written accounts of their children's spontaneous interest in death, a story completion test, and an intelligence test in which material relevant to death appeared (2). She found that approximately 50 per cent of the children

Reprinted by permission from *Journal of School Health,* Vol. 39, No. 4, April 1969.

tested on the story completion task made reference to death in completing their stories, although the concept did not appear in the story stem.

In a classic study, Schilder and Wechsler examined the attitudes of children toward death using such techniques as observation of play, spontaneous stories given to picture stimuli, and direct questioning (17). Subjects were 76 children between the ages of 5 and 15. Results indicated that children deal with death realistically and in a matter of fact way. While they are ready to believe that others can die, they do not believe their own death probable. It was the seventeenth century writer and moralist, La Rochefoucauld, who epitomized this viewpoint when he said that neither the sun nor death can be looked at steadily (21).

Several writers have been concerned with "fear of death" in children and its origin. Anthony relates it to the fear of retaliation . . . a fear of aggression of others (2). Children fear death when they realize that they can die which is usually past the age of five. Children under five also fear death more so as a reaction to their own aggressiveness. Yet Schilder and Wechsler state that the fear of death is rare among children. The child is not concerned with dying but rather with being murdered (17).

Alexander and Alderstein, in an attempt to test empirically the child's affective reaction to death, hypothesized that death stimulus words, matched on frequency of usage, number of letters, and number of syllables would elicit greater latencies and increased galvanic skin responses than either basal (neutral) or "a priori affective" stimulus words when used in a word-association test (1). Subjects were boys (N = 108) divided into three subgroupings: age 5 through 8 (N = 29), 9 through 12 (N = 48), and 13 through 16 (N = 31). Results indicated that the entire sample reacted to death words with increased latency and decreased skin resistance. There were, however, wide individual differences in response both among children and among age groups. These results were explained in line with Freudian developmental theory and cultural expectations.

To some adolescents, fear of death is often apparent. In his classic study of fears, G. Stanely Hall administered approximately 300 questionnaires to people of all ages (9). A young woman confessed that up to the age of fourteen she could never think of death "without tears." Often it would come to her with tremendous force . . . "what an awful thing death was . . . it cannot, it must not be, that we must die and give up this beautiful life" (4, 110). A boy of fifteen thinks death "unspeakably terrible and cannot talk about it without his voice trembling." Out of 6500 reported fears, death was mentioned fourth most frequently.

Kastenbaum subjected 260 young men and women to a variety of attitude tests including a variation of the Osgood Semantic Differential Test (12). He found: (1) The adolescent lives in an intense present; "now" is so real to him that both past and future seem pallid by comparison. Everything that is important and valuable in life lies either in the immediate life situation or in the rather close future.

(2) Extremely little explicit structuring is given to the remote future by most of the adolescents tested. Attitudes toward the future that do become manifest are distinctly negative. In other words, most of the subjects kept thoughts of death separate from their daily functioning. On the other hand, about 15 per cent of the adolescents tested were consciously concerned with *both* death and their remote future. Instead of keeping the thought of death separate from their present functioning, as did the majority, they attempted to structure their life in terms of goals and experiences far removed in time. The prospect of death was very much alive for them; it entered actively into the decisions they made while still in the transitional world of adolescence. These death-oriented students were more outspokenly religious, with church activities an important factor in their lives.

The problem of the adolescent in coming to terms with death is expressed by Maurer:

> Adolescence is a time of greater decision than has heretofore been given psychological attention. To the crucial questions of sexual adjustment and independence must be added the problems that have been labelled "identity" or "purpose," but which are fundamentally the need to find a satisfactory sublimation for the death anxiety either in religion or other altruistic choices (15, 89).

It is at the adolescent stage that suicide becomes a leading cause of death. Kiell writes:

> In the United States, figures for child and adolescent deaths by suicide are high. At least thirty boys and girls under the age of ten kill themselves each year. Between ten and fourteen, the number rises to about fifty. In the fifteen to nineteen year old group there are some 290 successful attempts. The suicide rate in colleges is high, too. One study sets the figure at 13 per 1,000,000 students. These are the reported figures. They do not include the "hidden suicides," those denied by families and classed as accidents. New York health officials feel that probably ten per cent of all fatal car accidents and fifteen per cent of home accidents (usually by poisoning) are actually suicide attempts (13, 178).

The point of this review is to show rather quickly that a body of literature does exist from which the interested health educator might develop appropriate teaching materials and a course of study. My own plan of teaching at the University follows a rather simple format. We meet with approximately 500 students in a lecture situation followed by a breakdown into subgroups to discuss the topic of the week. To add some continuity to the lectures, I have established a hero and heroine (Terry and Penny) with whom the audience can identify. During the 16 week semester, we follow them from their birth to their graduation from college. Topics include: birth control and population increase; human birth and reproduction; emotional health; suicide; thoughts on death and dying; life can be beautiful either as a bachelor or married; communication between the sexes . . . on sex; research on human sexual behavior, what is sexual perversion?; drug misuse, etc. . . .

The unit on suicide usually includes mention of the incidence of suicide (among the three leading causes of death) among college students followed by a film, "The Cry for Help" (5). "Cry for Help" is valuable for two reasons. First, it is the only film that I have seen on the topic appropriate and meaningful for students, and secondly, it elaborates on the theme that the individual contemplating suicide usually gives certain clues. Clues which, in many cases, may be detected by a keen, sensitive friend or loved one. During discussion periods, students have a chance to interact among themselves and my function is simply to answer questions. They soon begin to discuss their own feelings and to associate those feelings (especially acute depression) with the possibility of suicide or the use of suicidal gestures to gain withheld love or approval.

Questions asked concern how to cope with someone who is suicidal. Who does one call to help that individual? Who helps the person attempting suicide? Do those making suicide attempts appreciate being rescued or will they make another attempt as soon as possible? How can one avoid being stigmatized after a suicide attempt? Are there training programs in suicidology and the prevention of suicide? Usually, I find that the sources mentioned earlier enable me to answer their questions to a large degree. More important, we find that the fear element in discussing suicide and death is often reduced as we become familiar and comfortable with the language of death.

That our emotions are intimately associated with death is evidenced in our abundant use of euphemisms. One does not die, he "passes away," "goes to meet his Maker," or "goes to his eternal repose." Men killed in battle are referred to as "casualties" or the "deceased." Even though death is a taboo topic for discussion in our culture we find, paradoxically, that death is very much a part of our colloquial language. In sports, we use the language of death: "kill the ump," "murder the bum." A good fighter must have a "killer instinct." Who has not said after making some sort of error or blunder, "I could kill myself." Johnson, in another context, discusses how the inability to communicate honestly and effectively with oneself and others can affect healthy development and learning.

The area of sex education is ripe with examples of how language is a barrier to progress. How does one talk and teach about a subject which, uniquely, has no acceptable language associated with it? Even the white sterile medical terminology, the long dead Latin, is offensive to many people. And under circumstances, we permit ourselves to be rendered helpless and physiologically shaken as well as speechless and thoughtless by the four letter words of sex and other bodily functions. Incidentally, those words were in respectable usage in the English language until a few hundred years ago when the Puritan tradition made them unclean, unspeakable, and even unthinkable to nice people. Still, they are universally understood and highly efficient means of communication. The pathetic, self-defeating, demoralizing "battle between the sexes" as well as the widespread confusion concerning the sex roles of male and female are to a considerable extent confusions and misuses of language. (10, 25).

It is ironic that both the beginning and end of life should be so encased in taboos and mythology resulting in man being unsure, afraid, or embarrassed when in a death- or sexual-connoting situation.

The reduction in language "trauma" or "shock" during the unit on suicide leads us gently into the next area, "Thoughts on Death and Dying." The lecturee centers on a need for a period of grieving and other ways of coping with the loss of a loved one. The need to be guided by rational thought rather than emotion. The differences between "fear of death" and "fear of dying" are pointed out, and if time remains, some attention is given to the controversial aggressive instinct and "death instinct" theories. Often I will discuss differences between Eastern and Western philosophical thought on death and dying.

Student reaction has generally been quite favorable. In fact, they seemed quite appreciative of the opportunity to discuss a most realistic and pervasive problem. No one seemed traumatized by the topics judging by the contributions made by a wide variety of students. In fact, students have indicated their receptiveness by ranking the study of death second only to sexual behavior in terms of interest and worth.

Accompanying the need for teaching is always the need for research. Feifel wrote:

> Further investigations of attitudes toward death can enrich and deepen our grasp of adaptive and maladaptive reactions to stress and to personality theory in general.
>
> The price of denying death is undefined anxiety, self-alienation. To completely understand himself, man must confront death, become aware of personal death (6, 64).

While conducting research to determine the perception of death stimuli by participants in a hazardous and non-hazardous sports activity, I found that both groups of subjects (sports car racing drivers and bowlers) were more than happy to discuss their feelings toward death. (14). No evidence was available which painted the existence of a death wish; on the contrary, both groups of subjects were perceptually vigilant to any threat to life while consciously avoiding the thought of death and dying.

As in many health education areas, the possibilities for research on death, dying, and suicide are varied and abundant. It should be apparent that alleviating man's fear of the termination of life is a worthwhile, legitimate concern of health educators and other behavioral scientists.

REFERENCES

1. I. E. Alexander and A. M. Adlerstein, "Affective Responses to the Concept of Death," *J. Genet. Psychol.,* 1958, 93, 167-177.

2. S. Anthony, *The Child's Discovery of Death*, New York: Harcourt, Brace and Co., 1940.
3. J. Choron, *Death and Western Thought*, New York: Collier Books, 1953.
4. ――――, *Modern Man and Mortality*, New York: The Macmillan Co., 1964.
5. "The Cry for Help" may be ordered from: Film Distributor, Public Health Service, Audio-Visual Facility, Chamblee, Georgia 30005.
6. H. Feifel (ed.), "Death—Relevant Variable in Psychology" in R. May (ed.), *Existential Psychology*, New York: Random House Co., 1961.
7. ――――, *The Meaning of Death*, New York: McGraw-Hill Book Co., 1959.
8. R. Fulton (ed), *Death and Identity*, New York: John Wiley and Sons, Inc., 1965.
9. G. S. Hall, "A Study of Fears," *Amer. J. Psychol.*, 1897, 8, 147-150.
10. W. R. Johnson, "Psycholinguistics: Something New In Health Education," *JOHPER*, 1968, 39, 25.
11. R. A. Kalish and R. Kastenbaum (eds.), *Omega: A Newsletter Concerned with Time Perspective, Death and Bereavement*, Detroit: Wayne State University (Department of Psychology).
12. R. Kastenbaum, "Time and Death in Adolescence" in H. Feifel (ed.), *The Meaning of Death*, New York: McGraw-Hill Book Co., 1959.
13. N. Kiell, *The Universal Experience of Adolescence*, Boston: Beacon Press, 1967.
14. D. Leviton, *The Perceptual Defense of Amateur Sports Car Racing Drivers and Bowlers to Death- and Crash-Word Stimuli*, (Unpublished Ph.D. Dissertation, University of Maryland, College Park, Maryland, 1967).
15. A. Maurer, "Adolescent Attitudes Toward Death," *J. Genet. Psychol.*, 1964, 105, 75-90.
16. K. A. Menninger, *Man Against Himself*, New York: Harcourt, Brace and Company, Inc., 1938.
17. P. Schilder and D. Weschler, "The Attitudes of Children Toward Death," *J. Genet. Psychol.*, 1934, 45, 406-451.
18. E. S. Shneidman and N. L. Farberow (ed.), *Essays in Self Destruction*, New York: Science House, Inc., 1967.
19. ――――, *Clues to Suicide*, New York: McGraw-Hill Book Co., 1957.
20. E. S. Shneidman and D. D. Swenson (eds.), *Bulletin of Suicidology*, Washington, D. C.: National Institute of Mental Health (National Clearinghouse for Mental Health Information).
21. "Thanatology," quoted in *Time*, 1964, 84(21), 92.
22. A. D. Weisman and T. P. Hackett, "Predilection to Death," *Psychosomatic Med.*, 1961, 23, 232-256.

PREVENTION

Some might say that the decision as to whether we will or will not live is an inherent right. "Why shouldn't a man be able to suicide if he wants to? It's his life. There's a population explosion anyway. Let it be his decision whether he lives or not." Others claim there is irreverence in such thinking and that we should not allow ourselves to be calloused or indifferent to the stress periods of another human life.

If we agree that prevention is our obligation we must return to the compartments associated with etiology: (a) physical, (b) psychological, (c) interpersonal, (d) social, (e) religious, (f) economic.

Crisis intervention is possible in each of these spheres and each must also be inspected in terms of longer range problem solving. Crisis intervention implies temporary control of the individual or extraction from his immediate situation with the implied infringement on freedom which in the past has frequently meant hospitalization in a mental institution. At this point in time there is a collision between those who would provide hospitalization − asylum − protection or incarceration and those who insist upon freedom in the name of civil rights.

While crisis intervention is certainly important, the major

elements of prevention must concern themselves with basic problems which have longitudinal inference and concern themselves with resolution. The ultimate cure of physical infirmities, the understanding of depression at a biological-psychological level, early case finding, family therapy, and mental health services at a public school level are the types of efforts which will prove to be most meaningful. In the meantime, sociologists, economists, and religious leaders must find ways of reducing the problem areas of life to more compatible and functional terms — so easily said.

Responsibilities in Suicide Prevention

Jerome A. Motto

Suicidal behavior can be seen as a last resort effort to resolve unbearable pressures. These pressures can be generated by physical or emotional pain, or by symbolic needs, such as the need to rejoin some person who has died. The suicidal behavior becomes manifest when a person who is subjected to these unbearable pressures, first, feels isolated from other human beings, and second, perceives his situation as hopeless.

Suicide prevention starts with the identification of persons who experience their world in this way. When a physician or other health professional recognizes this state in a person, there is no question but that he should assume responsibility for coping with the possibility of suicide. This is related to the basic premise in the health professions that preservation of life is a primary goal. Within this framework it is appropriate to explore with the person alternate means of reducing both the pressures that are impinging on him and the pain these pressures produce.

When a suicidal state is recognized by other than health professionals, the assumption of responsibility for dealing with the possibility of suicide cannot be as readily taken for granted. The question is repeatedly raised whether intervening in a person's self-destructive actions—suicide prevention—is an unwarranted violation of that person's right to choose the time and manner of his own death. A person's birth, it is maintained, is beyond his control, but his death is his own to do with as he will.

SELF-DETERMINATION

This philosophy of self-determination as regards death is akin to many Western ideas about the value of individual rights and freedoms. It is consistent with attitudes which exalt rugged tenacity, stick-to-it-iveness, and the exertion of maximum efforts in exercising these freedoms. Such a philosophy puts a high value on one's ability to survive the traumas of life without relinquishing an independent role, that is, to be able to cope with life without help. A high degree of personal autonomy tends to be regarded in contemporary society not

Reprinted by permission from *California's Health,* July 1971.

simply as one desirable outcome of personal growth, but as a criterion for worthiness of respect and esteem.

Paradoxically, these views are especially prevalent among professional persons, who tend to express the idea, not always consciously, that it is certainly appropriate for persons in need of help to request and receive what assistance they need, but that this concept in no way applies to them, that is, to the professional.

One socially destructive result of this paradoxical attitude is that health professionals are as frequently lost through suicide as are persons in society at large, although one would anticipate that unusual personality strengths would be characteristic of this group.

Psychiatrists, who apparently have the greatest need to maintain this image of emotional independence, have the highest suicide rate among the medical specialties. Doctors as a group are notorious for being insensitive to their own needs even for physical care, to say nothing of their emotional health.

This issue poses a basic contradiction in our society. Moral progress increases our sense of duty toward our fellow man, yet efforts to discharge that duty are often referred to as "robbing of incentive," or "fostering dependency." We hear it is desirable to be our brother's keeper, but when we are, we are demeaning him. There are obviously exceptions, but this reflects a basic dependent-independent social conflict that impedes efforts in suicide prevention.

These attitudes about autonomy hamper the acceptance of individual responsibility for responding to communications of suicidal intent, by providing a ready rationalization for ignoring them. "He's not going to kill himself—he only wants some attention." "He's just looking for some reassurance." There's always the "just" or the "only," as though it were not acceptable to need attention or to receive reassurance from your environment that someone cares about you.

There is no way to estimate the frequency with which relatives, neighbors, colleagues, bartenders, taxi drivers, pharmacists and hairdressers are informed of a person's suicidal intent. We do know that such messages are pleas for assistance, sometimes eliciting it, but often not. Anxiety associated with taboos surrounding death and dying combine with social attitudes sanctifying autonomy to deny, rationalize or simply ignore the need for a response.

We can be encouraged by the fact that a large cadre of citizens is countering the tendency to leave suicide prevention to the health professionals. Suicide prevention center volunteers throughout the country are emerging as a new specialty group that is gaining recognition as a "true" professional resource in matters of suicide prevention. A trained, experienced volunteer can usually do as well as or better than the average mental health professional in the various aspects of suicide prevention work, specifically in such activities as assessment of suicidal risk, telephone counseling, referral to appropriate agencies, and public education and training in suicide prevention.

THE COMMUNITY ROLE

Traditionally, community resources have provided some form of general emergency psychiatric services. These have not set suicide prevention aside as a special aspect of their work, but include such emergencies along with other kinds of psychiatric problems. Although there have been various administrative and financial arrangements designed to include suicide prevention centers in community mental health programs, it has been very clear that most communities are reluctant to assume responsibility for suicide prevention facilities on an ongoing basis. Medical agencies tend to reject them as non-professional, resist collaborating with volunteer staff, and are generally hostile toward patients with injuries or disabilities that are self-inflicted.

PREVENTIVE APPROACH

Experience has also shown clearly that suicide prevention centers are used by the community mostly as a source of general counseling and emotional support rather than primarily for suicidal emergencies. Further development of suicide prevention centers along this line, with community administrative and financial support, would be an appropriate way to carry out suicide prevention responsibilities at the community level. This would entail true primary prevention, dealing with potential crises before they become difficult to manage, rather than the present focus on intervention after a crisis develops. This preventive approach would make it possible to communicate readily with a crisis center, and would encourage persons with difficult living problems to talk with a trained person skilled in counseling and in referral to appropriate community resources, *before* the problem has developed to suicidal dimensions.

A fundamental question is whether the values that are supported by the financial resources of the community are conducive to the development of stable life patterns, whether the quality of life of the members of the community are considered above commercialism, power, or economic gain. The community should exert pressure on newspapers, television, films, and radio to emphasize realistic ethical and social values. The tendency to sensationalize sexuality, notoriety, and violence that characterizes these media should be a concern in the community's role in suicide prevention. This means dealing with the problem on a long-term basis, starting with the developing value system of young people.

THE INDIVIDUAL'S ROLE

The community cannot identify high-risk or potential high-risk persons for suicide. This is an individual matter. Whether it's done by a minister, a physician, a social worker, pharmacist, or neighbor, one person must identify the potential suicide. It was mentioned above that some persons consider it a violation of another's freedom to interfere with his intended demise.

My own view is that if a person communicates his suicidal intent within the range of my senses—in my sight, or by sending me a letter, or by calling me on the telephone—or in any way indicates to me that he is considering killing himself, I must interpret it, rightly or wrongly, as a request for assistance that cannot be ignored.

Outside my awareness he may do with his life as he wishes, and I will feel responsible for his well-being only insofar as I am a fellow human being who wishes to assure that the conditions of life and society make it possible for every person to achieve a satisfying existence. Until that ideal is realized, I believe each individual shares the responsibility of responding to those who indicate that they feel unable to stick it out.

The next problem after identification is treatment and management. Theologians speak of the morality of loving concern. I don't think anyone questions but that this framework is essential to effective work in any kind of emotional problem. It is certainly a key issue in suicidal states.

FUSION

I would like to emphasize, however, that it is not enough to love or to care. It is not the loving or the caring; it is the effect of the loving and the effect of the caring on the person. Unfortunately, some persons do not perceive love when it is given, or do not feel cared about even when they are. So it is necessary in this stage of our work to try, and try, and try to find whatever it takes to generate in the person we are concerned about the feeling of worthiness of love.

It is necessary to establish what Hellmuth Kaiser referred to as the "delusion of fusion." He puts this in the most beautiful and simple way, referring to a "universal pathology," that we have a feeling of not being alone, or not being isolated, that we are part of a whole, that we have a sense of connection, or relatedness with family, with friends, with meaningful persons in our life. This sense of feeling "fused" with a larger entity than ourselves is essential to the maintenance of meaningful living.

Kaiser refers to man's manifold efforts to maintain or reestablish this delusion of fusion as a "universal symptom." It follows, of course, that the "universal therapy" is the facilitation of this process, a task approached in various ways, but with this common goal. When it is difficult for the goal to be achieved we find ourselves facing the dilemma of various emotional disorders, including suicidal states.

After identification, assessment, treatment, and management comes following-up. This is absolutely vital. Let me remind you of a Peanuts cartoon. Snoopy is sitting morosely out in the snow when Lucy and Violet approach him, saying to each other, "Snoopy looks sad. Let's cheer him up." So they go up to him and one after the other pat him on the head and say, "Be of good cheer, Snoopy." Then the two girls disappear over the horizon and Snoopy is still sitting there, now with a big question mark over his head, just as despondent as ever.

It is rarely enough to simply cheer someone up, or even to get him through a crisis. Follow-up is essential to assure development of as much stability as possible. I don't mean it's essential to maintain contact indefinitely in every instance, but the duration is potentially indefinite, depending on what one's clinical judgment dictates. In any case, the door should never be closed.

To work in the framework of concern for the quality and the preservation of human life, one of the most important requirements is an acceptance of our own limitations. We have to try and try and try and keep trying. And feel our own worthiness tied to the efforts, not to the result. There are very few human problems that are immutable; hence we can tackle, with a certain dogged optimism, many situations that we don't see any resolution to.

It's essential to maintain this firm, determined optimism, not in a Pollyanna sense, but in the conviction that if we keep looking long enough and hard enough some solution can be found. The effects of time alone often modify what persistent effort and spontaneous developments do not. Helping a person simply to endure a period of severe crisis can thus be a lifesaving procedure in what began as hopeless-looking circumstances. If our efforts in a given situation are in vain, we must, in spite of our dismay, accept our shortcomings and take some satisfaction from having done what we were able to, whether or not it was sufficient for the other's needs.

James Baldwin has expressed this very clearly: "for nothing is fixed, forever and forever and forever, it is not fixed; the earth is always shifting, the light is always changing, the sea does not cease to grind down rock. Generations do not cease to be born, and we are responsible to them because we are the only witnesses they have. The sea rises, the light fails, lovers cling to each other, and children cling to us. The moment we cease to hold each other, the moment we break faith with one another, the sea engulfs us and the light goes out."

REFERENCES

Kaiser, Hellmuth: *Effective Psychotheraphy.* New York: The Free Press, 1965.
Baldwin, James and Avedon, Richard: *Nothing Personal.* New York: Atheneum Press, 1964.

Preventing Suicide

Edwin S. Shneidman

In almost every case of suicide, there are hints of the act to come, and physicians and nurses are in a special position to pick up the hints and to prevent the act. They come into contact, in many different settings, with many human beings at especially stressful times in their lives.

A suicide is an especially unhappy event for helping personnel. Although one can, in part, train and inure oneself to deal with the sick and even the dying patient, the abruptness and needlessness of a suicidal act leaves the nurse, the physician, and other survivors with many unanswered questions, many deeply troubling thoughts and feelings.

Currently, the major bottleneck in suicide prevention is not remediation, for there are fairly well-known and effective treatment procedures for many types of suicidal states; rather it is in diagnosis and identification (2,4).

ASSUMPTIONS

A few straightforward assumptions are necessary in suicide prevention. Some of them:

Individuals who are intent on killing themselves still wish very much to be rescued or to have their deaths prevented. Suicide prevention consists essentially in recognizing that the potential victim is "in balance" between his wishes to live and his wishes to die, then throwing one's efforts on the side of life.

Suicide prevention depends on the active and forthright behavior of the potential rescuer.

Most individuals who are about to commit suicide are acutely conscious of their intention to do so. They may, of course, be very secretive and not communicate their intentions directly. On the other hand, the suicidally inclined

Reprinted by permission from *The American Journal of Nursing*, 65(5):19-15, 1965. Copyrighted by the American Journal of Nursing Company, New York.

person may actually be unaware of his own lethal potentialities, but nonetheless may give many indirect hints of his unconscious intentions.

Practically all suicidal behaviors stem from a sense of isolation and from feelings of some intolerable emotion on the part of the victim. By and large, suicide is an act to stop an intolerable existence. But each individual defines "intolerable" in his own way. Difficulties, stresses, or disappointments that might be easy for one individual to handle might very well be intolerable for someone else—in *his* frame of mind. In order to anticipate and prevent suicide one must understand what "intolerable" means to the other person. Thus, any "precipitating cause"—being neglected, fearing or having cancer (the fear and actuality can be equally lethal), feeling helpless or hopeless, feeling "boxed-in"—may be intolerable for *that* person.

Although committing suicide is certainly an all-or-none action, thinking about the act ahead of time is a complicated, undecided, internal debate. Many a black-or-white action is taken on a barely pass vote. Prof. Henry Murray of Harvard University has written that "a personality is a full Congress" of the mind. In preventing suicide, one looks for any indications in the individual representing the dark side of his internal life-and-death debate. We are so often surprised at "unexpected" suicides because we fail to take into account just this principle that the suicidal action is a decision resulting from an internal debate of many voices, some for life and some for death. Thus we hear all sorts of post-mortem statements like "He seemed in good spirits" or "He was looking forward to some event next week," not recognizing that these, in themselves, represent only one aspect of the total picture.

In almost every case, there are precursors to suicide, which are called "prodromal clues." In the "psychological autopsies" that have been done at the Suicide Prevention Center in Los Angeles—in which, by interview with survivors of questionable accident or suicide deaths, they attempt to reconstruct the intention of the deceased in relation to death—it was found that very few suicides occur without casting some shadows before them. The concept of prodromal clues for suicide is certainly an old idea; it is really not very different from what Robert Burton, over three hundred years ago in 1652, in his famous *Anatomy of Melancholy,* called "the prognostics of melancholy, or signs of things to come." These prodromal clues typically exist for a few days to some weeks before the actual suicide. Recognition of these clues is a necessary first step to lifesaving.

Suicide prevention is like fire prevention. It is not the main mission of any hospital, nursing home, or other institution, but it is the minimum ever-present peripheral responsibility of each professional; and when the minimal signs of possible fire or suicide are seen, then there are no excuses for holding back on lifesaving measures. The difference between fire prevention and suicide prevention is that the prodromal clues for fire prevention have become an acceptable part of our common-sense folk knowledge; we must also make the clues for suicide a part of our general knowledge.

CLUES TO POTENTIAL SUICIDE

In general, the prodomal clues to suicide may be classified in terms of four broad types: verbal, behavioral, situational, and syndromatic.

Verbal: Among the verbal clues we can distinguish between the direct and the indirect. Examples of direct verbal communications would be such statements as "I'm going to commit suicide," "If such and such happens, I'll kill myself," "I'm going to end it all," "I want to die," and so on. Examples of indirect verbal communications would be such statements as "Goodbye," "Farewell," "I've had it," "I can't stand it any longer," "It's too much to put up with," "You'd be better off without me," and, in general, any statements that mirror the individual's intention to stop his intolerable existence.

Some indirect verbal communications can be somewhat more subtle. We all know that in human communication, our words tell only part of the story, and often the main "message" has to be decoded. Every parent or spouse learns to decode the language of loved ones and to understand what they really mean. In a similar vein, many presuicidal communications have to be decoded. An example might be a patient who says to a nurse who is leaving on her vacation, "Goodbye, Miss Jones, I won't be here when you come back." If some time afterward she, knowing that the patient is not scheduled to be transferred or discharged prior to her return, thinks about that conversation, she might do well to telephone her hospital.

Other examples are such statements as, "I won't be around much longer for you to put up with," "This is the last shot you'll ever give me," or "This is the last time I'll ever be here," a statement which reflects the patient's private knowledge of his decision to kill himself. Another example is, "How does one leave her body to the medical school?" The latter should never be answered with factual information until after one has found out why the question is being asked, and whose body is being talked about. Individuals often ask for suicide prevention information for a "friend" or "relative" when they are actually inquiring about themselves.

Behavioral: Among the behavioral clues, we can distinguish the direct and the indirect. The clearest examples of direct behavioral communications of the intention to kill oneself is a "practice run," an actual suicide attempt of whatever seriousness. Any action which uses instruments which are conventionally associated with suicide (such as razors, ropes, pills, and the like), regardless of whether or not it could have any lethal outcome, must be interpreted as a direct behavioral "cry for help" and an indication that the person is putting us on our alert. Often, the nonlethal suicide attempt is meant to communicate deeper suicidal intentions. By and large, suicide attempts must be taken seriously as indications of personal crisis and of more severe suicide potentiality.

In general, indirect behavioral communications are such actions as taking a lengthy trip or putting affairs into order. Thus the making of a will under certain peculiar and special circumstances can be an indirect clue to suicidal intention. Buying a casket at the time of another's funeral should always be inquired after most carefully and, if necessary, prompt action (like hospitalization) taken. Giving away prized possessions like a watch, earrings, golf clubs, or heirlooms should be looked on as a possible prodromal clue to suicide.

Situational: On occasion the situation itself cries out for attention, especially when there is a variety of stresses. For example, when a patient is extremely anxious about surgery, or when he has been notified that he has a malignancy, when he is scheduled for mutilative surgery, when he is frightened by hospitalization itself, or when outside factors (like family discord, for example, or finances) are a problem—all these are situational. If the doctor or nurse is sensitive to the fact that the situation constitutes a "psychological emergency" for that patient, then he is in a key position to perform lifesaving work. His actions might take the form of sympathetic conversation, or special surveillance of that patient by keeping him with some specially assigned person, or by requesting consultation, or by moving him so that he does not have access to windows at lethal heights. At the least, the nurse should make notations of her behavioral observations in the chart.

To be a suicide diagnostician, one must combine separate symptoms and recognize *and label* a suicidal syndrome in a situation where no one symptom by itself would neccessarily lead one to think of a possible suicide.

In this paper we shall highlight syndromatic clues for suicide in a medical and surgical hospital setting, although these clues may also be used in other settings. First, it can be said that patient status is stressful for many persons. Everyone who has•ever been a patient knows the fantasies of anxiety, fear, and regression that are attendant on illness or surgery. For some in the patient role (èspecially in a hospital), as the outer world recedes, the fantasy life becomes more active; conflicts and inadequacies and fears may then begin to play a larger and disproportionate role. The point for suicide prevention is that one must try to be aware especially of those patients who are prone to be psychologically overreactive and, being so, are more apt to explode irrationally into suicidal behavior.

Syndromatic: What are the syndromes—the constellations of symptoms—for suicide? Labels for four of them could be: depressed, disoriented, defiant, and dependent-dissatisfied.

Depressed: The syndrome of depression is, by and large, made up of symptoms which reflect the shifting of the individual's psychological interests from aspects of his interpersonal life to aspects of his private psychological life, to some intrapsychic crisis within himself. For example, the individual is less interested in food, he loses his appetite, and thus loses weight. Or, his regular patterns of sleeping and waking become disrupted, so that he suffers from lack of energy in the daytime and then sleeplessness and early awakening. The habitual or regular patterns of social and sexual response also tend to change, and the individual loses interest in others. His rate or pace or speed of talking, walking, and doing the activities of his everyday life slows down. At the same time there is increased preoccupation with internal (intrapsychic) conflicts and problems. The individual is withdrawn, apathetic, apprehensive and anxious, often "blue" and even tearful, somewhat unreachable and seemingly uncaring.

Depression can be seen, too, in an individual's decreased willingness to communicate. Talking comes harder, there are fewer spontaneous remarks, answers are shorter or even monosyllabic, the facial expressions are less lively, the posture is more drooped, gestures are less animated, the gait is less springy, and the individual's mind seems occupied and elsewhere.

An additional symptom of the syndrome of depression is detachment, or withdrawing from life. This might be evidenced by behavior which would reflect attitudes, such as "I don't care," "What does it matter," "It's no use anyway." If an individual feels helpless he is certainly frightened, although he may fight for some control or safety; but if he feels hopeless, then the heart is out of him, and life is a burden, and he is only a spectator to a dreary life which does not involve him.

First aid in suicide prevention is directed to counteracting the individual's feelings of hopelessness. Robert E. Litman, chief psychiatrist of the Los Angeles Suicide Prevention Center, has said that "Psychological support is transmitted by a firm and hopeful attitude. We convey the impression that the problem which seems to the patient to be overwhelming, dominating his entire personality, and completely insidious, is commonplace and quite familiar to us and we have seen many people make a complete recovery. Hope is a commodity of which we have plenty and we dispense it freely" (3).

It is of course pointless to say "Cheer up" to a depressed person, inasmuch as the problem is that he simply cannot. On the other hand, the effectiveness of the "self-fulfilling prophecy" should never be underestimated. Often an integral part of anyone's climb out of a depression is his faith and the faith of individuals around him that he is going to make it. Just as hopelessness breeds hopelessness, hope—to some extent—breeds hope.

Oftentimes, the syndrome of depression does not seem especially difficult to diagnose. What may be more difficult—and very much related to suicide—is the apparent improvement after a severe depression, when the individual's pace of speech and action picks up a little. The tendency then is for everyone to think that he is cured and to relax vigilance. In reality the situation may be much more dangerous; the individual now has the psychic energy with which to kill himself that he may not have had when he was in the depths of his depression. By far, most suicides relating to depression occur within a short period (a few days to 3 months) after the individual has made an apparent turn for the better. A good rule is that any significant change in behavior, even if it looks like improvement, should be assessed as a possible prodromal index for suicide.

Although depression is the most important single prodromal syndrome for suicide—occurring to some degree in approximately one-third of all suicides—it is not the only one.

Disoriented: Disoriented people are apt to be delusional or hallucinatory, and the suicidal danger is that they may respond to commands or voices or experiences that other people cannot share. When a disoriented person expresses any suicidal notions, it is important to take him as a most serious suicidal risk, for he may be in constant danger of taking his own life, not only to cut out those parts of himself that he finds intolerable, but also to respond to the commands of hallucinated voices to kill himself. What makes such a person potentially explosive and particularly hard to predict is that the trigger mechanism may depend on a crazed thought, a hallucinated command, or a fleeting intense fear within a delusional system.

Disoriented states may be clearly organic, such as delirium tremens, certain toxic states, certain drug withdrawal states. Individuals with chronic brain syndromes and cerebral arteriosclerosis may become disoriented. On the other hand, there is the whole spectrum of schizophrenic and schizoaffective disorders, in which the role of organic factors is neither clearly established nor completely accepted. Nonetheless, professional personnel should especially note individuals who manifest some degree of nocturnal disorientation, but who have relative diurnal lucidity. Those physicians who see the patients only during the daytime are apt to miss these cases, particularly if they do not read nurses' notes.

Suicides in general hospitals have occurred among nonpsychiatric patients with subtle organic syndromes, especially those in which symptoms of disorientation are manifested. One should look, too, for the presence of bizarre behavior, fear of death, and clouding of the patient's understanding and awareness. The nurse might well be especially alert to any general hospital patient who has any previous neuropsychiatric history, especially where there are the signs of an acute brain syndrome. Although dyspnea is not a symptom in the syndrome related to disorientation, the presence of severe dyspnea, especially if it is unimproved by treatment in the hospital, has been found to correlate with suicide in hospitals.

When an individual is labeled psychotic, he is almost always disoriented in one sphere or another. Even if he knows where he is and what the date is, he may be off base about who he is, especially if one asks him more or less "philosophic" questions, like "What is the meaning of life?" His thinking processes will seem peculiar, and the words of his speech will have some special or idiosyncratic characteristics. In general, whether or not such patients are transferred to psychiatric wards or psychiatric hospitals, they should—in terms of suicide prevention—be given special care and surveillance, including consultation. Special physical arrangements should be made for them, such as removal of access to operable screens and windows, removal of objects of self-destruction and the like.

Defiant: The Welsh poet, Dylan Thomas, wrote, "Do not go gentle into that good night ˙ . . . rage, rage against the dying of the light." Many of us remember, usually from high school literature, Henley's *Invictus,* "I am the master of my fate: I am the captain of my soul." The point is that many individuals, no matter how miserable their circumstances or how painful their lives, attempt to retain some shred of control over their own fate. Thus a man dying of cancer may, rather than passively capitulate to the disease, choose to play one last active role in his own life by picking the time of his death; so that even in a terminal state (when the staff may believe that he doesn't have the energy to get out of bed), he lifts a heavy window and throws himself out to his death. In this sense, he is willful or defiant.

This kind of individual is an "implementer" (6). Such a person is described as one who has an active need to control his environment. Typically, he would never be fired from any job; he would quit. In a hospital he would attempt to control his environment by refusing some treatments, demanding others, requesting changes, insisting on privileges, and indulging in many other activities indicating some inner need to direct and control his life situation. These individuals are often seen as having low frustration tolerance, being fairly set and rigid in their ways, being somewhat arbitrary and, in general, showing a great oversensitivity to outside control. The last is probably a reflection of their own inability to handle their inner stresses.

Certainly, not every individual who poses ward management problems needs to be seen as suicidal, but what personnel should look for is the somewhat agitated concern of a patient with controlling his own fate. Suicide is one way of "calling the shot." The nurse can play a lifesaving role with such a person by recognizing his psychological problems and by enduring his controlling (and irritating) behavior—indeed, by being the willing target of his berating and demanding behavior and thus permitting him to expend his energies in this way, rather than in suicidal activities. Her willingness to be a permissible target for these feelings and, more, her sympathetic behavior in giving attention and reassurance even in the face of difficult behavior are in the tradition of the nurturing nurse, even though this can be a difficult role continually to fulfill.

Dependent-dissatisfied: Imagine being married to someone on whom you are deeply emotionally dependent, in a situation in which you are terribly dissatisfied with your being dependent. It would be in many ways like being "painted into a corner"—there is no place to go.

This is the pattern we have labeled "dependent-dissatisfied" (5). Such an individual is very dependent on the hospital, realizing he is ill and depending on the hospital to help him; however, he is dissatisfied with being dependent and comes to feel that the hospital is not giving him the help he thinks he needs. Such patients become increasingly tense and depressed, with frequent expressions of guilt and inadequacy. They have emotional disturbances in relation to their illnesses and to their hospital care. Like the "implementer," they make demands and have great need for attention and reassurance. They have a number of somatic complaints, as well as complaints about the hospital. They threaten to leave the hospital against medical advice. They ask to see the doctor, the chaplain, the chief nurse. They request additional therapies of various kinds. They make statements like, "Nothing is being done for me" or "The doctors think I am making this up."

The reactions of irritability on the part of busy staff are not too surprising in view of the difficult behavior of such patients. Tensions in these patients may go up especially at the time of pending discharge from the hospital. Suicide prevention by hospital staff consists of responding to the emotional needs and giving emotional support to these individuals. With such patients the patience of Job is required. Any suicide threats or attempts on the part of such patients, no matter how "mild" or attention-getting, should be taken seriously. Their demand for attention may lead them to suicide. Hospital staff can often, by instituting some sort of new treatment procedure or medication, give this type of patient temporary relief or a feeling of improvement. But most of all, the sympathetic recognition on the part of hospital staff that the complaining, demanding, exasperating behavior of the dependent-dissatisfied patient is an expression of his own inner feelings of desperation may be the best route to preventing his suicide.

COWORKERS, FAMILY, FRIENDS

Suicide is "democratic." It touches both patients and staff, unlettered and educated, rich and poor—almost proportionately. As for sex ratio, the statistics are interesting: Most studies have shown that in Western countries more men than women commit suicide, but a recent study indicates that in certain kinds of hospital settings like neuropsychiatric hospitals, a proportionately larger percentage of women kill themselves (1). The information in this paper is meant to apply not only to patients, but to colleagues, and even to members of our families as well. The point is that only by being free to see the possibility of suicidal potential in everybody can suicide prevention of anybody really become effective.

In our society, we are especially loathe to suspect suicide in individuals of some stature or status. For example, of the physicians who commit suicide, some could easily be saved if they would be treated (hospitalized, for example) like ordinary citizens in distress. Needless to say, the point of view that appropriate treatment might cause him professional embarrassment should never be invoked in such a way so as to risk a life being lost.

In general, we should not "run scared" about suicide. In the last analysis, suicides are, fortunately, infrequent events. On the other hand, if we have even unclear suspicions of suicidal potential in another person, we do well to have "the courage of our own confusions" and take the appropriate steps.

These appropriate steps may include notifying others, obtaining consultation, alerting those concerned with the potentially suicidal person (including relatives and friends), getting the person to a sanctuary in a psychiatric ward or hospital. Certainly, we don't want to holler "Fire" unnecessarily, but we should be able to interpret the clues, erring, if necessary, on the "liberal" side. We may feel chagrined if we turn in a false alarm, but we would feel very much worse if we were too timid to pull the switch that might have prevented a real tragedy.

Earlier in this paper the role of the potential rescuer was mentioned. One implication of this is that professionals must be aware of their own reactions and their own personalities, especially in relation to certain patients. For example, does he have the insight to recognize his tendency to be irritated at a querulous and demanding patient and thus to ignore his presuicidal communications? Every rescue operation is a dialogue: Someone cries for help and someone else must be willing to hear him and be capable of responding to him. Otherwise the victim may die because of the potential rescuer's unresponsiveness.

We must develop in ourselves a special attitude for suicide prevention. Each individual can be a lifesaver, a one-person committee to prevent suicide. Happily, elaborate pieces of mechanical equipment are not needed; "all" that is required are sharp eyes and ears, good intuition, a pinch of wisdom, an ability to act appropriately, and a deep resolve.

REFERENCES

1. Eisenthal, Sherman; Farberow, N. L.; and Shneidman, E. S. Follow-up of Neuropsychiatric Hospital Patients on Suicide Observation Status. *Public Health Reports,* 81:977-990, 1966.
2. Farberow, N. L., and Shneidman, E. S., eds. *The Cry for Help.* New York: McGraw-Hill Book Co., 1961.
3. Litman, R. E. Emergency response to potential suicide. *J. Mich. Med. Soc.* 62:68-72, 1963.
4. Shneidman, E. S., and Farberow, N. L., eds. *Clues to Suicide.* New York: McGraw-Hill Book Co., 1957.
5. _____. *Suicide-Evaluation and Treatment of Suicidal Risk Among Schizophrenic Patients in Psychiatric Hospitals.* (Medical Bulletin, MB-8) Washington, D.C.: Veterans' Administration, 1962, pp. 1-11.

6. U.S. Veterans' Administration, Department of Medicine and Surgery. *Suicide Among General Medical and Surgical Hospital Patients with Malignant Neoplasms,* Farberow, Norman L.; Shneidman, Edwin S.; and Leonard Calista. (Medical Bulletin, MB-9) Washington, D.C.: Veterans' Administration, 1963, pp. 1-11.

The Life You Can Save

Charles P. Weikel

Suicide is a leading cause of death in the United States among all ages, especially white, elderly males. The life-problems presented, especially among the elderly, are so filled with despair that dedicated older men and women all over the country have stepped in as volunteers to "handle" a suicidal crisis—and often save the life of an older friend.

These mature volunteers have proved so valuable that now they're at work in sixty nationwide suicide prevention centers. There they're becoming almost more successful than professionals in salvaging the despondent and encouraging them to regain faith in living. Because of their widespread success, every community is now seeking to recruit older volunteers in this vital work.

How many suicides occur each year? How many are elderly persons? Although the government reports 20,000 suicides annually, the toll may be over 60,000, according to Dr. Edwin S. Schneidman, Chief of the Center for Studies of Suicide Prevention, National Institute of Mental Health. The medical journal "Geriatrics" confirms the higher rate. As for suicide attempts, the rate jumps to a tragic 200,000 a year.

Who are the humans who've "given up" and would rather die than live? Here are the facts: more women than men try to end their lives . . . but it's the men who usually succeed. Twice more whites than blacks commit suicide. With college students, suicide is the third leading cause of death; the other two are accidents and cancer. In suicides, single people twice outnumber the married. Among adults, it's more frequently the elderly who kill themselves—and most of these are men, or "loners."

San Francisco has the sorrowful title, "suicide capital of the United States." But the Veterans Administration points out that another major city in the United States has a low number of suicides each year only because its coroner doesn't label a case "suicide" unless a note is found with the body. The truth is, most suicides don't leave notes. One researcher discovered that only one-third of all confirmed suicides left a "note."

Statistics, therefore, are rather shaky, differing from state to state, and even

Reprinted by permission from *Harvest Years*, June 1970.

from one coroner's jurisdiction to the next. Nevertheless, the sad and staggering number of people of all ages, color, and racial and economic background—and particularly the alarming number of elderly who prefer death to life—awoke the conscience of many, some years ago, to set up "suicide prevention centers."

The first such center was opened in New York City in 1906 by a clergyman, the Rev. Harry Marsh Warren, who'd been called to the bedside of a dying young woman who'd taken poison after being jilted on the verge of her marriage. Her last words to him were: "If I'd only had someone like you to talk with . . . Please keep others from making the same mistake."

This preventable tragedy shocked Dr. Warren. He founded the Save-a-Life League for suicide prevention. In 1924 it was incorporated as the National Save-a-Life League. Since 1925 his son, Harry M. Warren, Jr., has been its executive-in-charge. On its counseling staff are psychiatrists, psychologists, trained clergymen, psychiatric nurses, social workers—and volunteers. There's no charge for its counseling and aid to the discouraged, especially to the elderly, in whom the tendency to suicide is strongest after age sixty-five.

All suicide prevention centers are similar in their organized and instant response to an emergency. One lifeline is the telephone, manned round-the-clock, usually by volunteers. On the other end of the line it's not unexpected to hear a stricken voice say, "Thank God, there's someone to talk to." Some centers now are setting up their telephone circuits into a volunteer's home, so that when the center is called, the volunteer answers from his own phone at home.

In San Francisco's suicide prevention center, founded by Bernard Mayes in 1962, a corps of 125 dedicated, trained volunteers actually makes the system work for 1,400 emergency "lifeline" calls each month. "Experience has proved," says the Public Affairs pamphlet on suicide, "that lay volunteers can be very effective staff members." Selected and trained, these men and women volunteers are mature and usually have weathered psychological storms within their own lives. They are eagerly sought to help in the office or at home, at the hours they wish. Customarily, volunteers never identify themselves to callers, nor do they seek the caller's identity unless they suspect "a grave threat to life." Total anonymity is preferred by the suicide prevention center in a small town like Davis, Calif., for example, to avoid embarrassing, possibly unwelcome face to face confrontation. The rule of upholding anonymity on both ends of the telephone line may be inadvertently broken, of course, by a drop-in caller who may find himself face to face with a volunteer who'd previously responded to his phone call.

What can a volunteer in a suicide prevention service expect in the way of training? How is the volunteer prepared to cope with life-or-death phone calls?

The San Francisco experience gives some revealing answers. Its volunteers get two-hour training sessions together, led by an expert instructor or professionals on the center's advisory group. At these sessions they're schooled to pick up "clues" from callers. Fragments of conversation may disclose a caller's age, residence, marital status, number of children, sometimes a physician's name. From such slender threads, help may be rushed to a suicidal person in crisis.

A favorite question by callers, if a volunteer "sounds young" is: "How old are you?" Younger people want to talk to someone older. One caller asked desperately, "How old are you? I want to talk to someone over forty-nine; someone twenty-five couldn't understand me."

The older volunteer can "relate" better to callers, most centers agree. On his side is the approach, "Tell me all about it; we've both been through the mill." A youngster would find this an impossible role. Further, say center authorities, "the older volunteer hardly ever loses anyone on the line."

Volunteers are trained to keep their head, however tense a situation. One caller, to emphasize the grimness of his death threat, told the volunteer that he had "a gun in one hand and a knife in the other." Calmly the volunteer asked, "What hand are you holding the telephone with?" This promptly brought the conversation to a more realistic level.

Volunteers also learn that "suicidal people are ambivalent about living and dying, right up to the last moment. They remain open to other alternatives until death." Often the decision to commit suicide comes after months, years, even a lifetime of carrying a burden without relief. Very often the burdens are of such a nature they can't be shared or even mentioned in a person's usual outlets—immediate family, friends, business acquaintances; even doctors, priests, ministers, rabbis. One reason is that any of these people may have created the burden in the first place.

Basically, the view is that the volunteer's job is to take the role of a non-judging good listener who doesn't make demands on the caller. Once he's established a reasonably adequate link with the caller and discovered the problem, his job is to make an appropriate referral. "We aren't here to condemn them, but to help them," is the nationwide theme.

Training periods vary. In San Francisco, it's two months. Real-life situations presented to volunteers are interesting, thrilling, frightening.

Philosophical and Ethical Considerations of Suicide Prevention

Paul W. Pretzel

There are times when the esoterics of philosophical and ethical theory emerge from the classroom and take their place as issues of social concern. There are several ways in which this has been happening of late.

Television network news specials have lately examined such topics as "The Pursuit of Pleasure," asking the question, "How much individual indulgence can society withstand before the cohesion of that society is destroyed?" Corollary to this is the ethical question of how much action a society is entitled to take to demand conformity from its members. Demanding too much conformity stifles creativity, produces stagnation, and runs the danger of formenting revolution; too little control, on the other hand, results in anarchy and dissolution of the society. How much social dissent, then, are we to accept? How many do we permit to "turn on, tune in, and drop out"? How many do we permit to deviate from the social norm and in what ways?

This polarity between individual freedom and social cohesion is a social question, a religious question, a philosophical question, that has a long history which includes many different specific issues including birth control, capital punishment, abortion, euthanasia, and suicide and suicide prevention.

It is an unusual discussion on suicide in which someone does not pose the question, "But doesn't a person have the right to take his own life under certain circumstances?" Or, put more agressively, "What right do you have interfering with the person's decision to take his own life?"

This is no problem, of course, in those cases where the patient himself calls for help, or where he is obviously too mentally disturbed to be entrusted with such a final decision. The question arises in the minority of cases where the suicidal person is apparently in full possession of his faculties and where the circumstances of his life appear to make such a decision a "rational" one. This may occur in some situations when hope seems literally beyond any reasonable expectation.

The individual right of a person to kill himself for any reason has been the

Reprinted from *Bulletin of Suicidology*, July 1968. Published by National Institute of Mental Health.

object of philosophical discussion going back to the earliest roots of Greek philosophy and before.

> Socrates, for example, saw suicide as an evil in most cases and asserted that no man has a right to take his own life, but he must wait until God sends some necessity upon him, as he has now sent upon me. (1)

And as his own drinking of the hemlock indicates, there are such times of necessity.

Plato follows in this tradition, rigorously condemning the self-murder that takes place as a result of "slough or want of manliness" but tacitly approves of a suicide that takes place

> under the compulsion of some painful and inevitable misfortune which has come upon him or because he has to suffer from irremediable and intolerable shame. (2)

The second main tradition of Greek philosophy, that of the Epicureans, has a still more permissive stand in regard to the right of a person to take his own life. For the Epicureans death was not the terrifying object that it was to the other early Greeks. To them, death was simply the end of existence and an end that ought to be hastened whenever the individual wished it. Man is alive to enjoy life, was the Epicurean philosophy, and when life ceases to be enjoyable, there is no reason to continue to live. Lucretius, the Epicurean poet who himself died of suicide, expressed this point of view.

> If, one day, as well may happen, life grows wearisome, there only remains to pour a libation to death and oblivion. A drop of subtle poison will gently close your eyes to the sun and waft you smiling into the eternal night whence everything comes and to which everything returns. (3)

Perhaps the most famous quotation illustrating the Epicurean point of view is this one:

> Above all things remember that the door is open. Be not more timid than boys at play. As they, when they cease to take pleasure in their games, declare they will no longer play, so do you; when all things begin to pull upon you, retire. (4)

For the Epicureans, then, the door is always open. Life will be lived as long as it is enjoyed, but when the hope for happiness dims, the door to death is always open.

The third major tradition of Greek philosophy, that of the Stoics, again endorses the right of the individual to take his life when he wishes it, providing the act is one of reason, will, and integrity. Suicide as a result of despair was weakness and represented failure, but a rational suicide was not uncommon among the Stoics and was endorsed by the community. The Stoic Seneca expressed it this way:

> As I choose the ship in which I will sail and the house I will inhabit, so I will choose the death by which I leave life. In no matter more than in death should we act according to our own desire. (5)

According to Stoic philosophy, it would be far better for one to choose death rather than to see that noble part of him be eaten away by old age or disease. Seneca says in another place:

I will not relinquish old age if it leaves my better part intact, but if it begins to shake my mind, if it destroys its faculties one by one, if it leaves me not life but death, I will depart from the putrid or tottering edifice. I will not escape by death and disease as long as it may be healed and leaves my mind unimpaired. I will not raise my hand against myself on account of pain, for so to die is to be conquered, but if I know I must suffer without hope of relief, I will depart, not through fear of pain itself but because it prevents all for which I would live. (6)

Paul Tillich offers a good summary of the Stoic attitude toward suicide.

The Stoic recommendation of suicide is not directed to those who are conquered by life but to those who have conquered life and are able both to live and to die and can choose freely between them. Suicide as an escape dictated by fear contradicts the Stoic courage to be. (7)

Perhaps Stoicism received its best contemporary expression in the person of Ernest Hemingway who saw man's decision in life as being one of choosing defeat or destruction. Hotchner catches Hemingway in a pensive mood on the occasion of the serious injury of a much-admired matador:

He's a brave man and a beautiful matador. Why the hell do the good and brave have to die before everyone else?

Hotchner explains that Hemingway

did not mean die as in death, for Dominican was going to survive, but what was important is his living had died. I remember Ernest once telling me, "The worst death for anyone is to lose the center of his being, the thing he really is. Retirement is the filthiest word in the language. Whether by chance, or by fate, to retire from what you do—and what you do makes you what you are—is to back up into the grave." (8)

It would be better for man to be destroyed but undefeated, rather than to attempt a compromise with the inevitability of time and thus try to buy off destruction by accepting defeat.

These philosophical arguments defending man's right to kill himself under the "right circumstances" as expressed in the early Greek philosophy were re-examined and, in many cases, supported by the philosophers of the Enlightenment.

In his essay on suicide, Hume upheld man's freedom to do as he will with his own life. (9) Along with Hume, Montaigne (10) also affirmed the right of the suicide on the grounds that life is a blessing and when it ceases to be desirable, one should be free to give it up. Voltaire, (11) too, found the right of suicide in cases of extreme emergency to be an important individual right.

In our time, writers such as James Hillman not only defend the right of the person to kill himself, but he goes on to argue that everyone who is so presumptuous as to try to prevent a suicide is depriving the patient of what might be the most significant decision of his life; even if that decision is to die, it does not necessarily mean there is a failure. Hillman holds that no one has ever proven that the soul perishes after death, and the existential decision to kill oneself might be a necessary decision in terms of affirming the soul, in which case the analyst would be violating the right of his patient. Hillman:

> Usually the death experience is in the psychological mode, but for some, organic death through actual suicide may be the only mode through which the death experience is possible. (12)

But not all the philosophical thinkers of the past have been so vehement in defending the person's right to kill himself. One of the earliest Greek philosophers, the spokesman for the Orphic brotherhood, by the name of Pythagoras, saw suicide as an unmitigated evil. One of the important teachings of the Oprhic brotherhood was that of the transmigrations of the soul, its purification in the wheel of births, and its final reunion with the divine. Jacques Choron describes this teaching.

> The soul is imprisoned in the body and leaves it at death, and after a period of purification, re-enters another body. This process repeats itself several times, but to make sure that with every new existence the soul should retain its purity or become ever purer and better and thus come ever closer to the final stage where the reunion with the divine takes place, man must follow a certain discipline. Philosophy becomes with Pythagoras a way of life that assures salvation. (13)

To Pythagoras, then, suicide is a rebellion against the gods. It is an action that stems from perturbation which is a pollution of the soul and is therefore an unworthy act.

Aristotle, too, condemned suicide on the grounds that it is always a cowardly act.

> To seek death in order to escape from poverty or the pangs of love, or from pain or sorrow, is not the act of a courageous man but rather of a coward, for it is weakness to fly from troubles, and suicide does not endure death because it is noble to do so but to escape evil. (14)

But the main Aristotelian objection to suicide is on the basis that man is fundamentally the property of the state and he has no right to deprive the state of any of its property.

> Therefore the suicide commits injustice but against whom? It seems to be against the state rather than against himself, for he suffers voluntarily. Nobody suffers injustice voluntarily. This is why the state exacts a penalty. Suicide is punished by certain marks of dishonor as being an offense against the state. (15)

The period of the Enlightenment also had its philosophers who deny man's right to kill himself. Kant (16), for example, held that all human life was sacred and must be preserved at all costs. He stressed that suicide is inconsistent with reason and inconsistent with the categorical imperative by which every act should be judged. That is to say, the potential suicide should ask himself, "What would follow if everyone did what I am about to do?"

Schopenhauer (17) was another philosopher who doubted the authenticity of the suicidal person's wish to die. Although Schopenhauer is famous for his pessimism, characteristically dwelling on the evils and ills in life, he discarded suicide as a possible answer to the problem. The suicidal person is not really desiring to reject life, Schopenhauer held. He is rejecting the conditions under which he has been forced to live. He is indeed expressing a will to live, in his rebellion against all the conditions of his life which limit his basic freedom to enjoy life. We might be struck by a similarity between Schopenhauer's position and our own orientation toward suicide, namely that suicide can best be understood as an ambivalent cry for help.

In later times, William James (18) also denied the individual's right to take his own life, holding that the human task is to find the religious meaning in our own individual human lives, and it is only when this religious search is taken seriously that human life becomes meaningful.

This brings us to the consideration of the stand which the major religions of our own culture have taken on the question of suicide. Judaism, which, according to most available statistics, has usually enjoyed a comparatively low suicide rate, holds to the traditional view of the sacredness of all human life which *was* ultimately the property of the Creator rather than the individual person. In the Old Testament, for example, God was very angry with Onan for spilling his own seed on the ground rather than using it for procreation. There are six accounts of suicide in the Old Testament, (19) all of which are simply reported as historical facts without any judgment being attributed to them. In Biblical times, then, there seems to have been no express law against suicide unless the commandment Thou Shalt Not Kill can be interpreted to include self-murder.

There is some indication that during some of the wars, suicide rather than capture by the enemy was being accepted as a custom. Josephus put an end to this, however, by delivering a speech to his army which was considering suicide rather than capture during the siege of Jotaphata. Gathering his army before him, he delivered this stirring speech which he himself later recorded.

> Oh my friends, why are you so earnest to kill yourselves? Why do you set your soul and body which are such dear companions at such variance? It is a brave thing to die in war, but it should be by the hands of the enemy. It is a foolish thing to do that for ourselves which we quarrel with them for doing to us. It is a brave thing to die for liberty but still it should be in battle and by those who would take that liberty from us. He is equally a coward who will not die when he is obliged to die. What are we afraid of when we will not go and meet the Romans? Is it death? Why then inflict it on ourselves? Self-murder is a crime most remote from the common nature of all animals and an instance of impiety against God, our Creator. (20)

This eloquent speech is possibly the first expression of what has come to be accepted as a traditional Jewish view of suicide.

Perhaps even more characteristic than this prohibition are the words of the Mishnah, part of the Talmud. Speaking of a suicide, Rabbi Elizer says,

Leave him not in the clothes in which he died. Honor him not nor damn him. One does not tear one's garments on his account or take off one's shoes, nor does one hold funeral rites for him, but one does comfort his family, for that is honoring the living. (21)

Suicide, according to the Jewish tradition, implies freedom of choice and freedom of will. Almost by definition, a person who kills himself is not in control of his faculties, for it is not a rational act.

For several centuries, Christianity took no direct stand in regard to suicide. The New Testament makes no direct comment about it at all. There is some indication in its early years that certain suicidal deaths were receiving the approval of the Christian community. Martyrdom, for example, was deemed a worthy act commenting as it did on the cruelty of the pagan world, the lack of fear of death, and the strength of faith. Saint Cyprian (22) writes that the true Christians did not fear death and willingly gave their blood to escape from the cruel world. Tertullian (23), in defense of martyrdom, cites with approval some well-known suicides including those of Lucretia, Dido, and Cleopatra. Early Christian history is filled with stories of the faithful seeking out martyrdom as a sure means of eternal salvation.

In addition to the self-seeking martyrs, the early Christian community approved of those young women who took their own lives rather than lose their chastity. Saint Pelagia, a girl of 15, jumped from a roof to certain death to escape a Roman soldier and later was canonized for her action. Saint Ambrose said of her, "God was not offended by such a remedy and faith exalted it." Two other examples of such suicides include the death of Domena and her two daughters who accepted drowning in preference to loss of chastity, and Belsilla, a 20-year-old nun, who abused herself until she died and in so doing received the approval of Jerome.

The first clear statements against suicide in the Christian tradition came from the pen of Saint Augustine (24) who, in the *City of God,* put forth the view that suicide is never justified. He supports his opinion on the basis of four reasons: (1) The Christian is never without hope as long as a possibility of repentance remains alive, but with suicide the possibility of repentance is gone; (2) suicide is homicide, and this is a forbidden act; (3) there is no sin worthy of death. The Christian is not his own judge, for this is the prerogative of God alone; and (4) suicide is a greater sin, at any choice. The Christian is better advised to make any choice other than killing himself, for he will be guilty of a lesser sin and still be alive to repent.

St. Augustine had to modify his position somewhat since the Church had already canonized some suicides such as that of St. Pelagia. Augustine handles this by assuming that she had received special divine revelation which sanctioned her act, and thus this exceptional case did not invalidate his reasoning.

St. Augustine's view prevailed in the Church, and beginning with the

Council of Arles in 452, the Church issued a series of encyclicals defining their anti-suicide position and designating a series of punishments for the act. As time went on, the punishments became more intense and more cruel, reaching their culmination in the 18th century when it was not uncommon for the body of a suicide to be dragged nude through the streets, be buried at the crossroads with a stake in its heart, being deprived of the rights of burial, and having the state confiscate all the deceased's property, thereby depriving the heirs of their inheritance.

The trend toward such cruel punishment began to be reversed with the publication of *Biathanatos* by John Dunne, (25) Bishop of St. Pauls, in the mid-17th century. His thesis was that the power of God is great enough that we are in error in assuming that all suicides are irremissible sins. It was the first plea for moderation and understanding, and as a result, both secular and church law against suicide began to be modified.

In our own time, those like Edwin Shneidman, (26) who would defend suicide-prevention activities as being ethical, even imperative, and based on solid philosophical convictions, have stressed three basic points: (1) The ambivalence that is always present in any human action, including that of suicide; (2) the fact that suicide is impulsive; and (3) the effect that such an action has upon the survivors, including the general community.

To those like Hillman (27) who offer a mystical rationale defending the right of the individual to make this existential choice, other thinkers such as Robert E. Litman respond by pointing out that

From the medical point of view, questions of the soul and its destiny are rather irrelevant when confronted with a corpse. No matter how committed an analyst might be to the soul, it would seem his work, too, is stopped by physical death. (28)

Litman goes on to observe that if philosophical and ethical theory are to be relevant to the work of the clinician, they cannot be developed apart from the clinical setting, or (to use Freud's image) they will be like the whale and the polar bear who cannot carry on meaningful conversation since each being confined to his own element, they cannot meet.

Hemingway's suicide, for example, cannot be attributed simply to his philosophy of life while the signs of his personality difficulties in the last year or so of his life are ignored.

What is needed, according to Litman, to provide a meeting ground for scientists, theorists, philosophers and therapists who wish to discuss or argue suicide, is publication of the essential material of clinical psychology, a collection of detailed case reports on the lives and deaths of a variety of intensively studied individuals who committed suicide. (29)

Perhaps we can begin here to focus on the relationship between the clinical and philosophical fields. Our society often endorses the following four types of suicides as being "rational" and in regard to which the ethics of intervention might be open to question:

1. those suicides carried out for the good of some cause, as in the case of religious martyrdom, military heroism, or dramatic social witness;
2. those carried out as a reaction to what appears to be a literally hopeless, painful, and debilitating situation, as in the case of lingering terminal illness;
3. those in which the circumstances are not desperate, but in which the individual is no longer receiving the pleasure from life that he wants and so makes the decision to go through the "open door" away from life.
4. the so-called love-pact suicide where the double death is seen as having some aesthetic value, possibly being an expression of love, beauty, or dedication.

Let us examine some clinical illustrations of each of the categories. What we have designated as "suicide in support of a cause," Durkheim (30) described in terms of the "altruistic suicide."

Such a suicide, according to Durkheim, takes place when a person is overintegrated into his society and subordinates his own desires to the will of the group. One example of this is that of a captain going down with his ship to certain death in obedience to the social tradition that expects such behavior. Another example is that of a case reported by the press in 1965 of a young man who died of self-immolation in Washington, D.C., as part of his protest against the war in Vietnam. Norman Morrison was 32 years old, married, and a father. He was a college graduate and also held a degree from a recognized theological seminary. People who knew him described him in terms of his capacity to be a close personal friend, profound in his thinking, and sensitive to human suffering. They deny that he was an eccentric or a fanatic.

> But in fact he was a normal person in that he was genuinely concerned with other human beings, those in Vietnam and those who were with him. He was flattering to others as a conversationalist because he took what one had to say as something very important. Norman wasn't just a good listener but was truly concerned about the concerns of others. He loved people not in the sense of polite liberal abstractions but in the sense that other people got inside and affected him. He enjoyed carpentry around the house, gardening, softball, ice hockey, the things we all find normal. He was not a pious saint attempting some kind of fanatical purity. (31)

Morrison was a Quaker, and as such believed in a concerned and loving God, the sacredness of human life, and he shared the traditional Quaker abhorrence of war. We have available to us, then, a rather clear picture of Morrison's philosophical orientation, and a clear rationale for the act of self-destruction that he performed. If this were all that there was to say, Morrison could be cited as one of the rational suicides which comes about through dedication to some cause. What is missing, however, is a complete write-up of Morrison's personality development and a thorough appraisal of any psychiatric symptoms that might have been appearing in the last few years. What is needed, then, before any kind of accurate judgment might be made about the rationality of this type of suicide, is more complete data so that a more accurate evaluation can be made from several points of view.

The second type of suicide which our society may consider to be rational and ethical is that which stems from what appears to be an apparently hopeless situation. The prototype for this type is the elderly person who is suffering from a chronic, painful, and terminal disease. What is surprising to most people is that suicide among this population is as rare as it is. One case which might serve as an example is that of Joan Smith, a 24-year-old, attractive girl who has been suffering from Hodgkin's disease since the age of 12. The progress of the disease has been slowed down but yet continues with no real help of a cure.

Joan has been married for 4 years to a man by whom she had become pregnant prior to the marriage and who has continued since the marriage to have numerous affairs of which she was aware. She feels unloved by him and describes her home situation as being intolerable. Joan feels affectionate towards their 3½-year-old son, but she also feels that he deserves a mother who will be alive throughout his childhood and adolescence. She has strong feelings of self-depreciation and feels that anyone with whom she is closely involved is somehow going to be infected by her. She has thought about terminating her very unsatisfactory marriage but feels that her son deserves a father, even one as inadequate as this, and does not know what she would do if she did divorce him. She feels it would be unfair to her to consider marriage to any man.

In addition to her husband and her son, she has a mother, a stepfather, and a sister. The stepfather pays very little attention to her. Her mother, on the other hand, is a very "sweet" woman, long-suffering and double-binding. Joan has strong dependency feelings toward her mother and feels trapped and unable to cope with the kinds of demands that her mother subtly puts on her. Her sister is widowed and struggles to support herself and her three children. Joan and her sister have a fairly good relationship, but Joan feels guilty about accepting any help from this sister who has problems of her own. Joan has been suicidal for several years, and has made two very serious attempts in the last 6 months, both of which required hospitalization. She feels that she is nothing but a burden to those people who are near her and feels helpless and hopeless about ever attaining any significant degree of self-sufficiency and independence. The world, in general, and her son, in particular, would be better off if she were to die immediately and not burden everyone with several more years of emotional and financial stress. Her fantasy is that if she were to kill herself, her husband soon would remarry and her son would have a better mother almost regardless of whom the husband married.

In this case, as in the case of many such "hopeless" situations, the hopelessness, it later became clear, was more a function of Joan's emotional attitude than it was a function of the philosophical reality of the situation. As a result of her repeated suicide attempts, Joan was placed in therapy and with the help and support of the therapist was able to make certain decisions which changed the complexion of her life entirely. She left her husband, moved in with her sister, and began to reorientate her life around finding satisfactions for herself. She made appropriate and realistic plans for her own social life, accepted certain financial and social responsibilities that gave her a feeling of self-sufficiency and ability, and was able to continue functioning effectively as a member of the family and of society. To be sure, it might be expected that Joan will come across future crises in which she will seriously consider suicide, but if this happens, it will be the result of her emotional situation rather than a rational decision.

The third type of suicide which some consider rational concerns the exit through the "open door" of the Epicureans when life has failed to provide sufficient satisfaction to justify continuation of life, even though there is no overt or physical, hopeless situation. One example of such a type may be that of Ernest Hemingway, referred to earlier. Another example is that of Jim Johnson, a 60-year-old man whose wife had passed away several months earlier from cancer. The Johnsons had been married for some 35 years and although the marriage was childless, it was described by Jim as being a very close and a very happy marriage. Jim was steadily employed at one of the large manufacturing firms in the area where he held the position of skilled laborer. Four months prior to Mrs. Johnson's death they were told she had cancer and was given 6 months to a year. At that time Jim retired from his position at the manufacturing plant in order to be able to be at home and to nurse his ailing wife. When she died 2 months later he found himself without a job and without his wife—without his two main reasons for living. Being unable to tolerate the feelings he experienced in the house in which they had lived for many years, he sold it and purchased a trailer in a senior citizens' park.

Jim, himself, was in excellent physical health, had some interests, some hobbies, and was even able to formulate some plans for how he would spend his remaining years. He had no other family left, but had a close relationship with his wife's family. The problem was, as he put it, that he found no pleasure in anything anymore. He was chronically depressed and was unable to work through his grief. Life was flat and meaningless, and although there was no physical or mental agony, neither was there any pleasure or satisfaction in life. He began ruminating about suicide, considering several different plans. One night he came to the decision that life for him was no longer worth living, that he could no longer receive any satisfaction or pleasure from life, and so he killed himself.

To the Epicurean, this suicide might be seen as a rational act of a man who walked through the "open door," no longer willing to continue a life without satisfaction. To the clinician, however, the situation would seem quite different. The clinician would see an unresolved-grief reaction with difficulty in tolerating the depression which realistically follows such significant and important losses. The clinician's hope would be that although Jim would experience a residual sadness for the rest of his life, once the grief reaction had been dealt with, he would be able once again to experience satisfactions in certain aspects of living and that suicide was, for him, not the answer.

The fourth category of so-called rational suicide is that which we have called the love-pact suicide in which the double death is seen as having some esthetic value. Although not uncommon in romantic literature, such suicides are relatively rare in Western culture. They are more common in Far Eastern literature which characteristically portrays a pattern involving

a young merchant or craftsman and a young girl. Because of economic difficulties, problems preventing their marriage, such as their parents' or spouses' objections, poor living conditions such as pending criminal proceedings or inadaptability to rapid social change, one night in spring or summer of the Tokyo-Osaka area toward dawn, they stab themselves (occasionally hang or drown themselves) and almost never survive. (32)

The actual love-pact suicides in Japan, however, do not follow this romantic picture. According to Dr. Ohara's study, these suicides are characterized by unstable job situations, unsatisfying sexual relationships, social, economic, and emotional difficulties. Far from being a high expression of beauty or dedication, they can be described more accurately as desperate and unhappy resolutions of painful conflicts. Parties to a love-pact suicide are not dissimilar to people who commit suicide under less romantic circumstances.

One type of love-pact suicide is the murder-suicide pact where one party seeks to take a loved one into death with him. One such case involved an attractive 35-year-old mother who shot her 10-year-old son and then killed herself, after writing a 22-page suicide note expressing her fears for herself and her son and explaining at some length that this seemed to her to be the kindest thing to do and the only way to resolve the conflicts that life offered. But again, clinical investigation into the life of this person reveals increasing and intensifying symptoms of schizophrenia, terrible confusion and fear, paranoid ideation, and suspicion that had its climax in a double tragedy.

This, then, is the kind of investigation that needs to take place as the philosophical and ethical considerations of suicide and suicide prevention are being considered. The investigation must have the double focus of philosophical ideas and metaphysical continuity along with clinical evaluation of what is happening within the life of the person who would perceive his act as being rational and *justifiable.*

For the person who is working in the field of suicide and suicide prevention, as well as for the person who is confronted with a suicidal situation, the question is when, if ever, is the clinician willing to say:

Yes, I agree. It is the best thing for you to do, and I have no right to interfere, so I won't.

Where does he stop trying? How long does society desire to force continuation of life? Where is the point, if indeed there is one at all, at which the ambivalence inherent in any human action, including that of suicidal behavior, shades into self-determination? How far does the community want to go in forcing other people to adhere to life?

The purpose of this paper has been the limited one of attempting to set forth some of the basic considerations that should be weighed as the issue is being met.

REFERENCES

1. Plato. *Phaedo.*
2. Plato. *On Laws.*
3. Fedden, Henry Romily. *Suicide, A Social and Historical Study.* London: Peter Davies, 1938.
4. *Ibid.,* p. 87.
5. *Ibid.,* p. 74.
6. *Ibid.,* p. 76.
7. Tillich, Paul, *The Courage To Be.* New Haven: Yale University Press, 1952, p. 12.
8. Hotchner, A. E. *Papa Hemingway.* New York: Random House, 1966, p. 251.
9. Hume, David. *An Essay on Suicide* (1789). Yellow Springs, Ohio: Kahor and Co., 1929.
10. Montaigne. *That To Study Philosophy Is To Learn To Die.*
11. Dublin, L.; Bunzel, B. *To Be or Not To Be.* New York: Smith and Haas, 1933, p. 218.
12. Hillman, James. *Suicide and the Soul.* New York: Harper & Row, 1964.
13. Choron, Jacques. *Death and Western Thought.* New York: Collier Books, 1963, p. 32.
14. Aristotle. *Nicomachen Ethics, B&V.*
15. *Loc. cit.*
16. Kant, Immanuel. *The Metaphysics of Ethics.* Edinburgh: T&T Clark, 1871, p. 239.
17. Schopenhauer, Arthur. *The World as Will and Idea.* London: Degan, Paul, Trench, Tribune & Co., 1907.
18. James, William. Is life worth living? *The Will To Believe.* New York: Longmans, 1904.
19. These are:
    Abimelech (Judges 9:54)
    Sampson (Judges 16:28-31)
    Saul (I Samuel 31:1-6)
    Saul's Armor Bearer (Chronicles 10)
    Ahitophel (II Samuel 17:23)
    Zimri (I Kings 16:9, II Kings 9:30)
20. Dublin. *op. cit.,* p. 174.
21. *Loc. cit.*
22. *Ibid.,* p. 198.
23. *Ibid.,* p. 199.

24. St. Augustine. *City of God.*
25. Dunne, John. *Biathanatos.*
26. Shneidman, Edwin. Preventing suicide, *American Journal of Nursing,* 65:111-116, 1965.
27. Hillman, James. *op. cit.*
28. Litman, Robert E. Review of Hillman's "Suicide and the Soul." In: *Contemporary Psychology, 12:449-450, 1967.*
29. *Loc. cit.*
30. Durkheim, Emil. *Suicide.*
31. Memorial Service for Norman R. Morrison. Friends Coordinating Committee on Peace, November 21, 1965.
32. Ohara, K.; Reynolds, D. Love Pact Suicide. [Unpublished study]

Dr. Pretzel serves as psychologist and pastoral counselor at the Suicide Prevention Center, Los Angeles, California.

CRISIS INTERVENTION

The drama of crisis intervention has been exploited by the mass communication media and the public has a vague idea or image of the suicide prevention center. Manned by a central core of professional workers—usually psychiatrists, psychologists, social workers, nurses, the center depends upon a great number of volunteers whose prime duty is to answer telephone calls as they might relate to distressed individuals. These volunteers, usually lay people, represent a wide range of interests, sophistication and capability. It is their responsibility to weigh the significance of the call and make an appropriate referral either to one of the central workers or to a peripheral practitioner who has some affiliation with the center. Most of these volunteer workers are well motivated and service oriented. Unfortunately, however, some curiosity seekers and some morbid individuals are occasionally found in such projects.

Suicide Prevention Centers tend to vary in their operations and the quality depends upon the interest and funding available. These centers also look to the cooperation of the various professional societies in their region, and some states and counties enjoy excellent relations and cooperation in such a project.

It would seem that crisis intervention should be a well-defined element in the functioning of any good mental health center where there should be an awareness of the suicide problem and a growing acquaintance with the unstable members of each community.

It would also seem that any person who has continued exposure to individuals who are in varying degrees of crises may make a significant contribution in suicide prevention.

The Concept of Loss in Crisis Intervention

Martin Strickler and Betsy La Sor

INTRODUCTION

Crisis intervention has been steadily gaining in popularity since Gerald Caplan and Eric Lindemann first began describing the phenomenon of crisis. The usefulness of this work is particularly seen in the prevention of hospitalization of the individual. (3) Crisis, however, provides both special motivation and opportunity for a distressed person of any psychological, social or cultural level to attempt new ways of coping with particular life hazards. (6)

Caplan describes the crisis situation as involving a "relatively short period of psychological disequilibrium in a person who confronts a hazardous circumstance that for him constitutes an important problem which he can for the time being neither escape nor solve with his customary problem-solving resources." (1) Intervention consists of assisting the individual in solving this current problem by learning other and hopefully healthier ways of coping with the circumstances. Crisis intervention treatment, therefore, focuses on the immediate problem situation, not on long-standing pathology or well-established character patterns.

A trainee in crisis intervention must become accustomed to several alterations in his usual style of therapeutic assistance. Detailed assessment of the crisis requires clearcut determination of: (a) the actual precipitating event that transpired within the past few weeks; (b) the hazard or threat to a significant relationship or social role that emerged within the process of that event; (c) the loss to psychological needs that confronted the person as a consequence of the hazard (see below); (d) the customary and often very limited range of problem-solving resources or ego coping mechanisms employed to deal with the hazard; (e) the new factors or conditions involved in the recent situation that mitigated against the usefulness of habitual ways of coping with that hazard; and (f) the seemingly insoluble cognitive dilemma that derived from the impasse in resolving a vital life problem, eventuating in a state of crisis. (2)

Once this careful assessment has supplied the crisis picture, the treatment

Reprinted by permission from *Mental Hygiene* Vol. 54, No. 2, April 1970.

goal is then to communicate to the patient the essence of his dilemma, enabling him to be restored to an emotional equilibrium and to be ready for problem-solving. (5)

In the beginning contact the individual in crisis can occasionally identify a problem; much more often he can only describe feelings of despair and immobilization in his life. The short time limit of treatment, usually six weeks, and the urgency of the problem demand that the therapist understand and define the crisis situation for the patient in the first or second visit. Without a clear picture of all the elements leading to a crisis, utilization of the crisis intervention model is impossible and the sessions begin to resemble conventional short-term therapy with the focus on pathology rather than on the crisis itself.*

Strickler views crisis as occurring "only if the individual senses that he does not possess available means of coping with the hazard, which is seen consciously or unconsciously as a vital threat to his narcissistic, libidinal or dependency needs and supplies." (4) He has found that in every crisis three basic kinds of psychological needs are threatened to some degree; in each crisis situation, however, there is a predominant loss or threat of loss with respect to one or another of these three types of needs. Identifying the major loss suffered in a particular crisis (point "c" in the above assessment) can thereby greatly facilitate the overall assessment and intervention. It enables the crisis therapist to have a deeper awareness of the conflict or dilemma the individual is feeling and the reasons why previously used coping mechanisms are not sufficient to deal with the hazard.

This paper will define the three types of losses to which any adult in crisis, regardless of his level of mental health, is vulnerable. Following these definitions, case material will illustrate the predominant loss in each of three crisis situations and the value of this knowledge to the intervention.

LOSS OF SELF-ESTEEM

An individual enhances or bolsters his self-image and feelings of worthiness by receiving external supplies of recognition. A loss of self-esteem occurs when the person suddenly feels unable to maintain a sense of sufficient validation or confirmation of his self-worth. To a considerable degree this validation is dependent upon his ability to perform well in certain specific social roles or

---

*The Benjamin Rush Center, the Crisis Division of the Los Angeles Psychiatric Service of Los Angeles, has developed the theoretical and clinical model for the Individual or Specific type of crisis intervention as distinguished from the generic model of crisis intervention. (See Jacobson, Gerald F., Strickler, Martin, and Morley, Wilbur E., Generic and Individual Approaches to Crisis Intervention, American Journal of Public Health, Vol. 58, No. 2, February, 1968.

relationships; they are endowed by the individual with special importance on the basis of personal, social and cultural determinants in his history. A crisis can be triggered if the person's usual problem-solving resources are insufficient to protect the vital sources of external recognition required to supplement his inner sense of work.

LOSS OF SEXUAL ROLE MASTERY

In both sexes the ego has to arrive at an inner decision or solution regarding the level and type of success that the individual can comfortably attain and retain in the adult male or female role as defined by a society or sub-culture. Success in the adult male role is principally perceived in the larger American society in terms of performance in vocational and heterosexual areas; the adult female role is mainly assessed in terms of succes in maternal, heterosexual, and (increasingly) vocational areas. A loss of sexual role mastery occurs when a change in a significant relationship or role challenges or confronts the individual with the need to perform at a qualitatively new (higher or lower) level of success than he can accept in one or another of these areas.

The crisis intervention approach concerns itself with the various coping devices that the ego employs to provide and sustain "safe" compromise levels of investment in one or another area of the adult male or female role. A crisis may ensue when a situation will not permit the individual to function with the same relative sense of well-being he had previously enjoyed in a particular area of sexual role identity.

LOSS OF NURTURING

One of the major anxiety contents of life is the loss of love. A prime need of human beings is to be nurtured, and this requires the adult to find his own comfortable balance in the inter-relatedness between independence and dependence. Not only does our society provide less with each succeeding generation in the way of extended family emotional and social supports, but it continues to emphasize the values of independent strivings, competitiveness, and self-reliance. The problem that this engenders with respect to the need for nurturing requires the use of various ego mechanisms, such as projection and identification, sublimation, and forms of altruism, as well as conscious ego coping in particular social roles and relationships. The threat of loss of nurturing arises when a life event confronts the individual with actual or fantasied loss, or prospect of loss, of a nurturing object or role. A crisis state can then ensue if the habitual ways of coping designed to deal with such a threat are felt to be inadequate to perform this task.

CASE STUDY OF LOSS OF SELF-ESTEEM

Mrs. A, a 36-year-old divorced woman, came to the clinic to get help for her 16-year-old daughter. Joan was presenting a problem at home and particularly at school of increasingly uncooperative and disrespectful behavior. In describing this current situation it became evident that Mrs. A was herself in a state of crisis. A brief historical assessment revealed a series of stressful family events with which Mrs. A apparently had adequately coped until recently.

Mrs. A appeared youthful and attractive. She complained of feeling very weak and overwrought because of the behavioral problems her daughter was displaying. Currently Mrs. A was a student on scholarship at an excellent private music school. The family had been managing financially without a man for some years, with Mrs. A holding a number of low paying but difficult jobs. She could feel comfortable about her marginal breadwinner role, but any threat to her ability to maintain the image of student or promising musician had always aroused the greatest anxiety in her. Mrs. A had sustained herself for many years with the gratification she derived at being an outstanding student in her necessarily protracted, part-time higher educational pursuits.

One month before Mrs. A came to the clinic she found she could not work and also keep up her school work; she stopped working and had been drawing on a moderate amount of savings. Her decision to give up her job required the family to live within an even tighter budget. The problem with Joan began at about this time. Joan expressed resentment about a cut in her allowance and her no longer being able to keep up socially with her friends' social activities or clothing fads.

Because she had always worked before, Mrs. A felt she had been able to cope with her daughter's occasional unruly and demanding behavior with a combination of firmness and small gifts. Also, any conflict between the dual role of mother-student had apparently been inwardly justified by her hard-earned weekly paycheck. Although Joan's behavior seemed to require additional parental control, Mrs. A now felt a sudden and unusual powerlessness to exercise any control over Joan.

The therapist pointed out to Mrs. A the dilemma she was feeling, namely, that if she would continue with school while unemployed she could not cope effectively, in ways familiar to her, with Joan's needs and demands, but if she would go back to work she would again find that it would seriously interfere with her studies. The importance to her of her professional career was especially recognized in terms of her feelings of self-esteem. However, her sense of failure as a mother, which resulted from Joan's school misbehavior following Mrs. A's quitting her job, seemed to require her to sacrifice the professional plans that meant so much to her.

With the restoration of emotional equilibrium that followed this conceptualization of the dilemma, Mrs. A was able to see that finishing school could greatly enhance the future financial well-being of the family and she could actually provide better for her daughter's own higher educational needs. With this assurance she began again to be appropriately firm with Joan, and to utilize a new type of coping, namely, directly communicating with her daughter about her own needs and the impasse she was feeling. Joan responded to this firmness and communication with improved behavior which in turn reinforced Mrs. A's sense of adequacy in dealing with her. Mrs. A decided to complete her studies and was comfortable with this decision.

CASE STUDY OF LOSS OF SEXUAL ROLE MASTERY

Mr. D, a 27-year-old married man sought help at the clinic because he was not happy with his life, his marriage, or his wife. Mrs. D, a 24-year-old woman married to Mr. D for two and one half years, was seven months pregnant. In reviewing the history it seems to have been an unplanned but cautionless pregnancy. During the past three to four months Mr. D had been leaving home in the evening with weak, false alibis, and returning late at night or the next day. Women's letters were "accidently" found by Mrs. D and in general a pattern of infidelity was evident and not denied by Mr. D. Instead, he would shake his head and say there was really nothing to worry about and that he just couldn't help himself. He handled Mrs. D's nagging, accusing behavior with agreement or withdrawal in the treatment sessions, and by leaving the scene at home.

A clinical picture of Mr. D showed him to be a person whose usual behavior pattern in the marital area was that of a mildly delinquent boy. He had been able, though, to hold creative working positions, had done quite well, and liked his work. His capacity for adult management of household and marital responsibilities, however, seemed fairly minimal. His role of "naughty boy" at home had been permitted and even supported by Mrs. D's readiness to indulge him. He had been able, therefore, to enjoy marital status despite his little boy behavior at home.

Mrs. D had recently posed a serious challenge and threat to Mr. D by demanding that he now recognize he would soon be a father and that he take more responsibility in being "the man of the house." Mr. D began to feel an overwhelming panic that he could not define and it was at that point that he came to the clinic for help.

The problem or dilemma was outlined as involving Mr. D's intense fearfulness in being challenged to take on new responsibilities in the marriage that he felt unable to manage; at the same time his recent efforts to escape this situation were understandably unacceptable to his wife. Mr. D's distress diminished considerably with this conceptualization of the problem. Also, Mrs. D was able to see that this was indeed a critical emotional problem for her husband and not merely a continuance of his usual marital pattern. She began to display her more usual warmth and acceptance of him as a man. Mr. D then found that he could stay at home with his wife and discontinued the pattern of infidelity. This, in turn, proved to be sufficiently reassuring to Mrs. D. After the crisis itself was resolved, a referral to a family agency was arranged to work with the couple until after the baby arrived.

CASE STUDY OF LOSS OF NURTURING

Mrs. M was a 32-year-old married mother of two children, ages three and four. She came to the clinic in an extremely agitated state, feeling sure she had "lost her mind" and half expecting to be hospitalized. She had made a suicidal gesture three days before applying to the clinic by seizing a knife and threatening to stab herself. All this was in the context of a most unusual explosive type of behavior. She had experienced feelings of depression on one or two previous occasions during the past six months when she assumed more responsibility than she felt she could manage. She described herself as unable to say "no" to anyone who had a claim on her, and she ran herself ragged helping friends and relatives.

It was with much encouragement and insistent focusing on the therapist's part that Mrs. M could state that she made the suicidal gesture after her husband asked her to continue to engage in certain sexual acts which she found extremely repugnant. She had submitted on several previous occasions but had felt miserable and guilty afterward. She did not share her feelings with her husband. When it appeared that he expected her regular participation in these acts she exhibited the wild, irrational behavior which brought her to the clinic.

Mrs. M explained that she had been brought up in a strict Roman Catholic home and boarded at a parochial school during her adolescence so that her conscience "said" to her that certain sexual acts were sinful and undignified. While her conscience would not permit her to agree to certain acts, she felt that if she said "no" to her husband he would stop loving her.

The therapist pointed out that ministering, and even sacrificing, for others was important and characteristic for her, particularly with regard to her husband to whom she felt so indebted and emotionally needful. However, she recently found she could not in the instance of her husband's sexual expectations be everything he expected her to be because of her religious and moral background, and this presented her with the fearful thought that she might lose his love.

When Mrs. M returned to the clinic the following week she looked and behaved in a dramatically different way. She had color and life in her face and her manner was cheerfully animated and almost euphoric. She had talked with Mr. M about her problem, after getting up her "nerve." Mr. M had "lovingly" agreed not to make such demands again and said his request hadn't been of such importance to him. She now realized that the imperative command to conform came from "within my own mind."

SUMMARY

The phenomenon of loss is a fundamental issue in all crisis situations. We therefore consider that its particular nature be clearly defined and understood in the general and characteristic assessment process of crisis intervention treatment. This paper has therefore ventured to delineate, define and illustrate three kinds of adult losses: self-esteem, sexual role mastery and nurturing. Case material has been utilized to demonstrate the thesis that even though all three types of losses are involved to some degree in every crisis situation, one of these kinds of losses appears to be predominant and qualitatively more significant than the other two, in the etiology of any crisis reaction. The ability to identify the pertinent kind of loss in a particular crisis enhances the preventive goals of crisis intervention.

REFERENCES

1. Caplan, Gerald, Principles of Preventive Psychiatry, New York, Basic Books, Inc., 1964.
2. Jacobson, Gerald F., Wilner, Daniel M., Morley, Wilbur E., Schneider, Stanley, Strickler, Martin and Sommer, Geraldine J., The Scope and Practice of An Early Access Brief Treatment Psychiatric Center, American Journal of Psychiatry, 121:12, 1965.
3. Morley, Wilbur E., Treatment of the Patient in Crisis, Western Medicine, 77:3, 1965.
4. Strickler, Martin and Allgeyer, Jean, The Crisis Group: A New Application of Crisis Theory, Social Work, 12:3, 1967.
5. Strickler, Martin, Applying Crisis Theory in a Community Clinic, Social Casework, 46:3, 1965.
6. Strickler, Martin, Bassin, Ellen B., Malbin, Virginia and Jacobson, Gerald F., The Community-Based Walk-In Center: A New Resource for Groups Underrepresented in Outpatient Treatment Facilities, American Journal of Public Health, 55:3, 1965.

Crisis Intervention and Health Counseling: An Overview

Catherine M. Miller

Few educators would disagree that more students in today's world are in need of counseling services than ever before. Various reasons have been postulated for the increasing numbers of young people desperately searching for resolution of their problems through someone they can relate to as a "significant other person." Two decades ago, Paul Masoner drew a conclusion which seems even more relevant today:

> Counseling must show strong concern for helping individuals in personal problems, in the solution of emotional problems, in the exploration of social problems that are a common phenomenon in this world of tension and unrest. The increasing strains that grow out of a disordered international scene, the dislocations that arise from compulsory military service, the personal frustrations in respect to educational and vocational goals, the feelings of insecurity that develop in a complex world—all place upon the counselor a responsibility that is constantly growing in its seriousness.[1]

Regardless of the reasons behind the need for counseling services there are certain undeniable trends within the student population which need to be recognized. One, students tend to select a specific, liberal, yet objective individual whom they feel they can communicate with even though the principal role of that individual is not perceived as one of a counselor. Very often this "significant other person" is a health educator or another health related professional whose primary function is either instructional or health service oriented. The student chooses this professional for reasons other than title. In this instance the student initiates counseling rather than being selected for counseling. Two, problems of a socioeconomic or emotional nature by far outnumber physiological ones. Three, acts involving morality are often overshadowed by an extreme concern over the consequences of these acts. For example, the boy friend's dilemma is not over sexual relations but what to do about his pregnant girl friend. Four, young people are finding themselves involved in deep emotional relationships which have not or may not result in marriage. It would not be uncommon for the counselor to see one or both of

Reprinted by permission from *School Health Review*, Vol. 1, No. 4, September 1970.
[1]Paul H. Masoner, "The Role of the Counselor in the New World," *Journal of the National Association of Women's Deans and Counselors*, March 1950, p. 120.

these involved individuals. Five, the health professional can expect the student to need only a limited number of counseling sessions. Most likely one or two visits will suffice. Prolonged counseling is not the general pattern. This concept places a responsibility of utmost importance on the counselor for a successful outcome of the initial contact. Six, at the precise moment the student seeks professional help, he may realize that his usual coping mechanisms are inadequate, and what he feels is overwhelming to him now—today. What he needs is resolution of his problem and an immediate return to a state of equilibrium.

The terms "stress," "need," "problem," "crisis," are not new, nor are the concepts and practices of counseling. Health counseling has long been considered an integral part of health education, particularly as an aspect of school health services. On the other hand, crisis intervention is a relatively new field and one which is receiving increasing attention in the psychological, theological, and sociological disciplines. The following discussion will acquaint the health professional with the commonalities and the differences between health counseling and crisis intervention and the role of the health educator in these programs.

HEALTH COUNSELING

The generally accepted definition of health counseling is, "the procedure by which nurses, teachers, physicians, guidance personnel, and others interpret to pupils and parents the nature and significance of a health problem and aid them in formulating a plan of action which will lead to solution of the problem."[2] The process of health counseling may involve any or all of the following: organized classroom instruction pertaining to health problems which are common to practically all students or to groups of students; group health counseling; individual health counseling; and incidental health counseling. So as not to confuse health counseling with organized health instruction, health counseling, in this context, is concerned with health matters which pertain to the individual student.

The health counselor is the dynamic force in the health counseling setting. The student, displaying various manifestations of stress or distress, brings to this setting his problem which represents a state of uncertainty, perplexity, or difficulty. The question then is, "What are the expectations and characteristics of this health counseling experience for both the counselor and counselee?"

1. The duration of the problem may be as short as a few days or last over an indefinite span. The symptoms or feelings of the student may develop into a depression state or vacillate between depression and euphoria.
2. The sphere or periphery of the problem could encompass student-peer

[2] "Report of the Committee on Terminology in School Health Education," *Journal of Health, Phsyical Education, Recreation,* September 1951, p. 22.

relationships, student-parent relationships, or student-teacher relationships. More specifically, the immediate concern may be one of social maladjustment, emotional immaturity, or personal inadequacies.

3. The student will indicate various psychological and/or physiological symptoms of being "under stress." These signs may be overt, and thus observable, or covert, being uncovered as the counseling session progresses. A significant indication of concern has already been established when the student seeks out a counselor.

4. The problem-causing stimulus (causative agent) may not be profound, in and of itself, nor uncommon in others within the same age group. It may be a circumstance which presents itself to everyone at some time in life.

5. Although the student is in a state of disequilibrium at the moment, it can be expected that the usual reequilibrating mechanisms will reduce or eliminate the problem. Other individuals with similar problems may utilize habitual coping mechanisms successfully, but the student involved in a counseling experience needs supportive direction or redirection from the counselor.

6. The time span between the problem-related tension and the solution of the problem is usually short. This time will vary in proportion to the availability and/or accessibility of a counselor.

7. The student expects the counseling session to have a successful outcome. Either he will leave feeling relieved, or he will be equipped with some directives for appropriate actions which will achieve resolution.

8. Often the role of the counselor is only that of a listener. The need to dramatically intercede or become profoundly involved is not always desirable. The student may only be requesting and wanting to be heard.

9. The counselor, by virtue of his training, may be able to handle a majority of the problems with which he is confronted. However, regardless of his professional experiences and personal attributes, he should have a readily available list of referral personnel and services. He should recognize his limitations and utilize other resources.

10. When the problem is resolved, the behavior of the student will not appear to be significantly different. His outlook or life style will be much the same as prior to the problem. This is so because the student, with the aid of his counselor, has utilized established or habitual coping mechanisms to eliminate or control this temporary deviation from his normal life pattern.

The medium which stimulates or perpetuates health counseling experiences is the classroom in which health instruction takes place. The student, by selection or computer chance, is enrolled in a course directed toward cognitive learning of relevant health topics which will hopefully direct him toward and result in appropriate (for him) health behavior. At some point the student will relate to the topic, to the instructor, or to both. Under these conditions, health counseling experiences, whether numerous or few, are inevitable.

CRISIS INTERVENTION

Parad, a leading authority on crisis theory, defines crisis intervention as "entering into the life situation of an individual, family, or group to alleviate the impact of a crisis-inducing stress in order to help mobilize the resources of those directly affected."[3] The circumstances may be such that the crisis intervention process focuses on the individual or a composite of individuals. The base for the following discussion is the individual student who is in a "crisis state."

The student in an overpowering state of disequilibrium is driven by the situation toward the intervener-to-be. The selected intervener then becomes essential to the student. These two variables then formulate a counseling relationship with the counselee sensitive and susceptible to the help offered by the counselor. With this setting in mind, some concepts of crisis theory and crisis intervention can be identified.

1. The duration of the crisis is relatively short, often lasting from one to six weeks. The student is more likely to be somewhere between worry and depression on the continuum of psychological disequilibrium. There is a longer than usual period of subjective stress.
2. The crisis state may be a result of any one of the following hazardous circumstances: illness or death of a family member; pregnancy or birth; divorce; marriage; changing jobs, schools, or communities; or scholastic dismissal. Whatever the cause, the crisis stimulating experience is new to the student.
3. Depending on the severity of the crisis to the particular student and at what point the counselor sees him, the symptoms of tension may appear as is expected for someone under psychological stress. Or the student may be helpless, ineffectual, or completely disorganized.
4. The problem stimulus, often one of deprivation, loss, or change, is traumatic, unusual, and often abrupt in its appearance. It is a novel situation involving novel forces.
5. Beyond a certain point, habitual problem solving methods are ineffective and unsuccessful. Trial and error attempts by the student to cope with the crisis and subsequent failures lead him to seek counseling.
6. Steps taken in crisis intervention toward a crisis solution are complex and time consuming. A crisis may lead to other crises while current crises may involve other previous inadequately solved similar problems.
7. During a counseling session, the student may display displeasure, anxiety, guilt, fear, or shame. The expression of these feelings needs to be allowed.
8. The counselor needs to act, either for the student or with the student. Listening, without follow-up activity, will not suffice. Positive action could include: setting another time and date for counseling, having the student

[3]Howard J. Parad (ed.), *Crisis Intervention: Selected Readings* (New York: Family Service Assoc. of America, 1969), p. 2.

call or come into the office within a short time period, or referring the student to a more qualified professional. Ability to cope with a new crisis depends on successful resolution of previous ones.

9. A professional, working in crisis intervention programs in an educational setting, needs appropriate training in this area. A teaching, administrative, or medical degree does not prepare a person adequately to prevent or intercede in crisis unless follow-up training is specifically directed toward competencies in crisis theory and intervention. In many instances the crisis intervention counselor must rely on other school and community personnel for referral and assistance.

10. A different perspective on life or even a new living pattern may result from the crisis, the counseling, or both. It can be concluded that the counselee is, in fact, a different person.

Crises occur in the lives of all people, at all ages. Some experience more than others; some can cope with them better than others. A few are predictable; most are not. Crises related to certain developmental periods in school-age pupils are common enough that preventive services should be included in all schools for all students. One such service could be one or several health educators specifically and specially trained to handle these situations.

IMPLICATIONS FOR THE HEALTH EDUCATOR

A review of the theories of health counseling and crisis intervention reveals certain commonalities. They are alike in that a "significant other person" is a requisite; the student is undergoing various degrees of stress; the effectiveness of the student is minimized; normal coping mechanisms may be inadequate; referral is necessary in some cases, follow-up is essential in all; and the current problem or crisis may be the result of an accumulation of previous problems and crises.

Health counseling and crisis intervention differ in some respects. They are not similar in relation to the degree of problem stimulus; types of circumstances surrounding the problem; duration or intensity of discomfort or stress; length of time the problem persists; number of counseling sessions required for resolution; amount of significant activity required of the counselor; reliability of normal coping mechanisms; or subsequent behavior patterns following counseling.

Crisis intervention and health counseling are not abilities which go with a particular academic degree or come naturally with a specific number of years of teaching experience. Each necessitates some specialized training. With these competencies at hand, the health educator should do everything he can to encourage self-referral on the part of his students. When the student seeks his services, he should listen to the problem; evaluate the degree of severity of the situation; plan for further counseling or referral; and engage in follow-up activities.

Crisis Intervention by the Counseling Psychologist

Stanley Pavey

The dictionary defines the word "crisis" as a crucial situation or turning point. The definition hardly does justice to the strong or complex emotions which both the person in crisis and the person intervening in the crisis are likely to experience. While most of us have had to deal with at least mild crises, our own experiences may be poor preparation for dealing with people whose crises are so huge as to have propelled them to the edge of suicide or commitment to a mental hospital.

The mental health worker learns quickly that part of his job is crisis intervention. Most of his work tends to be routine and relatively uneventful. But, from time to time, he is going to have to deal with emergencies that require the quick, sure mobilization of all the knowledge, good judgment, and decision-making ability, not to mention good luck, that he can muster. The person before him may be undergoing a massive attack of anxiety. He may feel that his very existence is threatened, or that insanity is imminent. He may be experiencing pain more unendurable than any physical pain he has every felt. Or the crisis may involve suicide. There may be a phone call with the voice on the other end of the line expressing an unbreachable hopelessness and despair. The only way out appears to be the bottle of sleeping pills he has nearby. Or someone may bring in a student who has already passed over the dividing line into psychosis. He may be in an acute schizophrenic state, perhaps hearing the voices of enemies saying vile things and accusing him of deviant sexual practices.

The mental health worker has been trained to handle such crises. But to say that in every case he deals with them coolly, calmly, and with certainty and skill is more of a wish than a reality. Psychologists, psychiatrists, social workers, and others who come in contact with the emotionally disturbed as part of their daily work are bound to respond emotionally as well as intellectually, and because their emotions are involved and the situation may require decisions to be made on the spot, even the most highly trained professional, with many years of experience, may make mistakes. I would like to illustrate the hazards of dealing with crises by telling you of a young lady who is currently in treatment with me. I choose this particular case because it is complex enough to give a good picture

Reprinted by permission from *School Health Review*, Vol. 1, No. 4, September 1970.

of the many variables that enter into crisis intervention, and because I made some mistakes. More can be learned from such a case than from one which went by the book and was handled smoothly and without complications.

The young lady involved (I'll call her Lynn) had been in counseling with me for more than a year at the Counseling Center of the university where I am employed. Her greatest difficulty was that she mistrusted people, including me. She was isolated, alone, and from time to time very frightened. Before the incident I want to describe, there had already been a series of minor crises precipitated by Lynn in order to test whether she could trust me and rely on me. I had done everything I could in the normal course of counseling to instill in her the feeling that she could depend on me. Nevertheless, from time to time, there had been emergency phone calls followed by lengthy sessions in my office. I gave as generously as I could of my time to convince Lynn of the solidity of my commitment to her. There had been some positive results, but all my efforts had not reduced the frequency of the tests to which Lynn felt compelled to subject me.

As another way of giving Lynn a sense of interpersonal security, I had given her my home phone number and had told her to feel free to call me if she needed to. At first she was reluctant to impose on me, but then there began to be all too many calls. Once, when I was unable to come to the phone, and she was told that I would have to call her back, she felt rebuffed and stopped calling for a time. But the calls began again. I was somewhat ambivalent about them. On the one hand I felt that it was good for Lynn to have someone to speak to when she needed help, but on the other hand I recognized the calls as a sign of her dependence on me, and that I was playing some part in fostering it. The major crisis came after a series of phone calls complaining of increasing depression. Previously I had been able to get her to talk things through and to reassure her. She usually felt better by the end of the call, but now the depression seemed too powerful to yield that easily. The call to tell me that she was contemplating suicide seemed almost inevitable. She had the sleeping pills and she was going to take them.

Normally I believe in every individual's freedom to make his own choices in life. But that does not include the decision to do away with oneself. When someone feels as pushed to the wall and as hopeless as Lynn did, he is not, at that moment, free to make choices. Lynn was caught in a net of emotions which limited her freedom. Suicide for her, was not choice, but an imperative, and because she was not free, Lynn was in some sense my responsibility. Just how much of a responsibility was vague to me then, but I felt terribly responsible. My feelings of responsibility were only one part of the string of thoughts and feelings I had to cope with at that time, and which resulted in my telling her that I did not want her to commit suicide, that I was not going to let her do it, and that there was reason for her not to do it; that there was hope. I obviously wanted Lynn not to commit suicide. But the reason was not as simple and straightforward as my being responsible for her in some abstract way. I also liked her, cared about her, and did not want to see her do anything to hurt herself. But I cannot say that at that moment I did not share any of Lynn's utter despair. I did. I honestly doubted if she would ever work her way out of her apparently hopeless situation and achieve a life happy enough to justify efforts to save her. So, the questions, "Should I try to save her?" and "What right do I have to interfere with her?" raced through my mind. The way in which I handled the crisis was not a result of satisfactorily answering those questions. The questions smacked of more highminded considerations than the baldly selfish one that I did not want Lynn's suicide on my hands. I certainly did not want to suffer any of the guilt or remorse which would have been inevitable if Lynn did carry through her threat. I did not know how I would have lived with myself if I did not make every possible effort to save her. It was quite clear in my own mind that in trying to save Lynn I was also saving myself from eventual self-reproach.

There were more tangible considerations, too. I worried that if Lynn took her life, I might be faced by a suit for malpractice brought by her family. Any mental health worker is subject to such law suits, and in the case of a suicide it was not stretching the imagination too far to imagine that a bereaved family would seek damages if I had failed to do everything I could to save her. There also came to mind the fact that I was a psychologist working without medical supervision. I felt in a legally vulnerable position, and I wanted to get Lynn into the hands of medical authorities just as swiftly as I could. It should be apparent by now that Lynn's crisis was a crisis for me as well, and I was as interested in a happy resolution of my crisis as I was in doing the best I could for her.

I urged Lynn to admit herself to the psychiatric ward of the county general hospital. She had been there once before, for one night only, and had not liked it. At first she did not want to go, but after I told her what benefits I thought she could derive from it, she said she would consider it. I felt that her admission would give her a chance to get away from the pressures of her daily life. She would have time to think things through with less emotion than she had been experiencing, and she would also be able to receive medication which would help alleviate the depression. Lynn said she would call me back within a half hour to let me know her decision. The time until she did call was almost unendurably tense, not knowing whether she had already taken the sleeping pills or not. When she did call and told my she had decided to go the hospital, I was immensely relieved. Our common crisis was going to be resolved without tragedy. But I could not feel fully secure that I had discharged my responsibility until Lynn was safely in the hospital. I told her that I would drive her to the hospital. I picked her up at her apartment, went with her into the emergency room, and waited with her for more than two hours before she could be admitted to the ward. Though the crisis was over, the complications arising from how I had handled it were not.

Lynn remained in the hospital for two weeks, longer than either of us thought she would; but that is how long it took her to respond to the medication. While she was in the hospital I visited her twice. When I came the second time, Lynn ran up to me and threw her arms around me. She had done it impulsively, and the moment she did it she became embarrassed. It was at that point that it became apparent to both of us that as a result of her crisis, and the way I had handled it, something significant had happened to our relationship. A line had been crossed—the line that is so essential to keeping the professional and the personal separate in one's work. By being drawn so intimately into her life; by being as concerned about her ultimate fate as I was; by taking on as much responsibility for her life as I had; and by stepping in so actively, I had become personally involved in a way that did neither Lynn, nor me, nor our relationship any good. Conversations with my colleagues at the Counseling Center convinced me that I had unwittingly been badly manipulated and controlled by Lynn. She had made the ultimate threat of suicide and in response I had stepped beyond the bounds of my professional role. It was not only by what I had done, but by my feelings as well, that I knew something was wrong. I felt too close to her and too vulnerable to her demands. My permissiveness and understanding, and my desire not to impose any limits that would lead her to feel insecure, had all backfired. If I was going to be of any help to Lynn, I was going to have to establish a more realistic relationship.

Somewhat in anger, somewhat in self-defense, but mostly in the name of good therapy, I increased the emotional distance between Lynn and me when she resumed her counseling with me. In our sessions I was more matter-of-fact and businesslike. As I had expected, Lynn reacted badly to this, and in the face of what she must have experienced as withdrawal of my concern and affection for her, she began to test me again. I was accused of not caring, and there were once again angry scenes in the office. Then the phone calls began again, not to my home any more, but the office. She needed to come in to see me before her next regularly scheduled session. I had determined that no matter what the consequences, I was not going to go any further than good professional judgment dictated, and that was the once-a-week, fifty-minute hour in my office. Almost inevitably there came the anguished call in which she pleaded such desperation that I must see her immediately. It was not easy to deny her what she was asking for, because she was obviously suffering deeply. But I mustered all the strength I had and told her that I would see her the following week at her regular appointment time. As I put the phone down I could hear Lynn crying out my name in what must have been excruciating pain and terror at being deserted by me. I was not sure that Lynn would not then commit suicide. It was a chance I was taking and felt I had to take.

It worked. More than that, I had done exactly what needed to be done. And best of all, Lynn recognized it herself. At our next session Lynn told me that by finally setting limits and not responding to her unending demands, I had revealed myself to her as a human being. Now I was someone she could more easily believe in. Even in the face of the intense hunger for the things she had been asking from me, she recognized that for me to yield to her was not what she really needed. By this seeming denial of help, I had freed both Lynn and myself from one of the myths we had been laboring under. After the surprisingly insightful response, Lynn stopped making demands. From that point on, counseling proceeded much more smoothly and is still going on. Although Lynn has a long way to go, she has surmounted much of her hopelessness and has been able to begin to work productively on her problems in a way she could not before our crisis. For both Lynn and me, her crisis was an important learning experience.

There are a number of lessons I learned, and I would like to try to clarify them, as much for myself as for my readers. One thing that should be apparent from my account (and I hope it is reassuring rather than horrifying) is that even someone with ten years of counseling experience and some sense of how to handle crisis situations is liable to make serious errors of judgment. In telling the story of this particular crisis I have tried to give some clues about why this might be the case.

When a crisis involves someone we know well and are emotionally involved with, good sense is likely to desert us. What may seem to us like the finest of motives for how we handle a crisis, when examined in the cold light of day, are likely to turn out to be more self-serving than generous. At the time Lynn presented her numerous crises to me I felt that I was doing her a service by providing her with the time, attention, and concern she was begging for. I had it all neatly rationalized as an attempt to engender trust, which, if it could have worked, would have been worthy. But if I had really been engendering trust, I think there would not have been the ultimate confrontation. The fact of the matter is that I had been therapeutically blinded. My eyes were closed to the full import of Lynn's demands upon me. Had I seen more clearly, I would have done other than what I did. What blinded me was emotion. It may be creditable that I cared, that I was not standing off in an aloof therapeutic pose. But because I was so emotionally involved, I could not know what was best for her.

In any situation in which the helper is presented with a crisis, and his own emotions are involved, he needs to exercise extreme caution and to be very clear about his motives for how he handles the situation. The endangering emotions are likely to be a need to be needed by the person seeking help; the need to be omniscient or omnipotent ("I know what it is you need to get you through this crisis, and I can—and will—give it to you, or do it for you."); or sometimes even sexual interest in the person. In this particular case, there were at least some of these emotions in addition to the ones I have mentioned of guilt and the fear of legal and professional complications. These needs and fears undid me.

Another lesson that emerged for me from this crisis situation with Lynn was that what appears to be giving and generosity may be just the opposite. So often a crisis is a cry for help. People who gravitate to the field of mental health are humanitarians—or at least see themselves that way. Humanitarians are supposed to give. We rarely learn, either in our general upbringing or in our professional training, that knowing when to withold is as essential as knowing when to give.

The present emphasis, not only in the mental health fields but throughout society, on empathy, trust, and entering as fully as possible into relationships, is as full of peril as it is of possibility. The capacity to give unstintingly of oneself, and even temporarily to sacrifice oneself for another person, is laudable. But reality dictates that discrimination about when, and how, and to whom to give is equally important. Indiscriminate giving may simply be yielding to irrational needs which can never be filled. In handling a crisis it is as important to know how to set limits as it is to respond empathically. Parents eventually learn how necessary this is for their children. People who deal with emotional crises need to be even more aware of it.

I would not go so far as to say that Lynn's suicide call to me was precipitated by how generously I had been responding to her until then, but I have some suspicions that that was the case. Lynn undoubtedly felt much hopelessness and despair, but there is more than one way she could have dealt with these emotions. Once they were there, Lynn used them in the service of other strong, irrational needs. I think Lynn needed to draw me into her crisis, to have me participate and suffer with her, and particularly for me to demonstrate in some ultimate way how I felt about her. Nothing less than a suicide threat would provide the ultimate test. And had I not already taught her that when she asked, she was likely to receive? I mention this possibility of my complicity in bringing about the crisis because the genesis of a crisis is as important as how it is handled, and what I am suggesting is that sometimes misguided efforts to help may actually be a factor in bringing a crisis into existence.

I would also like to stress again what I mentioned in passing before: that Lynn's crisis was a crisis for me as well, and in this respect I am in a not very different position from the nonprofessional who may suddenly be confronted with someone in crisis and who may have to make important decisions about what to do. Despite years of training and experience, every crisis situation has its unique elements, and there is no such thing as a crisis which can be handled routinely. For the professional and nonprofessional alike, response to a crisis is going to depend upon a number of factors, and the response itself can vary considerably, from panic, aversion, and impatience on the one hand, to patience, understanding, and helpfulness on the other.

How an individual responds to a crisis may depend upon the nature of the relationship with the person undergoing the crisis, past experience in dealing with crises, insight into the nature of emotional disorders, but perhaps most of all, how much personal confidence and security one has. Personal strength and a sense of one's own ability to handle difficult situations, even in the absence of formal mental health training, can go a long way toward helping someone in crisis.

Particularly in milder crises the person may merely be looking for an anchor point, some mooring to which he can hold fast until the storm is past. I am sometimes amazed at how useful it is for someone in crisis merely to tell his story to someone who is willing to listen sympathetically. In fact, sometimes that is all there is to crisis intervention. Sometimes just listening, plus a common-sense suggestion which has escaped the person only because he is so panicky, is enough to restructure the person's perception of his situation so that it is transformed from a hopeless one to one which has some possibilities for resolution. To the extent that the person intervening in the crisis can avoid panic himself and not be bowled over by the intense emotions of the person suffering the crisis, he may be able to render as valuable a service as any trained mental health worker could.

In cases which are more complicated, however, referral would be made to someone equipped to deal with emotional crises. For the nonprofessional, the decision to refer or not to refer may not be clearcut. We usually either want to do all we can ourselves, which may lead to delaying a referral that should be made, or because of feelings of discomfort or overestimating the intensity of the person's problem, we may shunt the person away from us as quickly as possible. Professionals and nonprofessionals alike can make mistakes in estimating what a person in crisis needs.

But one rule above all should be observed, and that is that no one is obliged to put more of himself into a crisis situation than he is comfortable doing. Confronted with a crisis, no one is obliged to suffer anxiety and stress any longer than is absolutely necessary. There is no abstract need to help someone in crisis, except by getting him just as quickly as possible to someone who can provide that help. Nonprofessionals, then, should be aware of the resources in their institutions and communities for such referrals. Fortunately, there are more and more facilities offering crisis intervention services. The emergency telephone numbers and walk-in facilities mark an important step forward in our awareness that we must deal knowingly and swiftly with people in crisis.

I have tried to highlight some of the pitfalls of crisis intervention in this paper, but I would like to end it on a more optimistic note. There is yet one lesson I learned from my experience with Lynn, and that is that even when mistakes are made in efforts to be helpful, the resolution may still be an entirely satisfying one.

Crisis Intervention by the Health Educator

Dan Leviton

"May I come in? You said to call or drop by at any time . . . during your lecture . . . you said to come any time if we had a problem."

"Sit down, you're not interrupting anything. Let me light up a pipeful. Do you want some coffee?"

"No, thanks anyway."

"You're in my Health 5 lecture, aren't you?"

"Yea, that's what I'm here about."

"You mean you want to drop the course already?"

"No, the course isn't bad . . . in fact, it's kind of cool. I mean leveling about sex and people . . . I mean that's what's important . . . the course ought to be required of everyone. Who in hell would have expected lectures on death and suicide in a health ed course? Man, I was ready for the usual BS on 'don't blow grass,' 'don't smoke,' 'eat leafy green vegetables,' and 'take cold showers when you get excited thinking about girls.' "

"Obviously you don't want to drop the course . . . what's your name?"

"Mike. Have you ever blown grass? Well, if you need some, I supply the guys in the dorm."

This was my introduction to Mike, a tall, sensitive, likable freshman enrolled in a required health education class at the university. He had accepted an invitation offered to all of our students by both my graduate assistant and myself to call or visit at any time if the situation warranted it. Mike was in my office for a reason and it was not to compliment my teaching or to play the braggadocio about his role as a drug supplier, a role which turned out to be negligible and motivated by reasons other than monetary profit. He was there because he was contemplating his own self-destruction, hovering between what Freud called the libido (the striving for life drive) and mortido (the drive toward death). It was while in this state of psychic ambivalence that he came in for the first of many visits.

In a situation like that just described, the health educator has several options available to him in dealing with a student-client. He may overtly or covertly say, "Get out of here," or "I'd better call the police on this guy." He

Reprinted by permission from *School Health Review*, Vol. 1, No. 4, September 1970.

may shove off the responsibility to the vice-principal or the dean. On the other hand, he may conclude that Mike has a problem which may be drugs but the likelihood is that it is something more deep-seated. This article is for those who would opt for the last alternative. The many "Mikes" have taught some of us, our faculty and graduate students, that health educators can and must provide the very personalized and vital service of health counseling and crisis intervention.

The purpose of this article is to describe how health educators can appropriately intervene to ameliorate the most profound crisis of all—that crisis which includes suicidal ideation and intent.

The health educator needs training in the basics of crisis intervention and health counseling if any positive contribution is to be made in sensitive situations. An untrained person dealing with others while they are working through an emotional crisis could do a great deal of harm. At the University of Maryland, those familiar and experienced in this area lecture to one another's classes on the topic of suicide prevention and crisis intervention. In their in-service training program, our graduate assistants are given basic theoretical information, methodology, the names of available supportive agencies on campus, and an understanding of such concepts as medical confidentiality, privileged communication, psychological stress, homeostasis, etc. There is available a growing literature on crisis intervention theory for those interested (see the references at the end of this feature). This theory is the basis for contemporary community mental health programing and preventive psychiatry. Articles applying the theory to health education and public health models have begun to appear in the appropriate professional journals.

The health educator's counseling skills can be improved further by an understanding of the works of Carl Rogers, Viktor Frankl, and Abraham Maslow. They emphasize the concept that health is highly individualistic and that the client must be respected as he chooses alternatives or values in seeking his own brand of health. These alternatives and values need to be understood by the therapist if the client is to resolve his problem and become "healthy." The purpose of counseling is to help the client come to see different, more constructive, and healthier ways of dealing with a problem.

Each counselor will find the style which best suits him. Many adapt an eclectic approach based on Rogers' nondirective model and the more traditional one. "Client-centered psychotheraphy" as developed by Rogers (1) rests on two assumptions: (1) the individual has within him the capacity, at least latent, to understand the factors in his life that cause him unhappiness and pain, and to reorganize himself in such a way as to overcome those factors; (2) these powers will become effective if the therapist can establish with the client a relationship sufficiently warm, accepting and understanding. The counselor does not do something to the client. His case is not diagnosed nor is his personality evaluated. No treatment is prescribed nor does the therapist set the goals which shall be defined as a cure.

"Instead," writes Rogers, "the therapist approaches the client with a genuine respect for the person he now is and with a continuing appreciation of him as he changes during the association. He tries to see the client as the client sees himself, to look at problems through his eyes, to perceive with him his confusions, fears and ambitions. The therapist in such a relationship is not concerned with judging or making suggestions, but always strives to understand. In this atmosphere of complete psychological security the client can lay himself bare with no danger of being hurt. Protected by the conditions of therapy, he begins to reorganize the structure of self in accordance with reality and *his own needs.*"

The client's feelings are reflected by the therapist, thus enabling the client to see the possible problems and conflicts and other approaches to reconciling them.

In the traditional therapeutic model the therapist will often establish the goals (or the cure), and he tends to look at the client from his own perspective (he is the therapist and the patient is "sick"). Instead of an egalitarian relationship, in the traditional model the "patient" is usually asked to recline on a couch while the therapist sits in a position of authority. More importantly, in directive, supportive therapy, the therapist intervenes to "improve" the behavior of the client. The therapist represents the established societal order and thus hopes to "treat" the client so that he will act "appropriately" or "normally," that is, in a more socially acceptable manner.

Sometimes, as in the case of life and death, the counselor is forced to intervene in a strictly directive way. In discussing student suicide, Diamond writes, "Above all, I do not qualify as nondirective in the sense of being content that each client shall dispose of his own life as he sees fit. When I meet the possibility of suicide, I find myself wishing to prevent it." (2) This powerful, authoritarian type of intervention was not necessary in the case of Mike where the intent to kill himself was ambivalent, a point which we shall discuss later. It was necessary in the case of a young freshman coed who became psychotic during her first semester at the university.

Barbara was a student in the required health education course. A beautiful, sensitive girl, she had become increasingly talkative during the semester but in other ways her behavior was ordinary. She had good contact with reality, there were no noticeable mood swings (manic or "high" one moment and depressed or "low" the next), she related well to others, and in fact, appeared to be an extremely vivacious and loquacious student. Increasingly she talked about the cheerleader tryouts, a position she valued highly. In fact, when she was absent from my class I assumed it was due to the fatigue of excessive practice or nervousness. She wanted the job so badly that she placed ads in the school newspaper under ficitious names lauding her ability in an attempt to influence the judges. That was the first overt behavior which cued me to keep her under some degree of observation. I later learned that she had failed to make even the qualifying round in the elimination trials for the coveted position. Her failure to make the cheerleading team seemed to be the precipitating factor which affected her functioning. We can only take so much stress; each of us has a threshold of endurance.

I resolved to contact her after the weekend but she sought me out the following day. My wife and I were attending a Children's Physical Developmental Clinic staff meeting. Word reached me that a young lady was asking for me and that she was obviously in a quite agitated state. The three of us went over to the Student Union to talk over coffee. Barbara fantasized that her parents were spying upon her and engaged in a conspiracy to prevent her from winning the cheerleader's job. Further, some friends had published her life story in a school newspaper. Most of the time she was incoherent, out of touch with reality, and suffering from feelings of persecution. One did not have to be a Freud to recognize that Barbara was completely disorganized and disoriented in her functioning. How she found me at the clinic remains a mystery. After our talk I suggested that it would be best if she went to the Student Health Service to be seen by a physician. At first she refused but later reconsidered. In essence, she was gently but firmly persuaded to do as I requested. She was eventually hospitalized for several months, discharged, and is now continuing her education.

In this short description, several points should be noted. First, the troubled individual gives clues which the sensitive counselor can pick up. These clues may be verbal or nonverbal. In the case of Barbara her often illogical and ever increasing verbosity was a clue suggesting agitation and mania. The compulsive desire to attain a goal (cheerleader), a goal which was not realistic considering the girl's capabilities, was another. A more astute counselor would have asked himself, more quickly than did I, what would be the cost to Barbara if she failed to make the team? Her ads in the newspaper were a cry for help that should have been answered immediately by a concerned friend. In the case of crisis the clues are there if only we will see them.

Secondly, the fact that Barbara came to me rather than anyone else is important. Repeatedly, the crisis intervention literature emphasizes the role of the "significant other person." Investigations indicate that the troubled person, the person in crisis, will seek help from one who is meaningful and valued. A teacher, especially a health educator, by definition, may be that important someone. He is in the powerful and responsible position of being able to influence and help the tormented other. Thus, it was no accident that Barbara accepted my rather unequivocal direction to go to the Student Health Service. The next day, after she was released in the company of her parents, I again advised her that she needed the services which only a psychiatric hospital could offer. This was done in a quite supportive manner and on the basis of rationality and logic. She agreed that she was tired and "unable to think straight," but still was relectant about being hospitalized. She remembered my saying that a person's past or present physical or psychiatric history really has nothing to do with one's worth. "Do you think for a moment, Barbara, that our friendship will diminish one iota because you are going to a hospital?" I asked. Deliberations continued until finally I said, "Barbara, if we are friends and if you trust me, then I must ask you to agree to what we have discussed here today. I will stay in contact with you, and when you are finished with your stay we will have a celebration dinner . . . but we shall go to the hospital and that is final." For a person who is extremely suicidal or who has had a psychotic break (the two need not be related), the counselor needs to be directive. The situation is so overwhelming that the individual usually is in no position to act or think rationally.

A third principle that emerges from this case is that the counselor needs to be a good listener. The very fact that someone requests to be heard is important. You may suggest that some students seek a counselor, teacher, or nurse simply to get attention, and I could reply that that, too, is a significant problem. Loneliness, with its accompanying despair and depression, is one of the major problems of our time, and of our campuses. And this topic brings us back to Mike.

Mike continued to talk of drugs, of a variety of courses, and of other people, his dormitory mates in particular. When listening empathetically one tries to put himself in the place of the speaker. What is his problem? What is the *real* problem which may or may not be revealed in the ordinary verbal conversation? In Mike's case a noticeable change was apparent as he talked of his friends on the third floor of Epsom Hall.

"You know, one thing I can't stand is a phony," he said. "And I've got my share in Epsom."

"What kind of guys are they?" I asked.

"No good. Inconsiderate . . . pure selfishness. Can you imagine anyone playing their record player until three in the morning? I mean, man that's too much. Any guy with any sense knows that others have to sleep. And I've lent out money and things and have to go ask for it back. I mean, if I borrow something I'm going to return it as fast as I can with a thank you."

His hands twisted and turned on a nonexistent handkerchief. There was anger and yet a wistful quality in his voice. I felt that here in his relationships with his roommates, was the crux of the problem. "Mike, your roomies aren't as open and honest with you as you would like?"

That was the phrase, the stimulus, the cue that enabled us to bridge the hiatus between client and counselor. Mike had tried everything to win entry into the third floor clique. And it should have been easy for him. He was a well-built fellow, and handsome in a Germanic sort of way. Pushing drugs (primarily marijuana) had been an attempt to gain entry into the group, and he all but gave the substance away. He was the most savvy guy when it came to music and that which was "cool" and "in" and what was far out. But due to certain factors, some of which came out in our later sessions, he just could not gain acceptance. He was an outcast and this pattern of rejection had been common throughout his life. He had never been able to "make it" with the other fellows.

My wife and I (when appropriate, we often function as a team because her insights, perceptions, and counseling add much to the case) invited Mike home with us for supper and with that gesture established a bond of communication and friendship. It was later that he became quite depressed. He had made no progress in gaining acceptance. Mid-term grades had been returned and Mike found that he was dangerously close to failing those courses requiring some modicum of study and concentration. (As an aside, I should argue for the need for counseling those students who either fail or are placed on academic probation. Too often they are simply labeled "the dumb ones" and left to fend for themselves when, in reality, their inability to perform in the academic structure may be a behavioral clue that they need help. The "failing" student, by definition, needs counseling. For too long he has been neglected and even persecuted by school health authorities.)

The next time I saw Mike he entered the office and plopped in a nearby chair. His shoulders drooped and he spoke in a monotone with a trace of despair—a syndrome that rings alarm in my mind. After an exchange of pleasantries I asked, "Mike, are you thinking of killing yourself?"

"It's crossed my mind. What do I have to do to prove myself to those bastards? It's gotten to the point where I know that they're intentionally bugging me . . . trying to get on my nerves."

At this point he almost wailed his misery. Here was depression coupled with hostility, a classic prodromal clue to suicide. Karl Menninger has observed that the suicidal person has the wish to die, the wish to be killed, and the wish to kill. Mike wanted to kill those in his dormitory while also desiring to die. The aggression which should have been directed outward toward an object (dormitory mates) became reversed or directed inward toward the self. One of the first questions a knowledgeable therapist will ask of someone contemplating or who has attempted suicide is, "With whom are you angry?"

It is also important to determine why the environment has become so intolerable for the client. Death or the end of life was beginning to look attractive to Mike. Emile Durkheim, the French suicidologist and sociologist, believed that suicide was related to the degree to which an individual is integrated into society. Of the four types of suicide he discusses (egoistic, altruistic, anomic, and fatalistic), the egoistic type best "fits" Mike. Egoistic suicide occurs where there is slight integration of the individual into family life. If his peer group can be substituted for the "family" our comparison seems valid. Mike was an outcast and the resulting environment was becoming too unbearable. He was in need of help.

In counseling a potential suicide it is important to determine the lethal quality of the intent. I asked Mike rather matter-of-factly to what extent he was planning to take his life. Had he thought about the time, the day, the method? Had he actually the murder weapon in his possession? The individual who has a loaded revolver hidden in his bureau and says that he will end everything on a specific date and time presents a far more critical situation than a person who says he is thinking about suicide and has made no real plans about its implementation. Both situations require intervention but the former is of the greater urgency. Mike's case was somewhere in between. He did not have a weapon but he had developed some obsessive thinking about death and suicide.

It became apparent that I, as a health educator, needed to call upon those with greater training in psychotherapeutic techniques. Mike and I had discussed a strategy which might help him ameliorate his situation. It seemed that Mike was in the position of trying to "push" himself into a social group, an effort met with greater and greater rejection. We ascertained that there was no reason for Mike to value this particular group. Its members had no distinguishing character-istics one way or another and they did not share any of his interests. The group simply represented all of the other ones which had continually rejected Mike throughout his lifetime. Friendship, like wealth, is often best pursued indirectly. It was agreed that Mike might want to participate in some campus activities where the development of friendship was a secondary and not a primary goal. For the politically oriented, the Young Republicans or Democrats, Young Americans for Freedom, or Yippies were available. Skiing and sports car racing, bowling and sky-diving enthusiasts have clubs on campus. A variety of service organizations such as our Children's Physical Developmental Clinic also meaning-fully utilize students. Mike had options open to him.

As a second part of this strategy he agreed to visit a counseling psychologist at our highly regarded University Counseling Center. Fortunately our health education staff has developed an excellent relationship with the Center. A phone call will gain an immediate appointment for our client. Often the Center or the Student Health Service will request a confidential write-up of a particular case to help in their evaluation. The point here is that the health educator functions as part of a mental health team. He is the first line of defense, capable of handling many clients himself, yet he realizes the necessity of screening through those who need more sophisticated therapy.

I took the responsibility of checking out a few of the organizations. For example, our Clinic director made it quite clear that Mike was needed and would be put to work. Here is an example of the counselor taking action. He is saying to the client, "Look, I'm doing something for you; I and others care!" It is extremely important for the counselor and not someone else to take action on behalf of the student. If he says, "Look Mike, give me a call in a day or so" or "my secretary will check up on you tomorrow," the counselor becomes as rejecting as the other groups.

The client must be made to understand that the counselor cares to the extent that suicide will not be tolerated under any circumstances. Ludicrous as it sounds, he must say to Mike, "Look, I won't allow you to kill yourself. It's out of the question. Do you think I'm wasting my good time in developing our friendship to have you blow your brains out? Who will my wife prepare exotic meals for if you start playing fun and games?"

Mike responded well. As expected, he developed a good relationship with his psychologist. Our relationship continued with his periodic visits and some good "bull sessions" but they diminished as he found new interests and friends. We met again at spring term registration, and he exclaimed, with tongue-in-cheek and somewhat mischievously, how surprised he was that more people didn't commit suicide as a result of our tedious, frustrating registration process. When asked how things were going, he described a variety of friends and interests (he was in the company of three others at the time).

As could be expected, the dormitory group had opened up to Mike as his interests were directed elsewhere. He became a man of mystery to them, getting up at 7:30 a.m. on Saturdays (to work in our Clinic), and the possessor of an increasing number of rare and exotic jazz and rock records (he had joined a local collector's club). Of course, Mike had the brains to keep quiet about his new interests; in short, he became the quintessence, the epitome of the "cool cat." The worm had turned. The dormitory group wanted Mike but the passion was not reciprocated. Mike had learned several lessons, two of which were that it is impossible to be loved by everyone all of the time and that man can improve his own existence.

What may the health educator learn from this little vignette? First, the role of health counselor and crisis intervenor is a natural one for him to assume. One does not have to be a trained psychiatrist or psychologist to work in the area which has been described. One does have to be highly motivated, a good listener, perceptive to the varieties of "cries for help," trained, and at ease with and understanding of one's own personality and needs.

Second, health educators need to understand that this thing which is called "health" is a highly individualistic phenomenon, which varies among individuals and between individuals and cultures. What is one man's health may literally be another man's poison. Contemplation of this concept will tend to make health educators a little more tolerant of the idiosyncrasies of others and consequently better teachers, better counselors, and better human beings.

A County Mental Health Association's Hotline

School Health Review

When does a teenager's problem become a teenager's crisis? Ask him. He is likely to answer you this way. "Who is there to tell?" Label it lack of communication. "Who would understand?" Or, "Who would care?" Label it the generation gap. But now it can be labeled Hotline. That's what it's all about, the Montgomery County Mental Health Association's Crisis Intervention Program for troubled teenagers.

The MCMHA has been vitally concerned for a long time about improving communication for teenagers in Montgomery County and early in 1969 sought other agencies in various parts of the country who were dealing with problems of youth. Why was the association concerned? MCMHA acted on the belief that adolescence is a time of transition and disturbance, that the choices made by youth during this time of passing crisis, if unresolved, become another stumbling block in normal development and that properly structured guidance during this brief period may hold great influence in enhancing development. How he copes with today's crisis may become tomorrow's way of life. The important factor, MCMHA believes, is that any type of intervention in a moment of crisis must be readily available, professionally sound, yet acceptable to the youth who needs it.

The Montgomery County Mental Health Association turned to local statistics to substantiate the need for a crisis intervention program for teenagers. In January 1969, youth aged 12 to 24 made up 25% of Montgomery County's population. In 1968 there were 1,384 runaways between the ages of 12 and 17, out of a total population of 70,596 in that age bracket. During the same period there were 3,783 criminal arrests, and in three years, drug arrests rose 745%, according to police records. The National Institute of Mental Health contributed other statistics and suggested that Montgomery County, Maryland, may have the highest attempted suicide rate among adolescents anywhere in the country. During the past year, 41 teenagers attempted suicide and two succeeded. In a 1966-67 study by the Montgomery County schools, 3% or 2,287 public school children were described by teachers as in need of special services for the

Reprinted by permission from *School Health Review,* Vol. 1, No. 4, September 1970.

emotionally handicapped; only 624 were actually receiving adequate services at the time.

Another factor contributing to MCMHA's concern was the inadequate use of mental health resources by adolescents. Why weren't the available services being used more? All of these factors pointed toward the need for a communication line between teenagers and the community at large.

It was substantiated; there was a need for a program. What, then, would be the program's needs?

It was decided what was primarily needed was a readily available listening ear, with the ability to provide current information on request, and professional referral sources for those who sought "someplace to go" for help. After deliberation and consultation with numerous professional advisers, the Montgomery County Mental Health Association began to formulate plans for a 24-hour telephone service for troubled youth.

Funding was now the immediate need. The association took the proposed program to the Maryland State Department of Mental Hygiene and was granted financing through community mental health services monies. The state allocated $15,600 for the first year of operation, which would finance telephone lines, other necessary equipment, and paid personnel to answer the phones during "heavy use" periods and through the "desperate" night time hours when problems seem bigger than life.

To have available funds is to begin, and the association moved at once toward the next big step—substantial community support. Invitations went out to each agency that had any youth-oriented mental health service or program. Each was invited to send a representative to the first meeting. The response was an overwhelming recognition of the program's potential. These representatives of private and public agencies involved in mental health in Montgomery County met and formed the Montgomery County Council on Adolescents to help set up goals of the crisis intervention program.

Now to reach the teenager; without the consumer, how could such a service work? The association next invited representatives from all the high schools in the county. Each was asked to represent his or her school on a Youth Advisory Board, with this Board, in turn, having two representatives on the Montgomery County Council on Adolescents.

The Council on Adolescents established seven goals for the program:
1. To establish a 24-hour-a-day telephone crisis intervention program for teenagers
2. To establish a council on adolescents which would facilitate the exchange of information and the planning among agencies to provide needed services to adolescents
3. To serve as a referral source to existing services

4. To promote teenage exchanges (group discussion sessions on problems facing adolescents led by professional mental health workers)
5. To gather statistics regarding problems for which teens are seeking help
6. To initiate new service programs as warranted by documented needs
7. To continually evaluate the information secured from the service as well as the program itself.

The council then established six committees to carry out various tasks: selection and training of Hotline staff, development of resources and professional back-up, medical psychiatric back-up, publicity, evaluation, and exchanges.

The Youth Advisory Board began meeting regularly to handle numerous tasks: a dictionary on terms (the youth board learned that slang in one high school might mean something else entirely at another school, and might be completely unintelligible in a third!), publicity in school papers and in underground news media, and training which the advisory board enthusiastically attended to pose problems on the "other end of the line."

The teenagers on the Youth Advisory Board staged a real-life "hassle" for their advisors as they pondered over the design of the business "calling" cards. How could they say it without saying too much? The card was finally boiled down to eight words and a phone number: *Hotline to Help Youth* 949-6603 Professional Contacts Also Available.

The crux of the entire program now rested on the success of the next step: the selection of the staff. Though the actual academic requirement is high school graduation with preference given to those whose interest and/or extracurricular activity relates to the teenage culture, the initial recruitment was handled by sending applications (with explanation sheets) and a cover letter to chairmen of graduate and undergraduate behavioral science programs in the local colleges. It wasn't long before the MCMHA's mail was swelled to a burden with returning applications and additional application requests from the universities and colleges. Once the general public became aware—at this stage by word of mouth and later through all forms of communication media—of the prospect of Hotline, the association's telephone lines were jammed by calls from interested people willing to donate their services to this program.

Each applicant filed an application, provided references, and was interviewed with one other applicant by a team of mental health professionals. Chief qualities sought in the applicants are their ability to effectively communicate verbally with openness and empathy, and their knowledge of and ability to relate to the adolescent culture. Other qualities highly prized in applicants are their flexibility and ability to be nonauthoritarian. Once the needed applicants had been chosen to comprise the Hotline staff, certain individuals with seemingly outstanding personal qualifications were chosen for the paid staff and the others became the volunteer staff with seniority rights for paid positions as they became available. Since most of the chosen applicants were students, vacancies were inevitable.

Training then became the important (and ongoing) component of the program. Prior to any service, a six-hour training session is required. This session familiarizes the staff with the background of Hotline, the major developmental crises of adolescence, the specific problems of teenagers in Montgomery County, general principles regarding approach and procedures in answering the calls, and experience in handling calls through the use of role-playing techniques. An evening training session from 7:30 to 11:30 is scheduled once a week; each staff member *must* attend once a month and is invited to attend more if he or she chooses. Current problems, frequent callers, and other ongoing questions are discussed with mental health professionals at these meetings.

In addition to the initial and monthly training sessions, the entire staff must attend a training session once every six weeks at which lecture material is provided. During the first such meeting, the law and how it affects teenagers (e.g., marriage, pregnancy, runaways, parental support) were discussed in small groups following a presentation by a county lawyer. The questions posed by the Hotline staff revealed the degree of need. Some of the questions were so technical as to require additional research and a later report by the speaker!

Day-to-day back-up training is provided "on location." The executive director of Montgomery County Mental Health Association is on hand for observation and assistance of the telephone procedures. A trained social worker who serves on the board of MCMHA and is in charge of all Hotline training sessions also visits the Hotline phone staff regularly to observe and advise.

Each paid Hotline staff member works one eight-hour shift a week; volunteers work one three-hour shift a week. The 20 paid staff members receive $1.45 an hour; a total of 45 volunteers currently are on the work schedule. Any staff member who cannot take his shift must find his own replacement from the trained list of paid or volunteer staff. During office hours, back-up is provided by the Montgomery County Mental Health Association office staff. From 4 p.m. through 12 midnight every day of the week and continuously over the weekend, there are three individuals on duty during each shift. Week nights, midnight to 9 a.m. are covered by one individual.

Among the major aims of the staff are these: let the caller remain anonymous at all times, receive him warmly and low-keyed, be honest regarding your feelings and reactions to the caller, always urge the caller to reestablish lines of communication with those nearest him.

The golden rule of the Hotline staff remains, however, to never give personal advice (callers need a chance to explore and discuss their problems; they don't need an authoritarian solution handed to them). The staff is constantly reminded that if any doubts arise about calls, they must not hesitate to contact either of the two professionals who volunteer to be back-up for all nonoffice hours, a mental health professional and a psychiatrist (the latter of whom has admitting privileges at local hospitals). Specific back-up weeks are assigned to all agencies who are members of the Council. Each agency takes the responsibility for scheduling its own staff for this volunteer service and notifies MCMHA which professional is on duty which night and the telephone number at which he can be reached. These telephone numbers are always prominently displayed on the bulletin board.

As problems arise their solutions are sought in the county's professional community. The response has proven that the cynic's "nothing is done for free anymore" is actually false. Doctors, lawyers, and agency personnel have given their time, often the only free evening they have, to meetings and back-up; they have donated their services, measured in dollars, to the problems of these troubled teenagers.

Integral to each telephone call are two instructions: invite each caller to make a recontact with Hotline, and fill out the data card recorded on each call.

The data card briefly provides the statistical information which allows MCMHA to substantiate community need and to demonstrate community problems. Each caller is identified by type (person involved, relative, friend, acquaintance, professional person, or other), age, sex, general area from which he is calling, the date and time of call, and the length of the call. The card lists the nature of the problem, the strategy discussed in dealing with problems, and referrals given. Each operator is asked to make judgment on the caller's situation (highly emotional, thinking in circles, situations outside themselves, or emotionally ill). Space is also provided for other comments. These cards are reviewed regularly by the mental health professionals associated with the program.

A brief evaluation and interim report on Hotline data cards reported 2,500 calls in the first 30 days of operation. In a sampling of these 30 days, the average total calls was 117 and the average "real" (as opposed to crank or hang-up calls) calls totaled 83. Two and a half times as many girls called as did boys; one out of four of the callers was 13 or 14 years old. The ages calling were broken down into percentages: 12 and under, 16%; 13 through 15, 40%; 16 through 18, 32%; and 19 and over, 12%.

Chief reasons for calls tabulated during a one-week period were, in order of frequency: boy/girl relationships, family conflict, just to "talk," drugs, pregnancy, and social inhibition.

Hotline staff members quickly summed up immediate needs of Montgomery County: help for youngsters (age 12-14) on drugs; temporary (i.e., one-night) shelters for youngsters, more often thrown out of the home than runaway; and mental health resources in elementary schools similar to those available at junior high schools.

As the staff encountered these problems, they were concerned because they had no resources to offer these callers. A resource file which is maintained in the

Hotline office provides an extensive listing of community resources, but the file offered little consolation to the staff when no resources were available. A second problem occurred on occasion when the professional back-up failed to leave a change of phone number; professionals soon learned that their value was diminished if they were unavailable. Because major crises, such as suicide attempts, did not occur early in the development of Hotline, the importance of constant vigilance by the Hotline back-ups was quickly established.

A third problem arose mechanically; how can one quickly trace a call? What seemed impossible has become a methodical but learned routine, and calls can be traced during extreme emergencies. Manipulation of the telephones themselves was occasionally tricky. The two Hotline phones are used strictly for incoming calls, but long cords permit the staff to walk to other office phones to call back-ups as needed.

Montgomery County's youth have been uniquely receptive to Hotline. Perhaps because of the transient, affluent population and the nature of the teenage culture in the suburban community, Hotline has already provided a unique and badly needed insight into the problems of this group. Most promising, Hotline is reaching the teenage population of the county which has previously been resistant to the traditional services available. And tradition seems to be a key word in the Hotline operation, for the association believes Hotline's continuing evaluation of community problems may well demonstrate the irrelevance of some of the current traditional treatment services in the county.

Hotline has another service, the Hotline Speakers Bureau. When the general public became aware of Hotline there were many calls for someone from the association to speak to groups concerning the Hotline function; there were also calls from schools for Hotline staff members to speak directly to students about this service. The requests were numerous and so the Speakers Bureau gradually developed. It became necessary to set up a few rules: three staff members, with either the executive director or Hotline trainer, would speak to groups affiliated with teenagers or teenagers themselves, in the form of a panel; at least one-third of the time allotted must be devoted to a question and answer period; and a three-week notice is required. Speaking engagements are limited to the school year.

The Hotline—funded by a state concerned with its youth, backed by agencies and professionals working together for a community's need, and justifying its own existence through its increasing use by those it was meant to serve, Montgomery County's troubled teenager—has dramatized the first chapter of a success story. It has also served to warn of gaps in community resources and by documenting these further with additional statistics the MCMHA hopes to see new services developed. Crisis intervention for teenagers, as demonstrated by Montgomery County's Hotline, may well prove to be a crisis intervention for the community at large.

The Suicide Prevention Center in Los Angeles

Michael L. Peck

For most of us who are not directly involved with emotionally disturbed persons in a psychiatric setting, suicide is a remote and vaguely discomfiting act. We read about it in the newspapers and hear about it on the radio or television. For the most part, however, it has little personal significance. Only when it strikes close to home, to one's family or close friends, is the full emotional impact of suicidal behavior brought sharply into awareness.

It is, therefore, a great surprise to many people that, statistically, suicide is a problem of great magnitude. Among the listing of public health disorders, suicide ranks among the first ten causes of adult deaths in the United States. Among certain age groups (high school and college students) it is the third, and in some parts of the country, the second leading cause of death. It cuts across social, economic, racial, and religious lines, claiming its victims from all walks of life.

In the United States every year there are approximately 22,000 recorded suicides. The actual number is probably much higher. Some estimate the number to be well over 25,000. In Los Angeles County alone there are over 1,100 suicides a year. Staggering as these figures are, the magnitude of the problem is multiplied when we consider that for every completed suicide it is estimated that there are approximately ten suicide attempts. This maelstrom of unhappiness is further complicated when we stop to realize that committed suicides and suicide attempts cause untold grief and sadness in the many survivors and ultimately in the entire community.

Many communities lack adequate medical and psychiatric resources to cope with suicidal behavior and its subsequent emotional impact on the family and friends of the suicidal person. In these communities the suicidal person's "cry for help" often goes unheeded and a tragic, needless death results.

THE SUICIDE PREVENTION CENTER

To cope with the seriousness of this problem, the Suicide Prevention Center (SPC) was established in Los Angeles in 1958. Its efforts have been directed

Reprinted by permission from *School Health Review*, Vol. 1, No. 4, September 1970.

toward saving lives, learning more about the phenomenon of suicide, and disseminating information about suicide in training other professional and nonprofessional persons in suicide prevention.

The programs of the SPC are supported through various sources, such as the National Institute of Mental Health, the Los Angeles County Department of Mental Health, and, to a smaller degree, private contributions. The Center is affiliated administratively with the University of Southern California School of Medicine and has a close working relationship with the Psychiatry Department, in which many of the SPC staff members have faculty appointments.

The SPC co-directors are Norman L. Farberow, Ph.D., and Robert E. Litman, M.D. The staff is interdisciplinary and consists of psychiatrists, psychologists, psychiatric social workers, and biostatisticians; it maintains consultants in sociology, psychiatric nursing, anthropology, and logic. Students in medicine, psychology, social work, nursing, and pastoral counseling also receive intensive training at the SPC. Much of the clinical telephone services are handled by a cadre of clinical associates, who work part time and range in experience from professionals to nonprofessional volunteers. All receive extensive training and close supervision.

The SPC grew out of the research work in the early 1950's by Norman Farberow and Edwin Shneidman. After years of study, beginning with hundreds of suicide notes found in the coroner's files, their attention became directed toward helping the many suicidal patients they encountered. They formalized these efforts into a suicide prevention center.

Although the clinical activities of saving lives became of prime concern in the earlier years of the SPC, the research and training aspects have grown in importance in recent years. Numerous investigations have begun and papers have been published since 1958, oriented toward greater understanding of the whys of self-destructive behavior. Recently, these investigations have included studies on auto accident victims directed by Norman Tabachnick and excursions into the understanding of violence and drug usage as well.

Information is disseminated through the education and training section of the SPC in the form of community lectures, workshops and seminars to professional groups, both locally and throughout the country, and formal training institutes that not only provide for training and clinical aspects of suicide prevention but also encourage the establishment of other suicide prevention centers. In this last respect, it is clear that the Los Angeles SPC has served as a prototype.

The clinical aspect of the SPC most importantly provides easy availability to the person in need of help. There are no complex screening procedures, no fees, and no waiting list. There is an around-the-clock telephone service that provides that any suicidal person who needs help can readily receive it.

Although the persons who contact the SPC may be different in terms of personality and background, there is one striking similarity in the majority of cases: they are facing some kind of crisis. The crisis may be related to specific life situations, such as divorce or death of a loved one, financial loss, or some other event which involves the loss of self-esteem. In many suicidal persons there is no specific precipitating stress. A study of these persons often reveals a slow but consistent loss of the ability to cope with life. These people often experience a progression of small, but not insignificant, life failures until it finally manifests itself in a marked change in the person's picture of himself and a sharp decrease in the number and meaningfulness of his relations with other people. These kinds of changes are often clues to suicidal behavior.

Most people who call the SPC with desperate talk about suicide are actually communicating their need for help. All suicidal persons are, to some degree, ambivalent. Their cry for help is a reflection of their wish to live; at the same time, they are declaring their desire to die.

The telephone worker listens to the suicidal caller and first establishes a feeling of rapport and understanding. He lets the caller know that he is there to listen and to help. The worker then moves in the direction of the most appropriate action for the situation.

Appropriate action might best be thought of as a three-stage program: evaluation, mobilization of resources, and disposition. In attempting to evaluate the degree of suicidal behavior, the SPC staff have developed certain criteria from their research and clinical experience. Some of these are: (1) *age and sex*—older persons are regarded as more serious suicidal risks than the younger persons and since the suicide rate among men is higher than that of women, men are considered a higher suicide risk; (2) *availability of resources*—a friend, relative, family doctor, therapist. or anyone who cares can be of great help; when none of these is available the danger is greater; (3) *suicide method and plan*—a person who is contemplating a particular method such as shooting himself and has the means available is a much higher risk than someone who has no particular plan or method. Through the above and additional criteria, the worker makes an evaluation of the degree of lethality.

When we find any persons available in the suicidal individual's life situation, we encourage them to take an active role with their friend or relative and to provide him with the help he needs during this crisis. The higher the suicide risk the more important is this mobilization process. In many cases, in a low lethality situation, the caller can resolve some of the initial problems over the phone without the help of others. In a high risk situation the "significant others" of the suicidal person are often immobilized by the crisis and require an outside professional person to help them understand what is going on and to take active responsibility.

The SPC maintains good liaison with other psychiatric clinics, hospitals, law enforcement agencies and other social agencies in the community. It is through these relationships that we are best able to help the suicidal person find an appropriate resource for his particular problem and thereby lessen the likelihood of his becoming suicidal again.

About 10% of the persons who have been in contact with the SPC have been described as adolescents. They are not necessarily 19 and under, since the adolescent crisis often extends to college students who are over 20. Indeed, the adolescent crisis can be said to apply to persons up to the age of 25 who are experiencing problems and conflicts which are typical of the adolescent. The Center staff has published a number of studies about this group of young people. The staff also engages in consultation and training with various school administrators in Los Angeles County to help them understand and deal with the problems of suicide.

Some of the findings of the Center studies are briefly mentioned here. School pressures seem to play a relatively small role in committed suicide among adolescents. When they do, it is frequently a combination of high parental expectations and the sensitive student's inordinate fear of failure in the eyes of his parents which makes up the major dynamics of the death. The most common kind of suicide among adolescents tends to be a boy who is best described as sensitive, lonely, and unhappy. Although he may have had many acquaintances and even a few successes, basically he has lacked a close, meaningful relationship. One of the most often made comments about these young boys who commit suicide is, "No one really seemed to know him." These boys, in many cases, were so withdrawn that they were not even involved with the drug usage scene, so common among today's youth.

The female adolescents who committed suicide tended to have a much different personality description, being more typically outgoing and getting in trouble more frequently. They were known as emotionally disturbed by friends, family, and psychiatric agencies. Many more females than males, however, make suicide attempts in these age groups.

How can the professional person who works with youth be aware of suicidal problems and intervene positively and therapeutically in these crisis situations? First, there is the need to recognize the aforementioned clues and to learn to focus on persons who may, in fact, be disturbed. Second, a professional must learn to be unafraid to move in directly and ask questions. In this respect, the teacher, counselor, or school administrator can play an important, effective role with a young student who may be contemplating suicide. By asking first if the youngster is unhappy, and moving on to a successive series of questions in which he inquires about appetite, sleeping patterns, feelings of depression or hopelessness, self-worth, and finally, whether he has been contemplating self-injury or suicide, the teacher or counselor can help identify potential suicide. With a professional referral to help, he can thus make a major contribution in the field of suicide prevention.

SELECTED READINGS ON CRISIS INTERVENTION

BOOKS

G. Caplan. *Principles of Preventive Psychiatry*. New York: Basic Books, 1964.

G. Caplan and S. Lebovici (eds.). *Adolescence: Psychosocial Perspectives*. New York: Basic Books, 1969.

Louis Dublin. *Suicide: A Sociological and Statistical Study*. New York: Ronald Press, 1963.

E. Durkheim. *Suicide: A Study in Sociology*. New York: The Free Press, 1951.

A. Ellis and R. A. Harper. *A Guide to Rational Living*. Hollywood, Calif.: Wilshire Book Co., 1961.

E. H. Erikson. *Identity, Youth, and Crisis*. New York: W. W. Norton & Co., 1968.

N. L. Farberow and E. S. Shneidman (eds.). *The Cry for Help*. New York: McGraw-Hill, 1965.

D. L. Farnsworth. *Psychiatry, Education, and the Young Adult*. Springfield, Ill.: Charles C. Thomas, 1966.

V. E. Frankl. *Man's Search for Meaning*. New York: Washington Square Press, 1959.

N. Kiell. *The Universal Experience of Adolescence*. Boston: Beacon Press, 1964.

A. H. Maslow. *Toward a Psychology of Being*. 2nd edition. Princeton, N.J.: D. Van Nostrand Co., 1968.

H. Parad (ed.). *Crisis Intervention: Selected Readings*. New York: Family Service Association, 1965.

H. L. P. Resnik (ed.). *Suicidal Behaviors*. Boston: Little, Brown and Company, 1968. See especially chapters on "Suicide in Childhood and Adolescence" by James M. Toolan, "Suicide among Students" by James A. Knight, and "Suicide: A Public Health Problem" by Stanley Yolles.

C. R. Rogers. *Client-Centered Therapy*. Boston: Houghton Mifflin Co., 1951.

E. S. Shneidman and P. Mandelkorn. *How To Prevent Suicide*. Public Affairs Pamphlet No. 406. New York: Public Affairs Committee, 1967.

E. S. Shneidman and N. L. Farberow (eds.). *Clues to Suicide*. New York; McGraw-Hill, 1957.

PERIODICALS

H. H. Huessy and others. "The Indigenous Nurse as Crisis Counselor and Intervenor," *American Journal of Public Health* 59(11):2022-28, 1969.

N. L. Farberow and M. Simon. "Suicide in Los Angeles and Vienna," *Public Health Reports* 84(5), May 1969.

Elaine S. Feiden, "One Year's Experience with a Suicide Prevention Service" (White Plains, New York), *Social Work* 15(3):26-32, July 1970.

Dan Leviton. "Education for Death," *Journal of Health, Physical Education, Recreation* 40:46, September 1969.

Dan Leviton. "What the Peace Corps Has To Suggest About College Mental Health Education," *Journal of the American College Health Association* 16(1):74-79, 1967.

Michael Peck. "Suicide Motivations in Adolescents," *Adolescence* 3(9), spring 1968.

D. L. Robey and B. A. Dickey. "Health Counseling," *Journal of School Health* 36(4):179-82, 1966.

Mathew Ross. "Suicide Among College Students," *American Journal of Psychiatry* 126:2, 1969.

Albert Schrut. "Suicidal Adolescents and Children," *Journal of American Medical Association* 188:1103-107, 1964.

Albert Schrut. "Some Typical Patterns in the Behavior and Background of Adolescent Girls Who Attempt Suicide," *American Journal of Psychiatry* 125:1, July 1968.

The Selection and Training of Volunteers

Frances Pierce*

INTRODUCTION

The suicidal person is sometimes looking for a rescuer to serve as an alter ego at a time when his own ego functions are severely impaired. Ninety-five percent (13) of initial suicidal patient contacts begin on the telephone. These calls range from emergencies to situations of little or no suicidal risk. Regardless of the initial impression every call is treated seriously.

Efforts of volunteers must be directed toward living persons before they kill themselves. They need to be able to listen sympathetically and encourage the caller to discuss his feelings with his physician, minister, friend, or relative. The volunteer needs to be trained in how and what to say to persons who threaten suicide.

As a defensive or testing maneuver the caller will often begin in a joking or hostile way. The volunteer must accept and understand it for what it is (a defense against feelings of inadequacy). The caller may not go on to reveal his real suicidal feelings and the therapeutic opportunity may be lost.

The main purpose of a volunteer is to listen effectively with the end results of calming the person to a rational level and getting him to the point where he will follow through on the positive alternatives he has decided on. The volunteer does not give advice, but gives positive reinforcement and leads the person to work his own problems out.

The volunteer frequently offers a relationship to the patient which is on a more direct, friendly level than that of professionals. This is especially important in cases which contact rather than authority seems more important. (11)

Great care is given especially to the initial call. The time is spent carefully evaluating the situation, trying to form a positive relationship by moving into the situation rather than away from it. The volunteer must let the caller know quickly that they are interested, they wish to help him, and improvement is possible regardless of how desperate he feels. The volunteer must try to instill a

Reprinted by permission from *Self Destructive Behavior* – Workshop Proceedings, Health Science Department, Brent Q. Hafen Director, Brigham Young University, 1971.

*Prepared in association with: Lorraine Nielsen and Anita Louise Fager, Frances Pierce; Chairman.

feeling of hope, pointing out that there are several alternative ways of dealing with his problem may be found.

Specifically, the job on the telephone is to get information, to evaluate the situation, especially the suicidal potential, and to recommend a course of action.

This has to be done concomitantly and questions are woven in whenever possible at appropriate moments. The aim is to give the caller a therapeutic experience so the volunteer must avoid asking for information in a formal, routine way.

Volunteers should ask for identifying information as discreetly as possible and encourage the caller to discuss any current stress his is under. Suicidal feelings should be discussed openly as this helps relieve some of the anxiety. Should suggest action directed toward continued living. (16)

A program of public information on suicide problems would aim at reducing taboos surrounding the topic and making it possible and permissible for suicidal persons to reach out for help. Another objective is to secure early recognition of suicidal risk and cooperation in supporting the persons affected. Such education should lead to realization that certain information about suicide-prevention measures is already available and that its successful application depends to a considerable extent on the cooperation of society. This program would increase the need for more suicide prevention centers and therefore an increased need for volunteers.

The purpose in using volunteers in the Suicide Prevention Center is to find a means of alleviating the shortage of trained workers in the Mental Health field and of filling the community's needs for low-cost psychotherapy. The idea behind this purpose is similar to that of the public health nurse. A public health nurse can perform many duties with and for patients, thereby freeing the medical officer for tasks requiring greater training. So also, a corps of workers could be trained in the mental health field thereby freeing a significant amount of the psychiatrists time.(23)

SELECTION

The selection of volunteers in major crisis centers such as the Los Angeles Suicide Prevention Center usually begins with a telephone interview.

Initially the applicant has heard about the program from one of the other volunteers or by some other word-of-mouth source. After the initial phone contact, the staff worker begins the screening process. If the worker feels that the applicant may be appropriate for the program, he will invite the applicant into the center for a personal interview. If the staff worker still has the feeling that the applicant has potential, he will ask one or two other staff members to interview the applicant. The final decision about accepting the applicant is made through a consultation with the other staff workers.

The role for which the volunteers is needed is that of a clinical telephone therapist. The volunteer would be the person in direct telephone contact with the person calling the center. They are at times called upon to make rapid and important life and death decisions. The volunteer needs the skill and the ability to formulate a diagnostic impression and to accurately assess the suicidal danger the patient represents. (21)

The volunteers are called upon to be imaginative and often inventive in formulating a plan of crisis intervention and firm enough to help the patient carry it through. The volunteers need to be stable and secure that they would not be overcome by strong negative effect of some patients and could continue functioning in the face of the contagious feeling of despair and hopelessness. Even though the volunteers would usually have professional help within easy access, they would be depended upon to make reasonable assessments and decisions. (21)

Because of the experimental nature of the program at the beginning, it was decided that the criteria of selection would be of the broadest possible nature, and the applicants were judged clinically on the basis of seven general guidelines: (1) Strength of motivation—that is, did the applicant seem willing to make some sacrifices to work? (2) Responsibility—could the applicant be depended upon; could she take responsibility for her own feelings and her own actions? (3) Stability— was her life history reasonably stable; does her emotional life appear stable at this time? (4) Maturity—is the applicant realistic in her thinking; does she exhibit common sense in problem-solving? (5) Sensitivity—does the applicant appear to be aware of other persons' feelings and emotions; does she relate in an appropriate way? (6) Does the applicant demonstrate the ability to work as a member of a team? (7) Does the applicant demonstrate the ability to accept training and supervision? (21)

The volunteers for the newly formed "Crisis Line" in Utah County, Utah, are selected according to the following criteria: (1) their willingness to work; (2) their reasons for volunteering; (3) their hours available to work; (4) how they withstood and reacted to pressure at varying degrees and levels; and (5) their ability to communicate, in the aspect of listening rather than talking.

TRAINING

Training in suicide prevention has been influenced by two major factors: persons in need of training and new developments in mental health practice.

"The content covered in the training program varies with the format of the particular program and the time allocated to training." (12) Certain fundamentals are included in all the programs. "The four fundamental components of all training in suicide prevention are (1) basic concepts of suicide prevention, (2) recognition of suicidal persons and evaluation of lethality, (3) use of the telephone and techniques for telephone interviewing, and (4) mobilization of resources to implement an appropriate helping response." (12)

The first of the four fundamental components includes ambivalence, communication, lethality, stress, helplessness, hopelessness, and action response.

The most important single factor for training in suicide prevention is to teach how to make a careful evaluation of the danger, once a suicidal situation has been identified. (12)

In teaching the principles of telephone interviewing, covered are such items as maintaining contact and establishing a relationship, obtaining necessary information, evaluation of suicide potential, clarification of stress and focal problems. Also covered are assessment of strengths and resources, recommendation and initiation of an action plan, and closure. The use of the telephone in getting collateral persons to both provide information and help in the crisis is also discussed. (12)

Mobilization of resources is on three levels. They are: (1) personal resources; (2) professional resources available to a particular patient, and (3) the broad range community resources. (12)

The methods for training are primarily seminars in which prepared presentations are made, followed by discussions in small groups. (12)

Once accepted into training, the volunteers are told that if they find that they are not comfortable with the work, they should feel free to drop the program. It is stressed that they are under no obligation to the center. When the volunteers feel trapped into a position, somatic symptoms begin to develop. (21)

The training program itself is usually in three phases. The first phase has already been discussed. The second phase of training begins as the new volunteers start taking their first telephone calls. The volunteers are closely supervised and they discuss the content of each case and alternative ways of handling it in detail with their clinical supervisor. (21)

The third phase of the training consists of continued weekly volunteer meetings where the content varies from case conferences to the presentation of additional material. Although the need for close supervision diminishes as the volunteer .gains experience, both the volunteer and the professional staff function more comfortably within the context of frequent consultations. (21)

The following "don'ts" are included in the information taught in training volunteers: (1) do not set yourself up by answering a question that ends with "don't you?"; (2) do not give advice but lead them to working out their own problems; (3) do not go offensive or defensive; (4) do not condemn or be judgmental; (5) do not build up the caller falsely; and (6) never give out full names, especially last names, and never divulge the location of the center.

According to the director of the Utah County Crisis Line located in Provo, Utah, the volunteers are trained by the following: (1) they role play various situations and are required to read *Art of Listening* by Domnick A. Barbara; (2)

attend lectures on depression — its categories and how to recognize it; and (3) various other workshops and seminars to help in the recognition of a crisis. They are trained, in Utah County, to do the following: (1) be subtle and do not obviously give information; (2) listen effectively; (3) give positive reinforcement; and (4) calm the caller down to a rational level and help him determine where he will follow through in acquiring professional help.

CONCLUSION

One of the greatest problems experienced by the nonprofessional is role ambiguity or lack of role identity. He does not know who he is or who he is becoming. He is no longer a simple member of the community—if he ever was one—nor is he a professional. He is a highly marginal person, actually, just as the new programs he frequently represents are also highly marginal and lacking in a clear identity.

"Nonprofessional" describes what he is not, but does not clearly indicate what he is. He is not simply a citizen, nor a volunteer participating in the organization, although it is desired to have him represent the feelings of the neighborhood. He is not the traditional kind of employee because his participation and advice are sought; yet he is also an employee. He is not a professional, even though many people in the community may see the aide as a new kind of social worker. He is not a political action organizer, even though he does develop groups in the community concerned with various types of change. He has many roles and his trainers and the leaders of the community programs must understand and try to clarify this new role. He is the new marginal man. He must be selected with this in mind, trained and supervised in this fashion, and assisted in foregoing this new role.

This ambiguity of the nonprofessional is also related to the unclarity of goals and programs in the rapidly developing community programs. The newness of the programs, the vagueness of many of the goals, and the fact that the tasks for nonprofessionals are only beginning to be defined contribute to the total atmosphere of amorphousness and produce confusion and anxiety. All staff members, supervisory and nonprofessional, should be made honestly aware of the character of the situation; that is, the fact that it is rapidly changing and not highly structured and traditional. Structure and unity can be achieved by attempting to define as specifically as possible the job function, and the description of it should be provided in as much detail as possible without sounding overwhelming. (22)

"Our experience has been that as long as the Center staff can provide the volunteers with new horizons and further opportunity for learning, for self-development and for service, they retain a high sense of enthusiasm and loyalty to the program. What the average life of a volunteer in the Suicide Prevention

Center is, it is too early to determine. By defining the distinguishing characteristics of these men and women more precisely, their contributions to the field of
community mental health can be most effective." (21)

In general, it is apparent that nonprofessional volunteers, carefully selected
and trained in crisis intervention techniques and personal counseling can occupy
an important place in the field of mental health and make a significant
contribution to the mental health of the community. (11)

BIBLIOGRAPHY

1. Bartholomew, A. A., "The Personal Emergency Advisory Service", *Mental
   Hygiene*, 46:382-392, 1962.
2. _____,Kelley, Margaret F., and Staley, E. M., "An Analysis of 'Night
   Calls' Received by a Personal Emergency Telephone Service", *Social Service*,
   14(5):13, 1963.
3. Bellack, L. (ed.), *Handbook of Community Psychiatry and Community
   Mental Health*, New York: Grune and Stratton, 1964.
4. Brockepp, G. and Yasser, A., "Training the volunteer telephone therapist",
   Crisis Intervention Bulletin, Buffalo, New York: Vol. 2, pp. 65-72.
5. Cleaver, J. H., "Preventing Suicide", *Medical Herald* (St. Joseph), 49:47-95,
   1967.
6. Eidelman, J. R., "Prevention of Suicide", *Journal of Missouri Medical
   Association*, 48:441-446, 1951.
7. Farberow, Norman L., "Suicide Prevention Around the Clock", *American
   Journal of Orthopsychiatry*, 36(3):551-558, 1966.
8. _____,Heilig, Samuel M., and Titman, Robert E., "Training Manual for
   Telephone Evaluation and Emergency Management of Suicidal Persons",
   *Suicide Prevention Center, Inc., Technique In Crisis Intervention: A
   Training Manual*, Los Angeles, California, Dec., 1968, p. 2-16.
9. _____,and Shneidman, Edwin S., "A Survey of Agencies for the
   Prevention of Suicide", *Cry For Help*, New York, McGraw-Hill, 1961, p.
   6-18, 136-149.
10. Hankoff, L. D., "Suicide Prevention Service", *Medical Tribune*, 5(116):Oct.
    28, 1964.
11. Heilig, Sam M., "The Role of Non-Professional Volunteers in a Suicide
    Prevention Center," *Community Mental Health*, 1968, p. 4.
12. _____, "Training In Suicide Prevention", *Bulletin of Suicidology*, No. 6,
    Spring 1970, p. 41-44.
13. Hirsh, J., "Suicide (Part 5: The Trouble Shooting Clinic: Prototype of a
    Comprehensive Community Emergency Service)", *Mental Hygiene*,
    44:496-502, 1960, p. 8.
14. Kaphan, "Suicide Consultation: A Psychiatric Service to Social Agencies",
    American Journal of Psychiatry, 122(12):1357-1361, 1966.
15. _____, "Telephone Appraisal of 100 Suicidal Emergencies", *American
    Journal of Psychotherapy*, 16(4):591-599, 1962.
16. Klugman, David J., Titman, Robert E., and Wald, Carl, "Suicide: Answering
    Cry for Help", *Social Work*, 19(4):43-50, 1965.
17. McGee, R. K., "The Suicide Prevention Center or a Model for Community

Mental Health Programs", *Community Mental Health Journal,* 1(2):162-170, 1965.

18. Michenor, C., and Walzer, H., "Developing a Community Mental Health Volunteer System," *Social Work,* 1970 (Oct.), 15(4).

19. Peck, H. B., *"Extending and Developing Manpower for Urban Community Mental Health Centers.,* New York, Lincoln Hospital Mental Health Services, 1964.

20. Pines, M., "The Coming Upheaval in Psychiatry", *Harper's,* 1965 (Oct.) Vol. 231.

21. Pretzel, P., "The Volunteer Clinical Worker at the S.P.C", *Bulletin of Suicidology,* Spring 1970, No. 6, p. 29-34.

22. Reiff, R., and Reissman, F., "The Indigenous Non-Professional," *Community Mental Health Journal,* Monograph Series, No. 1.

23. Risch, Margaret et al., "NIMH Study in Training Mental Health Counselors", *American Journal of Orthopsychiatry,* 1963, p. 678-689.

24. Shneidman, E. S., et al., "Comprehensive Suicide Prevention Program", *California Mental Health Research Digest,* 1965, p. 37.

25. _____, "The Los Angeles Suicide Prevention Center", *American Journal of Public Health,* 1965, p. 21-26.

26. Wallace, M. A., "Nurse in Suicide Prevention", *Nursing Outlook,* XV, (March, 1967), p. 55-57.

27. Waltzer, Herbert, "One Year's Experience With A Suicide Prevention Telephone Service," *Community Mental Health Journal,* 1965, p. 309-315.

28. Weikel, Charles P., "The Life You Can Save", *Harvest Years,* June, 1970.